America's
TEST KITCHEN

America's
TEST KITCHEN

Cooking
for Two

2010

THE YEAR'S BEST RECIPES CUT DOWN TO SIZE

BY THE EDITORS OF
AMERICA'S TEST KITCHEN

PHOTOGRAPHY BY
CARL TREMBLAY, KELLER + KELLER, AND DANIEL J. VAN ACKERE

AMERICA'S TEST KITCHEN
17 Station Street, Brookline, MA 02445

Library of Congress Cataloging-in-Publication Data
The Editors at America's Test Kitchen

AMERICA'S TEST KITCHEN COOKING FOR TWO 2010:
The Year's Best Recipes Cut Down to Size

1st Edition

Hardcover: $35 US
ISBN-13: 978-1-933615-60-8   ISBN-10: 1-933615-60-5
1. Cooking. 1. Title
2010

Manufactured in the United States of America

10 9 8 7 6 5 4 3 2 1

Distributed by America's Test Kitchen
17 Station Street, Brookline, MA 02445

EDITORIAL DIRECTOR: Jack Bishop
EXECUTIVE EDITOR: Elizabeth Carduff
EXECUTIVE FOOD EDITOR: Julia Collin Davison
SENIOR EDITORS: Lori Galvin and Rachel Toomey
ASSOCIATE EDITORS: Elizabeth Emery and Kate Hartke
TEST COOKS: Adelaide Parker and Dan Zuccarello
EDITORIAL ASSISTANT: Elizabeth Pohm
DESIGN DIRECTOR: Amy Klee
ART DIRECTOR: Greg Galvan
DESIGNER: Beverly Hsu
STAFF PHOTOGRAPHER: Daniel J. van Ackere
ADDITIONAL PHOTOGRAPHERS: Christopher Churchill, Keller + Keller, Kate Kelley, and Carl Tremblay
FOOD STYLING: Marie Piraino and Mary Jane Sawyer
PRODUCTION DIRECTOR: Guy Rochford
SENIOR PRODUCTION MANAGER: Jessica Quirk
SENIOR PROJECT MANAGER: Alice Carpenter
TRAFFIC AND PRODUCTION COORDINATOR: Laura Collins
ASSET AND WORKFLOW MANAGER: Andrew Mannone
PRODUCTION AND IMAGING SPECIALISTS: Judy Blomquist and Lauren Pettapiece
COPYEDITOR: Barbara Wood
PROOFREADER: Jeffrey Schier
INDEXER: Elizabeth Parson

PICTURED ON THE FRONT COVER: Turkey and Green Chile Enchiladas (page 163)
PICTURED OPPOSITE TITLE PAGE: Grill-Smoked Pork Chops with Apple and Bibb Lettuce Salad (page 193)
PICTURED ON BACK OF JACKET: Classic Beef Chili (page 76), Skillet Pizza with Ricotta, Bacon, and Scallions (page 103), Slow-Roasted Beef with Horseradish Sauce (page 176), and Angel Food Cakes (page 272)

Contents

Introduction

THE FIRST *COOKING FOR TWO* COOKBOOK WAS published in 1919, and the subtitle reads "A Handbook for Young Housekeepers." The "two" was of course the newlyweds who, it seems, were so much in love that they preferred to dine alone. As was the custom at the time, the author, Janet McKenzie Hill, spoke about food much as one would consider filling up a car that was low on gas. Speaking of the need for a good midday meal, she wrote, "Your energy and motive power are gone. This waste must be renewed at once, or you will remain faint and inactive; or, if the renewal be deferred for days, you will cease to live." Wow! And all of that energy depletion happens between breakfast and lunch!

Our definition of cooking for two has less to do with doe-eyed newlyweds and the prospect of dying from starvation than with home cooks who enjoy good food but, given the modest audience seated around the dinner table, wish to produce less food to avoid endless leftovers and to also shorten lengthy recipe preparation that would be more suitable for a dinner party than a Tuesday night supper.

There are many creative answers to this conundrum. The first is to create recipes that use odd leftovers (from other recipes in the cookbook) such as half a can of black beans, a third of a cup of sour cream, or half a head of cabbage. How many times have you cut back a recipe only to throw out the unused ingredients a week later? We also suggest that you purchase a small handful of useful pieces of cookware, including a small cake pan or pie plate, a loaf pan, gratin dishes, ramekins—even small 1-cup Bundt pans and 2-cup tube pans. This means that one can bake up a manageable amount of pasta, cake, or casserole, just enough for two.

Smart cooking for two also makes good use of skillets for one-dish suppers, finds a way to downsize pasta dishes, invents truly innovative recipes such as skillet pizza, provides tricks, tips, and techniques for making casseroles for two, and even offers recipes for fancy meals—lobster, filet mignon, and even duck à l'orange. And since everybody appreciates a real dessert upon occasion, we might be inclined to shout, "Honey, we shrunk the desserts!" Yes, you can make Carrot Cake, Angel Food Cake, cobblers, gratins, and even Pineapple Upside-Down Cake for just one happy couple.

It is true that there are also cookbooks entitled *Cooking for One*, and that reminds me of a story, told by author Allen Foley, about the father of a well-known Vermonter, Senator George Aiken. The father was a member of the house and was being interrogated regarding his support of women's suffrage. As an example of the difficulties this would present a married couple, his opponent presented the following situation: "Well, Mr. Aiken, suppose in a criminal case that runs for four, five, or six days your wife was the only woman on the jury and had to be closely confined with those men during all this period. How would you like that, Mr. Aiken?"

"I think," mused Mr. Aiken, after carefully studying the chandelier in the center of the hall, "I think it would all depend on who we had for a hired girl at the time."

Finally, here is a cookbook that takes cooking in smaller households seriously, without compromising flavor or indulging in a lot of unsatisfying convenience foods. This is from-scratch cooking for two people who love a good meal and who also love each other's company.

CHRISTOPHER KIMBALL
Founder and Editor,
Cook's Illustrated and *Cook's Country*
Host, *America's Test Kitchen* and
Cook's Country from America's Test Kitchen

THE SMART SHOPPER'S GUIDE

MAKING THE MOST OF THE RECIPES IN THIS BOOK

LET'S FACE IT—WE ALL WASTE FOOD. AND WHEN YOU'RE cooking for two, this is an even bigger problem. Sure, there are some stores where you can buy loose leafy greens or a handful of Brussels sprouts, but usually you're stuck with prepackaged produce sold in large quantities. The same is true for canned goods and many other items used in everyday recipes. So what's the solution? Careful planning and shopping. To that end, we've prepared this guide to key ingredients, both perishable and canned, that are used throughout the book. So if you're making one recipe with half a can of kidney beans or half a bell pepper, you can see which other recipes in the book call for them so you don't have to toss the extras.

STOCKING THE COOKING-FOR-TWO KITCHEN

IN GENERAL, WHEN YOU'RE COOKING FOR TWO, you really don't need special equipment—the usual battery of pots, pans, knives, and tools will work just fine. (Although if your kitchen isn't stocked with smaller skillets—8- and 10-inch—or a small saucepan, you'll need them for a variety of recipes in this book.) But for some scaled-down entrées and desserts, we found we needed smaller baking dishes, cake pans, and more. Some dishes worked with common cookware—a loaf pan, we found, makes a great vessel for smaller casseroles. But for other recipes, like coffee cakes, mini loaves, and many desserts, special equipment was necessary. Fortunately, these dishes are inexpensive and widely available both online and at many retail stores. Plus, you'll never need more than two (and sometimes just one will suffice). Here's a list of the cookware we found most useful in this book.

BAKING DISHES

When you want to make a small sheet cake (such as Carrot Cake, page 277) or a scaled-down breakfast casserole (such as our 24-Hour "Omelet," page 219), this 3-cup baking dish (measuring about 7¼ by 5¼ inches) works perfectly since its capacity is about one-third that of a 13 by 9-inch baking pan. Likewise, an 8-inch square baking dish can be used to cook entrées like our Turkey Gratin (page 162).

SMALL CAKE PAN

With a 6-inch round cake pan, you can make cake or coffee cake for two (see our Pineapple Upside-Down Cake on page 270 or our Overnight Sour Cream Coffee Cake on page 209).

SMALL PIE PLATE

We found that a 6-inch pie plate works perfectly when you want to bake quiche or pie for two (see our Easy Cheesy Quiche on page 224 or our Icebox Strawberry Pie on page 263).

LOAF PANS

We use both traditional loaf pans (either 8- or 9-inch) and mini loaf pans (which measure about 5½ by 3 inches) in the for-two kitchen. We bake small casseroles in the larger loaf pan and scaled-down quick breads or cakes in the mini loaf pan.

SMALL TART PANS

When you want to make individual tarts, like our Smoked Salmon and Leek Tarts (page 122) or Pecan Tarts (page 282), two 4-inch tart pans (with removable bottoms) hold just the right amount of crust and filling.

GRATIN DISHES

For our Berry Gratins (page 258), we needed two mini broiler-safe gratin dishes with a 6-ounce (¾-cup) capacity that were shallow and wide so our desserts developed a lightly browned, caramelized crust. But for a main dish, such as our Lazy Man's Lobster (page 128), we needed larger 2-cup gratin dishes (measuring about 9 by 6 inches), although a dish of a comparable size could be used instead.

RAMEKINS

Ramekins are handy for making a number of savory and sweet dishes. In our testing, we found that 6-ounce ramekins were the perfect size for making our petite but rich Crème Brûlées (page 284) and Fallen Chocolate Cakes (page 278), and 12-ounce ramekins were ideal for making All-Season Peach Crisps (page 254).

SMALL BUNDT PANS

These 1-cup Bundt pans are ideal for making two scaled-down Bold and Spicy Gingerbread Cakes (page 275).

SMALL TUBE PANS

For two light and airy Angel Food Cakes (page 272), we found that 2-cup tube pans held just the right amount of batter.

BAKED SOLE WITH GARLICKY SPINACH

SKILLET MEALS

BEEF POT PIE

EVERYONE LOVES A GOOD BEEF POT PIE—WHAT'S NOT to love about tender pieces of beef and vegetables surrounded by a full-flavored sauce and baked under a flaky crust? But, as is true of a lot of home-style dishes, making it can take a good part of the day. Certainly there's nothing wrong with such a labor of love, but for a simple meal for two, we wanted a faster alternative. Our goal was a richly flavored beef pot pie—with all the nuance of a slow-simmered beef stew—made in a fraction of the time and using just one skillet.

We started our testing by turning to the primary concern: the choice of meat. Beef stew develops its rich flavor through the slow, deliberate simmering of an inexpensive yet flavorful cut of beef. Cooking these tougher cuts quickly over high heat usually results in bland chunks of meat with a rubbery texture. Clearly, if we wanted a quick-cooking cut of meat, we had to look elsewhere. Tender steaks were an obvious choice. Our first choice was blade steak, a reasonably priced steak we have used in the past for beef teriyaki and kebabs. It's also easy to buy in small quantities, which was ideal since we needed only 12 ounces of meat for two servings. Trimmed into small cubes, browned, and simmered in the oven underneath a crust, it was tender and flavorful. Pricey sirloin steaks treated in the same fashion yielded nearly identical results, but at a much higher cost. We would stick with blade steaks.

Confident in our meat selection, we began work on finessing the pie's flavor. Wanting to limit the number of vegetables, we included just onion, carrots, and peas. We sautéed the onion and carrots directly in the skillet after the meat was removed. The frozen peas, though, would have to wait; we added them, still frozen, to the sauce just before baking. Tasters enjoyed the flavor of this stew, but some wanted it heartier, so we added white mushrooms for more flavor and texture.

For the sauce in the stew, we wanted a hearty gravy. We started by making a roux with the vegetables in the skillet, then thinning it with broth. Focusing on the broth, we tried both chicken and beef broth to build the sauce. Chicken broth yielded a weakly flavored stew; beef broth was richer in flavor but the resulting sauce lacked complexity. Our solution was to fortify the flavor of the beef broth by adding a splash of red wine, 2 teaspoons of tomato paste, and a little thyme.

With our filling perfected, it was time for a topping. We began our testing with the test kitchen's single-crust pie dough, which calls for sour cream, flour, salt, and butter. Once we scaled down, however, we were down to 2 tablespoons of sour cream—a miniscule amount. So we switched to pantry-friendly shortening to retain the flakiness in our crust. We rolled out the dough to measure 10 inches across—the same size as the skillet. We then folded and crimped the dough around the edge (for looks and to support the outer rim of crust so it didn't melt into the filling during baking). To make transferring the crust to the top of the skillet easy, we froze the shaped crust on a baking sheet until stiff, then plopped it right onto the warm filling in the skillet.

NOTES FROM THE TEST KITCHEN

TRIMMING BLADE STEAKS

1. Halve each steak lengthwise, leaving the gristle on one half.

2. Cut away the gristle from the half to which it is still attached.

STORING MUSHROOMS

Gourmet markets usually sell loose mushrooms, but most of the time you'll find mushrooms prepackaged, shrink-wrapped in amounts that are too much for two people. Because of their high moisture content, raw mushrooms are very perishable. Packaged mushrooms, unopened, can be stored right in their original containers, which are designed to "breathe," balancing the retention of moisture and the release of ethylene gas. If you open a sealed package of mushrooms but don't use all the contents, simply rewrap the remaining mushrooms in the box with plastic wrap. If your market has loose mushrooms, store these in a partially open zipper-lock bag, which maximizes air circulation (and allows for the release of ethylene gas) without drying out the mushrooms.

We thought we were on the road to success, but we had trouble achieving a fully cooked crust; the underside was soggy. We found that using a 425-degree oven, and topping the pie while the ingredients were still piping-hot, allowed the crust to bake through more evenly and thoroughly, preventing a soggy underside. We had achieved our goal of making an easy, scaled-down beef pot pie for two. And not only was it convenient (and our kitchen wasn't piled high with dishes when we were done), but tasters weren't leaving a crumb behind.

Beef Pot Pie

SERVES 2

We prefer the buttery flavor and flaky texture of homemade pie dough here; however, you can substitute store-bought pie dough if desired. If using store-bought pie dough, fold back the rim, crimp the edges, cut vent holes, and freeze as directed in the Pot Pie Crust recipe. Make sure the filling is still hot when you place the frozen crust on top.

12	ounces blade steak, trimmed (see page 6) and cut into 1-inch pieces
	Salt and pepper
5	teaspoons vegetable oil
2	carrots, peeled and sliced ¼ inch thick
1	small onion, minced
4	ounces white mushrooms, halved if small, quartered if large
2	garlic cloves, minced
1	teaspoon minced fresh thyme or ¼ teaspoon dried
2	tablespoons unbleached all-purpose flour
2	teaspoons tomato paste
2	tablespoons dry red wine
1¾	cups beef broth
½	cup frozen peas
1	recipe Pot Pie Crust, frozen for at least 30 minutes (see note)

1. Adjust an oven rack to the lowest position and heat the oven to 425 degrees. Pat the steak dry with paper towels and season with salt and pepper. Heat 2 teaspoons of the oil in a 10-inch ovensafe skillet over medium-high heat until just smoking. Add the meat and cook, stirring occasionally, until well browned, 5 to 7 minutes. Transfer the meat to a bowl and set aside.

2. Heat the remaining 1 tablespoon oil in the skillet over medium heat until shimmering. Add the carrots, onion, and ¼ teaspoon salt and cook until the vegetables are softened, about 5 minutes. Stir in the mushrooms and cook until softened, 3 to 5 minutes.

3. Stir in the garlic and thyme and cook until fragrant, about 30 seconds. Stir in the flour and tomato paste and cook, stirring constantly, until the flour is incorporated, about 1 minute. Stir in the wine and cook until evaporated, about 30 seconds. Slowly stir in the broth, scraping up any browned bits, and bring to a simmer.

4. Off the heat, season the sauce with salt and pepper to taste, then stir in the browned beef, along with any accumulated juice, and peas.

5. Remove the frozen crust from the freezer, discard the plastic wrap and parchment paper, and, following the photo on page 8, place the crust on top of the filling. Bake the pot pie until the crust is golden brown and the filling is bubbling, 30 to 35 minutes. Let the pot pie cool for 10 minutes before serving.

VARIATION

Beef Pot Pie with Portobello Mushroom and Sherry
Follow the recipe for Beef Pot Pie, substituting 1 small portobello mushroom cap (about 4 ounces), gills removed, cut into ½-inch pieces, for the white mushrooms and 1 teaspoon minced fresh rosemary (or ¼ teaspoon dried) for the thyme. Substitute 2 tablespoons dry sherry for the wine in step 3 and stir in 2 tablespoons more dry sherry with the beef and peas in step 4.

Pot Pie Crust

MAKES 1 (10-INCH) ROUND

If you don't have a food processor, see the hand-mixing instructions on page 8.

1	cup (5 ounces) unbleached all-purpose flour
½	teaspoon salt
2	tablespoons vegetable shortening, cut into ½-inch pieces and chilled
4	tablespoons (½ stick) unsalted butter, cut into ¼-inch pieces and chilled
3–5	tablespoons ice water

1. Process the flour and salt together in a food processor until combined. Scatter the shortening over the top and process until the mixture resembles coarse cornmeal, about 10 seconds. Scatter the butter pieces over the top and pulse until the mixture resembles coarse crumbs, about 10 pulses. Transfer the mixture to a medium bowl.

2. Sprinkle 3 tablespoons of the water over the mixture. Using a stiff rubber spatula, stir and press the dough until it sticks together. If the dough does not come together, stir in the remaining water, 1 tablespoon at a time, until it does.

3. Turn out the dough onto a counter. Shape into a ball and flatten to a 5-inch disk; wrap with plastic wrap and refrigerate for 1 hour. Before rolling out the dough, let

it sit on the counter to soften slightly, about 10 minutes. (The wrapped dough can be refrigerated for up to 2 days or frozen for up to 1 month. If frozen, let the dough thaw completely on the counter before rolling it out.)

4. Roll out the dough to a 10-inch round, about ⅜ inch thick, on a large piece of parchment paper. Following the photos, fold back the outer ½-inch rim, then crimp the folded edge. Cut four oval-shaped vents in the center of the dough. Slide the parchment paper and dough onto a baking sheet, cover loosely with plastic wrap, and freeze until firm, at least 30 minutes or up to 24 hours.

NOTES FROM THE TEST KITCHEN

SHAPING POT PIE DOUGH FOR THE SKILLET

1. Fold back the outer ½-inch rim of the dough.

2. Using your knuckle and forefingers, crimp the folded edge of dough to make an attractive fluted rim.

3. Using a paring knife, cut four oval-shaped vents, each about 2 inches long and ½ inch wide, in the center of the dough.

HAND MIXING POT PIE CRUST

If you don't own a food processor, you can mix pie dough by hand. Freeze the butter in its stick form until very firm. Whisk together the flour and salt in a large bowl. Add the chilled shortening and press it into the flour using a fork. Grate the frozen butter on the large holes of a box grater into the flour mixture, then cut the mixture together, using two butter knives, until the mixture resembles coarse crumbs. Add the water as directed.

TOPPING SKILLET POT PIE

Gently lay the frozen pie crust on top of the hot filling in the skillet.

THE BEST STORE-BOUGHT PIE DOUGH

A flaky, buttery homemade pie crust is the ultimate crown for beef pot pie, but it's also a fair amount of work. How much would we sacrifice by using a store-bought crust instead? To find out, we tried several types and brands, including both dry mixes (just add water) and ready-made crusts, either frozen or refrigerated. The dry mixes, including Betty Crocker, Jiffy, Krusteaz, and Pillsbury, all had problems. Some were too salty, some were too sweet, and all required both mixing and rolling—not much work saved. Frozen crusts, including Mrs. Smith's (also sold as Oronoque Orchards) and Pillsbury Pet-Ritz, required zero prep, but tasters found them pasty and bland, and it was nearly impossible to pry them from the flimsy foil "pie plate" in which they are sold. The one refrigerated contender, **Pillsbury Just Unroll! Pie Crusts**, wasn't bad. Though the flavor was somewhat bland, the crust baked up to an impressive flakiness. Better yet, this fully prepared product comes rolled up and is just the right size for our Beef Pot Pie.

PAN-FRIED PORK CHOPS AND DIRTY RICE

IN THE SOUTH, PORK CHOPS ARE OFTEN PAIRED WITH dirty rice—a side dish of cooked rice, cured meats, vegetables, and seasonings that give the rice a "dirty" appearance. This pork and rice combination is no doubt a success when the components are prepared individually—the result is juicy pork chops and spicy, tender rice—but we wondered if it would work as well if we made it all in the same skillet to create a boldly flavored meal for two. There was only one way to find out.

We began by pan-frying two pork chops, then we set them aside while we prepared the rice. We cooked chorizo—cutting it into ¼-inch pieces and browning it in the skillet—then added the traditional dirty rice foundation of onion, bell pepper, and celery, followed by some garlic. After adding some chicken broth and the rice, we nestled in the browned chops, brought everything to a simmer, and allowed the pork and rice to finish cooking together. After tasting the results, we knew this approach certainly had potential, but there was plenty of room for improvement—the pork was tough and dry, and the rice was bland and mushy.

Because pork chops tend to be fairly lean, they require special treatment to prevent the meat from drying out. We typically favor bone-in rib chops, which are higher in fat than other chops and less prone to drying out. But even with the extra fat to protect these chops, the heat of pan-searing combined with the simmering time was still overcooking them. We tried pan-frying them for less time, but this left us with pale, bland chops. We were after moist, juicy chops with the deep flavor that comes only from a well-caramelized exterior. In the end, we found that pan-frying the chops until well browned on just one side—which took about 5 minutes—gave us the golden, crisp crust we sought (the browned side of the pork nestled into the rice lost its crispness anyway), while still ensuring juicy meat and deep flavor.

As for cooking a small amount of rice in a skillet, our research indicated that many recipes rely on quick-cooking instant rice. We find instant rice to be simply not as good as regular rice in flavor and texture, so we opted for long-grain rice, which offers more flavor and a consistently pleasant, chewy texture. This switch helped, but our skillet-cooked rice was still a little bit mushy. We found that sautéing the rice along with the cooked chorizo and vegetables (and before adding the cooking liquid) guaranteed distinct grains of perfectly cooked rice every time—and boosted the flavor of the rice in the process.

To add a little more depth to the rice, tasters favored a modest amount of thyme and cayenne. We also folded in a bit of sliced scallion for freshness. We transferred the rice to a platter, then topped it with our warm pork chops and watched as tasters sampled happily.

Pan-Fried Pork Chops and Dirty Rice
SERVES 2

If the pork is "enhanced" (see page 10 for more information), do not brine. If brining the pork, do not season with salt in step 1. If you can't find chorizo sausage, use andouille or linguiça. See page 10 for a recipe to use up the leftover celery and page 131 for a recipe to use up the leftover red bell pepper.

> 2 (12- to 14-ounce) bone-in pork rib chops, about 1½ inches thick, trimmed, sides slit (see page 10), brined if desired (see note; see page 162)
> Salt and pepper
> 2 tablespoons vegetable oil
> 4 ounces chorizo (see note), halved lengthwise and cut crosswise into ¼-inch pieces
> 1 small onion, minced
> 1 celery rib, minced
> ½ red bell pepper, stemmed, seeded, and chopped fine
> ½ cup long-grain white rice, rinsed
> 2 garlic cloves, minced
> ½ teaspoon minced fresh thyme or ⅛ teaspoon dried
> ⅛ teaspoon cayenne pepper
> 1¾ cups low-sodium chicken broth
> 2 scallions, sliced thin

1. Pat the pork chops dry with paper towels and season with salt and pepper. Heat the oil in a 10-inch skillet over medium-high heat until just smoking. Carefully lay the pork chops in the skillet and cook until well browned on one side, 4 to 6 minutes. Transfer the pork chops to a plate, browned-side up.

2. Pour off all but 1 tablespoon of the fat from the skillet and return the skillet to medium heat. Add the chorizo and cook until browned, 2 to 3 minutes. Add the onion, celery, and bell pepper and cook until the vegetables are softened, about 5 minutes. Stir in the rice, garlic, thyme, and cayenne and cook until fragrant, about 30 seconds.

3. Stir in the broth, scraping up any browned bits. Nestle the pork chops into the rice, browned-side up, and bring to a simmer. Cover, reduce the heat to medium-low, and cook until the pork chops register 140 to 145 degrees on an instant-read thermometer, 8 to 10 minutes.

4. Transfer the pork chops to a plate, browned-side up, brushing any rice that sticks to the chops back into the skillet. Tent loosely with foil and let rest for 10 minutes.

5. Cover the skillet and continue to cook the rice over medium-low heat, stirring occasionally, until the liquid has been absorbed and the rice is tender, about 15 minutes longer.

6. Off the heat, gently fold the scallions into the rice and season with salt and pepper to taste. Serve the pork chops with the rice.

NOTES FROM THE TEST KITCHEN

PREPARING PORK CHOPS

To get pork chops to lie flat and cook evenly, cut two slits about 2 inches apart through the fat and connective tissue.

ENHANCED OR UNENHANCED PORK?
Because modern pork is remarkably lean and therefore somewhat bland and prone to dryness if overcooked, a product called "enhanced" pork has overtaken the market. In fact, it can be hard to find unenhanced pork. Enhanced pork has been injected with a solution of water, salt, sodium phosphate, sodium lactate, potassium lactate, sodium diacetate, and varying flavor agents to bolster flavor and juiciness; these enhancing ingredients add 7 to 15 percent extra weight. After several taste tests, we have concluded that although enhanced pork is indeed juicier and more tender than unenhanced pork, the latter has more genuine pork flavor. Some tasters also picked up artificial, salty flavors in enhanced pork. It can also leach juice that, once reduced, will result in overly salty sauces. We prefer natural pork, but the choice is up to you.

USE IT UP: CELERY

Celery Salad with Red Onion and Orange
MAKES 2 CUPS

If you can find one, a blood orange, with its reddish-orange flesh, makes a colorful alternative to a regular orange. This salad pairs well with simply prepared fish and chicken dishes.

- 4 **celery ribs, sliced thin on the bias**
- 1 **orange, peeled, quartered, and cut into ¼-inch pieces (see note)**
- 3 **tablespoons minced red onion or shallot**
- 2 **tablespoons extra-virgin olive oil**
- 2 **tablespoons minced fresh parsley or mint**
- 1 **tablespoon cider vinegar**
- 1 **teaspoon honey**
- ⅛ **teaspoon celery seed**
  Salt and pepper

Combine the celery, orange, onion, oil, parsley, vinegar, honey, and celery seed in a medium bowl. Season with salt and pepper to taste. Let the salad sit for 15 minutes to allow the flavors to meld before serving.

PORK TENDERLOIN WITH SWEET POTATO

PORK TENDERLOIN IS A GREAT WEEKNIGHT CHOICE when you're cooking for two. The practical advantages of this supermarket cut are many: One 12-ounce pork tenderloin is just the right amount for two, it requires little in the way of prep, and it cooks relatively quickly. But because pork tenderloin is so incredibly lean, it is quick to dry out, and its mild flavor could benefit from a serious flavor boost. We hoped to solve both of these problems and create a juicy, flavorful pork tenderloin. While we were at it, we also wanted to make our pork tenderloin a complete skillet meal for two and thought sweet potatoes would be the ideal accompaniment.

First we worked with the tenderloin, and our initial tests quickly confirmed that a stovetop-to-oven technique was indeed the best approach to cooking this mild cut of pork: Searing the tenderloin on the stovetop

PAN-ROASTED PORK TENDERLOIN WITH SWEET POTATO AND SPICY MAPLE BUTTER

gave it a deep brown, caramelized crust that greatly enhanced its flavor, and transferring it to the oven allowed it to gently and evenly cook through without drying out. Testing various oven temperatures, we found that while cooler ovens produced evenly cooked and juicy tenderloins, they did little to help maintain the well-browned crust. Hotter oven temperatures enhanced the golden exterior and still produced an evenly cooked tenderloin, but the meat was slightly dry. In the end we found that a 425-degree oven was best, and taking the pork out of the oven when its internal temperature reached 140 to 145 degrees ensured that the meat remained juicy.

Although our tenderloin was now perfectly cooked and pan-searing had greatly enhanced its flavor, we still wondered if more could be done. The answer was simple: a dry rub of thyme, crushed rosemary, and ground cloves. Rubbed onto the tenderloin along with some salt and pepper before searing, our fragrant mix gained another level of flavor as the intense heat of the skillet toasted the rub.

Now that we had flavorful, juicy pork, we could turn our attention to the sweet potatoes—or rather, sweet potato, as we found that one large potato was plenty for two people. We already knew that cutting peeled sweet potatoes into wedges results in uneven cooking, as the thinner tips cook faster than the sides, whereas slicing the potatoes into rounds ensures pieces of even thickness that cook at the same rate. However, even with a uniform shape, simply dumping a handful of raw potato rounds into a hot skillet with a little oil left us chewing on charred potatoes with raw centers. Upping the amount of oil helped cook the potato slices a little more evenly, but not enough. The solution to our potato problem was to use the microwave to parcook them. While the tenderloin roasted in the oven, we popped the potatoes into the microwave to give them a head start, and by the time the pork was ready to rest, the potatoes were ready to finish up in the skillet with the flavorful fond left behind from the pork. They needed only about six minutes in the skillet, and placing the potatoes in a single layer ensured deeply caramelized exteriors and creamy, moist interiors.

As a final touch, we created a quick compound butter, mixing in maple syrup and a little cayenne. Spooned over the roasted pork tenderloin and potatoes just before serving, it slowly melted into a sauce and was the perfect complement.

Pan-Roasted Pork Tenderloin with Sweet Potato and Spicy Maple Butter
SERVES 2

Choose a sweet potato that is as even in width as possible. Make sure to use a 10-inch ovensafe nonstick skillet for this recipe.

- 2 tablespoons unsalted butter, softened
- 2 teaspoons maple syrup
- ⅛ teaspoon cayenne pepper
  Salt and pepper
- 1 teaspoon dried thyme
- 1 teaspoon dried rosemary, crushed
- ⅛ teaspoon ground cloves
- 1 (12-ounce) pork tenderloin, trimmed
- 5 teaspoons vegetable oil
- 1 large sweet potato (about 1 pound), peeled and sliced into ¾-inch-thick rounds (see note)

1. Beat the butter with a large fork in a small bowl until light and fluffy. Mix in the maple syrup, cayenne, ⅛ teaspoon salt, and ⅛ teaspoon pepper until well combined; set aside for serving.

2. Adjust an oven rack to the middle position and heat the oven to 425 degrees. Combine the thyme, rosemary, cloves, ¼ teaspoon salt, and ¼ teaspoon pepper in a small bowl. Pat the pork dry with paper towels, then rub the mixture evenly over the pork.

3. Heat 2 teaspoons of the oil in a 10-inch ovensafe nonstick skillet over medium-high heat until just smoking. Carefully lay the tenderloin in the skillet and cook until browned on all sides, about 6 minutes, turning as needed and reducing the heat if the spices begin to burn. Transfer the skillet to the oven and roast the tenderloin until it registers 140 to 145 degrees on an instant-read thermometer, 12 to 15 minutes.

4. Meanwhile, toss the potato slices with 1 teaspoon more oil, ⅛ teaspoon salt, and ⅛ teaspoon pepper in a microwave-safe bowl. Cover the bowl and microwave on high until the potato begins to soften, 5 to 7 minutes, gently stirring halfway through.

5. Using potholders (the skillet handle will be hot), remove the skillet from the oven. Transfer the tenderloin to a carving board, tent loosely with foil, and let rest for about 10 minutes.

6. Meanwhile, drain the microwaved potato rounds well. Add the remaining 2 teaspoons oil to the skillet and return to medium heat until shimmering. Add the drained potato rounds in a single layer and cook until golden brown on both sides, about 6 minutes, flipping them halfway through. (If the potato rounds are browning unevenly, use tongs to gently move them around as necessary.)

7. Transfer the potato rounds to a platter. Cut the pork into ½-inch-thick slices and transfer to the platter with the potato rounds; top with the butter and serve.

SAUTÉED CHICKEN WITH RATATOUILLE

FOR AN EASY WEEKNIGHT DINNER FOR TWO, it's hard to beat the ease and appeal of sautéed chicken breasts. But finding an interesting and equally convenient side dish that doesn't have you juggling multiple pans on the stovetop isn't so easy. We thought ratatouille—the flavorful French dish featuring eggplant, zucchini, onions, pepper, tomatoes, and fresh herbs—would make an ideal partner to simple chicken breasts. Ratatouille is colorful and inviting, the flavors are light and multilayered, and the variety of vegetables provides plenty of textural interest. We were confident that sautéing the chicken would be simple enough; the real challenge would be making our meal all in one skillet. Certainly we would be using small enough quantities of each vegetable to fit easily, but classic ratatouille preparation involves sautéing each vegetable separately, then combining them at the last minute so that each vegetable maintains its individual character. Could we find a way to streamline this technique and cook everything together?

Our plan was to first sauté the chicken to create a nicely browned, flavorful exterior, set it aside to start the vegetables, and finally return it to the pan to allow everything to finish cooking together. We found that the key to moist, tender meat when sautéing boneless, skinless chicken breasts (our cut of choice here since they require minimal prep) was pounding the chicken to an even thickness. This step allowed the chicken to cook evenly, which in turn preserved its flavor. We also found that lightly dredging the chicken in flour added even more flavor and encouraged further browning while protecting the delicate exterior of the chicken from the heat of the pan.

With the chicken browned and our skillet free, we could start the ratatouille. For textural contrast, we sliced the onion and pepper into strips and cut the zucchini and eggplant into 1-inch cubes (one small zucchini and

one small eggplant were just the right amount), leaving the skin on for extra stability. Fresh, ripe tomatoes would be ideal, but because good-quality tomatoes can be hard to come by most of the year, we settled on canned diced tomatoes for their reliable flavor.

With our key players in place, we could now address the cooking technique. Despite our skepticism, we thought it made sense to start with the simplest method—add the vegetables to the pan and begin stewing. We sweated the onions and peppers, then tossed in the rest of the vegetables, nestled the chicken into the mix, and simmered everything, covered, until the chicken was cooked through and the vegetables were tender. Although the chicken was perfectly cooked, the resulting ratatouille was mushy, soupy, and one-dimensional. We knew the eggplant and zucchini were responsible for releasing much of the liquid that led to the soupiness.

Eggplant and zucchini are often salted and set aside to release liquid before cooking, but for a simple week-night meal, an extra half hour of prep time wasn't really appealing. We wondered if browning them before the vegetables were combined would help reduce the amount of liquid and, at the same time, further concentrate their flavor. It took only five to seven minutes on medium-high heat for each vegetable to develop a well-browned exterior.

After transferring the eggplant and zucchini to a bowl, we sautéed the onions and peppers together, adding some garlic and fresh thyme for additional flavor. Finally, we gently folded in the tomatoes, zucchini, and eggplant, returned the chicken breasts to the skillet, and began simmering once again. This time when we removed the lid, we found that the vegetables had retained their shape much better and were surrounded by a judicious amount of liquid. We took the chicken out to rest and continued to cook the vegetables, uncovered, for an additional five minutes to allow the juices in the pan to reduce and thicken to just the right consistency. Finished with a little chopped fresh basil, our ratatouille was bright, fresh, and full of tender vegetables.

With our chicken perfectly cooked and the rata-touille showing a vast improvement on the soupy mess we'd made earlier, we had finally achieved a unique medley of chicken and vegetables with distinct textures and flavors.

Sautéed Chicken with Ratatouille
SERVES 2

Using fresh herbs is important here. If you can't find baby eggplant, you can use ½ globe eggplant (about 8 ounces) instead. Do not peel the eggplant, as the skin helps the eggplant hold together during cooking. It is important to cook the eggplant and zucchini until they are brown, but to stir them as little as possible to prevent them from turning mushy. See page 15 for a recipe to use up the leftover canned diced tomatoes and page 131 for a recipe to use up the leftover red bell pepper.

¼   cup unbleached all-purpose flour
2   (6- to 8-ounce) boneless, skinless chicken breasts, trimmed and pounded ½ inch thick
    Salt and pepper
3   tablespoons olive oil
1   baby eggplant (about 7 ounces), cut into 1-inch pieces (see note)
1   small zucchini (about 6 ounces), cut into 1-inch pieces
1   small onion, halved and sliced ¼ inch thick
½   red bell pepper, stemmed, seeded, and sliced into ¼-inch strips
2   teaspoons minced fresh thyme or rosemary
1   garlic clove, minced
½   cup drained canned diced tomatoes, ¼ cup juice reserved
¼   cup low-sodium chicken broth
1   tablespoon chopped fresh basil

1. Place the flour in a shallow dish. Pat the chicken breasts dry with paper towels and season with salt and pepper. Working with 1 breast at a time, dredge the chicken in the flour, shaking off the excess.

2. Heat 1 tablespoon of the oil in a 10-inch nonstick skillet over medium-high heat until just smoking. Carefully lay the chicken in the skillet and cook until lightly browned on both sides, 6 to 8 minutes, flipping the breasts halfway through. Transfer the chicken to a plate.

3. Wipe out the skillet with a wad of paper towels. Heat 2 teaspoons more oil in the skillet over medium-high heat until shimmering. Add the eggplant and cook, stirring occasionally, until browned, 5 to 7 minutes. Transfer the eggplant to a medium bowl. Repeat with 2 teaspoons more oil and the zucchini; transfer to the bowl with the eggplant.

4. Heat the remaining 2 teaspoons oil in the skillet over medium heat until shimmering. Add the onion, bell pepper, and ¼ teaspoon salt and cook until the vegetables are softened, about 5 minutes. Stir in the thyme and garlic and cook until fragrant, about 30 seconds.

5. Add the tomatoes with the reserved juice and broth, scraping up any browned bits. Gently stir in the browned eggplant and zucchini. Nestle the chicken into the vegetables and bring to a simmer. Cover, reduce the heat to medium-low, and cook until the chicken registers 160 to 165 degrees on an instant-read thermometer, 12 to 18 minutes.

USE IT UP: CANNED DICED TOMATOES

Spicy Chipotle Barbecue Sauce
MAKES ABOUT ¾ CUP

The sauce can be refrigerated in an airtight container for up to 4 days. Use it as you would any other barbecue sauce.

- 1 tablespoon unsalted butter
- 1 shallot, minced
- ½ teaspoon chili powder
- ½ cup drained canned diced tomatoes
- ¼ cup ketchup
- ¼ cup low-sodium chicken broth, plus extra as needed
- 2 tablespoons brown sugar
- 2 teaspoons white vinegar, plus extra to taste
- ½ teaspoon minced canned chipotle chile in adobo sauce, plus extra to taste

  Salt and pepper

1. Melt the butter in a medium saucepan over medium heat. Add the shallot and cook until softened, 2 to 3 minutes. Stir in the chili powder and cook until fragrant, about 30 seconds. Stir in the tomatoes and cook until softened and dry, about 1 minute. Add the ketchup, broth, sugar, vinegar, and chipotle. Bring to a simmer and cook until thickened, about 20 minutes.

2. Transfer the sauce to a blender and process until smooth, about 30 seconds, adjusting the consistency with extra broth as needed. Season with salt, pepper, vinegar, and chipotle to taste.

6. Transfer the chicken to a plate, tent loosely with foil, and let rest. Continue to cook the ratatouille, uncovered, until the sauce is thickened but the vegetables still retain their shape, about 5 minutes longer. Off the heat, gently stir in the basil and season with salt and pepper to taste. Serve the chicken with the ratatouille.

CHICKEN VESUVIO

CHICKEN AND POTATOES ARE A CLASSIC COMBINATION that can be prepared in a multitude of ways. One of the test kitchen's favorite preparations, however, is a Chicago-inspired dish with bone-in chicken and potatoes smothered in a garlicky white wine sauce and garnished with peas, known as chicken Vesuvio. Typically, this dish requires multiple pots and pans and trips back and forth to the oven, but we wanted something more appropriate for a dinner for two. Could we develop a recipe for chicken Vesuvio that stayed true to its roots but restricted the work to just one skillet on the stovetop? We stepped into the kitchen to find out.

Classic chicken Vesuvio starts with browning chicken parts in a hot skillet. The browned chicken parts are set aside and then potato wedges are browned in the rendered chicken fat. When the potatoes come out of the pan, it's time to build the sauce. Garlic is sautéed, oregano is added next, and the pan is deglazed with white wine. This mixture is combined with the browned chicken and potatoes in a roasting pan, and the whole thing is baked until cooked through. The sauce is then poured off into a pot and further reduced on the stovetop before being ladled over individual servings of chicken and potatoes.

For us, streamlining this dish meant starting with boneless, skinless chicken breasts. Bone-in, skin-on chicken parts are important in the traditional dish, where the bones and skin protect the meat from drying out during the lengthy cooking time. But we were hoping for a quick meal, and boneless, skinless breasts cook much faster. To get the most flavor from lean boneless breasts, we followed the method we had used for our Sautéed Chicken with Ratatouille (page 14), pounding the chicken to an even thickness and dredging it in flour before browning it in the skillet. After browning, we set the breasts aside until it was time to finish cooking them through with the potatoes and sauce.

Getting good browning on the potatoes was also important to flavor development. But we couldn't just grab any potato, as fluffy russets broke apart in the skillet. Yukon gold potatoes were a little firmer, but waxy red potatoes were the best choice, as they held their shape and texture throughout cooking. In Chicago recipes the potatoes are cut into wedges, but these small potatoes worked better cut into 1-inch chunks, which we browned and then removed from the pan while we built the sauce.

To stay true to tradition, we needed plenty of garlic, oregano, and white wine. For more assertive flavor, we added ½ teaspoon of fragrant rosemary, and to augment the chicken flavor we added chicken broth. Once the chicken was cooked through, we transferred it to a platter and tented it with foil to keep it warm. We continued simmering the potatoes until they were tender and the sauce had reduced to the proper consistency; the peas went into the pan off the heat.

Our skillet Vesuvio was almost there, but tasters thought the sauce needed some additional richness. A couple of tablespoons of butter and a squeeze of fresh lemon juice brought the sauce up to par. This Chicago favorite was now easy enough to prepare as a weeknight dinner for two—and it didn't require an army of dishwashers.

NOTES FROM THE TEST KITCHEN

SHIMMERING VERSUS SMOKING

Pan-searing and sautéing both require you to heat the oil in the skillet to a certain heat level. But how do you know when the pan is hot enough? We find visual cues helpful and offer them in our recipes, as follows: When searing or browning cuts of meat like a roast, steaks, bone-in chops, bone-in chicken breasts, and the like, you want the pan to be very hot. Searing over high heat gives your food a well-browned crust. Look for wisps of smoke rising from the oil—this means the pan is very hot and ready. By contrast, when sautéing thin, delicate cuts of meat like cutlets or thin fish fillets, or vegetables such as onions, you want the oil to be just moderately hot. You'll know the pan is ready when the oil shimmers. Why does it make a difference? If you put a thin fillet into a smoking hot pan, it will do more than sear—it will cook through before you've had time to flip it.

Chicken Vesuvio

SERVES 2

For a spicier dish, stir in ⅛ teaspoon red pepper flakes with the garlic in step 3.

- ¼ cup unbleached all-purpose flour
- 2 (6- to 8-ounce) boneless, skinless chicken breasts, trimmed and pounded ½ inch thick
  Salt and pepper
- 5 teaspoons olive oil
- 12 ounces red potatoes (about 3), cut into 1-inch chunks
- 1 garlic clove, minced
- 1 teaspoon minced fresh oregano or ¼ teaspoon dried
- ½ teaspoon minced fresh rosemary or ⅛ teaspoon dried
- 1 cup low-sodium chicken broth
- ¼ cup dry white wine
- ½ cup frozen peas, thawed
- 2 tablespoons unsalted butter
- 1 teaspoon fresh lemon juice

1. Place the flour in a shallow dish. Pat the chicken breasts dry with paper towels and season with salt and pepper. Working with 1 breast at a time, dredge in the flour, shaking off the excess.

2. Heat 1 tablespoon of the oil in a 10-inch nonstick skillet over medium-high heat until just smoking. Carefully lay the chicken in the skillet and cook until lightly browned on both sides, 6 to 8 minutes, flipping the breasts halfway through. Transfer the chicken to a plate.

3. Wipe out the skillet with a wad of paper towels. Heat the remaining 2 teaspoons oil in the skillet over medium-high heat until shimmering. Add the potatoes and cook, stirring occasionally, until golden brown, about 7 minutes. Stir in the garlic, oregano, rosemary, and ⅛ teaspoon salt and cook until fragrant, about 30 seconds. Add the broth and wine, scraping up any browned bits. Nestle the chicken, along with any accumulated juice, into the potatoes and bring to a simmer. Cover, reduce the heat to medium-low, and cook until the chicken registers 160 to 165 degrees on an instant-read thermometer, 12 to 18 minutes, flipping the chicken halfway through.

4. Transfer the chicken to a serving platter and tent loosely with foil to keep warm. Increase the heat to

CHICKEN VESUVIO

medium and continue to cook, uncovered, until the potatoes are tender and the sauce is thickened slightly, 5 to 7 minutes longer. Using a slotted spoon, transfer the potatoes to the platter with the chicken. Off the heat, stir in the peas, butter, and lemon juice, and season with salt and pepper to taste. Pour the sauce over the chicken and potatoes and serve.

BRAISED CHICKEN THIGHS

WHEN DONE RIGHT, BRAISED CHICKEN CAN BE THE ultimate comfort food: tender pieces of juicy meat surrounded by a rich, homey sauce and tender vegetables. But like most comfort foods, braised chicken is typically geared toward feeding the masses. We were looking for a smaller, simplified formula for braised chicken, one that could easily be made in a skillet and still make a fulfilling meal.

We first needed to address the issue of the chicken itself. The key to the success of any braise is cooking it slowly and over moderate heat. For our braised chicken, this meant we would need pieces that could withstand extended time in the pan. While many recipes start with whole leg pieces, for our smaller skillet braise we needed something more manageable, so we opted for convenient chicken thighs. The tough muscles of the legs are laced with fat and connective tissue, which provide a robust flavor and are better able to withstand longer cooking times than delicate breast meat. We found that four 6-ounce thighs were all we needed for our scaled-down version, and they fit nicely in a 10-inch skillet.

We know that most good braises start with browning the meat to establish flavor. We had chosen boneless, skinless thighs for their ease of preparation but quickly discovered that their problems outweighed their benefits—the meat toughened slightly and the flavor was weak. Switching to bone-in, skin-on thighs, we found that the bones added flavor to the braise and helped protect the chicken from overcooking, and the skin browned well (contributing flavor to the finished dish) and further protected the meat from drying out. (We decided to remove the skin once browned to avoid any flabby pieces in our final dish.) After about an hour

PREPARING FENNEL

1. Cut off the stems and feathery fronds. (The fronds can be minced and used for a garnish, if desired.)

2. Trim a very thin slice from the base and remove any tough or blemished outer layers from the bulb.

3. Cut the bulb in half through the base. Use a small, sharp knife to remove the pyramid-shaped core.

4. Slice each fennel half into thin strips. For chopped fennel, cut the strips crosswise into small pieces.

of slow simmering, our chicken was perfectly tender, but tasters still found the flavor to be fleeting; it was time to focus on the cooking liquid.

Although some braises use water (and seasonings) as the liquid base, we found that chicken broth and some wine lent our dish a welcome acidity and depth of flavor. In the end, we determined that 1¼ cups of chicken broth and ¼ cup of white wine yielded the right balance of chicken-y richness and bright flavor.

After browning the chicken, we set the thighs aside on a plate while we sautéed the vegetables—

another key step in developing flavor. We began with an onion and a few carrots (three were all we needed). Tasters requested a heartier dish, so we added a couple of red potatoes; not only did they add bulk, but the starch they released added body to our braising liquid. Stirring in some garlic and thyme also provided depth.

At this point, many braised chicken recipes have you add flour to help thicken the cooking liquid to a proper sauce-like consistency. While this step is necessary with larger braises that require a lot of liquid, we discovered that with our skillet braise, even the smallest amount caused the sauce to turn gloppy by the time the chicken was done cooking. We figured we could skip the flour and simply rely on a quick reduction of the sauce to develop the desired thickness.

After adding the broth and wine, we scraped the fond from the bottom of the pan, placed the chicken back in the skillet, and covered it to finish cooking. When the chicken was cooked through, we set it aside while we returned the liquid to a simmer and continued cooking until the vegetables were tender and the sauce had thickened slightly. Our braise was now fairly rich and heavy, so for a fresh touch, we added some thinly sliced fennel, which became perfectly tender in the short amount of time it took for the sauce to reduce. Asparagus worked equally well. We finished the dish with some fresh tarragon (dill with the asparagus) and decided we had developed the perfect formula for a small-scale, juicy, and flavorful braised chicken dish for two.

Braised Chicken Thighs with Potatoes, Carrots, Fennel, and Tarragon

SERVES 2

For this recipe you will need a 10-inch skillet with a tight-fitting lid. See page 99 for a recipe to use up the leftover fennel.

- 4   (6-ounce) bone-in, skin-on chicken thighs, trimmed
      Salt and pepper
- 2   teaspoons vegetable oil
- 3   carrots, peeled and sliced ½ inch thick
- 8   ounces red potatoes (about 2), scrubbed and cut into ½-inch chunks
- 1   small onion, minced

- 1   garlic clove, minced
- ½   teaspoon minced fresh thyme or ⅛ teaspoon dried
- 1¼ cups low-sodium chicken broth
- ¼   cup dry white wine
- ½   fennel bulb (about 6 ounces), trimmed of stalks, cored, and sliced thin (see page 18)
- 2   tablespoons minced fresh tarragon
- 1   teaspoon fresh lemon juice

1. Pat the chicken thighs dry with paper towels and season with salt and pepper. Heat the oil in a 10-inch skillet over medium-high heat until just smoking. Carefully lay the chicken in the skillet and cook until well browned on both sides, 10 to 15 minutes, flipping the thighs halfway through. Transfer the chicken to a plate; when cool enough to handle, remove and discard the skin.

2. Pour off all but 1 tablespoon of the fat from the skillet and return to medium heat. Add the carrots, potatoes, onion, and ¼ teaspoon salt and cook until the onion is softened, about 5 minutes.

3. Stir in the garlic and thyme and cook until fragrant, about 30 seconds. Stir in the broth and wine, scraping up any browned bits. Nestle the chicken, along with any accumulated juice, into the vegetables and bring to a simmer. Cover, reduce the heat to medium-low, and cook until the chicken is very tender and almost falling off the bone, about 1 hour, flipping the chicken halfway through.

4. Transfer the chicken to a serving dish and tent loosely with foil to keep warm. Increase the heat to medium, stir in the fennel, and continue to simmer, uncovered, until the vegetables are tender and the sauce has thickened slightly, about 8 minutes.

5. Off the heat, stir in the tarragon and lemon juice and season with salt and pepper to taste. Spoon the vegetables and sauce over the chicken and serve.

VARIATION

Braised Chicken Thighs with Potatoes, Carrots, Asparagus, and Dill

Follow the recipe for Braised Chicken Thighs with Potatoes, Carrots, Fennel, and Tarragon, substituting ¼ bunch asparagus (about 4 ounces), tough ends trimmed and cut on the bias into 2-inch lengths, for the fennel and 2 tablespoons minced fresh dill for the tarragon.

CHICKEN CURRY WITH CHICKPEAS AND GREEN BEANS

CHICKEN CURRY

CURRIES ARE NOTORIOUS FOR THEIR LONG ingredient lists, including all manner of spices and aromatics plus vegetables, meat, or fish and usually some amount of coconut milk or yogurt. Perhaps that is why most curries will serve a crowd. And since it's tricky to scale down a recipe dependent upon just the right balance of spices and dairy, it seemed like the ideal challenge for the test kitchen, one that we hoped would put a tasty but simple curry within reach of those cooking for just two. We wanted to create a chicken curry that was as deep and flavorful as authentic versions but much simpler and could cook in a skillet in less than an hour. Most streamlined recipes we tried, however, were either uninspired or overloaded with spices. We had our work cut out for us.

Some curries are made with exotic whole and ground spices (fenugreek, asafetida, dried rose petals, and so on), but we decided to limit ourselves to everyday ground spices typical in curries, such as cumin, cloves, cardamom, cinnamon, and coriander. We had been reluctant to use store-bought curry powder and garam masala—both common spice blends added to curries—assuming their flavor would be inferior to that of homemade spice mixtures, but since our goal was a streamlined curry we decided to give them a try. We were surprised when tasters liked the store-bought versions nearly as well as our homemade mix. It turns out that store-bought curry powder and garam masala contain some of the exotic spices we had dismissed at the outset. To improve the flavor of the curry powder and garam masala, we tried cooking them briefly with a little oil, a process known as "blooming," until their fragrance emerged. This simple step took less than a minute and turned commercial curry powder and garam masala into flavor powerhouses.

With the spices settled, we turned to building the rest of our base. Many curry recipes begin with a generous amount of sautéed onion, which adds depth and body to the sauce. We needed only one onion and added it to the spices and oil already in the pan. In almost all curry recipes, equal amounts of garlic and ginger are then added, and we found no reason to stray from this well-balanced method. Wanting to take our sauce to the next level, we stirred in half of a minced fresh jalapeño

chile for heat and a dab of tomato paste for contrasting sweetness. Though it is decidedly inauthentic, we felt the latter ingredient was a must for the depth it created. As for the liquid component, we were surprised to find that ½ cup of water and ½ cup of diced tomatoes, which we pureed, did a fine job. Typically we would reach for chicken broth instead of water for a recipe like this, but given the complexity of our curry spices, chicken broth proved unnecessary.

Confident of our base, we turned our focus to the chicken and vegetables. For the chicken, we preferred boneless, skinless breasts, which could be added, unseared, to the skillet and required less than 20 minutes of simmering to cook through. After simmering, we removed them from the sauce and shredded the meat, stirring it back into the curry before serving. Cubed chicken pieces, which are more traditional, were not only less appealing visually, but they didn't soak up the sauce as well as the shredded chicken did.

For the vegetables, we settled on a combination of bell pepper, cauliflower, and peas. Sautéing the pepper first with the onion, we then added the cauliflower to the skillet before the tomatoes to allow the spices to coat the florets. Adding the peas too soon caused them to turn an army green color, so we waited to stir them in at the end to ensure that their bright color lasted.

Finally, most authentic curry recipes we researched also included yogurt or coconut milk. Though we had trouble with both when adding them at the beginning of cooking, we found that if we added them at the end, we avoided curdling, and it was the perfect creamy finish to our curry (we liked the flavor of both, so we leave the decision to you). Cilantro stirred in at the end also lent a touch of brightness. With that, we had created a full-flavored, satisfying chicken curry that was simple to prepare and didn't require a laundry list of ingredients.

NOTES FROM THE TEST KITCHEN

SHOPPING AT THE SALAD BAR
Our recipe uses only ¼ head of cauliflower. While leftover cauliflower will keep in the crisper drawer of your refrigerator for five to seven days, another option is to get your cauliflower from a quality salad bar—not only is it already prepped, but you can buy just the amount you need.

Chicken Curry with Cauliflower and Peas

SERVES 2

To make this dish spicier, add the chile seeds. See page 15 for a recipe to use up the leftover canned diced tomatoes and page 131 for a recipe to use up the leftover red bell pepper. See page 157 for a recipe to use up the leftover coconut milk. Serve the curry over basmati rice.

- ½ cup drained canned diced tomatoes, ¼ cup juice reserved
- 2 tablespoons vegetable oil
- 1 tablespoon sweet or mild curry powder
- ½ teaspoon garam masala
- 1 small onion, minced
- ½ red bell pepper, stemmed, seeded, and sliced into ¼-inch strips
  Salt
- 2 garlic cloves, minced
- 2 teaspoons minced or grated fresh ginger
- ½ jalapeño chile, stemmed, seeded, and minced (see note)
- 2 teaspoons tomato paste
- ¼ head cauliflower (about 8 ounces), trimmed, cored, and cut into 1-inch florets (about 2 cups)
- ½ cup water
- 2 (6-ounce) boneless, skinless chicken breasts, trimmed and pounded ½ inch thick
- ¼ cup frozen peas
- ¼ cup coconut milk or plain whole milk yogurt
- 2 tablespoons minced fresh cilantro

1. Pulse the tomatoes with the reserved juice in a food processor until mostly smooth, about 8 pulses.

2. Heat the oil in a 10-inch nonstick skillet over medium heat until shimmering. Add the curry powder and garam masala and cook, stirring constantly, until fragrant, about 10 seconds. Add the onion, bell pepper, and ¼ teaspoon salt; cook until the vegetables are softened, about 5 minutes. Stir in the garlic, ginger, jalapeño, and tomato paste and cook until fragrant, about 30 seconds. Add the cauliflower and cook, stirring occasionally, until the spices coat the florets, about 2 minutes.

3. Stir in the processed tomatoes and water, scraping up any browned bits. Nestle the chicken breasts into the liquid and bring to a simmer. Cover, reduce the heat to medium-low, and cook until the chicken registers 160 to 165 degrees on an instant-read thermometer, 12 to 18 minutes, flipping the chicken halfway through.

4. Transfer the chicken to a carving board. When the chicken is cool enough to handle, shred the meat into bite-sized pieces.

5. Return the chicken, along with any accumulated juice, to the skillet. Stir in the peas and coconut milk and cook briefly over medium-low heat until hot, 1 to 2 minutes. Stir in the cilantro, season with salt to taste, and serve.

VARIATION

Chicken Curry with Chickpeas and Green Beans
Follow the recipe for Chicken Curry with Cauliflower and Peas, substituting one (15-ounce) can drained and rinsed chickpeas for the cauliflower in step 2. Add 3 ounces green beans, cut into 1-inch pieces, with the chickpeas and omit the peas.

PAN-SEARED SALMON WITH LENTILS AND SWISS CHARD

SALMON WITH LENTILS HAS BEEN A TRADITIONAL pairing in France for centuries. This match of earthy lentils and assertively flavored salmon has also become a restaurant favorite here in America in recent years. Our goal was to re-create the dish for the home cook, adding a leafy green used often in French cooking, Swiss chard, for a complete skillet dinner for two.

We started our testing with the lentils, looking for a way to cook them so that they were infused with flavor but not overpowered by any one ingredient. Working with readily available brown lentils, we knew we'd want to build a flavor base in the skillet and then add the lentils and the braising liquid. Experimenting with a variety of aromatics, we settled on onion for its sweetness. A clove of garlic rounded out the flavors.

Much of the flavor in the lentils, however, was to come from an unexpected ingredient, the chard stems. Chard stems possess an earthy, beetlike flavor that reveals the fact that chard is a relative of the beet. From the outset, we had decided that the stems would be braised with the lentils, and the more delicate leaves would be cooked separately. Since chard stems gain some richness when sautéed in butter, that is how we prepared them, cooking them with the onion prior to adding the lentils and cooking liquid. Fresh thyme complemented the other flavors, and chicken broth provided a neutral yet rich backdrop. A touch of lemon juice added brightness. When the lentils were tender, we transferred them to a bowl to free up the skillet for our Swiss chard leaves.

Our original intention was to wilt the chard leaves by cooking them in a hot pan with some butter until tender. Once wilted, they would go into the bowl with the cooked lentils. However, as we were adding the sautéed chard leaves to the lentils, we realized it would be just as easy to wilt the chard in the lentils, omitting an extra step. When we reheated the lentils after the salmon cooked, we folded in the chard and found that the sliced leaves wilted perfectly. Another pat of butter added a bit more richness.

Turning our attention to pan-searing the salmon, we gave the skillet a quick wipe with paper towels and patted the salmon dry before seasoning it with salt and pepper. We found that just 1 teaspoon of oil was enough to brown the fish and develop a nice crust. The salmon was cooked in a matter of minutes, and things were really coming together. We found that the fish, like most cuts of meat, had the best texture when we removed it from the pan before it was cooked through and allowed it to finish cooking as it rested.

With the salmon rested and the lentils reheated, we were now ready to assemble the dish. Tasters were impressed that such a meal could be whipped up so quickly and without a sink full of dirty pots and pans.

Pan-Seared Salmon with Braised Lentils and Swiss Chard
SERVES 2

If you can't find skinless salmon at the store, you can easily remove the skin yourself by following the photos below. Lentils lose flavor with age, and because most packaged lentils do not have expiration dates, try to buy them from a store that specializes in natural foods and grains. For this recipe you will need a 10-inch nonstick skillet with a tight-fitting lid. See page 24 for a recipe to use up the leftover Swiss chard.

- 2 **tablespoons unsalted butter**
- ½ **bunch Swiss chard (about 6 ounces), stems and leaves separated, stems chopped and leaves cut into 1-inch pieces (see page 239)**
- ¼ **cup minced onion**
- 1 **garlic clove, minced**
- ¼ **teaspoon minced fresh thyme or pinch dried**
- 2 **cups low-sodium chicken broth**
- ½ **cup brown lentils (about 3 ounces), picked over and rinsed (see note)**
- ½ **teaspoon fresh lemon juice**
  Salt and pepper
- 2 **(6-ounce) skinless center-cut salmon fillets, about 1½ inches thick (see note)**
- 1 **teaspoon vegetable oil**
  Lemon wedges, for serving

NOTES FROM THE TEST KITCHEN

SALMON 101
In season, we've always preferred the more pronounced flavor of wild-caught salmon to farmed Atlantic salmon. But with more species of wild and farmed salmon available these days, we decided to see what distinguishes one from the next. We tasted three kinds of wild Pacific salmon and two farmed kinds.

Farmed Atlantic ($9/lb., year-round) was bland and had a texture that some tasters disliked. Farmed king ($12/lb., year-round) had a richer yet still mild flavor, but it is not widely available. Wild coho ($13/lb., July through September) had a balanced flavor, but its texture was unimpressive. Boasting a strong flavor and a meaty texture, wild king ($20/lb., May through September) often winds up on restaurant menus. Our favorite is wild sockeye ($14/lb., May through September), which had a smooth, firm texture and an assertive flavor.

While we loved the generally stronger flavor of the wild-caught fish, our tasting confirmed: If you're going to spend the extra money on wild salmon, make sure it looks and smells fresh, and realize that high quality is available only from late spring through the end of summer.

HOW TO SKIN A SALMON FILLET

1. Insert the blade of a sharp boning knife just above the skin about 1 inch from the end of the fillet. Cut through to the nearest end, keeping the blade just above the skin.

2. Rotate the fish and grab the loose piece of skin. Carefully run the knife between the flesh and the skin, making sure the knife is just above the skin, until the skin is completely removed.

1. Melt 1 tablespoon of the butter in a 10-inch non-stick skillet over medium heat. Add the chard stems and onion and cook until the vegetables are softened, about 5 minutes. Stir in the garlic and thyme and cook until fragrant, about 30 seconds.

2. Stir in 1¾ cups of the broth, lentils, and lemon juice. Bring to a simmer, reduce the heat to low, cover, and cook until the lentils are tender, about 30 minutes. Season with salt and pepper to taste, transfer to a bowl, and cover to keep warm.

3. Pat the salmon fillets dry with paper towels and season with salt and pepper. Wipe out the skillet with a wad of paper towels, add the oil, and return to medium-high heat until just smoking. Carefully lay the salmon in the skillet, skinned-side up, and cook until well browned on the first side, about 5 minutes. Flip the fish

and continue to cook until the sides are opaque and the thickest part registers 125 degrees on an instant-read thermometer, 3 to 5 minutes longer. Transfer the fish to a plate, tent loosely with foil, and let rest while finishing the lentils.

4. Wipe out the skillet with a wad of paper towels and return to medium-high heat. Add the lentils and remaining ¼ cup broth and cook until hot, about 1 minute. Stir in the chard leaves and remaining 1 tablespoon butter and cook, stirring constantly, until the chard is wilted, 2 to 3 minutes. Serve the salmon and lentils with the lemon wedges.

USE IT UP: SWISS CHARD

Israeli Couscous Salad
SERVES 2

Israeli couscous is larger than traditional Moroccan couscous and therefore must be simmered. You can substitute orzo pasta for the Israeli couscous, but do not substitute traditional couscous.

- ½ **cup Israeli couscous (see note)**
  Salt
- ½ **bunch Swiss chard (about 6 ounces), stemmed, leaves cut into 1-inch pieces (see page 239)**
- 1 **ounce feta cheese, crumbled (about ¼ cup)**
- 1 **tablespoon extra-virgin olive oil**
- 2 **teaspoons fresh lemon juice**
  Pepper

1. Bring 2 quarts water to a boil in a large saucepan. Add the couscous and 1½ teaspoons salt and cook, stirring often, until al dente, about 7 minutes. Add the chard and cook until both the couscous and the chard are tender, 1 to 2 minutes.

2. Drain the couscous and chard, rinse under cold water until cool, and shake well to remove the excess water. Transfer the drained couscous and chard to a serving bowl, add the feta, oil, and lemon juice, and toss to combine. Season with salt and pepper to taste and serve.

BAKED SOLE WITH GARLICKY SPINACH

HOT ON THE HEELS OF OUR SUCCESSFUL PAN-SEARED Salmon with Braised Lentils and Swiss Chard (page 23), we set our sights on creating another skillet meal with a similarly popular fish, sole. After all, fish makes an ideal meal for two, as you can buy only the amount you need. While the combination of salmon and lentils is a hearty and satisfying one, for this dish we wanted something lighter and thought the mild, clean flavor of sole would pair well with some garlicky spinach. And since baking is a good way to preserve the buttery, succulent texture of sole, our thoughts turned to an oven-to-table-style dinner. We knew our main concern would be getting the timing just right; both fish and spinach cook quickly, and because sole is particularly lean, we would have to take special care to prevent it from emerging dry and overcooked.

Our first step was to choose the most suitable variety of spinach. Most markets sell two types: baby spinach and the more mature curly-leaf spinach, which has much bigger leaves. Baby spinach is undeniably more convenient, requiring no prep work, but it wilted to a mushy pile once baked with the fish. Curly-leaf spinach required a little more effort—the stems have to be removed—but it fared much better, retaining a pleasant resiliency throughout the cooking process. Briefly wilting the spinach on the stovetop before transferring it to the oven with the fish ensured that it emerged evenly cooked and perfectly tender.

After we determined that tasters favored the fruitier flavor of olive oil to vegetable oil for sautéing the spinach, it was time to focus on the garlic. We wanted bold garlic flavor, but because both sole and spinach are relatively mild, and because we were working with such small quantities of each, determining the best way to incorporate it into our dish proved to be a challenge. Garlic that was minced and briefly sautéed was overpowering and unappealing; garlic poached in oil (a technique we sometimes use for pasta) didn't meld well with the earthy flavor of the spinach; and raw garlic was simply too harsh. Two cloves of lightly browned, slivered garlic (sautéed before the spinach was added) was tasters' favorite—its sweet nuttiness paired well with the spinach. As a final touch, a pinch of red pepper flakes added some gentle heat.

For the fish, we generously seasoned four sole fillets (two 3-ounce fillets per person provided an ample dinner), then we rolled the fish into bundles and nestled them on top of the almost-tender spinach. (Because the fillets are so thin, rolling them into a bundle helps prevent them from overcooking and keeps them intact when serving.) After 15 minutes in a 450-degree oven, both the fish and the spinach were perfectly cooked. As the fish baked, it released its flavorful juice into the spinach, while at the same time the garlic subtly infused the fish with extra flavor.

Tasters enjoyed the sole and spinach combination but wanted some additional flavor and textural contrast. Toasted bread crumbs sprinkled on top of the sole before it was baked were exactly what our dish needed. Seasoned with a single shallot, some freshly grated lemon zest, and minced fresh thyme, the bread crumbs baked to a deep golden brown and added welcome flavor and crunch to the dish. Served with lemon wedges, this simple recipe makes a light, flavorful skillet meal for two.

Baked Sole with Garlicky Spinach

SERVES 2

You can substitute small flounder fillets or haddock for the sole.

- 1 slice high-quality white sandwich bread, torn into quarters
- 1 tablespoon unsalted butter
- 1 small shallot, minced
- 1 teaspoon grated lemon zest
- ½ teaspoon minced fresh thyme or ⅛ teaspoon dried

- 1 tablespoon olive oil
- 2 garlic cloves, sliced thin
- Pinch red pepper flakes
- 10 ounces curly-leaf spinach (about 8 cups), stemmed and torn into bite-sized pieces
- Salt and pepper
- 4 (3-ounce) boneless, skinless sole fillets, ¼ to ½ inch thick (see note)
- Lemon wedges, for serving

1. Adjust an oven rack to the middle position and heat the oven to 450 degrees. Pulse the bread in a food processor to coarse crumbs, about 10 pulses. Melt the butter in a 10-inch ovensafe skillet over medium heat. Add the bread crumbs and toast, stirring often, until golden brown, 5 to 7 minutes. Transfer the bread crumbs to a small bowl, stir in the shallot, lemon zest, and thyme; set aside.

2. Wipe out the skillet with a wad of paper towels. Add the oil, garlic, and pepper flakes and cook over medium-low heat until sizzling, about 1 minute. Increase the heat to medium-high and add the spinach, a handful at a time, and cook until just wilted and glossy, about 30 seconds. Off the heat, season with salt

NOTES FROM THE TEST KITCHEN

MAKING FISH BUNDLES

With the sole fillets skinned-side up, roll the fillets into tight bundles, starting at the tail end.

STORING BAGGED SPINACH

Fresh spinach used to come in perforated plastic bags that allowed the greens to breathe and stay fresh longer. These days, the bags of greens we buy no longer have the holes. Why the change? Plastic bag technology has come a long way over the years. Though they appear solid, the bags in which spinach and other greens are now sold are made of a polymer that allows the ripening gases that all produce emits to pass through freely. Because of this, leftover packaged spinach or greens will do much better stored in their original bags than when stored in ordinary plastic ones. To ensure freshness for as long as possible, fold the bag over and tape it shut.

and pepper to taste and arrange into an even layer in the skillet.

3. Pat the sole fillets dry with paper towels and season with salt and pepper. Roll the fillets into tight bundles (see page 25). Lay the fish bundles seam-side down on top of the spinach. Sprinkle each fish bundle with the bread crumb mixture. Transfer the skillet to the oven and bake until the crumbs are deep golden brown and the fish flakes apart when gently prodded with a paring knife, about 15 minutes. Serve with the lemon wedges.

BAKED SHRIMP AND ORZO

THOUGH CASSEROLE-STYLE DISHES ARE TYPICALLY meant to serve a crowd, we have found that with a little tweaking, a casserole can be turned into an incredibly satisfying one-dish meal for two. One of our favorite casseroles is Greek-style baked shrimp with orzo—tender shrimp paired with creamy orzo pasta in a garlicky broth. We think a dish this flavorful and satisfying shouldn't be limited to large gatherings and wondered if we could get it on the table as a simple skillet dinner for two.

For this casserole, orzo, the tiny rice-shaped pasta often found in Italian-style soups or pasta salad, is typically simmered until tender, then transferred to a baking dish with the other ingredients and placed in the oven. While this approach makes sense when cooking a large casserole, we thought for our smaller skillet meal we could use a different technique. Orzo can also be cooked "pilaf-style," or sautéed briefly in oil with flavorings before liquid is added, which deepens the pasta's flavor and color. And, if stirred occasionally as it simmers, the orzo releases starches into the cooking liquid and turns it creamy—not quite as creamy as risotto, perhaps, but rich and velvety nevertheless. This technique worked great with the small amount of orzo we were using.

With the method for cooking the orzo set, we turned our attention to the other elements of this one-dish meal. We wanted to limit the vegetables to a select few to keep preparation brief—nothing adds to prep time like cleaning and cutting a long list of vegetables. Red onion seemed like a natural for depth and body, as did the crisp, sweet crunch of red bell pepper; we

briefly sautéed both before toasting the orzo. For flavor, color, and acidity, we also decided to add tomatoes. Canned diced tomatoes kept things easy and flavorful. In order for the orzo to toast properly, we added the tomatoes after the orzo, instead of sautéing them with the other vegetables.

As for flavoring the pilaf, a healthy dose of garlic seemed essential, in keeping with the Mediterranean spirit of the dish. A sprinkling of fresh herbs seemed appropriate as well, and after testing a slew of options, tasters favored a simple combination of oregano and scallions.

After we had prepared a few batches of the pilaf, we realized that the straw-yellow color of the toasted orzo seemed pale against the deep red of the bell pepper and tomato. Though it isn't classically Greek, we took a cue from other Mediterranean cuisines and added a pinch of saffron to intensify the orzo's color. Toasted with the orzo, the saffron suffused the pasta with a sunny orange hue and its characteristic warm flavor.

As for the shrimp, we already knew we preferred larger shrimp, left whole, because they are less prone to overcooking. Searing the shrimp in the skillet before beginning the pilaf worked well, but we wondered if there was an easier solution. Baking the shrimp on top of the pilaf was easier, but the method dried the shrimp out and turned them rubbery. Embedding the raw shrimp in the pilaf and then baking it, however, was a whole different story. The orzo shielded the shrimp from the oven's direct heat, effectively preventing them from drying out and toughening. A relatively hot oven, 400 degrees, cooked the shrimp evenly in about 20 minutes—just enough time for the flavors of the pilaf and shrimp to meld.

While we liked the overall concept and flavor of the casserole, we thought it was a little bland. It needed a splash of acid, something sharp and pungent to provide an accent. Lemon wedges squeezed over the finished dish certainly helped. Capers and anchovies were both interesting additions, but tasters had mixed feelings in each case. We then decided to try feta cheese to keep with the Mediterranean flavors of the dish. The cheese's salty, briny bite was the perfect contrast to the sweetness of the shrimp and the fruitiness of the tomato and bell pepper. We normally shy away from combining cheese and fish, but in this instance it was a perfect pairing. At first, we crumbled it and scattered it over the finished dish, but we found that it actually tasted better if baked on top of the casserole, where it browned slightly and intensified in flavor. We had finally succeeded in creating a skillet casserole for two, with all the richness and satisfaction of a slow-baked casserole meant for a crowd.

Baked Shrimp and Orzo

SERVES 2

Make sure that the orzo is al dente, or slightly firm to the bite; otherwise it may overcook in the oven. If using smaller or larger shrimp, the cooking times may vary accordingly. The small amount of saffron makes a big difference to the flavor and look of the dish, so if you have some on hand, it's worth including. See page 131 for a recipe to use up the leftover red bell pepper and page 15 for a recipe to use up the leftover canned diced tomatoes.

- **8 ounces extra-large shrimp (21 to 25 per pound), peeled and deveined (see page 31)**
- **Salt and pepper**
- **1 tablespoon olive oil**
- **1 small red onion, minced**
- **½ red bell pepper, stemmed, seeded, and cut into ½-inch pieces**
- **3 garlic cloves, minced**
- **1 teaspoon minced fresh oregano or ¼ teaspoon dried**
- **1 cup orzo**
- **Pinch saffron threads, crumbled (optional; see note)**
- **1½ cups low-sodium chicken broth**
- **½ cup drained canned diced tomatoes, ¼ cup juice reserved**
- **⅓ cup frozen peas**
- **2 ounces feta cheese, crumbled (about ½ cup)**
- **2 scallions, sliced thin**
- **Lemon wedges, for serving**

1. Adjust an oven rack to the middle position and heat the oven to 400 degrees. Pat the shrimp dry with paper towels and season with salt and pepper. Cover and refrigerate while preparing the orzo.

2. Heat the oil in a 10-inch ovensafe skillet over medium heat until shimmering. Add the onion, bell pepper, and ¼ teaspoon salt and cook until the vegetables are softened, about 5 minutes. Stir in the garlic

and oregano and cook until fragrant, about 30 seconds. Stir in the orzo and saffron and cook, stirring frequently, until the orzo is coated with oil and lightly browned, about 4 minutes.

3. Stir in the broth and reserved tomato juice, bring to a simmer, and cook, stirring occasionally, until the orzo is al dente, 10 to 12 minutes. Stir in the shrimp, tomatoes, and peas, then sprinkle the cheese evenly over the top. Transfer the skillet to the oven and bake until the shrimp are cooked through and the cheese is lightly browned, about 20 minutes. Sprinkle with the scallions and serve with the lemon wedges.

NOTES FROM THE TEST KITCHEN

SIZING SHRIMP

Shrimp are sold by size (small, medium, large, and so on) as well as by the number needed to make 1 pound, usually given in a range. Choosing shrimp by the numerical rating is more accurate than choosing by a size label, which varies from store to store. Here's how the two systems line up.

SMALL
51 to 60 per pound

MEDIUM
41 to 50 per pound

LARGE
31 to 40 per pound

EXTRA-LARGE
21 to 25 per pound

SHRIMP STIR-FRIES

STIR-FRIES ARE AN IDEAL AND NATURAL WEEKNIGHT meal for two: The protein and vegetables are cooked in one skillet, and once all the ingredients are chopped and ready to go, the dish comes together very quickly. When done right, stir-fries offer a bright and fresh combination of tender meat and crisp vegetables tied together with a light, flavorful sauce. We wanted to develop a master recipe for a shrimp stir-fry, to which we could add a variety of vegetables and sauces. Shrimp are the perfect ingredient in the cooking-for-two kitchen—you can keep a bag of high-quality frozen shrimp on hand and use just as much as you need, so there's no waste.

Stir-fries are actually fairly easy to master at home. The key to a successful stir-fry is plenty of intense heat; the pan must be hot enough to caramelize sugars, deepen flavors, and evaporate unnecessary juices, all in a matter of minutes. And because stir-frying is such a quick-cooking method, organization is key to ensuring that the protein and vegetables are properly cooked and ready at the same time.

Because heat is key, the piece of cookware you use is critical to success. We found that the conical shape of woks, which are designed for a pit-style stove, don't work well on a conventional stovetop. Why? The heat becomes concentrated in the pan's bottom, and the larger surface area—the sides—simply doesn't heat as well. Instead, we like a large 12-inch skillet with a nonstick coating. Its flat-bottom design allows more of the surface area to come into direct contact with the flat burner, delivering more heat over a wider area. And while a stir-fry for two doesn't require a huge quantity of ingredients, we found that this larger pan prevents overcrowding.

For the shrimp, we determined that a simple yet flavorful marinade (tasters liked a combination of soy sauce and sherry) was all that was necessary to add flavor without overwhelming the finished dish. We cooked the shrimp over high heat, browning one side without stirring, then stirring once to quickly brown the second side. While many recipes had suggested constant stirring, we found that the continuous motion detracted from the browning.

After the shrimp were cooked, we removed them from the pan and added the vegetables. We found the combinations of vegetables to be limitless, from pineapple and red onion, to asparagus and carrots, to bok choy and red bell pepper. Once we became comfortable with the techniques of stir-frying and learned how long each vegetable needed to cook, we felt comfortable mixing and matching most any combination.

In most recipes the aromatics are added at the outset, when the pan is empty, and are doused with oil (which, in essence, fries them). By the time the stir-fry is done, the aromatics have burned, and all that unnecessary oil just makes the stir-fry greasy. We found we could avoid these problems by waiting to cook the aromatics—in this case, garlic and ginger—until after we had cooked the vegetables. When the vegetables were done, we pushed them to the sides of the pan, added the aromatics to the center, and cooked them until they were just fragrant, about 30 seconds. We then stirred them into the vegetables.

At this point, we were close to being finished. We had only one final component: the sauce. We found that chicken broth (or orange or tangerine juice when appropriate) made the best base because it was not overpowering. Soy and black bean sauces, as well as mirin, rice vinegar, and sesame oil, were all excellent flavor enhancers, and we discovered various combinations that worked well. We involved as few ingredients as possible; keeping the sauce simple is not only easier but allows the shrimp and vegetables to take center stage.

While determining options for flavoring the sauce was fairly easy, the sauce consistency needed work. Many of our stir-fry sauces were turning out too thin and would not adhere properly to the shrimp and vegetables. The solution was as simple as adding some cornstarch. Adding a little bit to these sauces, depending on the viscosity of the ingredients, helped them to coat the shrimp and vegetables.

Our components and process were set: We made the sauce, cooked the shrimp, and cooked the vegetables and aromatics; then we added the shrimp back to the pan along with the sauce and finally cooked the whole dish just until the sauce thickened, which took all of about 30 seconds. Incredibly quick and simple, any of these stir-fries makes a perfect meal for two.

STIR-FRIED SHRIMP, PINEAPPLE, AND RED ONION WITH SWEET-AND-SOUR SAUCE

Stir-Fried Shrimp, Pineapple, and Red Onion with Sweet-and-Sour Sauce

SERVES 2

If using smaller or larger shrimp, the cooking times may vary accordingly. Instead of purchasing a whole pineapple, you can often find prepackaged pineapple halves at the grocery store, ready to be cut and used in a recipe. You can substitute 1 cup drained canned pineapple chunks for the fresh pineapple. Serve the stir-fry over white rice.

SAUCE

- 3 tablespoons red wine vinegar
- 3 tablespoons fresh orange juice
- 3 tablespoons sugar
- 2 teaspoons ketchup
- ½ teaspoon cornstarch
- ¼ teaspoon salt

STIR-FRY

- 8 ounces extra-large shrimp (21 to 25 per pound), peeled and deveined (see page 31)
- 1 teaspoon soy sauce
- 1 teaspoon dry sherry
- 4 teaspoons vegetable oil
- 2 garlic cloves, minced
- 2 teaspoons minced or grated fresh ginger
- 1 small red onion, halved and sliced ½ inch thick
- ¼ medium pineapple, peeled, cored, and cut into ½-inch chunks (about 1 cup; see page 270) (see note)
- 1 scallion, sliced thin on the bias

1. FOR THE SAUCE: Combine all of the ingredients in a small bowl and set aside.

2. FOR THE STIR-FRY: Toss the shrimp with the soy sauce and sherry in a medium bowl and let marinate for at least 10 minutes, or up to 1 hour. In another bowl, mix 1 teaspoon of the oil, garlic, and ginger together.

3. Heat 1 teaspoon more oil in a 12-inch nonstick skillet over high heat until just smoking. Add the shrimp in a single layer and cook, without stirring, until the shrimp are browned at the edges, about 1 minute. Stir the shrimp and continue to cook until they are nearly cooked through, about 30 seconds longer. Transfer the shrimp to a clean bowl.

4. Add the remaining 2 teaspoons oil to the skillet and heat over medium–high heat until shimmering. Add

USE IT UP: PINEAPPLE

Pineapple Salsa
MAKES ABOUT 1 CUP

If you have any fresh jalapeño or serrano chiles, substitute ½ chile, stemmed, seeded, and minced, for the red pepper flakes. Serve with tortilla chips or grilled pork, chicken, or fish.

- ¼ medium pineapple, peeled, cored, and cut into ½-inch chunks (about 1 cup; see page 270)
- ½ red bell pepper, stemmed, seeded, and chopped fine
- ¼ cup minced red onion or shallot
- 2 tablespoons minced fresh cilantro, parsley, or mint
- 1 tablespoon fresh lime juice
- 1 garlic clove, minced
- ⅛ teaspoon red pepper flakes (see note)
- Salt and pepper

Combine the pineapple, bell pepper, onion, cilantro, lime juice, garlic, and pepper flakes in a medium bowl, and season with salt and pepper to taste. Let the salsa sit until the flavors meld, about 15 minutes, before serving.

the onion and cook until softened, 3 to 5 minutes. Add the pineapple and cook until heated through, about 1 minute.

5. Clear the center of the skillet, add the garlic mixture, and cook, mashing the mixture into the pan, until fragrant, 15 to 30 seconds. Stir the garlic mixture into the onion and pineapple.

6. Return the shrimp, along with any accumulated juice, to the skillet and stir to combine. Whisk the sauce to recombine, then add it to the skillet. Cook, stirring constantly, until thickened, about 30 seconds. Sprinkle with the scallion and serve.

VARIATIONS

Stir-Fried Shrimp, Asparagus, and Carrot with Tangerine Sauce

Orange juice and zest can be used in place of the tangerine juice and zest. If using smaller or larger shrimp, the cooking times may vary accordingly. See page 131 for a recipe to use up the leftover red bell pepper.

SAUCE

- ⅓ cup fresh tangerine juice plus 1 teaspoon grated tangerine zest from 2 tangerines (see note)
- 1 tablespoon soy sauce
- 1 tablespoon Chinese black bean sauce
- 1½ teaspoons sugar
- ½ teaspoon cornstarch
- ½ teaspoon toasted sesame oil
- ⅛ teaspoon red pepper flakes

STIR-FRY

- 8 ounces extra-large shrimp (21 to 25 per pound), peeled and deveined (see photos)
- 1 teaspoon soy sauce
- 1 teaspoon dry sherry
- 4 teaspoons vegetable oil
- 2 garlic cloves, minced
- 2 teaspoons minced or grated fresh ginger
- 1 scallion, minced
- ½ bunch asparagus (about 8 ounces), tough ends trimmed, cut on the bias into 2-inch lengths
- 1 carrot, peeled and cut into 2-inch-long matchsticks
- ½ red bell pepper, stemmed, seeded, and sliced into ¼-inch strips

1. FOR THE SAUCE: Combine all of the ingredients in a small bowl and set aside.

2. FOR THE STIR-FRY: Toss the shrimp with the soy sauce and sherry in a medium bowl and let marinate for at least 10 minutes, or up to 1 hour. In another bowl, mix 1 teaspoon of the oil, garlic, ginger, and scallion together.

3. Heat 1 teaspoon more oil in a 12-inch nonstick skillet over high heat until just smoking. Add the shrimp in a single layer and cook, without stirring, until the shrimp are browned at the edges, about 1 minute. Stir the shrimp and continue to cook until they are nearly cooked through, about 30 seconds longer. Transfer the shrimp to a clean bowl.

4. Add the remaining 2 teaspoons oil to the skillet and heat over medium-high heat until shimmering. Add the asparagus, carrot, and bell pepper and cook, stirring often, until the vegetables are crisp-tender, 4 to 6 minutes.

5. Clear the center of the skillet, add the garlic mixture, and cook, mashing the mixture into the pan, until fragrant, 15 to 30 seconds. Stir the garlic mixture into the vegetables.

6. Return the shrimp, along with any accumulated juice, to the skillet and stir to combine. Whisk the sauce to recombine, then add it to the skillet. Cook, stirring constantly, until thickened, about 30 seconds, and serve.

Stir-Fried Shrimp, Bok Choy, and Red Bell Pepper with Teriyaki Sauce

If you can't find baby bok choy, you can use ½ large head bok choy (about 12 ounces), stalks sliced crosswise into ¼-inch-wide pieces and greens cut into 1-inch-wide strips, instead; add the bok choy stalks to the skillet with the bell pepper in step 4, then add the bok choy greens to the pan with the sauce in step 6. Washing the bok choy after prepping it is the best way to completely remove all the dirt and sand. If using smaller or larger shrimp, the cooking times may vary accordingly. You can substitute 2 teaspoons white wine or sake mixed with ½ teaspoon sugar for the mirin. See page 131 for a recipe to use up the leftover red bell pepper.

SAUCE

- ⅓ cup low-sodium chicken broth
- 2 tablespoons soy sauce
- 1 tablespoon sugar
- 2 teaspoons mirin (see note)
- 1 teaspoon rice vinegar
- 1 teaspoon cornstarch
- Pinch red pepper flakes

STIR-FRY

- 8 ounces extra-large shrimp (21 to 25 per pound), peeled and deveined (see page 31)
- 1 teaspoon soy sauce
- 1 teaspoon dry sherry
- 4 teaspoons vegetable oil
- 3 garlic cloves, minced
- 2 teaspoons minced or grated fresh ginger
- 1 scallion, minced
- 3 (4-ounce) heads baby bok choy, greens and stalks sliced crosswise into ¼-inch-wide pieces (see note)
- ½ red bell pepper, stemmed, seeded, and sliced into ¼-inch strips

1. FOR THE SAUCE: Combine all of the ingredients in a small bowl and set aside.

2. FOR THE STIR-FRY: Toss the shrimp with the soy sauce and sherry in a medium bowl and let marinate for at least 10 minutes, or up to 1 hour. In another bowl, mix 1 teaspoon of the oil, garlic, ginger, and scallion together.

3. Heat 1 teaspoon more oil in a 12-inch nonstick skillet over high heat until just smoking. Add the shrimp in a single layer and cook, without stirring, until the shrimp are browned at the edges, about 1 minute. Stir the shrimp and continue to cook until they are nearly cooked through, about 30 seconds longer. Transfer the shrimp to a clean bowl.

4. Add the remaining 2 teaspoons oil to the skillet and heat over medium-high heat until shimmering. Add the bok choy and bell pepper and cook, stirring often, until the vegetables are crisp-tender, 4 to 6 minutes.

5. Clear the center of the skillet, add the garlic mixture, and cook, mashing the mixture into the pan, until fragrant, 15 to 30 seconds. Stir the garlic mixture into the vegetables.

6. Return the shrimp, along with any accumulated juice, to the skillet. Whisk the sauce to recombine, then add it to the skillet. Cook, stirring constantly, until the sauce is thickened and the greens are wilted, about 30 seconds, and serve.

POLENTA AND SAUSAGE DINNERS

SOFT, VELVETY, AND COMFORTING, POLENTA IS often used as a side dish—but it also makes a great basis for a baked dish or casserole. We imagined a baked polenta dish that would be a sophisticated skillet dinner for two, with a layer of soft polenta covered by meaty Italian sausage (its robust flavor is a classic pairing with polenta), hearty vegetables, and a touch of tangy cheese.

We knew that if we wanted to precook any of the topping ingredients, we would have to do it before making the polenta to limit our cooking to one skillet. After sautéing some sausage with a little onion, garlic, and fresh thyme, we had a great base of flavor, but the individual components didn't feel connected. Thinking of some of our favorite tomato-based meat sauces, we tried adding some canned diced tomatoes. Simmered with the sausage and aromatics, the tomatoes added a pleasant sweetness while their juice reduced to a sauce that brought everything together. And the addition of some Swiss chard further enhanced our topping's heartiness. With a splash of red wine vinegar for brightness, our topping was ready, and we moved on to the polenta.

Polenta must be added very slowly to boiling salted water to prevent clumping. To give the flavor of the polenta a boost, we tried cooking it in boiling milk. The milk complemented the flavor of the polenta nicely, but it also added an unwelcome slimy texture. Using a combination of roughly 1 part milk to 3 parts water, we were able to add some flavor to the polenta without ruining its creamy texture. We finished it with a little butter, which helped keep it smooth and soft, and a bit of garlic for more flavor.

When the polenta was fully cooked, we smoothed it into an even layer in the skillet, spread the sausage mixture over the top, and sprinkled on some Asiago—a tangy cheese that tasters thought paired well with the rich topping. (Cheese mixed directly into the polenta caused it to stiffen, a problem that would be compounded by the time in the oven.) After about 20 minutes in a 450-degree oven, the cheese was melted and golden.

Mildly flavored and easy to prepare, our baked polenta and sausage seemed like a great backdrop for a variety of toppings, so we decided to create some variations with broccoli and Parmesan as well as mushrooms and goat cheese.

Polenta and Sausage Dinner with Bell Pepper and Swiss Chard

SERVES 2

This recipe uses coarse-ground degerminated corn (it may be labeled as either polenta or yellow grits), often found alongside the rice and grains in the supermarket; do not substitute instant polenta. When stirring the polenta, make sure to scrape the sides and bottom of the skillet to ensure even cooking. See page 24 for a recipe to use up the leftover Swiss chard and page 131 for a recipe to use up the leftover red bell pepper. See page 15 for a recipe to use up the leftover canned diced tomatoes.

NOTES FROM THE TEST KITCHEN

BUYING AND STORING OLIVE OIL
Once opened, olive oil has a very short shelf life of about three months. When buying olive oil, we recommend checking the harvest date printed on the label of high-end oils to ensure the freshest bottle possible.

To store olive oil, don't keep it on the countertop or windowsill (even though it's easy to grab), but move it to a dark pantry or cupboard. Strong sunlight will oxidize the chlorophyll in the oil, producing stale, harsh flavors.

TOPPING

- 2 teaspoons olive oil
- 8 ounces sweet Italian sausage, casings removed
- 1 small onion, minced
- ½ bunch Swiss chard (about 6 ounces), stems and leaves separated, stems chopped and leaves cut into 1-inch pieces (see page 239)
- ½ red bell pepper, stemmed, seeded, and sliced into ¼-inch strips
- Salt
- 3 garlic cloves, minced
- ½ teaspoon minced fresh thyme or ⅛ teaspoon dried
- ⅛ teaspoon red pepper flakes
- ½ cup drained canned diced tomatoes, ¼ cup juice reserved
- 1½ teaspoons red wine vinegar
- Pepper

POLENTA

- 1⅔ cups water
- ½ cup whole milk
- Salt
- ½ cup coarse-ground cornmeal (see note)
- 2 tablespoons unsalted butter
- 1 garlic clove, minced
- Pepper
- 2 ounces Asiago cheese, grated (about 1 cup)

1. FOR THE TOPPING: Adjust an oven rack to the middle position and heat the oven to 450 degrees. Heat the oil in a 10-inch ovensafe skillet over medium heat until shimmering. Add the sausage and cook, breaking up the meat with a wooden spoon, until lightly browned, about 5 minutes.

2. Stir in the onion, chard stems, bell pepper, and ¼ teaspoon salt, and cook until the vegetables are softened, about 5 minutes. Stir in the garlic, thyme, and pepper flakes, and cook until fragrant, about 30 seconds. Stir in the tomatoes with the reserved juice and bring to a simmer, scraping up any browned bits.

3. Stir in the chard leaves, a handful at a time, and cook until bright green and slightly wilted, about 2 minutes. Off the heat, stir in the vinegar and season with salt and pepper to taste. Transfer the mixture to a medium bowl and set aside. (Do not wash the skillet.)

4. FOR THE POLENTA: Wipe out the skillet with a wad of paper towels and return to medium-high heat. Add the water, milk, and ½ teaspoon salt to the skillet and bring to a boil. Slowly add the polenta while whisking constantly in a circular motion to prevent clumping.

5. Bring to a simmer, stirring constantly. Reduce the heat to low, cover, and cook, stirring often and vigorously, until the polenta becomes soft and smooth, 10 to 15 minutes. Off the heat, stir in the butter and garlic and season with salt and pepper to taste.

6. Smooth the polenta into an even layer in the skillet. Spoon the sausage and chard topping evenly over the polenta, then sprinkle with the cheese. Bake the casserole until the cheese is melted and golden, 15 to 20 minutes. Let the casserole cool for 10 minutes before serving.

VARIATIONS

Polenta and Sausage Dinner with Broccoli

This recipe uses coarse-ground degerminated corn (it may be labeled as either polenta or yellow grits), often found alongside the rice and grains in the supermarket; do not substitute instant polenta. When stirring the polenta, make sure to scrape the sides and bottom of the skillet to ensure even cooking. See page 15 for a recipe to use up the leftover canned diced tomatoes.

TOPPING

½ cup water

8 ounces broccoli florets, cut into 1-inch pieces (about 3 cups)

2 teaspoons olive oil

8 ounces sweet Italian sausage, casings removed

1 small onion, minced

    Salt

3 garlic cloves, minced

½ teaspoon minced fresh thyme or ⅛ teaspoon dried

⅛ teaspoon red pepper flakes

½ cup drained canned diced tomatoes, ¼ cup juice reserved

1½ teaspoons red wine vinegar

    Pepper

POLENTA

1⅔ cups water

½ cup whole milk

    Salt

½ cup coarse-ground cornmeal (see note)

2 tablespoons unsalted butter

1 garlic clove, minced

    Pepper

2 ounces Parmesan cheese, grated (about 1 cup)

1. FOR THE TOPPING: Adjust an oven rack to the middle position and heat the oven to 450 degrees. Bring the water to a simmer in a 10-inch ovensafe skillet over medium-high heat. Add the broccoli florets, cover, and steam until the broccoli is bright green and beginning to soften, about 2 minutes. Uncover and cook until the water has evaporated, about 1 minute. Transfer the broccoli to a medium bowl and set aside.

2. Heat the oil in the skillet over medium heat until shimmering. Add the sausage and cook, breaking up the meat with a wooden spoon, until lightly browned, about 5 minutes. Add the onion and ¼ teaspoon salt and cook until softened, about 5 minutes. Stir in the garlic, thyme, and pepper flakes, and cook until fragrant, about 30 seconds. Stir in the tomatoes with the reserved juice and bring to a simmer, scraping up any browned bits.

3. Stir in the broccoli and cook until heated through, about 2 minutes. Off the heat, stir in the vinegar and season with salt and pepper to taste. Transfer the mixture to a medium bowl and set aside. (Do not wash the skillet.)

4. FOR THE POLENTA: Wipe out the skillet with a wad of paper towels and return to medium-high heat. Add the water, milk, and ½ teaspoon salt to the skillet and bring to a boil. Slowly add the polenta while whisking constantly in a circular motion to prevent clumping.

5. Bring to a simmer, stirring constantly. Reduce the heat to low, cover, and cook, stirring often and vigorously, until the polenta becomes soft and smooth, 10 to 15 minutes. Off the heat, stir in the butter and garlic and season with salt and pepper to taste.

6. Smooth the polenta into an even layer in the skillet. Spoon the sausage and broccoli topping evenly over the polenta, then sprinkle with the Parmesan. Bake the casserole until the Parmesan is melted and golden, 15 to 20 minutes. Let the casserole cool for 10 minutes before serving.

Polenta and Sausage Dinner with Mushrooms

This recipe uses coarse-ground degerminated corn (it may be labeled as either polenta or yellow grits), often found alongside the rice and grains in the supermarket;

do not substitute instant polenta. When stirring the polenta, make sure to scrape the sides and bottom of the skillet to ensure even cooking. See page 15 for a recipe to use up the leftover canned diced tomatoes.

TOPPING

- **2 teaspoons olive oil**
- **8 ounces sweet Italian sausage, casings removed**
- **1 small onion, minced**
- **Salt**
- **8 ounces portobello mushroom caps (about 2 small caps), sliced ¼ inch thick**
- **8 ounces white mushrooms, sliced ¼ inch thick**
- **3 garlic cloves, minced**
- **½ teaspoon minced fresh thyme or ⅛ teaspoon dried**
- **⅛ teaspoon red pepper flakes**
- **½ cup drained canned diced tomatoes, ¼ cup juice reserved**
- **1½ teaspoons red wine vinegar**
- **Pepper**

POLENTA

- **1⅔ cups water**
- **½ cup whole milk**
- **Salt**
- **½ cup coarse-ground cornmeal (see note)**
- **2 tablespoons unsalted butter**
- **1 garlic clove, minced**
- **Pepper**
- **4 ounces goat cheese, crumbled (about 1 cup)**

1. FOR THE TOPPING: Adjust an oven rack to the middle position and heat the oven to 450 degrees. Heat the oil in a 10-inch ovensafe skillet over medium-high heat until shimmering. Add the sausage and cook, breaking up the meat with a wooden spoon, until lightly browned, about 5 minutes.

2. Stir in the onion and ¼ teaspoon salt and cook until just beginning to soften, about 2 minutes. Stir in the portobello and white mushrooms and cook, stirring often, until the mushrooms have released their liquid and are well browned, about 5 minutes. Stir in the garlic, thyme, and pepper flakes, and cook until fragrant, about 30 seconds. Stir in the tomatoes with the reserved juice

and bring to a simmer, scraping up any browned bits. Off the heat, stir in the vinegar and season with salt and pepper to taste. Transfer the mixture to a medium bowl and set aside. (Do not wash the skillet.)

3. FOR THE POLENTA: Wipe out the skillet with a wad of paper towels and return to medium-high heat. Add the water, milk, and ½ teaspoon salt to the skillet and bring to a boil. Slowly add the polenta while whisking constantly in a circular motion to prevent clumping.

4. Bring to a simmer, stirring constantly. Reduce the heat to low, cover, and cook, stirring often and vigorously, until the polenta becomes soft and smooth, 10 to 15 minutes. Off the heat, stir in the butter and garlic and season with salt and pepper to taste.

5. Smooth the polenta into an even layer in the skillet. Spoon the sausage and mushroom topping evenly over the polenta, then sprinkle with the cheese. Bake the casserole until the cheese is melted and golden, 15 to 20 minutes. Let the casserole cool for 10 minutes before serving.

NOTES FROM THE TEST KITCHEN

BUYING POLENTA

Polenta can refer to both the dish that hails from the northern region of Italy and the cornmeal used to make it. Polenta (the dish) is really nothing more than this cornmeal cooked in water and sometimes milk to form a soft mush. Sounds pretty straightforward, right? Not when you hit the grocery store and see that there are various kinds of polenta and cornmeal to choose from—everything from the color of the corn to the level of grind and whether the corn has been degerminated can be specified on the label. And just to complicate matters, your supermarket might shelve polenta in a number of places, from the pasta aisle to the baking section; most likely, though, you'll find it stocked with rice and grains.

Because of these variables, it's hard to choose a product based on the front of the package. That's why we recommend reading the ingredients; you're looking for coarse-ground degerminated cornmeal, which will make a smooth and creamy polenta. It may be labeled as either polenta or yellow grits. Be sure to stay away from anything identified as instant or quick-cooking cornmeal or polenta, which is too powdery and will make gummy, gluey polenta; this is cornmeal that has actually been cooked and dried, so it rehydrates within a minute or two of cooking and will overcook in the time specified in our recipes. You'll also want to avoid regular or stone-ground cornmeal, as it keeps its rough texture, even after cooking.

RISOTTO WITH CHICKEN, ARTICHOKES, AND PEAS

POPULAR ON RESTAURANT MENUS, RISOTTO HAS A reputation for being difficult and fussy, but it is actually quite easy to prepare, and like many pasta dishes, it is endlessly variable. We wanted to both take the fear out of making risotto and come up with an approachable, easy weeknight recipe for those cooking for two since scaling a risotto recipe can be tricky. We wanted this risotto to be a main course, so we chose chicken as the starring ingredient.

Starting with the chicken, we wanted to keep the process simple and streamlined since we were using only two chicken breasts. We opted for a half-sautéing, half-poaching technique. First we browned the chicken on one side to develop flavor and create a fond in the pan, then we flipped the chicken, added some liquid (a combination of water and broth was best) to the skillet, reduced the heat, and covered the skillet until the chicken was cooked through. This method yielded moist, flavorful chicken breasts and, at the same time, a broth in which to cook the risotto. Best of all, it took just 15 minutes. With our chicken cooked to perfection and our broth ready, we moved on to the risotto.

Having made countless batches of risotto in the past, we had already learned a few key points. An Italian medium-grain rice was a must, and tasters preferred the Arborio variety for its firm bite. We also found that while most recipes require adding the broth in painstakingly small increments and stirring continuously for up to 30 minutes, there was a simpler route. We found we could add about half of the broth at the beginning, allowing it to simmer and stirring only occasionally. Once the rice absorbed this broth, we added more, ½ cup at a time. At this point, stirring every minute or so was important; if we didn't stir, the rice stuck to the bottom of the pan.

With the risotto cooking method in order, we aimed to refine the cooking time to achieve a perfect combination of creamy risotto and tender chicken. Throughout testing, we had been shredding the chicken into bite-sized pieces and adding it roughly five minutes before we thought the rice would be cooked through, but occasionally this led to overcooking, as the cooking time of the risotto varied slightly from batch to batch. Then a fellow test cook suggested stirring the chicken into the risotto, reducing the heat to low, and covering

the risotto. This allowed the chicken to heat through and the risotto to gently finish cooking.

Tasters were enjoying our risotto with chicken, though some felt incorporating a couple of fresh ingredients might help balance the richness of the dish; artichoke hearts and peas filled the bill perfectly. (For added flavor, we browned the artichokes in the skillet before the chicken.) Added along with the chicken at the end, they quickly heated through and brought just the right amount of bright flavor.

For the final touch, Parmesan and butter are typically added to risotto right before serving, and we certainly didn't want to break tradition there. Grated cheese proved best, as it melted almost instantaneously, and because its flavor is so prominent, we found that a high-quality Parmesan really made a difference in this dish.

Risotto with Chicken, Artichokes, and Peas
SERVES 2

To quickly thaw frozen artichoke hearts, place them in a microwave-safe bowl, cover, and microwave on high for about 3 minutes. Drain thoroughly and pat dry with paper towels before using. Serve this dish with extra grated Parmesan cheese on the side, if desired.

- 4 teaspoons olive oil
- 1 (9-ounce) package frozen artichoke hearts, thawed and patted dry with paper towels (see note)
- 2 (6-ounce) boneless, skinless chicken breasts, trimmed Salt and pepper
- 1¾ cups low-sodium chicken broth, plus more as needed
- 1 cup water
- 2 tablespoons unsalted butter
- 1 small onion, minced
- ⅔ cup Arborio rice
- ½ cup dry white wine
- 1 ounce Parmesan cheese, grated (about ½ cup)
- ¼ cup frozen peas, thawed

1. Heat 2 teaspoons of the oil in a 10-inch nonstick skillet over medium-high heat until shimmering. Add the artichoke hearts and cook until lightly browned and tender, 4 to 5 minutes. Transfer the artichoke hearts to a small bowl and set aside.

2. Pat the chicken breasts dry with paper towels and season with salt and pepper. Heat the remaining 2 teaspoons oil in the skillet over medium-high heat

RISOTTO WITH CHICKEN, ARTICHOKES, AND PEAS

until just smoking. Carefully lay the chicken in the skillet and cook until well browned on the first side, 6 to 8 minutes. Flip the chicken, add the broth and water, and bring to a simmer. Cover, reduce the heat to medium-low, and cook until the chicken registers 160 to 165 degrees on an instant-read thermometer, 6 to 8 minutes.

3. Transfer the chicken to a carving board and pour the cooking liquid into a large glass measuring cup. Add more broth as needed to equal 2½ cups, then transfer to a small saucepan, bring to a simmer, cover, and set aside off the heat to keep warm. When the chicken is cool enough to handle, shred the meat into bite-sized pieces.

4. Melt 1 tablespoon of the butter in the skillet over medium heat. Add the onion and ¼ teaspoon salt and cook until softened, about 5 minutes. Stir in the rice and cook, stirring often, until the ends of the rice kernels are transparent, about 2 minutes. Stir in the wine and cook until it has been completely absorbed, 1 to 2 minutes.

5. Stir in 1 cup of the hot broth mixture and continue to simmer, stirring every few minutes, until the liquid is absorbed and the bottom of the pan is almost dry, 7 to 9 minutes.

6. Stir in ½ cup more broth every few minutes as needed to keep the pan bottom from drying out (you may not need all of the broth mixture) and cook, stirring often, until the rice is al dente, 10 to 12 minutes.

7. Off the heat, vigorously stir in the remaining 1 tablespoon butter and cheese, then gently fold in the chicken, artichokes, and peas. Cover the skillet, reduce the heat to low, and cook until the chicken and vegetables are heated through, about 5 minutes, stirring once halfway through. Season with salt and pepper to taste and serve.

VARIATION

Risotto with Chicken, Radicchio, and Walnuts
Any mild blue cheese will work here.

Follow the recipe for Risotto with Chicken, Artichokes, and Peas, substituting 1 head radicchio (about 8 ounces), cored and cut into 1-inch pieces, for the artichokes in step 1 and reducing the cooking time to 2 to 3 minutes, until the radicchio is beginning to wilt and brown. Substitute 2 tablespoons toasted and chopped walnuts for the peas in step 7. Omit the Parmesan and sprinkle 1 ounce crumbled Gorgonzola cheese (about ¼ cup) over the risotto before serving.

WHITE BEAN AND ROSEMARY GRATIN

A TUSCAN-STYLE HEARTY WHITE BEAN CASSEROLE, with a pile of lightly dressed mixed greens on the side, makes the perfect supper when you're not in the mood for the usual steak, chicken, or pasta entrée. This dish boasts creamy, tender white beans flavored with garlic and tomatoes and accentuated by intense, salty bits of pancetta, but the downside is that casseroles feed a crowd and can be time-consuming to make. We liked the concept and flavors of the dish, but we didn't feel like eating leftovers for a week. We sought to rework this classic into a faster-to-the-table casserole for two by making it entirely in a skillet.

Traditionally, white bean casseroles are prepared with dried cannellini beans, which accounts for much of the long cooking time. We generally prefer the superior flavor and texture of dried beans, but milder-tasting, softer-textured canned beans are an acceptable substitute when time is tight. The trick, however, is infusing them with flavor before they become mushy. Canned beans simply cannot withstand an extended cooking time.

With that in mind, we knew we had to establish a base for this dish and develop much of its flavor prior to the beans' introduction. Following the lead of conventional recipes, we prepared a flavorful base using sautéed onion, carrot, and celery. Cooked over moderate heat, the vegetables developed a sweet flavor, which we enhanced with minced garlic and rosemary.

We next considered including tomatoes, another traditional ingredient. For convenience, we hoped that canned diced tomatoes would work. We added the tomatoes to the cooked vegetables to soften and intensify in flavor before the beans and any liquid were added. Tasters liked the tomatoes for the fruity and acidic notes they added to the dish.

Still in search of another hearty ingredient or two to play off the still-to-come beans in our one-skillet meal, we hit on earthy kale leaves, also a Tuscan favorite, along with pancetta. We sautéed the pancetta in the skillet with the vegetables, which helped enrich our flavor base. To cook the kale, we chopped the leaves into 1-inch pieces and simmered them for just five minutes in the skillet once the liquid had been added.

To build the sauce, we tried adding just water, but this flavorless base lacked any richness. When we tried half water, half chicken broth, the flavor of the dish was right on—the only complaint was that the sauce seemed too thin. We considered adding cream, but that seemed out of place in this olive oil–based Italian dish. More oil wasn't the answer either. We needed to thicken our casserole so it was more of a hearty stew, rather than a broth-based soup. Looking for a thickening agent that would keep the tone of the dish, we realized there was an obvious solution: beans pureed with broth or water, a common thickener used in many soup and stew recipes. We pureed ½ cup of the beans with the chicken broth. This creamy mixture added just the right amount of body to the dish, while the remaining whole rinsed beans filled out the sauce.

Since the original dish is typically served with a crusty loaf of bread, we thought a bread topping would be an interesting twist that would contribute a similar flavor and texture. Finely ground bread crumbs didn't quite cut it; they were too sandy in texture and tasted bland. We wanted heartier, more rustic texture and flavor—the crunchy crust of a high-quality loaf, with a flavorful interior to match. We opted to toss chunks of baguette in olive oil and Parmesan before scattering them over the beans. The baguette gave us a higher crust-to-crumb ratio, making for a textured topping. The croutons browned attractively in a 450-degree oven and had a flavorful combination of crisp crust and tender, sweet crumb.

A modern take on an old-world standby, our white bean casserole was still fully rustic, with buttery beans that contrasted nicely with the crisp, salty Parmesan croutons.

White Bean and Rosemary Gratin with Parmesan Croutons

SERVES 2

Canned navy or great Northern beans can be substituted for the cannellini beans. If pancetta is unavailable, substitute 2 ounces bacon (about 2 slices). See page 10 for a recipe to use up the leftover celery and page 15 for a recipe to use up the leftover canned diced tomatoes.

- 1 (15-ounce) can cannellini beans, drained and rinsed (see note)
- 1 cup low-sodium chicken broth
- 2 ounces pancetta, cut into ¼-inch pieces (see note)
- 2 tablespoons olive oil
- 1 small onion, minced
- 1 celery rib, chopped medium
- 1 carrot, peeled and chopped medium
- 3 garlic cloves, minced
- ½ teaspoon minced fresh rosemary or ⅛ teaspoon dried
- ½ cup drained canned diced tomatoes, ¼ cup juice reserved
- ¼ cup water
- ¼ bunch kale or collard greens (about 4 ounces), stemmed (see page 239), leaves cut into 1-inch pieces
  Salt and pepper
- 4 ounces French or Italian bread, cut or torn into 1-inch cubes (about 2 cups)
- 1 ounce Parmesan cheese, grated (about ½ cup)

1. Adjust an oven rack to the middle position and heat the oven to 450 degrees. Puree ½ cup of the beans and broth together in a blender until smooth, about 30 seconds; set aside.

2. Cook the pancetta and 1 tablespoon of the oil in a 10-inch ovensafe skillet over medium heat, stirring occasionally, until the pancetta is lightly browned, 3 to 5 minutes. Stir in the onion, celery, and carrot and cook until the vegetables are softened, about 5 minutes.

3. Stir in the garlic and rosemary and cook until fragrant, about 30 seconds. Stir in the tomatoes and cook until softened and dry, about 2 minutes. Stir in the broth mixture, remaining 1 cup beans, reserved tomato juice, and water. Increase the heat to high, bring to a simmer, and cook until the beans are heated through, about 5 minutes.

4. Stir in the kale leaves, a handful at a time, and continue to cook until the liquid has thickened slightly and begins to fall below the level of the vegetables, and the mixture measures about 3 cups, about 5 minutes. Season with salt and pepper to taste.

5. Toss the bread with the remaining 1 tablespoon olive oil and cheese and sprinkle over the top. Bake the casserole until the cheese has melted and the croutons are golden brown, about 15 minutes. Let the casserole cool for 10 minutes before serving.

SINGAPORE NOODLES WITH SHRIMP

CHAPTER 2

PASTA FOR DINNER

SPAGHETTI WITH GARLIC AND OLIVE OIL

PASTA WITH GARLIC AND OIL, OR *AGLIO E OLIO*, is among the most satisfying (and simplest) of pasta dishes. Composed of kitchen staples—pasta, olive oil, garlic, and red pepper flakes—it is the perfect last-minute pantry supper for two. However, if not made with care, the dish either is dominated by the flavor of burnt garlic or, worse, has no garlic presence at all. We headed to the test kitchen to create a recipe that made the most of its simple flavors.

We first pursued the perfect garlic flavor, working down the list of possibilities from whole crushed cloves to grated raw garlic and using half a pound of pasta for all tests. We didn't care for sautéed whole or slivered garlic, whether ultimately removed from the dish or left in. In fact, no one cared for browned garlic at all—tasters found it acrid and one-dimensional in this dish. Raw minced or grated garlic alone was zingy and harsh.

We then thought to try a different technique, in which a large amount of minced garlic is sautéed slowly until it turns golden and becomes mellow, thus producing a garlic flavor far more complex than does a simple sauté. We tried this with five cloves of minced garlic (about 5 teaspoons) and were delighted to discover that, with low heat and constant stirring, the garlic became sticky and straw-colored, with a flavor that was deep, nutty, and rich. But alone, this slow-sautéed garlic lacked brightness. We decided to combine the forces of cooked and raw by stirring 1 teaspoon of raw garlic into the cooked pasta to release its perfume and sharpness. The effect of this one-two garlic punch was outstanding, creating layers of garlic flavor in this simple dish.

While we were conducting our garlic experiments, it became obvious that the amount of oil we used had to be established carefully. Too much oil made our pasta greasy, but if we used too little, the garlic flavor wasn't distributed evenly throughout the dish. The oil contributes much of the freshness and verve to this dish, so extra-virgin olive oil is a must. We settled on 3 tablespoons: 2 to cook the garlic and 1 tossed into the pasta at the end for flavor.

To finish, some minced parsley, fresh lemon juice, and a dash of red pepper flakes brightened this simple pasta dish. Best of all, we discovered that this sauce plays host to a couple of easy variations using vegetables like artichoke hearts and fennel.

Spaghetti with Garlic and Olive Oil
SERVES 2

See page 43 for tips on how to measure out long strands of pasta without using a scale.

- **3 tablespoons extra-virgin olive oil**
- **1 garlic clove, minced to a paste (see page 43), plus 5 garlic cloves, minced**
- **⅛ teaspoon red pepper flakes**
- **Salt**
- **½ pound spaghetti (see note)**
- **2 tablespoons minced fresh parsley**
- **1 teaspoon fresh lemon juice**
- **Pepper**
- **Grated Parmesan cheese, for serving**

1. Combine 1 tablespoon of the oil and the garlic paste in a small bowl and set aside. Cook the remaining 2 tablespoons oil, minced garlic, pepper flakes, and ¼ teaspoon salt in a 10-inch nonstick skillet over low heat, stirring often, until the garlic is sticky and golden, about 10 minutes. Set aside off the heat.

2. Meanwhile, bring 4 quarts water to a boil in a large pot. Add the pasta and 1 tablespoon salt and cook, stirring often, until al dente. Reserve ½ cup of the cooking water, then drain the pasta and return it to the pot.

3. Add the raw garlic–oil mixture, sautéed garlic mixture, parsley, lemon juice, and 1 tablespoon of the reserved pasta cooking water to the pasta, and toss to combine, adjusting the sauce consistency with the remaining reserved cooking water as desired. Season with salt and pepper to taste and serve with the Parmesan.

VARIATIONS

Spaghetti with Garlic, Olive Oil, and Artichokes
To quickly thaw frozen artichoke hearts, place them in a microwave-safe bowl, cover, and microwave on high for about 3 minutes. Drain thoroughly and pat dry with paper towels before using.

Follow the recipe for Spaghetti with Garlic and Olive Oil, transferring the sautéed garlic mixture to a small bowl in step 1. Add 2 teaspoons extra-virgin olive oil to the skillet and return to medium-high heat until shimmering. Add 1 (9-ounce) package frozen artichoke hearts, thawed and patted dry with paper towels, and ⅛ teaspoon salt to the skillet. Cook until the artichokes are lightly browned and tender, 4 to 6 minutes. Add the

HOW TO COOK PASTA

If you ask 10 cooks how they cook pasta, you're likely to get 10 answers. In an effort to standardize pasta cookery, we've come up with these guidelines that will guarantee perfect pasta every time.

Use plenty of salt. Many people dump oil into boiling pasta water, thinking it will keep pasta from sticking together, but this is a myth. Adding oil does not prevent sticking. Frequent stirring does. Skip the oil but make sure to add salt—roughly 1 tablespoon for 4 quarts of water—or the pasta will taste bland.

Use 4 quarts of water in a large pot. This may sound like a lot of water for just two servings, but this amount will ensure that the pasta cooks evenly and won't clump.

Taste pasta often for doneness. Reading the instructions on the box is a good place to start, but for al dente pasta, you may need to shave a few minutes off the recommended time. When you start to get close to the recommended cooking time, begin tasting for doneness.

Save some cooking water. Wait! Before you drain that pasta, measure about ½ cup of the cooking water from the pasta pot with a liquid measuring cup. Then drain the pasta and immediately toss it with the sauce. (Don't let the pasta sit in the colander too long; it will get very dry very quickly.) When you toss your sauce with the pasta, add some (or all) of the reserved pasta cooking water to thin the sauce as needed.

MINCING GARLIC TO A PASTE

In some recipes that use garlic raw, it is important that the garlic be smooth for even distribution. Adding a pinch of salt, then dragging a chef's knife over the mixture to make a fine paste, helps break down the garlic further.

ALL ABOUT GARLIC

We go through a lot of garlic in the test kitchen, so we know firsthand that peeling and mincing many cloves can be tedious. We tested two convenience garlic products—peeled whole cloves and minced jarred bits—against fresh garlic in our spaghetti with garlic and oil. The minced product, which is garlic preserved in a solution of water and phosphoric acid, ruined the recipe with musty, bitter flavors. The peeled cloves, however, were an acceptable substitute almost as good as the fresh garlic. But consider this: While a whole head of garlic will keep for at least a few weeks (if not longer) stored in a cool, dry place with plenty of air circulation, prepeeled garlic in a jar (which must be kept refrigerated) lasts only about two weeks before developing an overly pungent aroma. Our verdict? Fresh garlic is the best choice, especially when cooking for two.

MEASURING PASTA

Guessing how much pasta you *really* need to cook can be tricky when cooking for just two people. Of course you can always judge by how full the box is (most pasta is packaged in 1-pound boxes), but we think it's easier to simply measure shaped pasta using dry measuring cups and to measure strand pastas by diameter. Here are the cup measurements of the most common short pasta shapes, as well as the diameter of some strand pastas.

PASTA TYPE	⅓ POUND	½ POUND
Campanelle, Farfalle, Medium Shells, Fusilli, Cavatappi, and Rigatoni	2 cups	3 cups
Penne, Ziti, Orecchiette, and Small Shells	1⅔ cups	2½ cups
Macaroni	1½ cups	2 cups
Orzo	1 cup	1¼ cups

When ½ pound of uncooked linguine, thin spaghetti, spaghettini, or soba noodle strands are bunched together into a tight circle, the diameter measures about 1¼ inches. When ⅓ pound of uncooked linguine, thin spaghetti, spaghettini, or soba noodle strands are bunched together into a tight circle, the diameter measures about 1 inch.

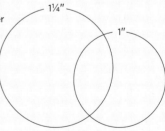

cooked artichokes to the pasta with the sautéed garlic mixture in step 3.

Spaghetti with Garlic, Olive Oil, and Fennel

Follow the recipe for Spaghetti with Garlic and Olive Oil, transferring the sautéed garlic mixture to a small bowl in step 1. Add ½ cup water, 2 teaspoons extra-virgin olive oil, and 1 thinly sliced fennel bulb (see page 18) to the skillet. Cover and cook over medium-high heat until the fennel is crisp-tender, about 3 minutes. Uncover and continue to cook until the water has evaporated and the fennel is lightly browned and fully tender, about 5 minutes longer. Add the cooked fennel to the pasta with the sautéed garlic mixture in step 3.

PASTA WITH RICOTTA

PASTA WITH A CREAMY, SLIGHTLY SWEET RICOTTA sauce is a naturally quick and convenient meal for two, but such a simple sauce can require expert execution—all too often the sauce is grainy and its flavor is bland. We set out to develop a pasta recipe that would highlight ricotta's creamy texture and milky flavor. Ricotta, peas, and prosciutto are a familiar combination in Italian cooking, and the simplicity of this trio appealed to us.

We tackled the issue of the pasta sauce first. In most recipes ricotta is simply added in small bits to hot drained pasta, but this method did not work well. Although the cheese melted slightly, it failed to sufficiently coat the pasta and resulted in grainy bits of ricotta. A few recipes suggested whisking the ricotta with a small amount of reserved pasta cooking water before mixing it with the pasta. This technique was a success. The hot water smoothed out the graininess of the ricotta and created a uniform coating for our pasta. However, the sauce was not quite rich or flavorful enough for our tastes. The addition of just 1 tablespoon of butter was all it took to enrich the sauce. We also decided to add some Parmesan to the mixture; its bold, nutty profile gave our simple pasta dish a serious flavor boost. Tasters also liked the addition of a little lemon juice and lemon zest for brightness.

We then turned to the prosciutto. While we liked the flavor of the prosciutto in the dish generally, some tasters felt its texture was bothersome. Raw prosciutto is silky, but warm prosciutto can be slightly rubbery and chewy. We tried cutting it into smaller pieces but found that it didn't impart enough flavor that way. We then considered using the prosciutto in a manner more along the lines of bacon or pancetta. We hoped we could cook the prosciutto in a little oil, crisping its texture and rendering some of its fat. We would then sauté onion and garlic in the remaining oil. This technique turned out to be the best option. By sautéing the aromatics in the rendered fat from the prosciutto, we retained the salty meatiness tasters liked but avoided the texture problems. Topping the completed dish with crispy bits of prosciutto provided a welcome textural contrast to the creamy ricotta sauce.

Next, we moved on to the peas. While we normally avoid frozen vegetables, peas are an exception. Peas are so delicate that their flavor is compromised as soon as they are picked; their sugars, like those of corn,

instantly begin converting to starch after harvesting. Fortunately, frozen peas are processed within hours of being picked, when their flavor is at its peak. We knew that if we thawed them, they would need just a hint of heat to warm through and maintain their fresh flavor, so we added them to the hot pasta. Finally, for a flavor reminiscent of spring, we finished our dish with some fresh mint, the perfect complement to the creamy ricotta, zesty lemon, salty prosciutto, and sweet peas.

Shells with Ricotta, Peas, and Prosciutto
SERVES 2

Do not substitute fat-free ricotta here. Other pasta shapes can be substituted for the shells; however, their cup measurements may vary (see page 43). See page 45 for a recipe to use up some of the leftover ricotta cheese.

- 4 ounces whole milk or part-skim ricotta cheese (about ½ cup)
- 1 ounce Parmesan cheese, grated (about ½ cup)
- 1 tablespoon unsalted butter, cut into 4 pieces
- ¼ teaspoon grated lemon zest plus 1½ teaspoons fresh lemon juice
- Salt and pepper
- 1½ teaspoons olive oil
- 8 thin slices prosciutto (about 2 ounces), cut into ¼-inch strips
- 1 small onion, minced
- 1 garlic clove, minced
- ½ pound small shells (about 2½ cups; see note)
- 1 cup frozen peas, thawed
- 1 tablespoon minced fresh mint

1. Mix the ricotta, Parmesan, butter, lemon zest, lemon juice, ⅛ teaspoon salt, and ¼ teaspoon pepper together in a medium bowl; set aside.

2. Cook the oil and prosciutto in an 8-inch nonstick skillet over medium heat until the prosciutto is well browned and crisp, about 5 minutes. Using a slotted spoon, transfer the prosciutto to a paper towel–lined plate, leaving the fat in the skillet. Add the onion and cook over medium heat until softened and lightly browned, 5 to 7 minutes. Stir in the garlic and cook until fragrant, about 30 seconds. Transfer the onion mixture to the bowl with the ricotta mixture.

3. Meanwhile, bring 4 quarts water to a boil in a large pot. Add the pasta and 1 tablespoon salt and cook, stirring often, until al dente. Reserve ½ cup of the cooking water, then drain the pasta and return it to the pot. Stir the peas into the pasta and cover to warm through.

4. Whisk ¼ cup of the reserved pasta cooking water into the ricotta mixture until smooth. Pour the ricotta mixture over the pasta and peas and toss to combine, adjusting the sauce consistency with the reserved cooking water as desired. Season with salt and pepper to taste. Sprinkle individual portions with the crisped prosciutto and mint and serve.

VARIATIONS

Shells with Ricotta, Roasted Red Peppers, Goat Cheese, and Basil

Follow the recipe for Shells with Ricotta, Peas, and Prosciutto, substituting ½ cup crumbled goat cheese for the Parmesan, 1 tablespoon balsamic vinegar for the lemon juice and lemon zest, 1 cup jarred roasted red peppers, drained, patted dry, and chopped medium, for the peas, and 2 tablespoons chopped fresh basil for the mint.

Shells with Ricotta, Arugula, and Pine Nuts

The arugula will wilt when tossed with the hot pasta.

Follow the recipe for Shells with Ricotta, Peas, and Prosciutto, substituting 1 ounce Asiago cheese, grated (about ½ cup), for the Parmesan, 4 ounces baby arugula (about 4 cups) for the peas, and 1 tablespoon toasted pine nuts for the mint.

USE IT UP: RICOTTA CHEESE

Sweet Ricotta Cheese Dip
MAKES ABOUT ¾ CUP

This sweet dip is similar to cannoli filling. Serve it with cinnamon-sugar pita chips, biscotti, or toast, or spoon it into a bowl with fresh berries. The dip can be refrigerated in an airtight container for up to 4 days.

4–6 ounces whole milk or part-skim ricotta cheese
2–3 tablespoons confectioners' sugar
 ½   teaspoon vanilla extract
 ¼   teaspoon grated lemon zest

Stir the ricotta, sugar, vanilla, and lemon zest together in a bowl until smooth. Serve.

THE BEST PROSCIUTTO

Americans have long looked to Italy for the best prosciutto. After all, Italy invented the method used to produce this salt-cured and air-dried ham. So when we heard about a prosciutto on the market that is crafted not in Italy but in Iowa, we were more than curious. Tasted side by side with prosciutto di Parma and prosciutto San Daniele, the newcomer from Iowa, **La Quercia Prosciutto Americana**, was the hands-down winner. Tasters marveled at the deep, earthy flavor and creamy texture of this prosciutto, which can be found at specialty and gourmet grocery stores. The other domestic brands we tasted simply aren't worth buying.

STORING PROSCIUTTO

Prosciutto, salt-cured and air-dried ham, is essentially a high-end deli meat—so keep this in mind when storing any extra, and store it the way you bought it. Whether freshly sliced at an Italian market or purchased prewrapped at the supermarket, prosciutto usually comes layered between sheets of waxed paper. To store extra prosciutto, keep it in its original packaging and either slide the container into a zipper-lock bag and press the air out or wrap it tightly with plastic wrap. Use it within five to seven days or else it will dry out and the flavor will be compromised. If you have just a few scraps left, you can wrap the strips around slices of melon or thin breadsticks for a quick appetizer.

PASTA WITH TOMATO AND ALMOND PESTO

THIS SIDE OF THE ATLANTIC, "PESTO" IS SYNONYMOUS with lots of basil, Parmesan cheese, garlic, pine nuts, and good olive oil blended into a rich, grassy, no-cook concoction. However, throughout Italy, you can find countless variations on this theme, with ingredients ranging from parsley and arugula to almonds, walnuts, pecans, sun-dried tomatoes—even fennel. We've always been intrigued by a "red" variation that hails from Trapani, a village on the western tip of Sicily. Here almonds replace pine nuts, but the big difference is the appearance of fresh tomatoes—not as the main ingredient, but just enough to tint the sauce and lend fruity, vibrant sweetness. This seemed to us a great place to start for a flavor-packed pasta dinner for two.

The Trapanese pesto recipes we found in Italian cookbooks seemed to use a similar technique and stuck to a core list of ingredients: tomatoes, almonds, basil, garlic, olive oil, and cheese. But when we mixed up a few, the results were distinctly different. One resembled chunky tomato salsa, while another was thin and watery. The most promising recipe was a creamy, reddish-ocher pesto. Like most pestos, this one came together in just minutes: Pulse tomatoes, basil leaves, toasted almonds, garlic, salt, and red pepper flakes together in a food processor; add olive oil in a slow, steady stream to emulsify; adjust the seasonings; toss with pasta and cheese; and serve. The tomatoes contributed bright flavor, and the almonds thickened the sauce and offered their own delicate flavor and richness.

Focusing first on the tomatoes, we thought farmers market tomatoes would surely be best, but we wanted a year-round pesto, which meant relying on year-round tomatoes. We plucked plum tomatoes, round tomatoes, grape tomatoes, and cherry tomatoes from the produce aisle and dropped them into the food processor, batch by batch. The plum and round tomatoes were out—their quality was inconsistent. The cherry and grape tomatoes proved equal contenders, sharing a similar brightness and juiciness that was far more reliable. We settled on a generous 1 cup for two servings.

Almonds, just like pine nuts in other pestos, are integral to this pesto because they contribute body while retaining just enough crunch to offset the tomatoes' pulpiness. Toasting was a must to release oils and flavor prior to blending. We found that slivered almonds browned more evenly than whole nuts and avoided the muddy flavor often contributed by papery skins. Two tablespoons of slivered almonds plus a relatively modest 3 tablespoons of extra-virgin olive oil added plenty of pleasant grittiness and creamy texture without too much richness.

Basil is the star of many pestos, but its role in the Trapanese version is a supporting one. One-quarter cup provided just enough flavor to work in tandem with the tomatoes. For a variation, we swapped out the almonds for pine nuts and the basil for peppery arugula.

Save for boiling the pasta, our pesto was all but on the table. But something was missing—something small. A pinch of salt and red pepper flakes came close, but we wanted something more bracing. Just ¼ teaspoon of red wine vinegar provided the zing the sauce needed.

By the time we dressed the dish and showered on a handful of grated Parmesan cheese, Trapanese pesto fit our tastes perfectly.

Pasta with Tomato and Almond Pesto
SERVES 2

See page 43 for tips on how to measure out long strands of pasta without using a scale. You can substitute grape tomatoes for the cherry tomatoes.

6	ounces cherry tomatoes (about 1 cup)
¼	cup fresh basil
2	tablespoons slivered almonds, toasted (see page 210)
1	small garlic clove, minced
¼	teaspoon red wine vinegar
⅛	teaspoon red pepper flakes
	Salt
3	tablespoons extra-virgin olive oil
½	pound linguine or spaghetti (see note)
¼	cup grated Parmesan cheese, plus extra for serving

1. Process the tomatoes, basil, almonds, garlic, vinegar, pepper flakes, and ½ teaspoon salt in a food processor until smooth, about 1 minute. Scrape down the sides of the bowl with a rubber spatula. With the machine running, slowly drizzle in the oil until incorporated, about 30 seconds.

2. Meanwhile, bring 4 quarts water to a boil in a large pot. Add the pasta and 1 tablespoon salt and cook, stirring often, until al dente. Reserve ½ cup of the cooking water, then drain the pasta and return it to the pot.

3. Add the pesto and ¼ cup of the Parmesan to the pasta and toss to combine, adjusting the consistency with the reserved pasta cooking water as desired. Season to taste with salt and serve with extra Parmesan.

VARIATION
Pasta with Tomato, Pine Nut, and Arugula Pesto
Follow the recipe for Pasta with Tomato and Almond Pesto, substituting ½ ounce baby arugula (about ½ cup) for the basil and 2 tablespoons toasted pine nuts for the almonds. Add ¾ teaspoon grated lemon zest plus ½ teaspoon fresh lemon juice to the food processor in step 1.

PASTA WITH TOMATO AND ALMOND PESTO

SPAGHETTI WITH MARINARA SAUCE

MARINARA, MEANING "SAILOR-STYLE," IS THE NAME given to a tomato-based pasta sauce that first became popular in the seafaring town of Naples. Compared to a fast and fresh tomato sauce, marinara is complex and rich, thanks to long, slow simmering. Unfortunately, this complexity of flavor comes at the price of hours in the kitchen, which is just fine if you're simmering a large pot for Sunday dinner—but not so practical when preparing a weeknight dinner for two. We wondered if we could achieve that authentic, long-cooked flavor in less than an hour.

We started our testing with the main ingredient, the tomatoes. Because prime fresh tomatoes are available for such a limited time during the year, we opted for canned. Canned whole tomatoes were our first choice for fresh tomato flavor and optimum texture; however, the big drawback of using whole tomatoes in a sauce is that they have to be cut up. Chopping them on a cutting board was a mess. Our solution was to dump them into a strainer over a bowl and hand-crush them, removing the hard core and any stray bits of skin. One 28-ounce can of whole tomatoes yielded enough sauce to coat ½ pound of pasta. Instead of adding all of the juice from the can, we reserved just 1¼ cups (rather than the full 1¾ cups we had collected), which helped shorten the simmering time since the sauce didn't need to cook for as long to thicken.

Up until now we had been following the standard marinara procedure of sautéing aromatics (in this case, onions and garlic) in olive oil before adding the tomatoes, liquid, and flavorings, then simmering. To concentrate the tomato flavor quickly, we sautéed the tomatoes until they glazed the bottom of the pan. Only then did we add the liquids, which deglazed the pan and added crucial flavor. Since we were cooking a small amount of sauce, we switched from a saucepan to a 10-inch skillet—the greater surface area encouraged faster evaporation and, thus, faster concentration of flavors. This turned out to be the key step in giving our quick sauce the complexity of a long-simmered one.

With the tomato flavor under control, it was time to develop more depth of flavor. Onion added a pleasant sweetness; carrots, not uncommon in marinara, added an earthy flavor but contributed too much sweetness. Sugar, added at the end of cooking, proved to be the working solution to balance the flavors: Too much and our sauce began to taste like it came out of a jar; too little and the acidity overwhelmed the other flavors. Tasters loved the robust, complex flavor of red wine, and a mere 2 tablespoons was just the right amount. But not just any bottle: Wines with a heavy oak flavor rated lower than those with little to no oak presence. (Chianti and Merlot scored particularly high marks.)

We now had a good marinara ready for two to ladle and serve in less than an hour. Could we further bolster the complexity without adding minutes? On a hunch, we tried reserving a few of the uncooked canned tomatoes and adding them near the end of cooking. Tasters were unanimous in their preference for the new sauce; just ⅓ cup of tomatoes pureed into the sauce at the end added enough brightness to complement the deeper profile of the cooked sauce.

So far the sauce had little flavor from herbs beyond oregano. Fresh basil, also added at the end, contributed a floral aroma that complemented the sauce's careful balance of sweet and acid. A tablespoon of extra-virgin olive oil rounded out the flavors.

Spaghetti with Marinara Sauce
SERVES 2

See page 43 for tips on how to measure out long strands of pasta without using a scale. Be sure to use whole tomatoes packed in juice (not puree). If you prefer a chunkier sauce, give it just three or four pulses in the food processor in step 4.

- 1 (28-ounce) can whole tomatoes (see note)
- 2 tablespoons olive oil
- 1 small onion, minced
- 2 garlic cloves, minced
- ¼ teaspoon dried oregano
- 2 tablespoons dry red wine
- 1½ tablespoons chopped fresh basil
- 1 tablespoon extra-virgin olive oil
- Salt and pepper
- ½–1 teaspoon sugar
- ½ pound spaghetti (see note)
- Grated Parmesan cheese, for serving

1. Drain the tomatoes in a strainer set over a medium bowl. Open the tomatoes with your hands and remove and discard the fibrous cores. Let the tomatoes sit to drain excess liquid, about 3 minutes. Measure out and reserve ⅓ cup of the tomatoes from the strainer. Reserve 1¼ cups of the tomato juice and discard the remainder.

2. Heat 1 tablespoon of the olive oil in a 10-inch skillet over medium heat until shimmering. Add the onion and cook until softened and lightly browned, 5 to 7 minutes. Stir in the garlic and oregano and cook until fragrant, about 30 seconds.

3. Add the remaining 1 tablespoon olive oil and the remaining tomatoes from the strainer to the skillet and increase the heat to medium-high. Cook, stirring occasionally, until the liquid has evaporated and the tomatoes begin to stick to the bottom of the pan and brown around the pan edges, 8 to 10 minutes. Add the wine and cook until nearly evaporated, about 30 seconds. Add the reserved tomato juice and bring to a simmer. Reduce the heat to medium and cook, stirring occasionally and scraping up any browned bits, until the sauce is thick, 7 to 9 minutes.

4. Transfer the sauce to a food processor and add the reserved raw tomatoes. Pulse until the sauce is mostly smooth, about 8 pulses. Return the sauce to the skillet and stir in the basil and extra-virgin olive oil. Season with salt, pepper, and sugar to taste.

5. Meanwhile, bring 4 quarts water to a boil in a large pot. Add the pasta and 1 tablespoon salt and cook, stirring often, until al dente. Reserve ½ cup of the cooking water, then drain the pasta and return it to the pot.

6. Add the sauce to the pasta and toss to combine, adjusting the sauce consistency with the reserved pasta cooking water as desired. Serve with the Parmesan.

NOTES FROM THE TEST KITCHEN

THE BEST SPAGHETTI
In the not-so-distant past, American pasta had a poor reputation, and rightly so. It cooked up gummy and starchy, and experts usually touted the superiority of Italian brands. To find out if this was still the case, we tasted eight leading brands of spaghetti—four American and four Italian. Ultimately, American-made **Ronzoni Spaghetti** was the top finisher; tasters praised its nutty, buttery flavor and superb texture. The two most expensive brands came in last, so save your money and don't bother with the expensive imported pastas— American-made is just fine.

PASTA WITH ROASTED CHERRY TOMATOES

PASTA WITH A BRIGHT FRESH TOMATO SAUCE, HEADY with garlic and basil, is an appealing weeknight meal— it's quick (no long simmering required), easy to prepare, and requires few ingredients. But except for a short time in the summer, the supermarket options are limited to vibrantly red specimens that deliver mealy texture and almost no discernible flavor. Yes, we could start with canned tomatoes for a quick sauce—and most often we do—but we thought that a really good fresh tomato sauce any time of year was a worthy goal.

When we want to find an off-season tomato with at least some positive attributes, we usually turn to cherry tomatoes. We decided to sample both no-cook and quick sauté recipes. The no-cook concept is simple enough: Toss halved cherry tomatoes with a little olive oil, fresh herbs, and salt; allow them to sit and give off their juice; then toss with pasta. This method works with sweet, tender, summertime tomatoes, but with tart off-season varieties the sauce was flat and watery. The quick sauté method, which exposes the halved tomatoes to just enough high heat to warm them through, was equally disappointing. Not only does it require precision timing to avoid overcooking, but it failed to improve the meager flavor of the tomatoes.

The obvious place to turn was roasting, a method that would concentrate and sweeten their flavor. We found recipes that called for two to three hours of roasting, an absurd amount of time for a quick sauce. In addition, these recipes produced tomatoes with a leathery texture that seemed more oven-dried than slow-roasted. We wanted a quicker recipe and a juicier end result.

Roasting the tomatoes in high heat (400 to 450 degrees) took considerably less time, but the high oven temperature caused the tomatoes to explode out of their skins, something that did not translate into a palatable sauce. They were juicy, yes, but they were also mushy and quickly disintegrated when mixed with the pasta. We needed to test lower oven temperatures. In the end, the best choice was 350 degrees. The tomatoes became sweet and concentrated in just 30 minutes.

When it came to seasoning, garlic was a must, but we wanted to add it the easy way, roasting it along with the tomatoes. Minced garlic was too strong, but garlic cut into slivers was just right. Although onions added a harsh flavor, delicate shallot was sweet enough to complement the tomatoes. But when we mixed the larger slices of shallot with the tomatoes, as we had done with the garlic slivers, the shallot didn't cook quickly enough. Simply sprinkling the slices on top of the tomatoes helped them to roast more quickly.

By the time we reached the 20th batch of pasta, we noticed that the sweetness level of the tomatoes tended to vary. Sometimes they leaned to the sweeter side (much like in-season cherry tomatoes or their cousins, grape tomatoes), but most were exceedingly tart. We added a small amount of sugar to the recipe to adjust for this tartness (the sugar can be easily reduced or even omitted

when using sweeter tomatoes). Two other ingredients that boosted flavor were a modest 1½ teaspoons of balsamic vinegar and a pinch of red pepper flakes, both added to the tomatoes before roasting. Fresh basil and Parmesan cheese, added just before serving, completed the sauce.

In the end, then, is a fresh tomato sauce in late winter a good idea? Yes. This relatively quick and simple roasting method guarantees rich tomato flavor, even with third-rate supermarket tomatoes, so we can enjoy this simple pasta dish any time of year.

NOTES FROM THE TEST KITCHEN

ROASTING TOMATOES
Tomatoes roasted in a low oven for a long time will dry out and become leathery (left). And while a high oven temperature will shorten the roasting time, it will also cause the tomatoes to explode out of their skins, creating a mushy sauce. The key to perfectly cooked tomatoes that retain their juiciness—and shape—is to roast them in a moderate oven for about 30 minutes (right).

| TOO MUCH | JUST RIGHT |

STORING NUTS
Because of their high fat content, nuts can go rancid very quickly. A cool, dark pantry might seem like the perfect place to store your walnuts and pecans, but the only place to really guarantee their freshness is the refrigerator. Keep all nuts in the freezer, where they will stay fresh for at least six months.

PASTA PARAPHERNALIA
For the most part, our opinion of pasta gadgets is pretty low. Pasta pots with perforated inserts, a favorite on late-night infomercials, tend to boil over if filled with the necessary amount of water. And a pot with a strainer lid might look promising, but we found that if your grip isn't secure, the lid pops off and pasta can end up all over your sink. The only pasta tool we've come across through the years that we've actually liked is a pasta fork, which is a long-handled spoon with ridged teeth. But no need to rush out and buy one; basic tongs work just fine.

Pasta with Roasted Cherry Tomatoes, Garlic, and Basil
SERVES 2

You can substitute grape tomatoes for the cherry tomatoes. Other pasta shapes can be substituted for the penne; however, their cup measurements may vary (see page 43).

- 1 **small shallot, sliced thin**
- 2 **tablespoons olive oil**
- 1 **pound cherry tomatoes (about 2½ cups), halved**
- 3 **garlic cloves, sliced thin**
- 1½ **teaspoons balsamic vinegar**
- ¾ **teaspoon sugar**
-   **Salt and pepper**
- ⅛ **teaspoon red pepper flakes**
- ½ **pound penne (about 2½ cups; see note)**
- 2 **tablespoons chopped fresh basil**
-   **Grated Parmesan cheese, for serving**

1. Adjust an oven rack to the middle position and heat the oven to 350 degrees.

2. Toss the shallot and 1 teaspoon of the oil together in a small bowl. In a medium bowl, gently toss the remaining 5 teaspoons oil, tomatoes, garlic, vinegar, sugar, ¼ teaspoon salt, ⅛ teaspoon pepper, and pepper flakes together. Spread the tomatoes in a single layer in a 13 by 9-inch baking dish and scatter the shallot over the tomatoes. Roast, without stirring, until the edges of the shallot begin to brown and the tomato skins are slightly shriveled but the tomatoes still retain their shape, about 30 minutes. Remove the tomatoes from the oven and let cool slightly, about 5 minutes.

3. Meanwhile, bring 4 quarts water to a boil in a large pot. Add the pasta and 1 tablespoon salt and cook, stirring often, until al dente. Reserve ½ cup of the cooking water, then drain the pasta and return it to the pot.

4. Scrape the tomato mixture on top of the pasta, add the basil, and toss to combine, adjusting the sauce consistency with the reserved pasta cooking water as desired. Season with salt and pepper to taste and serve with the Parmesan.

VARIATIONS

Pasta with Roasted Cherry Tomatoes, Olives, Capers, and Pine Nuts

You can substitute grape tomatoes for the cherry tomatoes. See page 43 for tips on how to measure out long strands of pasta without using a scale.

 1 **pound cherry tomatoes (about 2½ cups), halved**
 2 **tablespoons drained capers, rinsed**
 2 **tablespoons olive oil**
 3 **garlic cloves, sliced thin**
 ¾ **teaspoon sugar**
    Salt and pepper
 ¼ **teaspoon red pepper flakes**
 ½ **pound spaghetti (see note)**
 2 **tablespoons chopped pitted kalamata olives**
 1 **tablespoon minced fresh oregano**
 2 **tablespoons pine nuts, toasted (see page 210)**
    Grated Pecorino Romano cheese, for serving

1. Adjust an oven rack to the middle position and heat the oven to 350 degrees.

2. Gently toss the tomatoes, capers, oil, garlic, sugar, ¼ teaspoon salt, ⅛ teaspoon pepper, and pepper flakes together in a medium bowl. Spread the tomatoes in a single layer in a 13 by 9-inch baking dish and roast, without stirring, until the tomato skins are slightly shriveled but the tomatoes still retain their shape, about 30 minutes. Remove the tomatoes from the oven and let cool slightly, about 5 minutes.

3. Meanwhile, bring 4 quarts water to a boil in a large pot. Add the pasta and 1 tablespoon salt and cook, stirring often, until al dente. Reserve ½ cup of the cooking water, then drain the pasta and return it to the pot.

4. Scrape the tomato mixture on top of the pasta, add the olives and oregano, and toss to combine, adjusting

the sauce consistency with the reserved pasta cooking water as desired. Season with salt and pepper to taste. Sprinkle individual portions with the pine nuts and serve with the Pecorino Romano.

Pasta with Roasted Cherry Tomatoes, Arugula, and Goat Cheese

You can substitute grape tomatoes for the cherry tomatoes. Other pasta shapes can be substituted for the farfalle; however, their cup measurements may vary (see page 43).

 1   **small shallot, sliced thin**
 2   **tablespoons olive oil**
 1   **pound cherry tomatoes (about 2½ cups), halved**
 3   **garlic cloves, sliced thin**
 1½ **teaspoons sherry or red wine vinegar**
 ¾   **teaspoon sugar**
     Salt and pepper
 ⅛   **teaspoon red pepper flakes**
 ½   **pound farfalle (about 3 cups; see note)**
 2   **ounces baby arugula (about 2 cups)**
 2   **ounces goat cheese, crumbled (about ½ cup)**

1. Adjust an oven rack to the middle position and heat the oven to 350 degrees.

2. Toss the shallot and 1 teaspoon of the oil together in a small bowl. In a medium bowl, gently toss the remaining 5 teaspoons oil, tomatoes, garlic, vinegar, sugar, ¼ teaspoon salt, ⅛ teaspoon pepper, and pepper flakes together. Spread the tomatoes in a single layer in a 13 by 9-inch baking dish and scatter the shallot over the tomatoes. Roast, without stirring, until the edges of the shallot begin to brown and the tomato skins are slightly shriveled but the tomatoes still retain their shape, about 30 minutes. Remove the tomatoes from the oven and let cool slightly, about 5 minutes.

3. Meanwhile, bring 4 quarts water to a boil in a large pot. Add the pasta and 1 tablespoon salt and cook, stirring often, until al dente. Reserve ½ cup of the cooking water, then drain the pasta and return it to the pot. Stir the arugula into the pasta until wilted.

4. Scrape the tomato mixture on top of the pasta and arugula and toss to combine, adjusting the sauce consistency with the reserved pasta cooking water as desired. Season with salt and pepper to taste. Sprinkle individual portions with the goat cheese and serve.

PASTA WITH CHICKEN AND VEGETABLES

PASTA WITH CHICKEN AND VEGETABLES MAKES A hearty, satisfying weeknight dinner (think chicken, broccoli, and ziti). But sometimes the familiar becomes a bit humdrum. So in an effort to step away from the same old, we set out to come up with a few fresh, inspired pasta dishes with moist chicken, crisp-tender vegetables, and a light, well-seasoned sauce.

First, we reacquainted ourselves with our fail-safe cooking method for pasta with chicken and vegetables. We thinly slice one large boneless, skinless chicken breast—they're great when cooking for two because they are easy to prepare and you can either buy them one at a time or buy more and freeze the rest—and cook it with butter in a skillet until golden, then remove it from the pan just before it is done. Next, we sauté the vegetables, then transfer them to the bowl with the chicken. For the sauce, we cook garlic, thyme, red pepper flakes, and a little flour in the skillet, whisk in chicken broth and white wine (which gives us a lighter, brighter sauce than one made with cream), and simmer the mixture until thickened slightly. We then return the chicken and vegetables to the sauce to finish cooking (this sauté-then-poach technique for cooking the chicken provides the best balance of flavor and tenderness) before tossing the mixture with the pasta and any quick-cooking vegetables. Finally, we round out the dish with a tablespoon of butter, a handful of cheese, and a sprinkling of fresh herbs.

Now we were ready to customize each recipe with additional ingredients. For our first combination, we chose sweet butternut squash with pleasantly bitter radicchio, nutty Parmesan, and basil. Next, we matched earthy spinach with sweet and creamy Gorgonzola and crunchy toasted almonds. Last, we dusted off the classic combination of pasta with chicken and broccoli and paired assertive broccoli rabe with sweet red bell pepper, Pecorino Romano, and toasted pine nuts.

When it came to cooking the vegetables, we discovered that not all should be treated the same. We found that the butternut squash, radicchio, and bell pepper could be cooked in the pan before building the sauce. However, when it came to cooking the broccoli rabe, we found that it was best to blanch it. Spinach, a tender leafy vegetable, needed only a few seconds in the pot to wilt, so we stirred it into the pasta just before serving. We now had three new pasta-and-chicken recipes in our repertoire.

Pasta with Chicken, Butternut Squash, and Radicchio
SERVES 2

Other pasta shapes can be substituted for the campanelle; however, their cup measurements may vary (see page 43). See page 54 for a recipe to use up the leftover butternut squash. If using prepeeled and seeded squash from the supermarket, you will need 8 ounces for this recipe.

- 4 tablespoons (½ stick) unsalted butter
- 1 (8-ounce) boneless, skinless chicken breast, trimmed and sliced thin
- ⅓ medium butternut squash, peeled, seeded, and cut into ½-inch cubes (about 1½ cups) (see note)
- 1 head radicchio (about 8 ounces), cored and cut into 1-inch pieces
- 1 small onion, minced
- 3 garlic cloves, minced

NOTES FROM THE TEST KITCHEN

PREPARING BUTTERNUT SQUASH
With its tough outer skin, bulbous base filled with seeds and fibers, and long, skinny neck, butternut squash can be formidable to prepare. Here's how we get the squash ready to cut into evenly sized pieces.

1. After cutting off both ends of the squash and removing the skin with a vegetable peeler, cut the squash in half, separating the bulb from the neck.

2. Then cut the bulb in half through the base and remove the seeds with a spoon. Cut the peeled and seeded squash as directed in recipes.

PASTA WITH CHICKEN, BUTTERNUT SQUASH, AND RADICCHIO

1 teaspoon minced fresh thyme or ¼ teaspoon dried
1 teaspoon unbleached all-purpose flour
⅛ teaspoon red pepper flakes
1 cup low-sodium chicken broth
½ cup dry white wine
⅓ pound campanelle (about 2 cups; see note)
  Salt
1 ounce Parmesan cheese, grated (about ½ cup),
  plus extra for serving
¼ cup shredded fresh basil (see page 57)
  Pepper

1. Melt 1 tablespoon of the butter in a 10-inch nonstick skillet over high heat until beginning to brown. Add the chicken in a single layer, break up any clumps, and cook without stirring until it begins to brown, about 1 minute. Stir the chicken and continue to cook until it is almost cooked through, about 2 minutes longer. Transfer the chicken to a bowl, cover, and set aside.

2. Melt 1 tablespoon more butter in the skillet over medium heat. Add the squash and cook, stirring occasionally, until spotty brown and tender, 7 to 10 minutes. Transfer the squash to the bowl with the chicken. Add the radicchio to the skillet and cook until beginning to wilt and brown, 2 to 3 minutes. Transfer the radicchio to the bowl with the chicken and squash.

3. Melt 1 tablespoon more butter in the skillet over medium heat. Add the onion and cook until softened and lightly browned, 5 to 7 minutes. Stir in the garlic, thyme, flour, and pepper flakes, and cook until fragrant, about 30 seconds. Stir in the broth and wine, bring to a simmer, and cook until the sauce has thickened slightly and reduced to ⅔ cup, about 10 minutes. Set aside and cover to keep warm.

4. Meanwhile, bring 4 quarts water to a boil in a large pot. Add the pasta and 1 tablespoon salt and cook, stirring often, until al dente. Reserve ½ cup of the cooking water, then drain the pasta and return it to the pot.

5. Return the vegetables and chicken, along with any accumulated juice, to the skillet with the remaining 1 tablespoon butter and ½ cup of the Parmesan. Bring to a simmer and cook until the chicken is cooked through, about 1 minute.

6. Add the chicken mixture and basil to the pasta and toss to combine, adjusting the sauce consistency with the reserved pasta cooking water as desired. Season with salt and pepper to taste and serve with extra Parmesan.

USE IT UP: BUTTERNUT SQUASH

Butternut Squash Puree
SERVES 2

Serve with roasted chicken or pork. The squash puree can be refrigerated in an airtight container for up to 4 days.

⅔ medium butternut squash, peeled, seeded, and
  cut into 1½-inch pieces (about 3 cups)
1 tablespoon half-and-half
1 tablespoon unsalted butter
1 teaspoon brown sugar
  Salt and pepper

1. Place the squash in a large microwave-safe bowl. Cover the bowl and microwave on high until the squash is tender and easily pierced with a dinner fork, 6 to 10 minutes, stirring halfway through.

2. Drain the squash, then transfer it to a food processor. Add the half-and-half, butter, sugar, and ½ teaspoon salt. Process until the squash is smooth, about 30 seconds, scraping down the sides of the bowl as needed. Season with salt and pepper to taste and serve.

VARIATIONS

Pasta with Chicken, Spinach, and Gorgonzola
Other pasta shapes can be substituted for the farfalle; however, their cup measurements may vary (see page 43).

3 tablespoons unsalted butter
1 (8-ounce) boneless, skinless chicken breast,
  trimmed and sliced thin
1 small onion, minced
3 garlic cloves, minced
1 teaspoon minced fresh thyme or ¼ teaspoon dried
1 teaspoon unbleached all-purpose flour
⅛ teaspoon red pepper flakes
1 cup low-sodium chicken broth
½ cup dry white wine
⅓ pound farfalle (about 2 cups; see note)
  Salt
6 ounces baby spinach (about 6 cups)
1 ounce Gorgonzola cheese, crumbled (about ¼ cup)
  Pepper
1 tablespoon sliced almonds, toasted (see page 210)

1. Melt 1 tablespoon of the butter in a 10-inch nonstick skillet over high heat until beginning to brown. Add the chicken in a single layer, break up any clumps, and cook without stirring until it begins to brown, about 1 minute. Stir the chicken and continue to cook until it is almost cooked through, about 2 minutes longer. Transfer the chicken to a bowl, cover, and set aside.

2. Melt 1 tablespoon more butter in the skillet over medium heat. Add the onion and cook until softened and lightly browned, 5 to 7 minutes. Stir in the garlic, thyme, flour, and pepper flakes, and cook until fragrant, about 30 seconds. Stir in the broth and wine, bring to a simmer, and cook until the sauce has thickened slightly and reduced to ⅔ cup, about 10 minutes. Set aside and cover to keep warm.

3. Meanwhile, bring 4 quarts water to a boil in a large pot. Add the pasta and 1 tablespoon salt and cook, stirring often, until al dente. Reserve ½ cup of the cooking water, then drain the pasta and return it to the pot. Stir the spinach into the pasta until wilted.

4. Return the chicken, along with any accumulated juice, to the skillet with the remaining 1 tablespoon butter. Bring to a simmer and cook until the chicken is cooked through, about 1 minute.

5. Add the chicken mixture and Gorgonzola to the pasta and spinach and toss to combine, adjusting the sauce consistency with the reserved pasta cooking water as desired. Season with salt and pepper to taste, sprinkle individual portions with the almonds, and serve.

Pasta with Chicken, Broccoli Rabe, and Bell Pepper

Other pasta shapes can be substituted for the ziti; however, their cup measurements may vary (see page 43). Parmesan cheese can be substituted for the Pecorino Romano. See page 56 for a recipe to use up the leftover broccoli rabe.

½   **bunch broccoli rabe (about ½ pound), tough ends trimmed, cut into 1½-inch lengths**
    Salt
4   **tablespoons (½ stick) unsalted butter**
1   **(8-ounce) boneless, skinless chicken breast, trimmed and sliced thin**
1   **red bell pepper, stemmed, seeded, and sliced into ¼-inch strips**

1   **small onion, minced**
3   **garlic cloves, minced**
1   **teaspoon minced fresh thyme or ¼ teaspoon dried**
1   **teaspoon unbleached all-purpose flour**
⅛   **teaspoon red pepper flakes**
1   **cup low-sodium chicken broth**
½   **cup dry white wine**
⅓   **pound ziti (about 1⅔ cups; see note)**
1   **ounce Pecorino Romano cheese, grated (about ½ cup), plus extra for serving (see note)**
    Pepper
1   **tablespoon pine nuts, toasted (see page 210)**

1. Bring 4 quarts water to a boil in a large pot. Add the broccoli rabe and 1 tablespoon salt and cook, stirring often, until the broccoli rabe turns bright green, about 2 minutes. Using a slotted spoon, transfer the broccoli rabe to a paper towel–lined plate and set aside.

2. Melt 1 tablespoon of the butter in a 10-inch nonstick skillet over high heat until beginning to brown. Add the chicken in a single layer, break up any clumps, and cook without stirring until it begins to brown, about 1 minute. Stir the chicken and continue to cook until it is almost cooked through, about 2 minutes longer. Transfer the chicken to a bowl, cover, and set aside.

3. Melt 1 tablespoon more butter in the skillet over medium heat. Add the broccoli rabe and bell pepper and cook until the vegetables are tender and beginning to brown, about 4 minutes. Transfer the vegetables to the bowl with the chicken.

4. Melt 1 tablespoon more butter in the skillet over medium heat. Add the onion and cook until softened and lightly browned, 5 to 7 minutes. Stir in the garlic, thyme, flour, and pepper flakes, and cook until fragrant, about 30 seconds. Stir in the broth and wine, bring to a simmer, and cook until the sauce has thickened slightly and reduced to ⅔ cup, about 10 minutes. Set aside and cover to keep warm.

5. Meanwhile, return the water to a boil, add the pasta, and cook, stirring often, until al dente. Reserve ½ cup of the cooking water, then drain the pasta and return it to the pot.

6. Return the vegetables and chicken, along with any accumulated juice, to the skillet with the remaining 1 tablespoon butter and ½ cup of the Pecorino Romano.

Bring to a simmer and cook until the chicken is cooked through, about 1 minute.

7. Add the chicken mixture to the pasta and toss to combine, adjusting the sauce consistency with the reserved pasta cooking water as desired. Season with salt and pepper to taste. Sprinkle individual portions with the pine nuts and serve with extra Pecorino Romano.

USE IT UP: BROCCOLI RABE

Italian Sweet-and-Sour Broccoli Rabe
SERVES 2

Sweet golden raisins balance the somewhat bitter broccoli rabe. If using dark raisins, increase the amount of brown sugar by 1 teaspoon.

½   **bunch broccoli rabe (about ½ pound), tough ends trimmed, cut into 1½-inch lengths**
    Salt
1   **tablespoon olive oil**
1   **small onion, minced**
1   **garlic clove, minced**
3   **tablespoons red wine vinegar**
2   **tablespoons golden raisins (see note)**
1   **tablespoon fresh orange juice**
1   **tablespoon brown sugar**
    Pepper

1. Bring 3 quarts water to a boil in a large saucepan. Add the broccoli rabe and 1 tablespoon salt and cook, stirring often, until the broccoli rabe turns bright green, about 2 minutes. Drain, transfer the broccoli rabe to a paper towel–lined plate, and set aside. Dry the pan with a wad of paper towels.

2. Heat the oil in the pan over medium heat until shimmering. Add the onion and cook until softened, 3 to 5 minutes. Stir in the garlic and cook until fragrant, about 30 seconds. Add the vinegar, raisins, orange juice, and sugar, and cook until syrupy, 3 to 5 minutes. Add the broccoli rabe to the pan and cook, stirring occasionally, until well coated and fully tender, about 2 minutes. Season with salt and pepper to taste and serve.

SKILLET PASTA PRIMAVERA

DESPITE THE ITALIAN NAME, PASTA PRIMAVERA originated in the United States, not Italy. This fresh-flavored pasta dish, full of crisp vegetables, was created in the 1970s by the owner of Le Cirque, New York's famed French restaurant. It was dubbed spaghetti primavera—*primavera* is Italian for "spring"—and became a sensation in a New York minute.

This dish is a sure winner, but if you're making dinner for two, it's simply not practical. For one thing, it calls for blanching the green vegetables separately so that they retain their individual character. Then, once the vegetables are blanched, you need five more pots: one to cook the vegetables in garlicky olive oil, one to sauté mushrooms, one to make a fresh tomato sauce flavored with basil, one to make a cream sauce with butter and Parmesan, and one to cook the pasta. While these steps aren't difficult, the timing is complicated—and if you're going to go to all that trouble, you might as well make enough to serve a crowd. But we love pasta primavera, so we wanted to see if we could simplify the process enough that it made sense to make it for just two people—in just one skillet.

When cooking for two, it doesn't make sense to buy 10 different vegetables only to use a portion of each in a recipe, so our first issue was to decide which vegetables were essential. Many of the ingredients in the original dish, such as broccoli and green beans, are not actually spring vegetables, so we eliminated them. Other vegetables, like artichokes, overpowered the other flavors in the dish. Asparagus, on the other hand, was a hit, so we included it along with peas (we liked the convenience and quality of frozen peas), zucchini, and mushrooms.

The next step was cooking and incorporating the vegetables into the dish. Knowing we didn't want to spend extra time blanching each vegetable individually, we searched for a different method. Sautéing the vegetables individually in the skillet worked, but tasters felt that the expected fresh and crisp qualities were now missing. We then tried pan-steaming the green vegetables briefly in a splash of water and a pat of butter until they were crisp, tender, and bright green. Now we were on the right track—this dish was clean and fresh-tasting. The mushrooms, however, would still need to be browned to cook off their moisture and bring out their flavor. As for the fresh tomato sauce, we took a hint from other streamlined primavera recipes and skipped this ingredient. Instead, we focused on the cream sauce.

To build flavor in the sauce, garlic and butter proved essential. Tasters preferred the sweet, rich flavor of the butter to the flavor of olive oil. We then added a combination of vegetable broth and water (4 cups total) and our pasta (⅓ pound) to the skillet.

For the pasta, we chose trumpet-shaped campanelle, which stands up well to the vegetables. As we've done in other skillet pasta dishes in the past, we cooked the pasta right in the sauce where it absorbs most of the liquid as it simmers, and the remainder of the liquid reduces to a nice saucy consistency. We added the reserved vegetables and ¼ cup of cream and let the cream reduce for just a minute before stirring in a generous amount of Parmesan cheese and a couple of tablespoons of fresh basil. The sauce was silky and creamy, but some tasters found it a tad too rich. A bit of fresh lemon juice cut through the richness and gave the dish some needed brightness.

Our recipe was just as delicious as the more laborious original, and we had just one pan to clean, not six. We had also reduced total preparation and cooking time by more than half. Our Skillet Pasta Primavera is a perfect weeknight meal for two when you are craving fresh vegetables and pasta.

Skillet Pasta Primavera

SERVES 2

Low-sodium chicken broth can be used instead of the vegetable broth. Other pasta shapes can be substituted for the campanelle; however, their cup measurements may vary (see page 43). See page 229 for a recipe to use up the leftover heavy cream.

- 3 tablespoons unsalted butter
- ¼ bunch asparagus (about 4 ounces), tough ends trimmed, cut on the bias into 1-inch lengths
- 1 small zucchini (about 6 ounces), ends trimmed, quartered lengthwise and cut into ½-inch chunks
- 2¼ cups water
    Salt
- 3 ounces white mushrooms, quartered
    Pepper
- 2 garlic cloves, minced

- 2 cups low-sodium vegetable broth (see note)
- ⅓ pound campanelle (about 2 cups; see note)
- ¼ cup heavy cream
- ½ cup frozen peas
- ¼ cup grated Parmesan cheese, plus extra for serving
- 2 tablespoons shredded fresh basil (see photo)
- 1½ teaspoons fresh lemon juice

1. Melt 1 tablespoon of the butter in a 12-inch nonstick skillet over medium heat. Add the asparagus, zucchini, ¼ cup of the water, and a pinch of salt. Cover and cook until the vegetables are crisp-tender, 3 to 4 minutes. Uncover and continue to cook until the vegetables are just tender and the liquid has nearly evaporated, 1 to 2 minutes longer. Transfer the vegetables to a bowl, cover to keep warm, and set aside.

2. Melt 1 tablespoon more butter in the skillet over medium heat. Add the mushrooms and a pinch of salt and cook until they have released their moisture and are golden brown, about 5 minutes. Transfer the mushrooms to the bowl with the asparagus and zucchini, season with salt and pepper to taste, and cover to keep warm.

3. Wipe out the skillet with a wad of paper towels. Melt the remaining 1 tablespoon butter in the skillet over medium heat. Stir in the garlic and cook until fragrant, about 30 seconds. Stir in the remaining 2 cups water, broth, and ¼ teaspoon salt, then add the pasta. Increase the heat to high and cook at a vigorous simmer, stirring often, until the pasta is tender and the liquid has thickened, 15 to 18 minutes.

4. Stir in the cooked vegetables, cream, and peas, and cook until the cream has thickened and the vegetables are warmed through, about 1 minute. Off the heat, stir in ¼ cup of the Parmesan, basil, and lemon juice, and season with salt and pepper to taste. Serve with extra Parmesan.

PASTA ALLA NORMA

PASTA ALLA NORMA IS A LIVELY COMBINATION OF tender eggplant and robust tomato sauce, seasoned with herbs, mixed with al dente pasta, and finished with shreds of salty, milky ricotta salata (salted and pressed ricotta cheese). But often this classic faces pitfalls. The eggplant is a big production to prepare, usually requiring salting before frying, and it often ends up soggy and slick with oil. The tomatoes tend to coagulate into a heavy, overwhelming sauce, or there are so few tomatoes that they don't form an adequate foundation. The flavors in the dish can also easily drown out the subtle essence of the eggplant. Determined to do better, we went into the kitchen to develop a bold, complex pasta, one with rich tomato and eggplant flavors and smooth texture. While we were at it, we hoped to streamline the amount of work involved and make pasta alla Norma an ideal dish for two.

Most pasta alla Norma recipes advise salting cubed eggplant to draw out its excess moisture, sometimes for up to two hours. Since we were keen to streamline at every opportunity, this was the place to start. After a side-by-side tasting of versions that were salted from 15 minutes to two hours, we concluded that salting for an hour was best; it drew out the most moisture, which helped the eggplant brown better and cook faster.

Next, we considered how to cook the eggplant. We first tried frying it, but it soaked up about half its weight in oil and made for a heavy, greasy sauce. We briefly considered roasting the eggplant, but this method seemed slow for a weeknight meal. The remaining option was sautéing in a lesser amount of oil. Unfortunately, when we tried this approach, the eggplant was almost always underdone.

Looking for new ideas, we recalled an ingenious method for removing moisture from eggplant that was developed in the test kitchen for another recipe. Instead of salting the eggplant and then leaving it to drain on paper towels on the counter, we zapped the salted cubes in the microwave for 10 minutes. The salt draws out moisture that microwaving turns into steam, all the while causing the eggplant to collapse and compressing its air pockets. The collapsed air pockets, in turn, meant that the eggplant soaked up less oil in

the pan. Put into practice for pasta alla Norma, this method was a resounding success. This time sautéing worked perfectly, browning the eggplant and adding rich flavor.

The base for pasta alla Norma is a simple tomato sauce to which the eggplant is added. Canned diced tomatoes yielded a bright-tasting sauce with a coarse texture, and one 14.5-ounce can was just the right amount, but since the eggplant was already cut into cubes, the sauce was too chunky. Tasters preferred a smoother sauce, so we processed the canned diced tomatoes in the food processor.

To season the sauce, we kept things simple: Two garlic cloves added depth, a small measure of red pepper flakes lent a suggestion of heat, a generous dose of chopped basil brought fresh flavor, and 2 teaspoons of extra-virgin olive oil stirred in at the end with the basil gave the sauce rich, round, fruity notes. The sauce tasted fine tossed with the pasta, especially when sprinkled with ricotta salata cheese, yet something was missing. It seemed to lack backbone. We were considering breaking with tradition and adding pancetta or prosciutto when

---

NOTES FROM THE TEST KITCHEN

THE BEST FOOD PROCESSOR

What should a food processor be able to do? For starters, it ought to chop, grate, and slice vegetables; grind dry ingredients; and cut fat into flour for pie pastry. If it can't whiz through these tasks, it's wasting precious counter space. Recently, we tested inexpensive food processors to find out which one performed best. Unfortunately, many brands failed basic tests: vegetables were torn into mangled slices, soup leaked from the workbowl, and attempts to make pizza dough resulted in seriously strained motors and an acrid, smoky smell. We realized it would be necessary to open our wallet and check out the more expensive options.

After we put the high-priced machines through a battery of tests, it was obvious that more money does indeed buy a better food processor—though you don't need to buy the most expensive one. Our top pick is the **KitchenAid 12-cup Food Processor**, $199.95. It has a sturdy, sharp blade and a weighty motor that did not slow under a heavy load of dough. It performs almost every task as well as (or better than) its pricier competition.

PASTA ALLA NORMA

one taster offered a novel suggestion: anchovies. Cooked in oil with garlic and red pepper flakes, one minced fillet was perfect, giving the sauce a deep, savory flavor without any trace of fishiness.

So far, we had well-browned eggplant and a flavorful tomato sauce. To bring these elements together, we set the browned eggplant aside, made the sauce in the same skillet, and then added the eggplant to the sauce and simmered the two together only long enough to heat through, no more than five minutes. Now all the components—the pasta, the tomato sauce, and the eggplant—were perfectly in tune. Our pasta alla Norma was on the table in well under an hour with bold and balanced flavors.

Pasta alla Norma

SERVES 2

We call for both regular and extra-virgin olive oil in this recipe. The higher smoke point of regular olive oil makes it best for browning the eggplant; extra-virgin olive oil stirred into the sauce before serving lends fruity flavor. Do not peel the eggplant as the skin helps the eggplant hold together during cooking. Other pasta shapes can be substituted for the rigatoni; however, their cup measurements may vary (see page 43). Ricotta salata is traditional, but French feta, Pecorino Romano, and *cotija* (a firm, crumbly Mexican cheese) are acceptable substitutes.

- 1 (14.5-ounce) can diced tomatoes
- 1 globe eggplant (about 1 pound), cut into ¾-inch pieces
  Salt
- 2 tablespoons olive oil
- 2 garlic cloves, minced
- 1 anchovy fillet, rinsed, patted dry, and minced
- ⅛ teaspoon red pepper flakes
- 1 cup water
- ½ pound rigatoni (about 3 cups; see note)
- 3 tablespoons chopped fresh basil
- 2 teaspoons extra-virgin olive oil
  Pepper
- 1½ ounces ricotta salata cheese (see note), shredded (about ⅓ cup)

1. Process the tomatoes with their juice in a food processor until smooth, about 10 seconds. Set aside.

2. Line a large microwave-safe plate with a double layer of coffee filters and lightly coat with vegetable oil spray. Toss the eggplant with ¼ teaspoon salt in a medium bowl. Spread the eggplant in a single layer over the coffee filters. Wipe out and reserve the bowl. Microwave the eggplant on high, uncovered, until dry to the touch and slightly shriveled, 8 to 10 minutes, tossing halfway through. Let the eggplant cool slightly.

3. Return the eggplant to the bowl, drizzle with 1 teaspoon of the olive oil, and toss gently to coat; discard the coffee filters and reserve the plate. Heat 1 tablespoon more olive oil in a 12-inch nonstick skillet over medium-high heat until shimmering. Add the eggplant in a single layer and cook, stirring occasionally, until well browned and fully tender, about 8 minutes. Return the eggplant to the plate and set aside.

4. Let the skillet cool slightly, about 1 minute. Add the remaining 2 teaspoons olive oil, garlic, anchovy, and pepper flakes to the skillet, and cook over medium heat until fragrant, about 30 seconds. Stir in the processed tomatoes and water and simmer until thickened slightly, about 8 minutes.

5. Meanwhile, bring 4 quarts water to a boil in a large pot. Add the pasta and 1 tablespoon salt and cook, stirring often, until al dente. Reserve ½ cup of the cooking water, then drain the pasta and return it to the pot.

6. Return the eggplant to the skillet with the tomatoes and continue to simmer, gently stirring to combine, until the eggplant is heated through, 3 to 5 minutes. Stir the basil and extra-virgin olive oil into the sauce and season with salt and pepper to taste. Add the sauce to the pasta and toss to combine, adjusting the sauce consistency with the reserved pasta cooking water as desired. Serve, sprinkling individual portions with the ricotta salata.

VARIATION

Pasta with Eggplant, Olives, and Capers

Follow the recipe for Pasta alla Norma, substituting 1 tablespoon minced fresh parsley for the basil and adding ¼ cup thinly sliced pitted kalamata olives and 1 tablespoon drained and rinsed capers to the sauce with the parsley and extra-virgin olive oil in step 6.

SKILLET SHRIMP SCAMPI

SHRIMP IS A GREAT OPTION WHEN YOU'RE COOKING for two. You can buy just what you need from your local fish market, or you can keep a bag of frozen shrimp in your freezer for a last-minute dinner. We wanted to create a skillet version of the Italian-American classic shrimp scampi—for two. Off the bat, we realized our main concern was the star ingredient—too many scampi dishes are ruined by overcooked, rubbery shrimp.

Our established skillet pasta method, which relies on building a sauce and cooking the pasta in the sauce (see Skillet Pasta Primavera on page 57), presented a serious issue for our scampi. A typical scampi-style sauce is based on just olive oil and garlic; the sauce would need more liquid to allow the pasta to cook through, but we hoped to find something that wouldn't mute the other flavors. We had to devise a way to combine all of these elements and still retain the individual bright flavors, while also making sure the shrimp stayed plump and tender.

To prevent the shrimp from becoming tough, we knew they would have to be cooked quickly and at high heat. We sautéed them in a single layer, without moving them, just long enough for the shrimp to become spotty brown on one side. We also amplified the flavor—and enhanced the browning—by tossing the shrimp with a little sugar prior to cooking. The shrimp were then stirred and cooked for an additional 30 seconds until almost, but not quite, done. We put them aside while we built the sauce, planning to finish them up in the skillet, where they could absorb the flavor of a garlicky sauce.

For the sauce, we began our tests with clam juice and water, thinking that the clam juice would naturally enhance the shellfish flavor. Much to our surprise, the clam juice made a sauce that was so strongly flavored it masked the subtle complexity of the shrimp. Chicken broth turned out to be a much better choice, in spite of our initial reservations (it seemed a bit unusual to use chicken broth in a seafood dish).

We were now ready to incorporate the garlic and lemon flavors so essential to scampi. The garlic was too bitter if simply sautéed in olive oil, so we returned to a technique that we had used in our recipe for Spaghetti with Garlic and Olive Oil (page 42)—sautéing the garlic over very low heat until pale golden and sticky to develop a nutty flavor. For further flavor, we added spicy red pepper flakes and deglazed the pan with white wine. We were closing in on finalizing our sauce, but it still lacked the garlicky punch our tasters craved, so again we turned to our recipe for Spaghetti with Garlic and Olive Oil. We made a paste with salt and one clove of raw garlic, which we combined with 1 tablespoon of extra-virgin olive oil. Added to our skillet after the pasta was done, this fresh burst of garlic did the trick.

The last element to be determined was the pasta shape. We began our testing with linguine, the pasta that we tend to find in scampi dishes. After making many batches of scampi, each using a different amount of liquid, we were still unhappy with the consistency of the sauce—it just felt too slick for the long strands of pasta and ended up being either too heavy or too loose. Campanelle, a short, trumpet-shaped pasta, worked better; the smaller pasta offered many nooks and crannies to trap the sauce and afforded the dish a better balance overall. We were now able to return the sautéed shrimp to the skillet to finish. With a little fresh lemon juice, lemon zest, and minced parsley added at the very end, this shrimp scampi boasted bright, garlicky flavor and tender shrimp.

NOTES FROM THE TEST KITCHEN

FRESH OR FROZEN SHRIMP?

We're often asked whether it's better to cook with fresh or frozen shrimp. It's somewhat of a trick question—almost all shrimp are frozen after being harvested, so the "fresh" shrimp you see at the market have very likely been frozen and then thawed by your fishmonger. Since there's no way to know for certain when these "fresh" shrimp were defrosted, quality varies dramatically. In the test kitchen, we find that buying frozen shrimp and defrosting them at home yields superior results. And when cooking for two, it's convenient to keep a bag of frozen shrimp on hand, so you can take just what you need for a quick dinner. To defrost shrimp, place them in a colander under cold running water; they will be thawed and ready to cook in a few minutes (always thoroughly dry them first). Make sure to buy frozen shrimp with their shells on; shelled shrimp don't survive the freezing and thawing process very well and will surely be mushy (and the shrimp shells can be used to make a quick and flavorful shrimp stock).

Skillet Shrimp Scampi with Campanelle

SERVES 2

Other pasta shapes can be substituted for the campanelle; however, their cup measurements may vary (see page 43). If using smaller shrimp, the cooking times may vary.

      3 tablespoons extra-virgin olive oil
      1 garlic clove, minced to a paste (see page 43),
         plus 5 garlic cloves, minced
      8 ounces extra-large shrimp (21 to 25 per pound),
         peeled and deveined (see page 31)
         Salt and pepper
      ⅛ teaspoon sugar
      ⅛ teaspoon red pepper flakes
      ¼ cup dry white wine
      3 cups water
      1 cup low-sodium chicken broth
      ⅓ pound campanelle (about 2 cups; see note)
      2 tablespoons minced fresh parsley
     1½ tablespoons fresh lemon juice
         plus ¼ teaspoon grated lemon zest

1. Combine 1 tablespoon of the oil and garlic paste in a small bowl and set aside. In a medium bowl, toss the shrimp with ⅛ teaspoon salt, ⅛ teaspoon pepper, and sugar.

2. Heat 2 teaspoons more oil in a 12-inch nonstick skillet over high heat until just smoking. Add the shrimp in a single layer and cook, without stirring, until beginning to brown, about 1 minute. Stir the shrimp and continue to cook until spotty brown and just pink around the edges, about 30 seconds longer. Transfer the shrimp to a bowl, cover, and set aside.

3. Let the skillet cool slightly, about 1 minute. Add the remaining 4 teaspoons oil, minced garlic, and pepper flakes, and cook over low heat, stirring often, until the garlic is sticky and pale golden, about 4 minutes. Stir in the wine, increase the heat to medium-high, and simmer until nearly evaporated, about 1 minute.

4. Stir in the water, broth, and ¼ teaspoon salt, then add the pasta. Increase the heat to high and cook at a vigorous simmer, stirring often, until the pasta is tender and the liquid has thickened, 15 to 18 minutes.

5. Return the shrimp, along with any accumulated juice, to the skillet and cook until warmed through, about 30 seconds. Off the heat, stir in the garlic paste mixture, parsley, lemon juice, and lemon zest. Season with salt and pepper to taste and serve.

SKILLET PASTA PUTTANESCA

THOUGH ITS FLAVOR PROFILE IS BRIGHT AND FRESH, traditional Italian puttanesca sauce relies on ingredients that require minimal preparation such as anchovies, capers, and olives, making it an ideal last-minute, full-flavored supper. Unfortunately, many home cooks buy this lusty sauce premade, which can be disappointing. Even restaurant versions sometimes fall short, overpowered by one flavor, whether it's too fishy, too garlicky, too briny, or just plain too salty. On the opposite end of the spectrum, it can also be incredibly dull and monochromatic. We were searching for a satisfying sauce with aggressive but well-balanced flavors, and it had to fit the bill as a handy one-pot skillet supper for two.

Because puttanesca features intense flavors, we wanted a simple sauce with minimal ingredients as a base. Using a test kitchen recipe for skillet tomato sauce as our starting point, we briefly processed a can of diced tomatoes in a food processor until nearly smooth before cooking them with olive oil in a large skillet. After simmering for a mere 10 minutes (any longer, and the flavor was dulled), we continued with our skillet pasta-cooking method, adding 2 cups of water and ½ pound of pasta (tasters liked thin spaghetti) to the skillet. We covered the pan to minimize evaporation and keep the dish saucy, then cooked the pasta until it was tender.

For our first test we simply added the pungent ingredients that make up puttanesca—minced garlic, minced olives, whole capers, chopped anchovies, and red pepper flakes—to the skillet with the tomatoes and simmered. The result was a dull sauce with underdeveloped flavors. Clearly, we needed to rethink our method.

A technique we often use to develop a deeper flavor is to sauté the ingredients in oil, or bloom them, so that their flavors permeate the oil. We decided to see if this method would improve our dish. First up were the anchovies. Not wanting bits of anchovy creating an uneven, fishy taste, we finely minced them and sautéed them together with oil, garlic, and red pepper flakes. In just minutes, the anchovies melted into the oil, and we had a full, rich flavor base to build on. Anchovies can be intimidating, but here the flavor serves to bring together all the other assertive ingredients in the sauce. Though it may seem like a lot for a dish that serves only two people, we found that six anchovy fillets were ideal and did not create a fishy sauce.

The next question we faced was how hot the sauce should be. We started testing with a full teaspoon of red pepper flakes. Our tasters were unanimous—the finished dish had way too much heat. After tasting batches of pasta made with reduced quantities of red pepper flakes, tasters were split down the middle between ¼ teaspoon and ½ teaspoon. Leaving the recipe with a range of amounts kept everyone happy.

Finally, we had to incorporate the olives. We determined that it was best to coarsely chop them and toss them into the sauce at the very last minute, allowing the residual heat of the tomatoes to warm them. This preserved their flavor and texture and prevented them from disappearing into the sauce. The capers, rinsed thoroughly to keep the saltiness of the dish in check, were added along with the olives. Finished with fresh parsley, our one-skillet puttanesca was bright, boldly flavored, and perfectly balanced.

Skillet Pasta Puttanesca

SERVES 2

Use the smaller amount of pepper flakes if you want a milder dish. See page 43 for tips on how to measure out long strands of pasta without using a scale. Be sure to simmer the tomatoes gently in step 2 or the sauce will become too thick.

1	(28-ounce) can diced tomatoes
2	tablespoons extra-virgin olive oil
6	anchovy fillets, rinsed, patted dry, and minced
4	garlic cloves, minced
¼–½	teaspoon red pepper flakes (see note)
	Salt
2	cups water
½	pound thin spaghetti or spaghettini (see note), broken in half
⅓	cup pitted kalamata olives, chopped coarse
⅓	cup minced fresh parsley
2	tablespoons capers, rinsed and drained
	Pepper
	Grated Parmesan cheese, for serving

1. Process the tomatoes with their juice in a food processor until smooth, about 15 seconds. Set aside.

2. Cook 4 teaspoons of the oil, anchovies, garlic, and pepper flakes in a 12-inch nonstick skillet over medium-low heat, stirring constantly, until the garlic is fragrant

but not browned, 1 to 2 minutes. Stir in the processed tomatoes and ½ teaspoon salt and simmer until thickened slightly, about 10 minutes.

3. Stir in the water, then add the pasta. Cover, increase the heat to medium-high, and cook, stirring often and adjusting the heat to maintain a vigorous simmer, until the pasta is tender, 12 to 15 minutes.

4. Stir in the remaining 2 teaspoons oil, olives, parsley, and capers, and season with salt and pepper to taste. Serve with the Parmesan.

SKILLET PASTA QUATTRO FORMAGGI

MACARONI AND CHEESE IS GREAT FOR DINNER WITH the kids, but sometimes we crave a more sophisticated cheesy pasta dish. Enter *pasta quattro formaggi*. This rich, refined blend of pasta and four cheeses is decidedly adult, perfect when you don't have to worry about pleasing a crowd of picky eaters or being kid-friendly. Although the dish is simple in concept, the preparation of pasta quattro formaggi is fussy, requiring multiple pots to cook the pasta, make a sauce, and bake the casserole. Our goal was to scale down and streamline this recipe, reinventing it as an easy skillet pasta without losing the flavor or silkiness of the sauce.

The first issue we encountered—in terms of both flavor and texture—was, naturally, the cheese. The recipes we found called for varying combinations and amounts of Italian cheeses. Recipes contained anywhere from 1 cup to 6½ cups of cheese for 1 pound of pasta and served from four to eight people. The selection of cheeses that turned up in our research was just as dizzying: Asiago, fontina, Taleggio, Pecorino Romano, mascarpone, mozzarella, Gorgonzola, Parmesan, and ricotta. Some initial testing reduced the scope quickly: Mascarpone and ricotta added neither flavor nor texture, and Asiago was bland. Pasta tossed with mozzarella was gooey and greasy, and Taleggio not only was difficult to obtain but also made the pasta too rich. Tasters favored a combination of Italian fontina, Gorgonzola, Pecorino Romano, and Parmesan. We found that 2½ ounces of cheese in total (about ¾ cup) was the right amount for ⅓ pound of pasta, an appropriate portion for two people.

With our winning cheese combination selected, we turned our attention to incorporating it into the dish.

NOTES FROM THE TEST KITCHEN

WHAT IS REAL PARMESAN?

The buttery, nutty, slightly fruity taste and crystalline crunch of genuine Parmigiano-Reggiano cheese is a one-of-a-kind experience. Produced using traditional methods for the past 800 years in one government-designated area of northern Italy, this hard cow's-milk cheese has a distinctive flavor that comes from the highly codified production process. Made with leftover whey from the previous day's cheese-making process and raw milk from cows that graze outdoors, the cheese is aged a minimum of 12 and usually 24 months to allow its flavor to develop fully. The process is laborious and time-consuming, which explains the high price tag for this cheese. There are also plenty of places to cut corners, which is one reason why domestic Parmesans are less expensive. In the United States, the federal standard for aging is a mere 10 months. Most cows are given a concentrated feed and are not pastured, and Parmesan is made with manufactured enzymes and pasteurized milk.

At the grocery store, authentic Parmigiano may not be labeled as such. Fortunately, you can shop with your eyes. To ensure that you're buying a properly aged cheese, examine the condition of the rind. It should be a few shades darker than the light interior and be about half an inch thick (younger or improperly aged cheeses will have a paler, thinner rind). Also, check for the pin-dot writing—it should spell out some portion of the words *Parmigiano-Reggiano*.

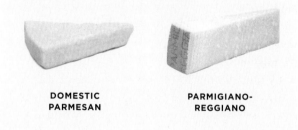

DOMESTIC PARMESAN   **PARMIGIANO-REGGIANO**

Using our skillet method of cooking the pasta right in the sauce, we knew this would be tricky. Heating the cheeses and cream together, then adding the pasta and water to the sauce to cook through, produced an ugly mess with curdled or separated cheese that had lost its flavor. The cheese would need to wait until the end.

Instead, we began by sautéing a shallot (preferred over onion for its delicate flavor) in butter until softened, then we added wine to deglaze the pan and cut through the richness of the sauce. Water, heavy cream, and penne were added to the skillet and simmered until the pasta was tender. After cooking our way through dozens of batches of pasta quattro formaggi with varying amounts of water and cream, we settled on 4 cups of water combined with ½ cup of cream. This provided just the right amount of sauce for the cheese to melt into after the pasta was finished cooking.

We had learned that to create the best flavor, the cheeses had to be added off the heat. A quick toss melted the cheeses without cooking them. This satisfying dish was simplified and packed with flavor.

Skillet Pasta Quattro Formaggi
SERVES 2

If you don't have both Parmesan and Pecorino, you can omit one and use ¼ cup of the other. Other pasta shapes can be substituted for the penne; however, their cup measurements may vary (see page 43). See page 229 for a recipe to use up the leftover heavy cream.

- 1 **tablespoon unsalted butter**
- 1 **shallot, minced**
  Salt
- ⅓ **cup dry white wine**
- 4 **cups water**
- ½ **cup heavy cream**
- ⅓ **pound penne (about 1⅔ cups; see note)**
- 1 **ounce Gorgonzola cheese, crumbled (about ¼ cup)**
- 1 **ounce Italian fontina cheese, shredded (about ¼ cup)**
- 2 **tablespoons grated Pecorino Romano cheese**
- 2 **tablespoons grated Parmesan cheese**
  Pepper

1. Melt the butter in a 12-inch nonstick skillet over medium heat. Add the shallot and ¼ teaspoon salt and cook until softened, 2 to 3 minutes. Stir in the wine, increase the heat to medium-high, and simmer until nearly evaporated, about 1 minute.

2. Stir in the water and cream, then add the pasta. Increase the heat to high and cook at a vigorous simmer, stirring often, until the pasta is tender and the liquid has thickened, 15 to 18 minutes.

3. Off the heat, stir in the Gorgonzola, fontina, Pecorino Romano, and Parmesan, one at a time, until melted and combined. Season with salt and pepper to taste and serve.

SKILLET PASTITSIO

EVERY GREEK COOKBOOK HAS A RECIPE FOR *PASTITSIO*, a hearty layered casserole consisting of ground meat, tomato sauce, pasta, a creamy béchamel, and a sprinkling of cheese. When well prepared, it is comfort food at its finest, but making pastitsio is a lot of work—the pasta, meat sauce, and béchamel are cooked in separate pots, then layered in a casserole and baked. If you are feeding a crowd, this effort may seem justified, but it's simply too time-consuming (and produces a week's worth of leftovers) when cooking for two. However, we don't think comfort food should be limited to large gatherings, so we set out to simplify and scale down this classic Greek dish into an easy skillet supper for two.

We began by selecting the meat. Some of the recipes we came across called for ground beef or veal, and more traditional recipes called for ground lamb. Not surprisingly, those made with beef didn't taste terribly authentic, and those made with veal lacked deep flavor. Lamb, on the other hand, contributed a rich, meaty flavor. We have learned over the years that ground lamb can be incredibly fat-laden, making a dish greasy. To remedy this potential problem, we cooked the ground lamb until it was just cooked through and then drained the excess fat before adding the other ingredients.

With the meat chosen and its cooking technique established, we turned to our aromatics. Onion and garlic were a given, but getting the spices set proved to be more of a puzzle. Several recipes called for a whole array of spices, including cumin, coriander, cardamom, cinnamon, nutmeg, and cloves, but tasters found this abundance overpowering. We aimed for a lighter touch, and the simple combination of a small amount of freshly grated nutmeg, a little cinnamon, and some fresh oregano did the trick.

Next, we had to decide which tomato product to use. Diced tomatoes were acceptable, but tasters did not care for the overly assertive chunks, which stood out in the sauce. We then tried crushed tomatoes, but again tasters were not happy—they wanted a deeper flavor, but less tomato presence. We turned to tomato paste, which provided the perfect backbone of flavor. It helped thicken the meat sauce slightly and rounded out the flavors.

It was time to add the pasta to the skillet, along with some chicken broth and heavy cream, to simmer until tender. In addition to ¼ cup heavy cream (for richness), we found that we needed 3 cups of liquid to cook ⅓ pound pasta. Three cups of chicken broth, however, made the final dish too salty and overwhelmed the lamb flavor. Replacing some of the broth with water (we settled on a 2-to-1 ratio) balanced the sauce and cut the saltiness.

As for pasta type, we tried spaghetti, because some recipes call for long-strand pasta. However, tasters complained that the long strands were difficult to eat in this dish. So we turned to more manageable pasta shapes and tested elbow macaroni, penne, and ziti. The penne and ziti bulked up the dish unnecessarily and produced a pasta-heavy casserole that didn't have the balance we wanted. The elbow macaroni gave tasters bites of all the elements of the dish with every forkful.

In lieu of preparing the béchamel sauce separately, we decided to simply finish the dish with a quick replication: more heavy cream thickened with cornstarch. The addition of ¾ cup of Pecorino Romano (a substitute for the traditional Greek cheese *kefalotyri,* which is hard to find and not worth hunting down for such a small amount) enriched the sauce while intensifying the flavor of the lamb. We stirred ¼ cup into the sauce, which was just enough to give it the richness we wanted; the remaining ½ cup we sprinkled on top for the finishing touch.

We then slid the skillet into a hot oven briefly to melt the cheese—and once it came out, no one could tell that this typically time-consuming Greek classic had taken us just minutes to prepare.

SKILLET PASTITSIO

Skillet Pastitsio

SERVES 2

Ground lamb is traditional in this dish, but you can substitute 90 percent lean ground beef if you prefer. If using ground beef, do not drain the meat in step 1. You can substitute ⅓ pound small shells (about 1⅔ cups) for the macaroni. Make sure to use a 12-inch ovensafe nonstick skillet for this recipe. See page 229 for a recipe to use up the leftover heavy cream.

8	ounces ground lamb (see note)
1	onion, minced
¼	teaspoon ground cinnamon
⅛	teaspoon freshly grated nutmeg
4	garlic cloves, minced
1½	tablespoons tomato paste
2	teaspoons minced fresh oregano or ½ teaspoon dried
2	cups low-sodium chicken broth
1	cup water
½	cup heavy cream
	Salt
⅓	pound elbow macaroni (about 1½ cups; see note)
1	teaspoon cornstarch
1½	ounces Pecorino Romano cheese, grated (about ¾ cup)
	Pepper

1. Adjust an oven rack to the middle position and heat the oven to 475 degrees. Cook the lamb in a 12-inch ovensafe nonstick skillet over medium heat, breaking apart the meat, until no longer pink and the fat has rendered, 3 to 5 minutes. Transfer the lamb to a strainer set over a medium bowl and let drain, reserving 1 tablespoon of the fat.

2. Heat the reserved fat in the skillet over medium heat until shimmering. Add the onion, cinnamon, and nutmeg, and cook until the onion is softened, about 5 minutes. Stir in the garlic, tomato paste, and oregano, and cook until fragrant, about 30 seconds.

3. Stir in the broth, water, ¼ cup of the cream, and ¼ teaspoon salt, then add the drained lamb and pasta. Increase the heat to high and cook at a vigorous simmer, stirring often, until the pasta is tender, 9 to 12 minutes.

4. Whisk the remaining ¼ cup cream and cornstarch together in a small bowl, then stir into the skillet

and continue to simmer until thickened slightly, about 1 minute. Off the heat, stir in ¼ cup of the Pecorino Romano; season with salt and pepper to taste. Sprinkle the remaining ½ cup Pecorino Romano over the top; bake until the cheese is melted, about 5 minutes. Serve.

GNOCCHI WITH MUSHROOMS AND CREAM SAUCE

ALTHOUGH NOTHING BEATS THE FLUFFY, CREAMY texture of handmade potato gnocchi, homemade pasta can be a time-consuming process and isn't something we want to attempt most nights of the week. The convenience of store-bought gnocchi is undeniable, especially when you are cooking for two people, but is this convenience product any good? We set out to answer this question and see how we could transform store-bought gnocchi into a satisfying weeknight pasta dish for two.

We started by taking a closer look at the three types of gnocchi sold in supermarkets: frozen, fresh in the refrigerated section, and dry in vacuum-sealed packages in the pasta aisle. We prepared several batches of each with a simple sauce to find out which one was best. The frozen gnocchi did not fare well. They were heavy, dense, flavorless balls; moreover, some of them developed a slimy coating. The fresh gnocchi from the refrigerator case weren't much better. They had a strange springy quality and never seemed to become properly tender. The vacuum-packed gnocchi, sold with the dried pasta, were the best of the bunch. These gnocchi were much lighter and didn't have an off-putting artificial flavor, although tasters complained that the texture was somewhat doughy. Our next step was to improve this gnocchi's texture.

We took a closer look at our cooking method. We had been following the package directions, boiling the gnocchi in salted water for a few minutes until they floated to the surface, draining them, and tossing them with a simple cream sauce. Clearly this approach wasn't working. What if we browned the gnocchi in a pan to get a crust on the exterior, then poached them in the sauce to finishing cooking? We wouldn't have to boil a pot of water, the browning step might eliminate any gumminess, and the sauce would flavor the gnocchi. At first our plan appeared to be successful: A few minutes of sautéing gave the gnocchi an attractive, golden crust. But by the time the gnocchi had cooked through in the sauce, the crust was soggy and blown out.

We backed up and took another look at the package directions. Maybe combining our rogue method with the conventional cooking method would work. We boiled the gnocchi in water until just tender, drained them, and then sautéed them in a little butter. Success! The gnocchi were tender in the middle but had a browned, pleasantly chewy exterior.

Having solved the gnocchi's textural problem and pinned down our cooking method, we concerned ourselves with the sauce. After tasting the gnocchi with tomato and butter sauces, we decided to stick with the cream-based sauce we had been using. Tasters liked the way the velvety sauce clung to the browned gnocchi but felt the dish needed another component. We chose mushrooms, which pair well with cream sauce. Tasters favored meaty creminis, which we sautéed in the skillet after removing the gnocchi. Covering the mushrooms until they had released their liquid sped up the cooking process.

When the mushrooms were browned, we continued building the sauce. For aromatics, we added shallot, thyme, and garlic, along with a teaspoon of flour for thickening. We stirred 1 cup of chicken broth and ¼ cup of cream into the skillet, and found that a touch of white wine helped to cut the richness of the sauce. After 10 minutes of simmering, which was ample time for our small amount of sauce to reduce and thicken, we folded in the browned gnocchi.

All that was left were a few final tweaks. In the test kitchen when we want to bump up the flavor of supermarket mushrooms, we often use dried porcini mushrooms. We tried it here and it worked well. Half a cup of frozen peas, stirred into the sauce with the browned gnocchi, added color and a fresh, vegetal flavor to the sauce. For a finishing touch, a sprinkling of minced fresh parsley was all that was needed.

Gnocchi with Mushrooms and Cream Sauce
SERVES 2

For optimal texture, be sure to brown the gnocchi shortly after draining them, while they are still warm. See page 229 for a recipe to use up the leftover heavy cream.

- ½ **pound vacuum-packed gnocchi (about 1½ cups)**
  Salt
- 2 **tablespoons unsalted butter**
- 6 **ounces cremini mushrooms, sliced thin**
- 1 **shallot, minced**
- ⅛ **ounce dried porcini mushrooms (about 2 tablespoons), rinsed and minced**
- 1 **garlic clove, minced**
- 1 **teaspoon unbleached all-purpose flour**
- ½ **teaspoon minced fresh thyme or ⅛ teaspoon dried**
- 1 **cup low-sodium chicken broth**
- ¼ **cup heavy cream**
- 2 **tablespoons dry white wine**
- ½ **cup frozen peas, thawed**
  Pepper
- 1 **tablespoon minced fresh parsley**

1. Bring 4 quarts water to a boil in a large pot. Add the gnocchi and 1 tablespoon salt and cook until the gnocchi float to the surface and are just tender, about 2 minutes. Drain the gnocchi.

2. Melt 1 tablespoon of the butter in a 10-inch nonstick skillet over medium-high heat. Add the gnocchi and cook, stirring occasionally, until golden brown, about 5 minutes. Transfer the gnocchi to a plate; set aside.

3. Melt the remaining 1 tablespoon butter in the skillet over medium heat. Add the cremini mushrooms, shallot, and porcini mushrooms, cover, and cook until the cremini mushrooms have released their liquid, about 4 minutes. Uncover and continue to cook, stirring often, until the cremini mushrooms are well browned, 5 to 7 minutes longer.

4. Stir in the garlic, flour, and thyme, and cook until fragrant, about 30 seconds. Stir in the broth, cream, and wine, and simmer until the sauce has thickened slightly and reduced to 1 cup, 8 to 10 minutes.

5. Fold in the browned gnocchi and peas and continue to cook until the gnocchi are well coated and the peas are heated through, about 1 minute. Season with salt and pepper to taste, sprinkle with the parsley, and serve.

SINGAPORE NOODLES WITH SHRIMP

WHILE NOT AS UBIQUITOUS ON CHINESE RESTAURANT menus as pork lo mein or beef with broccoli, stir-fried rice vermicelli noodles with curry (often called "Singapore noodles") is a dish with a devoted following. At its best, this is Asian comfort food: a big bowl of tender, moist noodles swathed in a savory sauce laced with fragrant curry. Bad versions of Singapore noodles we've had have been greasy tangles of rice noodles with so much curry we couldn't taste anything else. We set out to develop a flavorful, balanced version of this takeout dish, scaled down for two.

The curry powder and thin rice stick noodles (also called rice vermicelli) are the defining threads of the dish. The sauces we uncovered in our research varied, but they all had three major components: something salty, something sweet, and a base that provided moisture and flavor. Basing our recipe on 4 ounces of rice noodles (what we thought was a good portion for two people), we first selected a salty ingredient. Soy sauce was an obvious choice, and we started with ¼ cup. As for the sweet element, we agreed on a small amount of mirin (sweetened Japanese rice wine). Tasters thought it provided a desirable, subtle sweetness that didn't overpower the nuances of the dish as granulated sugar did. Half a cup of chicken broth worked best as a base for our sauce (better than coconut milk and water, as some recipes instructed) to flavor and moisten the noodles. Because the chicken broth contributed saltiness, we found it necessary to reduce the amount of soy sauce to 3 tablespoons.

With our basic sauce in order, we were ready to prepare the rice noodles for stir-frying. We found three different methods for softening them: boiling them, soaking them in room-temperature water, and soaking them in hot water. We began with boiling and quickly realized this was a bad move. Drained and waiting in the colander, the noodles glued themselves together, then wound up soggy and overdone in the finished dish. Noodles soaked in room-temperature water remained fairly stiff. After lengthy stir-frying, they became tender, but longer cooking made them drier and stickier. We finally tried soaking the noodles in water that had been brought to a boil and then removed from the heat. They softened, turning limp and pliant, but were not yet fully tender. Drained, they were loose and separate,

and they cooked through easily with stir-frying. The result? Noodles that were at once pleasantly tender and resilient.

Most recipes we found for Singapore noodles included a protein of some kind, frequently barbecued pork or shrimp. For simplicity we zeroed in on shrimp. By quickly searing ½ pound of shrimp and setting them aside before proceeding with the rest of the recipe, we found that we could cook everything in one skillet in minimal time. To boost flavor, we tossed the shrimp with curry powder, and to encourage browning, we added a scant amount of sugar as well.

Next we looked for other additions to round out our noodle dish. Sliced shallots added a mellow onion flavor, and red bell pepper contributed sweetness. We added the curry powder (a little more than 1 teaspoon was flavorful but not overwhelming for our scaled-down dish) to the pan with the vegetables, to ensure that it had direct contact with the heat of the skillet to deepen its flavor. After sautéing the vegetables, we returned the drained rice noodles and browned shrimp to the skillet, added our liquid ingredients, and tossed everything together for a few minutes over medium heat. This last

NOTES FROM THE TEST KITCHEN

RICE NOODLES
In Southeast Asia and southern regions of China, a delicate pasta made from rice flour and water is used in an array of dishes, including soups, stir-fries, and salads. Unlike other pasta, these delicate noodles should not be boiled because they have a tendency to overcook very quickly, resulting in a mushy, sticky mess. Instead, it is best to bring a pot of water to a boil, then remove the pot from the heat and steep the noodles gently in the hot water.

SRIRACHA HOT CHILI SAUCE
Sriracha is a Southeast Asian hot sauce from Thailand. It is named after the seaside town Si Racha, where it was first produced in small batches as a local product. It is made from sun-ripened chile peppers, vinegar, garlic, sugar, and salt and has a consistency like slightly thick ketchup. We use Sriracha hot chili sauce to bump up the flavor in stir-fries and sauces.

step allowed the noodles and shrimp to finish cooking through and also helped integrate the flavors of the dish and thicken the sauce.

So far our noodle dish was good, but tasters still wanted more flavor. The addition of ½ teaspoon Sriracha hot chili sauce contributed depth as well as heat. Finally, we stirred in some minced cilantro and crunchy, peppery bean sprouts for bright, fresh flavor and textural contrast. One bite and we knew we had achieved something far better than takeout—but just as fast.

Singapore Noodles with Shrimp

SERVES 2

If rice vermicelli is unavailable, substitute 4 ounces capellini; in step 1, cook the capellini in the boiling water until al dente. You can substitute 2 teaspoons white wine or sake mixed with ½ teaspoon sugar for the mirin. If using smaller shrimp, the cooking times may vary.

- 4 ounces dried rice vermicelli (see note)
- 8 ounces extra-large shrimp (21 to 25 per pound), peeled and deveined (see page 31)
- 1½ teaspoons curry powder
- ⅛ teaspoon sugar
- 4 teaspoons vegetable oil
- 3 shallots, sliced thin
- 1 red bell pepper, stemmed, seeded, and sliced into ¼-inch strips
- 1 garlic clove, minced
- ½ cup low-sodium chicken broth
- 3 tablespoons soy sauce
- 2 teaspoons mirin (see note)
- ½ teaspoon Sriracha hot chili sauce
- 1 cup bean sprouts (about 2 ounces)
- ¼ cup minced fresh cilantro

1. Bring 4 quarts water to a boil in a large pot. Remove the boiling water from the heat, add the rice noodles, and let sit, stirring occasionally, until the noodles are tender, about 10 minutes. Drain the noodles and set aside.

2. Meanwhile, toss the shrimp with ¼ teaspoon of the curry powder and sugar. Heat 2 teaspoons of the oil in a 12-inch nonstick skillet over medium-high heat until just smoking. Add the shrimp in a single layer and cook, without stirring, until beginning to brown, about

1 minute. Stir the shrimp and continue to cook until spotty brown and just pink around the edges, about 30 seconds longer. Transfer the shrimp to a bowl, cover, and set aside.

3. Heat the remaining 2 teaspoons oil in the skillet over medium heat until shimmering. Add the remaining 1¼ teaspoons curry powder, shallots, and bell pepper, and cook until the vegetables are softened, 3 to 5 minutes. Stir in the garlic and cook until fragrant, about 30 seconds.

4. Stir in the drained rice noodles and shrimp, along with any accumulated juice, broth, soy sauce, mirin, and Sriracha and cook, tossing constantly, until the noodles, shrimp, and vegetables are well coated and heated through, about 2 to 3 minutes. Stir in the bean sprouts and cilantro and serve.

SPICY BASIL NOODLES WITH CRISPY TOFU

WHEN WE GET TAKEOUT FROM A THAI RESTAURANT and want something that's not too rich but still bright and full of flavor, we order spicy basil noodles. Consisting of tender rice noodles, fragrant basil, and a spicy, aromatic sauce, this dish is satisfying without being heavy. Having developed a streamlined version of a favorite Chinese restaurant noodle dish, Singapore Noodles with Shrimp, we hoped to successfully re-create this Thai specialty at home. And since we were cooking for just two, we didn't want to track down exotic ingredients and hoped to stick to items we could get at the supermarket.

We selected the noodles first. Flat rice noodles come in several different widths, from extra-small to extra-large. For this dish, we liked the extra-wide flat noodles, as they seemed to be the closest supermarket approximation to the homemade rice noodles that Thai restaurants serve. (That being said, any size of flat rice noodles will work with this recipe; just use the widest ones you can find.)

As with our Singapore Noodles with Shrimp, we prepared the rice noodles for stir-frying by soaking them for 10 minutes in hot water and draining them. The parcooked noodles then took only a few minutes of stir-frying to become tender.

Most recipes for spicy basil noodles that we researched called for similar flavorings, including chiles, shallots, garlic, fish sauce, and lime juice. Thai chiles, the classic choice for this recipe, were our favorite, but more readily available serranos and jalapeños were also good. We found that four minced chiles contributed good chile flavor and moderate heat. We then added three minced shallots and four minced garlic cloves to the mix, and it started to feel as if we were doing a lot of chopping for two people. We decided to simplify the preparation by tossing the chiles, garlic, and shallots into the food processor.

In Thai cooking, the success of many dishes is contingent upon the proper balance of sweet, salty, sour, and spicy elements. The aromatic chile mixture had established the spiciness in our sauce; now we needed to incorporate the other components. After some experimentation we arrived at a working recipe consisting of 2½ tablespoons of fish sauce (salty), 1½ tablespoons of lime juice (sour), and 2 tablespoons of brown sugar (sweet). While the flavor of the sauce was good, there wasn't enough of it, and our noodles were dry. Increasing the amounts of these ingredients made the final dish too pungent. Instead, we supplemented our sauce with chicken broth, which provided much-needed moisture without upsetting the careful balance of flavors. Half a teaspoon of cornstarch thickened our sauce to just the right consistency.

Our recipe was close to completion, but it was feeling a bit skimpy for dinner, so we added tofu. We took half a block of tofu (the perfect amount for two), cut it into cubes, patted it dry, and coated it with cornstarch, a technique that we've found gives tofu a crispy crust with minimal effort. Next we looked for one or two quick-cooking vegetables to add to the mix, and tasters like the sweetness of bell pepper and the crunch of snap peas.

Following the test kitchen's method for stir-fries, we cooked the tofu and vegetables in separate batches and set them aside before continuing with our recipe. The processed chile mixture went into the skillet next. We cooked it just enough to allow excess moisture to evaporate, then we added the drained noodles and sauce to the skillet, along with the browned tofu and vegetables and a generous amount of fragrant Thai basil. After a few minutes the noodles were tender and well coated with sauce. One bite confirmed that our noodles tasted as good as they looked.

Spicy Basil Noodles with Crispy Tofu, Snap Peas, and Bell Pepper
SERVES 2

Flat rice noodles come in a variety of widths. While we like the wider, ⅜-inch noodle for this recipe, any flat rice noodles will work. To make this dish spicier, add the chile seeds. If you can't find Thai basil leaves, regular basil will work fine. See page 72 for a recipe to use up the leftover tofu.

SAUCE
- 4 fresh Thai, serrano, or jalapeño chiles, stemmed and seeded (see note)
- 4 garlic cloves, peeled
- 3 shallots, peeled
- ⅓ cup low-sodium chicken broth
- 2½ tablespoons fish sauce
- 2 tablespoons brown sugar
- 1½ tablespoons fresh lime juice
- ½ teaspoon cornstarch

NOODLES
- 6 ounces flat rice noodles (see note)
- ¼ cup cornstarch
- ½ (14-ounce) block firm or extra-firm tofu, patted dry and cut into 1-inch cubes
- 5 tablespoons vegetable oil
- 1 cup snap peas (about 3 ounces), ends trimmed and strings removed
- 1 red bell pepper, stemmed, seeded, and sliced into ¼-inch strips
- 1½ cups fresh basil, preferably Thai basil (see note)

1. FOR THE SAUCE: Pulse the chiles, garlic, and shallots in a food processor to a coarse paste, about 15 pulses, scraping down the sides of the bowl as needed; set aside. In a small bowl, whisk the broth, fish sauce, sugar, lime juice, and cornstarch together; set aside.

2. FOR THE NOODLES: Bring 4 quarts water to a boil in a large pot. Remove the boiling water from the heat, add the rice noodles, and let sit, stirring occasionally, until the noodles are tender, about 10 minutes. Drain the noodles and set aside.

3. Spread the cornstarch in a shallow dish, then dredge the tofu in the cornstarch and transfer to a plate. Heat 2 tablespoons of the oil in a 12-inch nonstick skillet over medium-high heat until just smoking. Add the tofu and cook, turning every few minutes, until all sides are crisp and browned, about 8 minutes. Transfer the tofu to a paper towel–lined plate and set aside. Wipe out the skillet with a wad of paper towels.

4. Heat 1 tablespoon more oil in the skillet over medium-high heat until just smoking. Add the snap peas and bell pepper and cook, stirring frequently, until the snap peas are crisp-tender and begin to brown, 2 to 4 minutes. Transfer the vegetables to a small bowl.

5. Heat the remaining 2 tablespoons oil in the skillet over medium heat until shimmering. Add the processed chile mixture and cook until the moisture evaporates and the color deepens, 3 to 5 minutes.

6. Whisk the broth mixture to recombine, then add it to the skillet. Stir in the drained rice noodles, cooked tofu and vegetables, and basil, and cook, tossing constantly, until the sauce has thickened and the noodles and vegetables are well coated and heated through, 2 to 3 minutes. Serve.

USE IT UP: TOFU

Marinated Tofu
SERVES 2

Serve this marinated tofu on its own, or over a salad, rice, or Asian noodles.

- 2 tablespoons soy sauce
- 1 tablespoon rice vinegar
- 1 teaspoon minced or grated fresh ginger
- 1 teaspoon sugar
- ½ teaspoon toasted sesame oil
- ¼ teaspoon red pepper flakes
- ½ (14-ounce) block firm or extra-firm tofu, patted dry and cut into 1-inch cubes
- 2 scallions, sliced thin on the bias
- 2 teaspoons sesame seeds (optional), toasted (see page 210)

1. Whisk the soy sauce, vinegar, ginger, sugar, sesame oil, and pepper flakes together in a medium bowl. Add the tofu and gently stir to combine. Let sit for 15 minutes, stirring halfway through.

2. Drain the tofu and discard the marinade. Sprinkle the tofu with the scallions and sesame seeds (if using) and serve.

SOBA NOODLES WITH PORK

JAPANESE SOBA NOODLES ARE MADE WITH BUCKWHEAT flour, which adds a hearty nuttiness and springy chew to the noodles. Soba are typically served hot in a simple broth along with vegetables or meat, or cold with a simple dipping sauce. Because of their unique rich flavor and chewy texture they need little adornment, so we thought these noodles could easily become a quick, substantial meal for two. After some consideration, we decided that the natural sweetness of pork would make a great foil to the earthy soba. It would be simple enough to prepare a pork stir-fry, which we'd then toss with the boiled noodles.

First we took a closer look at soba noodles. Although it is buckwheat flour that gives the noodles their unusual flavor, buckwheat flour contains no gluten, so a binder, usually wheat, is added to give the noodles structure and hold them together during cooking. Like other noodles, soba noodles require an ample amount of water for cooking; we achieved the best results by cooking the noodles in 4 quarts of salted water.

Starting with ⅓ pound of soba for two people, we determined that 8 ounces of pork would provide a good noodle-to-meat ratio. Pork tenderloin is our usual choice for stir-fries, but even a small tenderloin was much more meat than we needed. Because they can be purchased individually (or purchased in bulk and frozen individually), boneless pork chops were a better choice. We found that one boneless center-cut chop yielded just the right amount of meat for our recipe. The drawback of boneless pork chops is that the meat has a tendency to dry out during cooking. Cooking the pork until it's almost cooked through, removing it from the pan, setting it aside, and reintroducing it later to finish cooking through with the vegetables ensured tender, moist slices of pork.

Next we selected the vegetables for the stir-fry. Sticking with the Japanese theme, we selected full-flavored shiitake mushrooms. After sampling both sliced and quartered stir-fried mushrooms, tasters unanimously preferred the more substantial quartered pieces. For a second vegetable, we liked bok choy. We gathered three heads of baby bok choy, which gave us the perfect amount for two, and cut the stalks and leaves into thin pieces. We added the bok choy to the skillet with the mushrooms after browning the pork so the stalks could cook down and the leaves could wilt slightly.

For our sauce, we started with a base of 2 tablespoons each of soy sauce, hoisin, and mirin (sweetened Japanese rice wine). To balance the sweetness of the hoisin and mirin we added rice vinegar, a teaspoon at a time, until we settled on 4 teaspoons. Garlic and minced fresh ginger are typical in stir-fries; tasters liked them here.

We finished the dish with sliced scallions and bean sprouts for texture and crunch. Although we don't usually season soy-based dishes with salt and pepper, we found that sprinkling some salt and a generous portion of freshly ground pepper enhanced this dish tremendously.

Soba Noodles with Pork, Shiitake Mushrooms, and Bok Choy
SERVES 2

Freezing the pork for 15 minutes before slicing makes it easier to cut thin strips. If you can't find baby bok choy, you can use ½ large head bok choy (about 12 ounces) instead; add the bok choy stalks to the skillet with the mushrooms in step 2, then add the greens to the pan with the pork in step 3. You can substitute 2 tablespoons white wine or sake mixed with 1½ teaspoons sugar for the mirin. See page 43 for tips on how to measure out long strands of pasta without using a scale.

- 2 tablespoons vegetable oil
- 3 garlic cloves, minced
- 1½ teaspoons minced or grated fresh ginger
- 1 (8-ounce) boneless center-cut pork chop, about 1 inch thick, trimmed and sliced thin (see note; see photos)
- 5 ounces shiitake mushrooms, stemmed and quartered
- 3 (4-ounce) heads baby bok choy, greens and stalks sliced crosswise into ¼-inch-wide pieces (see note)
- 2 tablespoons soy sauce
- 2 tablespoons hoisin sauce
- 2 tablespoons mirin (see note)
- 4 teaspoons rice vinegar
- ⅓ pound soba noodles (see note)
  Salt
- 1½ cups bean sprouts (about 3 ounces)
- 4 scallions, sliced thin
  Pepper

1. Mix 1 teaspoon of the oil, garlic, and ginger together in a small bowl; set aside. Heat 2 teaspoons more oil in a 12-inch nonstick skillet over high heat until just smoking. Add the pork in a single layer, break up any clumps, and cook without stirring until it begins to brown, about 1 minute. Stir the pork and continue to cook until it is almost cooked through, about 2 minutes longer. Transfer the pork to a bowl, cover, and set aside.

2. Heat the remaining 1 tablespoon oil in the skillet over medium-high heat until shimmering. Add the mushrooms and bok choy and cook until the vegetables are browned, 5 to 7 minutes.

3. Clear the center of the skillet, add the garlic mixture, and cook, mashing the mixture into the pan, until fragrant, about 30 seconds. Stir the garlic mixture into the vegetables. Return the pork, with any accumulated juice, to the skillet along with the soy sauce, hoisin, mirin, and vinegar. Cook, tossing constantly, until the pork is cooked through, about 1 minute. Set aside and cover to keep warm.

4. Meanwhile, bring 4 quarts water to a boil in a large pot. Add the noodles and 1 tablespoon salt and cook, stirring often, until al dente, about 4 minutes. Reserve ½ cup of the cooking water, then drain the noodles and return them to the pot.

5. Add the pork-mushroom mixture, bean sprouts, scallions, and ¼ teaspoon pepper to the pasta, and toss to combine, adjusting the sauce consistency with the reserved pasta cooking water as desired. Season with salt and pepper to taste and serve.

NOTES FROM THE TEST KITCHEN

SLICING PORK FOR STIR-FRIES

1. Using a sharp chef's knife, slice the partially frozen pork chop crosswise into ¼-inch-thick slices.

2. Cut each slice into ¼-inch-wide strips.

CLASSIC BEEF CHILI

EVERYDAY MAIN DISHES

CLASSIC BEEF CHILI

GO TO ANY SUPER BOWL PARTY AND YOU'RE LIKELY to find a large pot of chili (the kind made with ground meat, beans, tomatoes, and chili powder) simmering on the stove. Although chili should come together easily, it should taste fairly complex. The flavors should be rich and balanced, the texture thick and lush. Unfortunately, many "basic" recipes yield a pot of underspiced, under-flavored chili reminiscent of Sloppy Joes. We had two goals for our chili recipe: We wanted to develop a no-fuss chili that tasted far better than the sum of its common parts, and we wanted a recipe that would serve two. Since most recipes for chili could feed a small army, we knew scaling this dish down would require a careful balancing act.

We began our chili with a base of sautéed onion and garlic. Tasters liked the addition of red bell pepper to this mix but rejected other options, including green bell pepper, celery, and carrots. The next issues to tackle were the spices (how much and what kind) and the meat (how much ground beef). There were also the cooking liquid (what kind, if any) and the proportions of tomatoes and beans to consider.

After experimenting with quantities of chili powder, we eventually settled on 1½ tablespoons. Though this seems like a modest amount for chili (even for just two servings), we found that if we used any more it simply overpowered the other layers of flavor in our chili. Cumin, coriander, red pepper flakes, and oregano rounded out our spices, but something was missing. Although we didn't want a chili with killer heat, we did want real warmth and depth of flavor, so we added just a touch of cayenne. Adding the spices early—along with the aromatics—helped develop their flavors fully.

It was now time to consider the meat. Eight ounces of beef was the right amount for two servings, and half of a 15-ounce can of beans provided a good meat-to-bean ratio. Tests using 90 percent, 85 percent, and 80 percent lean ground beef showed that fat content makes a big difference. Pools of orange oil floated to the top of the chili made with ground chuck (80 percent lean beef). At the other end of the spectrum, the chili made with 90 percent lean beef was a tad bland—not bad, but not as full-flavored as the chili made with 85 percent lean beef, which was our final choice.

As for the type of liquid to add to our chili, we tried batches made with water (too watery), chicken broth (too chicken-y and dull), and no liquid at all except for that in the single can of diced tomatoes we had been using (by far the best). This gave us the perfect amount of flavor, and the chili was rich and rounded.

Looking more closely at the tomatoes, tasters liked the amount of tomato chunks provided by a 14.5-ounce can of diced tomatoes, but the chili needed more body. We paired the diced tomatoes with a small can of tomato sauce, and without exception, tasters preferred the thick consistency of this combination of tomato products.

For our modest pot of chili, one hour of gentle sim-mering was enough to meld the flavors. But should we cook it with or without a lid? With other chili recipes, we've had success covering the pot during the first half of the cooking time and uncovering it for the final portion to thicken it nicely. However, following this method with our small amount of chili resulted in dry chili. We tried simply cooking the chili for less time, but the flavor wasn't as good. Covering it the entire time made the chili soupy. Keeping the lid on for most of the cooking time and then removing it for the last 15 minutes gave our chili the ideal consistency—rich and thick, but not dry. Although our chili may be simple in style and the size scaled down, the flavor is big, meaty, and satisfying.

Classic Beef Chili

SERVES 2

Serve with lime wedges, minced fresh cilantro, sliced scallions, minced onion, diced avocado, shredded cheddar or Monterey Jack cheese, and/or sour cream. See page 131 for a recipe to use up the leftover red bell pepper and page 178 for a recipe to use up the leftover beans.

- 1 tablespoon vegetable oil
- 1 small onion, minced
- ½ red bell pepper, stemmed, seeded, and cut into ½-inch pieces
- 3 garlic cloves, minced
- 1½ tablespoons chili powder
- 1 teaspoon ground cumin
- ¾ teaspoon ground coriander
- ¼ teaspoon red pepper flakes
- ¼ teaspoon dried oregano
- ⅛ teaspoon cayenne pepper
- Salt

8 ounces 85 percent lean ground beef

¾ cup drained and rinsed canned
red kidney or pinto beans

1 (14.5-ounce) can diced tomatoes

1 (8-ounce) can tomato sauce

1. Heat the oil in a medium saucepan over medium heat until shimmering. Add the onion, bell pepper, garlic, chili powder, cumin, coriander, pepper flakes, oregano, cayenne, and ¼ teaspoon salt, and cook, stirring often, until the vegetables begin to soften and the spices are fragrant, 3 to 5 minutes.

2. Stir in the beef and cook, breaking up the meat with a wooden spoon, until no longer pink, about 2 minutes.

3. Stir in the beans, diced tomatoes with their juice, and tomato sauce, and bring to a boil. Cover, reduce the heat to low, and simmer, stirring occasionally, for 45 minutes.

4. Uncover and continue to simmer, stirring occasionally, until the beef is tender and the chili is dark, rich, and slightly thickened, about 15 minutes longer. (If at any time the chili begins to stick to the bottom of the pot, stir in ¼ cup water.) Season with salt to taste and serve.

VARIATIONS

Beef Chili with Bacon

Cook 4 slices bacon, cut into ¼-inch pieces, in a medium saucepan over medium heat until crisp, about 8 minutes. Follow the recipe for Classic Beef Chili, omitting the oil and adding the vegetables and spices to the pan with the bacon and bacon fat; continue to cook as directed in step 1.

NOTES FROM THE TEST KITCHEN

THE BEST CHILI POWDER

A good-quality chili powder is an essential ingredient in any respectable chili. Chili powder is typically a blend of ground red chile peppers, cumin, oregano, garlic, and salt; sometimes cloves or allspice or both are included. Avoid chili powders labeled "pure," which are solely one kind of ground chile pepper (typically ancho or chipotle) with no added seasonings—they can be assertively hot and smoky. The test kitchen's favorite brand of chili powder is **Spice Islands**, praised by tasters for its sweet, smoky flavor that was deemed very potent.

Beef Chili with Moroccan Spices and Chickpeas

See page 140 for a recipe to use up the leftover chickpeas.

Follow the recipe for Classic Beef Chili, omitting the chili powder and red pepper flakes and adding 1 teaspoon paprika, 1 teaspoon ground ginger, and ⅛ teaspoon ground cinnamon with the other spices in step 1. Substitute ¾ cup drained and rinsed canned chickpeas for the kidney beans. Add ¼ cup raisins (if desired) to the pot with the beans and tomatoes in step 3. Stir in ¼ teaspoon grated lemon zest and 1 teaspoon fresh lemon juice before serving.

Smoky Southwestern Chili with Chipotle, Black Beans, and Corn

Follow the recipe for Classic Beef Chili, omitting the red pepper flakes and cayenne pepper and adding 1 teaspoon minced chipotle chile in adobo sauce with the spices in step 1. Substitute ¾ cup drained and rinsed canned black beans for the kidney beans. After the chili is thickened in step 4, stir in ½ cup frozen corn kernels and continue to simmer until heated through, about 2 minutes. Stir in 1 to 2 teaspoons more minced chipotle to taste before serving.

BEEF ENCHILADA CASSEROLE

THE APPEAL OF CASSEROLES IS UNDENIABLE: THEY are rich and hearty, can be transported easily, and feed a crowd. But if you make a casserole for just two people, you're guaranteed to face leftovers. We don't think the satisfying and comforting nature of casseroles should be out of reach when cooking for two, so we aimed to downsize one of our favorites: beef enchilada casserole, a Tex-Mex lasagna of sorts. The dish is modeled on beef enchiladas but streamlined in technique (the casserole version features quick-cooking ground beef and a simple, layered approach to assembly), though some recipes take the streamlining too far, including convenience products such as canned sauce or condensed tomato soup. We wanted our scaled-down version to be easy, but not at the expense of flavor.

We started with the sauce, adapting a beef enchilada sauce the test kitchen has made in the past. We sautéed onion and garlic in oil, then stirred in a small amount of chili powder and ground cumin. Next we poured in canned tomato sauce, followed by beef broth. After the sauce had simmered for a few minutes to thicken and concentrate, we mixed half of it with beef we'd browned (tasters preferred the flavor of 85 percent lean ground beef over anything leaner) and turned up the heat by stirring in minced jalapeño and hot sauce.

Everybody agreed that deep corn flavor would be key to a successful beef enchilada casserole, but from past tastings we knew that corn tortillas straight from the plastic bag turn slimy in a casserole, and baking renders them tough, chewy, and flavorless. Instead we tried toasting them in a dry skillet. As the tortillas blistered and charred, we knew we were headed in the right direction.

Now that it was time to start building the casserole, we had to figure out what to build it in. After several tests with baking dishes of varying size, we determined that a 9 by 5-inch loaf pan was the ideal baking dish for a casserole that would serve two generously. The only problem was that the 6-inch tortillas didn't fit in the loaf pan. Cutting them in half left us with awkward half-moons. The solution was as simple as trimming the rounded edges off the tortillas, leaving us with squares that fit perfectly in the pan. We layered three levels of toasted tortillas with two of beef filling, poured the sauce on top, and finally sprinkled the cheese over everything. The casserole smelled fantastic in the oven, but the middle layer of tortillas developed a papery, unpleasant texture. When we tried eliminating it, the simplest fix, tasters missed both its toasty corn flavor and the cohesiveness it had given the casserole.

We decided to keep the top and bottom layers of tortillas, but also incorporate more tortillas in another manner. To keep the full flavor of the tortilla trimmings and use them as a thickener, we put them, plus one additional whole tortilla, in the food processor with a can of Ro-Tel tomatoes (flavored with green chiles). We processed the mix until it was smooth, then folded it into the browned beef, along with some of the sauce and a little Colby-Jack cheese. This time we sandwiched the filling between just two tortilla layers and poured the remaining enchilada sauce over the top. After the casserole had baked for 15 minutes, we sprinkled it with more cheese and some minced jalapeño. After another 10 minutes in the oven, the casserole had set up, and we cut hefty squares for our tasters. Finally, we had a small casserole with a big payoff.

Beef Enchilada Casserole

SERVES 2

Two tortillas are placed on the bottom of the baking dish, but 3 tortillas are used for the top layer because the pan widens slightly at the top. If you can't find Ro-Tel tomatoes, substitute 1¼ cups canned diced tomatoes plus an additional jalapeño. Monterey Jack cheese may be substituted for the Colby-Jack. To make this dish spicier, add the chile seeds. Serve with sour cream, thinly sliced scallions, and lime wedges, if desired.

- **6** (6-inch) corn tortillas
- **1** (10-ounce) can Ro-Tel tomatoes (see note)
- **8** ounces 85 percent lean ground beef
- **2** teaspoons vegetable oil
- **1** small onion, minced
- **4** garlic cloves, minced
- **1** jalapeño chile, stemmed, seeded, and minced (see note)
- **2** teaspoons chili powder
- **½** teaspoon ground cumin
- **1** (8-ounce) can tomato sauce
- **½** cup beef broth
- **6** ounces Colby-Jack cheese (see note), shredded (about 1½ cups)
- **¼** cup minced fresh cilantro
- **1** teaspoon hot sauce
  Salt and pepper

1. Adjust an oven rack to the middle position and heat the oven to 450 degrees. Grease a 9 by 5-inch loaf pan. Toast 2 of the tortillas in a 10-inch nonstick skillet (they will overlap) over medium-high heat until bubbling and spotty brown, about 2 minutes, flipping them halfway through. Transfer to a plate and repeat twice more with the remaining 4 tortillas.

2. Following the photo on page 79, trim 5 of the tortillas into 4½-inch squares, reserving the trimmings. Tear the trimmings and remaining tortilla into small pieces, combine with the Ro-Tel tomatoes and their juice in a food processor, and process until smooth, about 1 minute. Transfer to a medium bowl.

3. Cook the beef in the skillet over medium heat, breaking up the meat with a wooden spoon, until no longer pink, about 2 minutes. Transfer to the bowl with the processed tortilla mixture.

4. Add the oil and onion to the skillet and cook over medium heat until softened, about 5 minutes. Stir in the garlic, 2 teaspoons of the minced jalapeño, chili powder, and cumin, and cook until fragrant, about 30 seconds. Stir in the tomato sauce and beef broth and simmer until slightly thickened and reduced to 1 cup, 5 to 7 minutes. Remove from the heat.

5. Stir ½ cup of the tomato sauce mixture, ½ cup of the cheese, cilantro, and hot sauce into the tortilla-beef mixture. Season with salt and pepper to taste.

6. Arrange 2 toasted tortillas in the bottom of the prepared loaf pan. Spread the beef filling evenly in the dish, then top with the remaining 3 tortillas (they may overlap slightly) and the remaining tomato sauce mixture. Bake until the filling bubbles lightly around the edges and the top of the filling begins to brown, 15 to 20 minutes.

7. Sprinkle with the remaining 1 cup cheese and remaining minced jalapeño and continue to bake until the casserole is hot throughout and the cheese is browned in spots, about 10 minutes longer. Let cool for 15 minutes before serving.

NOTES FROM THE TEST KITCHEN

TRIMMING TORTILLAS

Trim 5 of the toasted tortillas to make 4½-inch squares, reserving the scraps for use in the filling.

RO-TEL TOMATOES

A spicy, tangy blend of tomatoes, green chiles, and spices, Ro-Tel tomatoes are an easy way to add flavor to a variety of dishes. They're also particularly ideal when cooking for two—not only do they eliminate the prep work of chopping both tomatoes and chiles, but the relatively small 10-ounce can is just right for scaled-down recipes.

STEAK TACOS

BEEF TACOS MADE INDOORS ARE TYPICALLY THE pedestrian ground beef kind, stuffed into a crisp corn tortilla and loaded with cheese and shredded lettuce. There are also steak tacos, modeled after authentic Mexican carne asada and generally reserved for the grill. Here a thin cut of beef, typically skirt or flank steak, is marinated, grilled, then sliced thin and served in a soft corn tortilla with simple garnishes. Done properly, the meat has rich, grilled flavor, and the tacos themselves are simple to throw together.

Given the choice, we'd almost always prefer the beefier (and let's face it—better) flavors of a steak taco over a ground beef one, but what about those times when cooking outdoors isn't possible? We wanted to develop an indoor method for tender, juicy steak tacos. And since steak is easy to buy in small portions, we figured steak tacos would make a satisfying meal for two.

Our first task was to choose the right cut of meat. Traditional Mexican recipes typically call for skirt or flank steak for taco meat, both of which come from the belly of the cow. Skirt steak is well marbled, but we found that the availability of this cut is spotty. Flank steak is more widely available, has a nice beefy flavor, and, when sliced thinly against the grain, is very tender. About 12 ounces of flank steak seemed an ideal portion for two.

Unadorned, flank steak is good, but we wondered if the meat could be even juicier. In the past, we have found that sprinkling steak with salt and allowing it to sit for an hour boosts juiciness, similarly to brining. But an hour seemed like a long time to wait for a relatively quick weeknight supper for two. Poking holes into the steak with a fork allowed the salt to sink more quickly into the meat's interior and reduced that time by half—to 30 minutes.

Wanting to mimic the browned exterior and crisp, caramelized edges of grilled meat as much as possible, we figured that the intense heat of the oven's broiler would be the best option for cooking our steak. But the broiler proved to be a failure for a thin cut like flank steak; by the time the exterior was browned, the interior was overcooked.

Pan-searing proved to be a much more promising method that achieved some decent browning. But we wanted more. Looking to increase the surface area of

STEAK TACOS WITH SWEET AND SPICY PICKLED ONION

the steak, we tried cutting it lengthwise with the grain into strips about 1½ inches wide. The results were great. Now the steak could be browned on four sides instead of two, and we had more exposed edges that became crisp and super-flavorful. As a final trick to boost browning, we sprinkled the steak pieces with a little sugar before searing.

With a successful cooking method squared away, we looked at adding some other flavor dimensions to the steak. We liked the idea of a wet rub or paste, provided it was removed before cooking so it wouldn't impede browning. After looking into traditional marinades, we settled on a combination of cilantro, scallions, garlic, and jalapeño. Processed into a pesto-like paste with some oil, this marinade added fresh flavors to the steak. And when coupled with the salt, the oil-based marinade was pulled into the steak, flavoring it throughout. We reserved some of the marinade to toss with the steak after it was sliced. This brightened the flavor and presentation considerably.

For garnish, we experimented with making some quick pickled vegetables, which we loosely based on *curtido* (a relish commonly served in Latin America). Tasters loved the onion we "pickled" in a mixture of sugar and red wine vinegar enlivened by a jalapeño, and it took only 30 minutes for the flavors to meld. We now had a lively alternative to the ubiquitous ground beef taco, and it was incredibly easy and tasted great.

NOTES FROM THE TEST KITCHEN

WARMING TORTILLAS

Warming tortillas over the open flame of a gas burner or in a skillet gives them a toasted flavor, but the oven or microwave also work. If your tortillas are dry, pat them with a little water first.

If using a gas stove, toast the tortillas, one at a time, directly on the cooking grate over a medium flame until slightly charred around the edges, about 30 seconds per side. If using a skillet, toast the tortillas, one at a time, over medium-high heat until softened and speckled with brown, 20 to 30 seconds per side. Wrap the warmed tortillas in foil or a kitchen towel to keep them warm and soft until serving time.

If using an oven, stack the tortillas in a foil packet and heat at 350 degrees until warm and soft, about 5 minutes. Keep them in the foil until serving time.

To use a microwave, stack the tortillas on a plate, cover with microwave-safe plastic wrap, and heat on high until warm and soft, 1 to 2 minutes. Remove the plastic wrap and cover the tortillas with a kitchen towel or foil to keep them warm.

Steak Tacos

SERVES 2

We prefer this steak cooked to medium-rare, but if you prefer it more or less done, see our guidelines in "Testing Meat for Doneness" on page 109. To make this dish spicier, add the chile seeds. Serve the tacos with lime wedges, additional cilantro, thinly sliced radishes, or cucumber. See page 163 for a recipe to use up the leftover corn tortillas.

HERB PASTE

- ½ **cup fresh cilantro**
- 3 **garlic cloves, peeled**
- 3 **scallions, roughly chopped**
- 1 **jalapeño chile, stemmed and seeded (see note)**
- ½ **teaspoon ground cumin**
- ¼ **cup vegetable oil**
- 1 **tablespoon fresh lime juice**

STEAK AND TACOS

- 12 **ounces flank steak**
  Salt
- ¼ **teaspoon sugar**
- ¼ **teaspoon pepper**
- 2 **teaspoons vegetable oil**
- 6 **(6-inch) corn tortillas, warmed**
- 1 **recipe Sweet and Spicy Pickled Onion (see page 82)**

1. FOR THE HERB PASTE: Pulse the cilantro, garlic, scallions, jalapeño, and cumin in a food processor until finely chopped, 10 to 12 pulses. Add the oil and process until the mixture is smooth and resembles pesto, about 15 seconds, scraping down the sides of the bowl as necessary. Transfer 2 tablespoons of the herb paste to a medium bowl, whisk in the lime juice, and set aside.

2. FOR THE STEAK: Pat the steak dry with paper towels. Following the photos on page 82, cut the steak with the grain into 1½-inch-wide strips. Using a fork, poke each piece of steak 10 to 12 times on each side. Rub the steak with ¾ teaspoon salt, place in an 8-inch square baking dish, then coat evenly with the remaining herb paste. Cover the dish with plastic wrap and refrigerate for at least 30 minutes, or up to 1 hour.

3. Scrape the herb paste off the steak and sprinkle evenly with the sugar and pepper. Heat the oil in a 10-inch nonstick skillet over medium-high heat until just smoking. Brown the steak pieces well on all sides and cook until the steak registers 125 degrees on an instant-read thermometer (for medium-rare), 7 to 10 minutes. Transfer the meat to a carving board and let rest for 5 minutes.

4. Slice the steak thinly across the grain into small pieces, add to the bowl with the reserved herb paste–lime juice mixture, and toss to coat. Season with salt to taste. Spoon a small amount of sliced steak into the center of each warm tortilla and serve, passing the pickled onion separately.

NOTES FROM THE TEST KITCHEN

PREPARING THE STEAK FOR TACOS

1. Cut the flank steak into strips about 1½ inches wide. This provides extra surface area for additional browning.

2. Pierce the steak strips with a fork, then season the meat, coat with the herb paste, and let sit for at least 30 minutes to allow the flavors to penetrate.

3. Sear the steak on all sides to maximize browning.

4. Cut the steak thinly across the grain into small pieces, then toss with the additional herb paste and lime juice.

Sweet and Spicy Pickled Onion
MAKES ABOUT 1 CUP

To make this dish spicier, add the chile seeds.

- 1 **small red onion, halved and sliced thin**
- ½ **cup red wine vinegar**
- 2½ **tablespoons sugar**
- 1 **jalapeño chile, stemmed, seeded, and sliced into thin rings (see note)**
- ⅛ **teaspoon salt**

Place the onion in a medium heat-resistant bowl. Bring the vinegar, sugar, jalapeño, and salt to a simmer in a small saucepan over medium-high heat, stirring occasionally, until the sugar dissolves. Pour the vinegar mixture over the onion, cover loosely, and let cool to room temperature, about 30 minutes. When cool, drain the onion, discarding the liquid, and serve. (The pickled onion can be refrigerated in an airtight container for up to 1 week.)

STEAK PIZZAIOLA

DON'T BE CONFUSED BY THE "PIZZA" IN ITS NAME because this bold, saucy steak dish is definitely not pizza parlor fare. As legend has it, Italian pizza makers used to slow-simmer cheap cuts of beef in their extra pizza sauce to create a hearty, satisfying lunch for themselves. Once their customers noticed what was happening on the other side of the counter, they wanted in, too, and thus the dish known as steak pizzaiola was born. Italian-American restaurants have modernized this recipe by ladling slow-simmered marinara sauce enriched with sautéed onions, peppers, and mushrooms over tender seared steaks. Searing the steaks would be quick enough, but we didn't want to wait all day for the sauce to come together. Could we streamline this recipe, creating a quick scaled-down sauce with the same complexity as a long-cooked marinara in the time it takes to cook two steaks?

We started with the steak. Strip steaks were a natural choice because they are extremely flavorful and ideal for pan-searing. We chose steaks that were 1 inch thick—thin enough to cook quickly, but thick enough to develop a nice sear on the outside while still retaining a rosy, tender interior. We seared the steaks for three to

STEAK PIZZAIOLA

five minutes per side, then transferred them to a plate (tented with foil) while we started the sauce in the unwashed pan—we hoped the browned bits left behind from searing the steaks would contribute important flavor and complexity to our quick sauce. We sautéed chopped onion, green pepper, and white mushrooms before adding a splash of red wine to deglaze the fond. When the wine had reduced, we poured in some crushed tomatoes. After 10 minutes of cooking, the sauce had reduced to the right consistency but lacked the long-simmered flavor we were after.

Looking to develop deeper flavor, we decided to try a technique developed recently in the test kitchen for a quick marinara sauce. This recipe calls for draining a can of whole tomatoes, breaking the tomatoes apart, and caramelizing the dry tomato chunks in a skillet before adding the juice. We found that just three minutes in the hot pan deepened the flavor of half a can of drained whole tomatoes (the right amount for our scaled-down sauce).

To achieve even more complexity, we replaced the white mushrooms with earthy creminis and used smoky roasted red peppers instead of fresh green bell peppers. Swapping out the traditional red wine for balsamic vinegar as the deglazing liquid added another dimension of richness; 1 tablespoon of vinegar was all that was needed. A little garlic rounded out the flavors.

We were getting close but wanted to add even more depth to our quick sauce. We tried adding tomato paste, but with such a short cooking time it tasted raw and bitter. Searching for another tomato product to lend depth to the sauce, we decided to add chopped sun-dried tomatoes. Just a tablespoon lent bright, complex flavor. Off the heat, a sprinkle of fresh basil contributed a welcome freshness.

Although the sauce was ready in just 15 minutes, the steaks were no longer hot by the time they got to the table. Holding the seared steaks in a 200-degree oven only dried them out. Instead, we found that if we seared the steaks more quickly (just three minutes per side), we could then finish them in a 350-degree oven while we prepared the sauce. This potent combination of tomatoes, onion, mushrooms, and peppers had all the flavor of a slow-simmered sauce and was the perfect complement to our juicy, seared steaks.

Steak Pizzaiola

SERVES 2

We prefer this steak cooked to medium-rare, but if you prefer it more or less done, see our guidelines in "Testing Meat for Doneness" on page 109.

- 2 **(8-ounce) boneless strip steaks, about 1 inch thick**
  Salt and pepper
- 2 **tablespoons vegetable oil**
- 1 **small onion, minced**
- 3 **ounces cremini mushrooms, quartered**
- 2 **garlic cloves, minced**
- 1 **tablespoon sun-dried tomatoes packed in oil, rinsed, patted dry, and minced**
- 1 **tablespoon balsamic vinegar**
- ⅓ **cup drained canned whole tomatoes (about 3 tomatoes), chopped medium, ⅓ cup juice reserved**
- 2 **ounces jarred roasted red peppers, drained, patted dry, and chopped medium (about ¼ cup)**
- 2 **tablespoons chopped fresh basil**

1. Adjust an oven rack to the middle position and heat the oven to 350 degrees.

2. Pat the steaks dry with paper towels and season with salt and pepper. Heat 2 teaspoons of the oil in a 10-inch skillet over medium-high heat until just

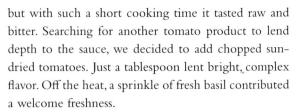

smoking. Brown the steaks well on both sides, about 6 minutes, flipping them halfway through.

3. Transfer the steaks to a wire rack set inside a rimmed baking sheet and roast until the steaks register 125 degrees on an instant-read thermometer (for medium-rare), about 10 minutes. Transfer the steaks to a platter, tent loosely with foil, and let rest while preparing the sauce.

NOTES FROM THE TEST KITCHEN

CHOOSING THE RIGHT SIZE SKILLET

When cooking for four or more, a large 12-inch skillet does the job, but using the same skillet to cook for two can result in disaster. Certain dishes, like Steak Tacos (page 81) and Pan-Fried Pork Chops and Dirty Rice (page 9), would scorch in a 12-inch skillet because there would be too much hot surface area (and heat) for too little food. Instead, we reach for an 8- or 10-inch skillet for these dishes. (Stir-fries and some pasta dishes are the exceptions, as the large surface area is necessary to accommodate either all the vegetables and protein for adequate browning or ample sauce and liquid to cook the pasta.) With a mix of skillet sizes on hand, you'll be able to make anything from Pasta alla Norma (page 60) to Steak Pizzaiola. (See below and page 31 for information on our top-rated traditional and nonstick skillets.)

OUR FAVORITE TRADITIONAL SKILLET

We use our skillets all the time, for everything from pan-roasting chicken breasts and searing steaks to cooking pasta. While nonstick skillets can be purchased at a reasonable price (see page 31), traditional skillets can cost anywhere from $30 to $150 or more. Preliminary tests of traditional skillets confirmed our suspicions that cheap was not the way to go, but how much do you really need to spend? We tested eight pans from well-known manufacturers. All of the pans tested had flared sides, and most had uncoated stainless steel cooking surfaces, which we prize for promoting a fond (the browned, sticky bits that cling to the interior of the pan when food is sautéed, which help flavor sauces).

We concluded that medium-weight pans (not too heavy and not too light) are ideal—they have enough heft for heat retention and structural integrity, but not so much that they are difficult to manipulate. For its combination of excellent performance, optimum weight and balance, and overall ease of use, the **All-Clad Stainless Steel Fry Pan**, which comes in 8-inch ($85), 10-inch ($100), and 12-inch ($135) sizes, was the hands-down winner.

4. While the steaks are cooking, add 2 teaspoons more oil, the onion, mushrooms, and ⅛ teaspoon salt to the skillet, and cook until the vegetables are softened, about 5 minutes. Add the garlic and sun-dried tomatoes and cook until fragrant, about 30 seconds. Stir in the vinegar and cook until nearly evaporated, about 30 seconds. Transfer the mushroom mixture to a bowl.

5. Add the remaining 2 teaspoons oil and tomatoes to the skillet and cook over medium heat until the tomatoes begin to brown and stick to the pan, about 3 minutes. Stir in the reserved tomato juice, roasted peppers, and mushroom mixture. Reduce the heat to medium-low and simmer until the sauce is slightly thickened, about 4 minutes.

6. Off the heat, stir in the basil and season with salt and pepper to taste. Spoon the sauce over the steaks and serve.

PORK SCHNITZEL

WIENER SCHNITZEL, OR VIENNESE CUTLET (NAMED for Wien, or Vienna, the capital of Austria), features a thin, tender veal cutlet coated with fine bread crumbs and fried until puffy and golden brown. What separates wiener schnitzel from ordinary breaded cutlets is the coating's rumpled appearance. But in our experience the coating is often soggy and oily, and the meat is too tough for a knife to slice. To avoid this toughness, not to mention the high price of veal, many recipes substitute pork to move this dish into weeknight dinner territory. Sadly, these recipes yield dry cutlets with greasy coatings, but we wanted a tender pork cutlet with a crisp, greaseless coating.

Focusing on the pork, we first considered pork chops. However, pounding them proved laborious, and the cooked cutlets had a dry, mealy texture. Another option was prepackaged pork cutlets, but when we managed to find these at the supermarket, they were sinewy and fatty. The last option was pork tenderloin. Pounded thin and fried, cutlets made from tenderloin were far superior to the others. They were remarkably tender and had a mild flavor that was similar to that of veal. We found that a small 12-ounce pork tenderloin was just the right size for two servings.

CUTTING TENDERLOIN FOR PORK SCHNITZEL

Cut the tenderloin in half on a severe bias (at about a 20-degree angle). Once pounded, these cutlets will fit easily in a Dutch oven.

KEYS TO A CRISP AND PUFFY COATING

1. Microwave the bread then process it in a food processor to create ultra-fine crumbs.

2. Add oil to the eggs to keep the coating from fusing with the meat.

3. Fry in 2 cups of oil to allow the eggs to set quickly and trap steam, creating the puff.

4. Carefully shake the Dutch oven to bathe each cutlet in hot oil, which helps the egg to set faster, enhancing the puff.

The only drawback to the tenderloin was its long, cylindrical shape. Cutting the tenderloin crosswise into two equal chunks (each 2 to 3 inches long) and then pounding them replicated the typical dinner plate–sized veal cutlets, but these were so large we could cook only one at a time. We tried again with just a slight variation, cutting at an angle. We ended up with oblong pieces that, when pounded, were twice as long as they were wide. Two fit perfectly in a pan.

The standard breading method for wiener schnitzel is no different from that for most other breaded cutlets. The meat is dredged in flour, then egg, and finally bread crumbs. The bread-crumb coating is the crucial part, so we started testing our options. The most convenient options, such as seasoned store-bought bread crumbs, panko (Japanese-style bread crumbs), ground Melba toasts, ground stuffing mix, and ground saltine crackers, were all unappealing with our pork. Drying bread in a low-temperature oven before processing it into crumbs was time-consuming, and the bread turned brown, making the crumbs taste too much like toast. We wondered if microwaving would dry the bread without developing a toasted flavor. After some testing we had success: Cubing slices and microwaving them for five minutes produced ultra-parched bread. After 45 seconds in the food processor, we had super-fine, super-dry bread crumbs that fried up extra-crisp.

So far our cutlets were crisp and tender, but we had not achieved the wrinkled, puffy exterior that is wiener schnitzel's signature. Some recipes suggested adding oil to the egg wash. Whisked into the eggs, just 1 tablespoon of oil made the coating crisper and helped it slide free of the meat, making it puff—but just slightly.

Frustrated, we turned back to our research. One recipe used a shallow pot similar to a Dutch oven (we'd been using a skillet); the cutlets were cooked in an inch of oil—a very generous amount—and the pot shaken the entire time. We tried this approach and were astounded; the coating was perfectly crinkled and beautifully browned. Now that the cutlets were finally crisp, rumpled, and properly puffed, all they needed was a spritz of lemon, some parsley, and capers (and for truly authentic flavor, a sieved hard-cooked egg). The result: a cutlet so tender we could cut it with a fork.

PORK SCHNITZEL

Pork Schnitzel

The 2 cups oil called for in this recipe may seem like a lot, but they're necessary to achieve an authentic crinkled, puffed texture on the finished cutlets. When properly cooked, the cutlets absorb very little oil. To ensure ample cooking space, a large Dutch oven is essential.

PORK

- **4** slices high-quality white sandwich bread, crusts removed, cut into ¾-inch cubes (about 4 cups)
- **¼** cup unbleached all-purpose flour
- **2** large eggs
- **2** cups plus 1 tablespoon vegetable oil (see note)
- **1** (12-ounce) pork tenderloin, trimmed and cut on the bias into 2 equal pieces (see page 86)
- Salt and pepper

GARNISHES

- **½** lemon, cut into wedges
- **1** tablespoon minced fresh parsley
- **1** tablespoon capers, rinsed
- **1** large hard-cooked egg, yolk and white separated and passed separately through a fine-mesh strainer (optional)

1. Place the bread cubes in a single layer on a large microwave-safe plate. Microwave on high until the bread is dry and a few pieces start to brown lightly, 4 to 6 minutes, stirring halfway through. Process the dry bread in a food processor to very fine crumbs, about 45 seconds.

2. Transfer the bread crumbs to a shallow dish (you should have about ⅔ cup crumbs). Spread the flour in a second shallow dish. Beat the eggs with 1 tablespoon of the oil in a third shallow dish. Place each piece of pork between 2 sheets of plastic wrap and pound to an even ⅛- to ¼-inch thickness, then season with salt and pepper.

3. Working with 1 cutlet at a time, dredge the pork cutlets in the flour, shaking off the excess, then coat with the egg mixture, allowing the excess to drip back into the dish, and coat evenly with the bread crumbs, pressing on the crumbs to adhere. Place the breaded cutlets on a wire rack set inside a rimmed baking sheet; let the coating dry for 5 minutes.

4. Heat the remaining 2 cups oil in a large Dutch oven over medium-high heat until it registers 375 degrees on an instant-read thermometer. Carefully lay the cutlets in the hot oil, without overlapping, and cook, shaking the pot continuously and gently, until the cutlets are wrinkled and light golden brown on both sides, 2 to 4 minutes, flipping them halfway through.

5. Transfer the cutlets to a paper towel–lined plate and blot well on both sides to absorb the excess oil. Serve with the garnishes.

HERBED ROAST CHICKEN BREAST

WITH GOLDEN, BURNISHED SKIN AND JUICY, flavorful meat, a roasted chicken with fresh herbs represents what's best about home cooking: It's simple and satisfying and appeals to everyone. But when "everyone" refers to just you plus one, it's time to rethink traditional roast chicken. And while adding herb flavor to roast chicken sounds easy, the reality is that the herbs rarely make much of an impression on the chicken. The most common approach—spreading herb butter under the skin of the breast—isn't enough. We set out to develop a retooled roast chicken recipe for two that would produce crisp skin, moist meat, and serious herb flavor.

Right off the bat, we decided our best bet was to roast a bone-in, skin-on whole chicken breast—a 1½-pound breast is right for two servings, and it eliminates the challenge of cooking both the white and dark meat, which cook at different rates. We usually split the breast, but decided against it here, as having the skin intact might mean better retention and distribution of herb butter next to the skin.

We started by making a basic rosemary-parsley paste, gently loosening the skin, and spreading the paste over the meat. For more herb flavor, we also decided to slather the chicken breast with more of the paste midway through cooking. (Any earlier and the herbs would scorch.) The results were mixed: The very top of the breast had an herb-infused crust, but most of the paste slid right off the sides.

In an effort to give the paste a better chance of sticking, we pressed on the breastbone to get the whole breast to lie flat. We also moved the chicken from the V-rack we'd been roasting it in to a flat roasting pan. This time when the butter in the paste melted and ran off, the herbs mostly stayed put. Our method was working; tasters were pleased by the herb-to-meat ratio.

While we were making headway in the herb department, the skin of the breast wasn't as brown or crisp as we'd hoped. Figuring that the moisture in both the herbs and the butter (butter is nearly 20 percent water) were slowing down the melting of fat in the skin, it made sense to speed things up by starting the chicken on the stovetop. Now that we had flattened the breast, a good portion of the skin made contact with the skillet to brown and develop a good crust. We then transferred the whole skillet to the oven. This pan-roasting technique worked perfectly: Browning the chicken in the skillet made the fat render more easily, giving us the crisp, golden crust we were after.

NOTES FROM THE TEST KITCHEN

PREPARING THE CHICKEN FOR ROASTING

1. Use the heel of your hand to press firmly on the breastbone so the chicken will lie flat.

2. Gently lift the skin at the top of each side of the breast to form a pocket.

3. Using a spoon, slide 1 tablespoon of herb butter into each pocket and push it off with your fingers as you pull the spoon out.

4. Use the back of a spoon (or your fingers) to spread the butter evenly over the meat on each side of the breast.

With the cooking technique settled, we turned our attention to the best herb combination. Dried herbs were not an option, as their potency weakened dramatically during roasting and their texture turned gritty. For a balance of flavors and textures, we tried pairings of soft, delicately flavored herbs like parsley and tarragon with bold, potent herbs like rosemary and thyme.

After numerous tests we found at least one herb that tasters could agree on: scallions. A couple of scallions contributed a fresh, grassy flavor that everybody loved. This, combined with a handful of tarragon and thyme, two other herbs our tasters favored, worked incredibly well, and a little minced garlic mixed into the paste boosted all of its flavors. We made this combination the main recipe and created a brightly flavored variation with parsley, rosemary, and Dijon mustard.

Just to make sure that every bite of chicken was bursting with herb flavor, we made a quick pan sauce using the drippings in the skillet, finishing it off with a tablespoon of extra herb butter and a few drops of lemon juice. Now, with triple layers of herb flavor—roasted into the meat, spread over the skin, and drizzled onto each serving—our version of roast chicken was scaled down in size, but not in flavor.

Herbed Roast Chicken Breast
SERVES 2

Do not use dried herbs, which lose potency during cooking and turn the dish gritty. If using a kosher chicken, do not brine. If brining the chicken, do not season with salt in step 2. The chicken may seem snug in an 8-inch skillet, but once browned it will fit.

- 4 tablespoons (½ stick) unsalted butter, softened
- 1 tablespoon minced fresh tarragon
- 2 scallions, minced
- 1½ teaspoons minced fresh thyme
- 1 small garlic clove, minced
  Salt and pepper
- 1 (1½-pound) whole bone-in, skin-on chicken breast, trimmed, brined if desired (see note; see page 162)
- 1 teaspoon vegetable oil
- 1 teaspoon unbleached all-purpose flour
- ¾ cup low-sodium chicken broth
- ½ teaspoon fresh lemon juice

1. Adjust an oven rack to the middle position and heat the oven to 450 degrees. Mash the butter, tarragon, scallions, thyme, garlic, ⅛ teaspoon salt, and ⅛ teaspoon pepper together in a medium bowl. Measure out and reserve 1 tablespoon of the herb butter for the sauce and refrigerate until needed.

2. Pat the chicken dry with paper towels. Following the photos on page 89, flatten the chicken and separate the skin from the top of each side of the breast to form a pocket. Place 1 tablespoon of the softened herb butter in each pocket. Using the back of a spoon or your fingers, spread the butter over each side of the breast. Reserve the remaining butter to brush over the skin partway through roasting. Season the chicken with salt and pepper.

3. Heat the oil in an 8-inch ovensafe skillet over medium-high heat until just smoking. Carefully lay the chicken, skin-side down, in the skillet and reduce the heat to medium. Cook until lightly browned, 3 to 5 minutes. Transfer the skillet to the oven and roast the chicken for 20 minutes.

4. Flip the chicken skin-side up, brush the remaining butter over the skin, and continue to roast until the skin is golden and the breast registers 160 to 165 degrees on an instant-read thermometer, 10 to 15 minutes longer. Transfer the chicken to a carving board and let rest while making the sauce.

5. Using a potholder (the skillet handle will be hot), discard all but 1 teaspoon of the fat in the pan. Add the flour and cook over medium heat, stirring constantly, until golden, about 1 minute. Stir in the broth and bring to a simmer, scraping up any browned bits. Cook until the sauce is slightly thickened and reduced to ½ cup, 3 to 5 minutes.

6. Stir in any accumulated chicken juice and return to a brief simmer. Off the heat, whisk in the lemon juice and reserved chilled herb butter and season with salt and pepper to taste. Following the photos, carve the chicken and serve, passing the sauce separately.

VARIATION

Mustard and Rosemary Herbed Roast Chicken Breast

Follow the recipe for Herbed Roast Chicken Breast, substituting 1 tablespoon minced fresh parsley for the tarragon and 1½ teaspoons minced fresh rosemary for the thyme. Add 1½ tablespoons Dijon mustard to the softened butter in step 1.

NOTES FROM THE TEST KITCHEN

CARVING A BONE-IN BREAST

1. To remove the meat, cut straight down along one side of the breastbone.

2. Run the knife down along the rib cage to remove the entire breast half.

3. Slice each breast half crosswise on the bias, making thin slices.

TANDOORI CHICKEN

THE BEST RENDITIONS OF THIS INDIAN SPECIALTY feature lightly charred pieces of juicy chicken infused with smoke, garlic, ginger, and spices for a dish that manages to be exotic and homey at the same time. Authentic versions call for a 24-hour marinade and a tandoor, the traditional beehive-shaped clay oven that fires up to 900 degrees—requirements that keep the dish mainly in the realm of restaurants, even in India. We decided to take on the challenge of reinventing this Indian classic as a weekday dish that we could tailor for two.

Traditional recipes for tandoori chicken are all fairly similar. They start with skinless, bone-in chicken marinated for 24 hours in yogurt flavored with ginger, garlic, and garam masala, a spice mix that typically includes cumin, cardamom, coriander, and cinnamon.

Before we worried about marinating times, we wanted to pin down the larger issue of cooking method. We prepped some chicken pieces according to a standard recipe and put them in the refrigerator to marinate for a day. We decided to use split bone-in chicken breasts, a natural choice when cooking for two because they are usually sold individually or by the pair.

Although the grill would be the most obvious means to approximate the tandoor's fierce heat, we wanted a dish we could make year-round, so we decided to simply crank the oven as high as it would go. We took out the long-marinated chicken breasts and slid them into a 500-degree oven. The chicken that emerged 30 minutes later was a big disappointment: pasty and hopelessly dry. Broiling the chicken was also a disaster, leaving some parts of the chicken charred and dry to the bone and others underdone.

Maybe it was time to stop mimicking a tandoor and go for something different. In the test kitchen, we've preserved the juiciness of thick-cut steaks by starting them in a low oven and searing them at the end. Following this approach, we baked the chicken until almost done in a 325-degree oven, then gave it a quick broil to char the exterior. This was the winning method—the meat was nicely charred on the outside and decidedly not dry within. In fact, we had another problem: Tasters complained it was too tender—almost mushy.

When chicken is left in an acidic marinade for too long, the meat starts to break down and become mushy. It seemed that the lactic acid in the yogurt was having this very effect on our chicken breasts. We tested marinating times significantly shorter than 24 hours, even as short as a brief dip. We were surprised when tasters strongly preferred the chicken that had been dipped versus soaked for even just 30 minutes.

Without the extended marinade, we still needed a way to get the flavors of the other spices into the chicken and make it juicy. A salt-spice rub seemed promising: Salt draws juices out of the meat, then the reverse happens and the salt, along with the spices and moisture, flows back in, bringing flavor deep into the meat.

We created a rub with the same spices we'd used in the marinade (garam masala, cumin, and chili powder), then cooked them in oil with some grated ginger and garlic to amplify their flavor. We added a teaspoon of salt and some lime juice, massaged the rub into the chicken pieces, which we'd scored for better flavor absorption,

and let them sit for half an hour. After a dunk in yogurt—all we needed was ½ cup flavored with the same spice mixture, the chicken was ready for the oven.

The results were terrific: juicy, lightly charred, well-seasoned meat with concentrated flavor and the right degree of tenderness. All the chicken needed was a dollop of yogurt sauce and a few lime wedges, and that clay oven and 24-hour marinade were finally history.

Tandoori Chicken with Yogurt Sauce
SERVES 2

We prefer this dish made with whole milk yogurt, but low-fat yogurt can be substituted. If garam masala is unavailable, substitute 1 teaspoon ground coriander, ¼ teaspoon pepper, ⅛ teaspoon ground cardamom, and ⅛ teaspoon ground cinnamon. It is important to remove the chicken from the oven before switching to the broiler setting to allow the broiler element time to come up to temperature. Serve with basmati rice and a chutney or relish.

SAUCE
- ½ cup plain whole milk yogurt
- 1 tablespoon minced fresh cilantro
- 1 tablespoon minced fresh mint
- 1 small garlic clove, minced
- Salt and pepper

CHICKEN
- 2 tablespoons vegetable oil
- 3 garlic cloves, minced
- 1 tablespoon grated or minced fresh ginger
- 1½ teaspoons garam masala (see note)
- 1 teaspoon ground cumin
- 1 teaspoon chili powder
- ½ cup plain whole milk yogurt
- 2 tablespoons fresh lime juice
- 1 teaspoon salt
- 2 (12-ounce) bone-in, skin-on split chicken breasts, trimmed (see page 148), skin removed, cut in half
- Lime wedges, for serving

1. FOR THE SAUCE: Combine the yogurt, cilantro, mint, and garlic in a small bowl. Season with salt and pepper to taste, cover, and refrigerate while preparing the chicken.

2. FOR THE CHICKEN: Heat the oil in an 8-inch non-stick skillet over medium heat until shimmering. Add the garlic and ginger and cook until fragrant, about 30 seconds. Stir in the garam masala, cumin, and chili powder, and cook until fragrant, 30 to 60 seconds. Remove from the heat.

3. Combine 1 tablespoon of the garlic-spice mixture, yogurt, and 1 tablespoon of the lime juice in a medium bowl and set aside.

4. In a medium bowl, combine the remaining garlic-spice mixture, remaining 1 tablespoon lime juice, and salt. Following the photo, score each piece of chicken twice with a sharp knife, then add to the bowl with the spice-salt mixture. Rub the mixture into the chicken until all of the pieces are evenly coated and let stand at room temperature for 30 minutes.

5. Adjust an oven rack to the upper-middle position and heat the oven to 325 degrees. Set a wire rack inside a foil-lined rimmed baking sheet. Transfer the chicken to the bowl with the spice-yogurt mixture and gently toss to coat. Lay the chicken, skinned-side down, on the prepared baking sheet. Discard any remaining yogurt mixture. Bake until the chicken registers 125 degrees on an instant-read thermometer, 15 to 25 minutes.

6. Remove the chicken from the oven, position the rack 6 inches from the broiler element, and heat the broiler. Flip the chicken pieces skinned-side up and broil until the chicken is lightly charred in spots and registers 160 to 165 degrees on an instant-read thermometer, 8 to 15 minutes. Transfer the chicken to a platter, tent loosely with foil, and let rest for 5 minutes. Serve with the yogurt sauce and lime wedges.

NOTES FROM THE TEST KITCHEN

SCORING TANDOORI CHICKEN

Score each piece of chicken with a sharp knife, making 2 shallow cuts about 1 inch apart and ⅛ inch deep.

SOUTH CAROLINA SHRIMP BOIL

WHILE NEW ENGLAND HAS ITS CLAMBAKES AND NEW Orleans its crawfish boils, the coastal towns of South Carolina boast a unique seafood boil that features local shell-on shrimp, smoked sausage, corn on the cob, and potatoes simmered in a broth seasoned with Old Bay. When it's time to eat, the broth is discarded and the shrimp and vegetables are heaped onto newspaper-covered picnic tables cluttered with paper towels and "waster" buckets for spent cobs and shells.

Though it's meant to feed the masses, we saw no reason this dish should be limited to large social gatherings. However, downsizing this feast wouldn't be our only challenge—its rustic, one-pot aspect is often its downfall. Home cooks are apt to add everything to the pot at the same time, or let everything boil away madly, often resulting in blown-out potatoes, mealy corn, and rubbery shrimp. The seasonings are also hit-or-miss: Sometimes the Old Bay hits you over the head; other times it's just a rumor. We set out to develop a smaller version of the shrimp boil that would have well-balanced seasoning and properly cooked components and would make just enough for two.

Most recipes we found included several pounds of shrimp and a dozen ears of corn, so before we addressed cooking technique, we first had to scale down the ingredients. We decided that 6 ounces of sausage, half a pound of shrimp, three small potatoes, and two ears of corn made up a balanced combination and a good portion for two. To make cooking and serving easier, we cut the sausage and corn into 2-inch pieces and halved or quartered the potatoes (depending on size).

With our key players in place, we were ready to cook. The most promising recipe we tested browned smoky, spicy andouille sausage to render fat and boost flavor, so we followed suit. Then we set the browned sausage aside and added 6 cups of water and 2 teaspoons of Old Bay to the pot. The potatoes and corn went in next; when the potatoes were barely tender, we added the sausage back to the pot, followed five minutes later by the shrimp. The staggered cooking ensured intact potatoes, plump corn, and nicely cooked sausage and shrimp. Unfortunately, the flavors were washed out.

SOUTH CAROLINA SHRIMP BOIL

You don't eat the broth in a South Carolina shrimp boil, but if the broth has no flavor, the stuff you *do* eat won't either. We tested adding garlic, onion, celery, and bell pepper to the broth, but only the garlic added any flavor, given the short cooking time of our downsized boil. Rather than increasing the amount of Old Bay to boost flavor, we reduced the amount of water to 2 cups, barely enough to cover the sausage and vegetables. With less water to dilute the seasonings, the flavor of our broth was now more intense.

For even more flavor, we tried replacing a cup of the water with an equal amount of clam juice, chicken broth, or beer. Tasters preferred the clam juice, which reinforced the brininess of the shrimp. Some recipes call for tomato. Since we wouldn't need much tomato for our scaled-down version, we wanted something easy; tasters liked a teaspoon of boldly flavored tomato paste. We then wondered if it was necessary to remove the browned andouille from the pot, only to add it back in later, so we tried leaving it in to cook with the other ingredients. After 20 minutes, the potatoes were tender,

and the sausage was still perfectly moist. Best of all, the extra simmering time for the sausage imparted a huge amount of flavor to the corn and potatoes. And the broth, which is usually discarded, is so flavorful it can be used to make Creole Rice (see page 95).

We had been adding the shrimp to the simmering liquid during the last few minutes of cooking, but that gave them scant time to soak up flavor. We tossed the shrimp with ½ teaspoon of Old Bay and scattered them directly on the simmering vegetables and sausage. With our reduced liquid amount, the shrimp stayed elevated above the liquid, and the seasoning stayed put. After simmering them for a minute, we covered the pot and set it off the heat to gently finish cooking the shrimp. A couple of minutes later, they were juicy and much more flavorful. Plus, cooking them this way was foolproof and relaxed, right in spirit with a casual seafood boil.

NOTES FROM THE TEST KITCHEN

DEVEINING SHELL-ON SHRIMP

To devein shell-on shrimp, use a pair of small scissors, which can cut through the shell to expose the underlying vein, then use the tip of the scissors to free the vein.

SITTIN' ON THE DOCK OF THE (OLD) BAY

Old Bay seasoning is a spice mix that's essential for shrimp boils, crab cakes, and many other seafood dishes. Created in the 1940s, this spice mix is a regional favorite in Maryland and Virginia along the coast. The predominant flavors in Old Bay are celery, mustard, and paprika. We like to use Old Bay to season steamed or boiled crustaceans and bivalves, in coatings for fried chicken and seafood, and in gumbos and seafood stews.

South Carolina Shrimp Boil

SERVES 2

This dish is made with shell-on shrimp; if you prefer peeled shrimp, use only ¼ teaspoon Old Bay in step 2. If you can't find andouille sausage, kielbasa can be substituted. If desired, reserve 1½ cups of the broth to make the recipe on page 95.

- 1 teaspoon vegetable oil
- 6 ounces andouille sausage, cut into 2-inch lengths
- 1 (8-ounce) bottle clam juice
- 1 cup water
- 2½ teaspoons Old Bay seasoning
- 2 garlic cloves, smashed
- 1 teaspoon tomato paste
- 1 bay leaf
- 2 ears fresh corn, husks and silk removed, cut into 2-inch rounds
- 8 ounces red potatoes, halved if small, quartered if large
- 8 ounces extra-large (21 to 25 per pound) shell-on shrimp (see note), deveined (see photo)
- 1 tablespoon minced fresh parsley or scallions (optional)

PAN-ROASTED HALIBUT STEAK WITH CHERMOULA

TUNA, SALMON, AND SWORDFISH ARE THE FISH STEAKS most American home cooks know best, but halibut is a nice option for a change of pace. With its lean, firm texture and clean, mild flavor, halibut plays well with the brightness of an aromatic raw sauce. This combination is naturally quick to prepare, making it a perfect candidate for a weeknight dinner for two. But halibut's leanness also presents a problem for the cook—sautéing and roasting tend to dry it out, and the lack of browning from braising produces a lackluster fish. Our goals were to find a cooking method that added flavor and also achieved a perfectly cooked, tender piece of fish, and to create a bold sauce to pair with it.

Before addressing the questions of technique and sauce, we took to the supermarkets and fishmongers to find the best cut of halibut for our recipe. We had already settled on steaks rather than fillets based on availability, but steaks can vary considerably in size. We found the best size steak to be between 10 and 12 inches in length and roughly 1¼ inches thick. This size steak weighs about 1¼ pounds, so we would need only one to serve two people. Frozen halibut steaks should be avoided; while the flavor matched that of the fresh fish, tasters were disappointed in the mushy texture, so we crossed them off our list.

Keeping in mind that we wanted to brown the fish to develop flavor, we tested two different techniques: skillet-cooking on the stovetop and roasting in the oven. Neither was ideal. The skillet-seared fish browned nicely but the end result was dry. The roasted sample was moist and evenly cooked, but it barely browned and had little flavor. To achieve intense, rich flavor, we chose a common restaurant technique and combined the methods. First we seared the fish in a heavy-duty ovensafe nonstick skillet on the stovetop, and then we put the whole thing—pan and fish—in the oven to finish. This approach was an improvement, but we still had a problem. Our efforts to brown the fish to enhance flavor usually caused it to overcook.

After much additional testing, we finally hit on the solution. Instead of searing the fish on both sides, we seared it on one side only, then flipped it seared-side up and moved the skillet to the oven. After testing a range of oven temperatures, we opted for 325 degrees because it cooked the halibut in under 10 minutes but still allowed for a reasonable margin of error. (The lower the temperature, the slower the fish cooks, and therefore the longer the window of time for doneness.) This worked beautifully, combining the flavor of browned fish with the moist interior that comes from finishing in the oven's even heat.

With the fish properly cooked, we turned our attention to the sauce. We wanted something aromatic and a bit off the beaten path. Chermoula, a Moroccan sauce of cilantro, lemon juice, garlic, olive oil, and spices, fit the bill perfectly. Using it as a sauce rather than a marinade worked perfectly with our halibut—and it took just five minutes to prepare.

Pan-Roasted Halibut Steak with Chermoula
SERVES 2

This recipe will work with salmon and swordfish steaks as well; however, the cooking times may vary slightly depending on their thickness. Make sure to use a 12-inch ovensafe nonstick skillet for this recipe.

CHERMOULA

- ¼ cup minced fresh cilantro
- 3 tablespoons extra-virgin olive oil
- 1 tablespoon fresh lemon juice
- 1 small garlic clove, minced
- ½ teaspoon ground cumin
- ½ teaspoon paprika
- ⅛ teaspoon cayenne pepper
- ⅛ teaspoon salt

HALIBUT

- 1 (1¼-pound) full halibut steak, about 1¼ inches thick
- Salt and pepper
- 1 tablespoon vegetable oil

1. FOR THE CHERMOULA: Combine all of the ingredients in a bowl and set aside.

2. FOR THE HALIBUT: Adjust an oven rack to the middle position and heat the oven to 325 degrees. Following the photo on page 98, trim the fish, then pat dry with paper towels and season with salt and pepper.

3. Heat the oil in a 12-inch ovensafe nonstick skillet over medium-high heat until just smoking. Carefully lay the fish steak in the skillet and cook until well browned on one side, about 5 minutes.

TRIMMING AND SERVING FULL HALIBUT STEAKS

A. Before cooking, cut off the cartilage at the ends of the steak to ensure that it will fit neatly in the pan and to diminish the likelihood that the small bones located there will end up on your plate.

B. To serve, remove the skin from the cooked steaks and separate each quadrant of meat from the bones by slipping a knife or spatula gently between them.

THREE KINDS OF HALIBUT STEAK

Most halibut steaks consist of four pieces of meat attached to a central bone (top). It is not uncommon, however, to encounter a steak with just two pieces, both located on the same side of the center bone (center). These steaks were cut from the center of the halibut, adjacent to the belly cavity. The belly, in effect, separates the two halves. We prefer full steaks with four meat sections when cooking for two because a full steak serves two perfectly. If you can find only the belly steaks, you will have to purchase two steaks instead of one to make our pan-roasted halibut recipe. Avoid very small, boneless steaks (bottom) cut entirely free from the bone and each other. Most boneless steaks won't serve even one person.

FULL STEAK
4 sections

BELLY CUT
2 sections

BONELESS STEAK
1 section

4. Off the heat, gently flip the halibut. Transfer the skillet to the oven and roast the halibut until the flesh is opaque and the fish flakes apart when gently prodded with a paring knife, 6 to 9 minutes.

5. Using a potholder (the skillet handle will be hot), remove the skillet from the oven. Transfer the halibut to a carving board, tent loosely with foil, and let rest for 5 minutes. Following the photo, separate the skin and bones from the fish with a spatula or knife. Transfer the fish to a platter and serve with the chermoula.

STUFFED TOMATOES

WARM SUMMER NIGHTS CALL FOR A SIMPLE SUPPER that makes the most of the season's best produce. We wanted to make a vegetable-based entrée from our favorite offerings at the farmers market—ripe, full tomatoes, firm zucchini, and fragrant basil. Stuffed tomatoes naturally came to mind—with the addition of nuts and some cheese, two tomatoes plus lightly dressed greens and a few slices of fresh baguette would make a satisfying and fresh meal for any diner.

We began testing by following a typical recipe: Stuff a hollowed-out raw tomato with filling (usually bread crumbs or rice) and bake it at 375 degrees for 30 minutes. The outcome was a soggy mess. The tomato was completely devoid of flavor, and the stuffing was dull and wet. We concluded that perhaps the same element that lends majesty to a tomato—water— was the source of our failure.

Ridding the tomato of its excess liquid was our goal. First we tested oven-drying, rationalizing that the slow, low heat would concentrate the tomato's sweetness and vaporize the water. The dried tomato was laden with rich flavor notes, but it was also shriveled and shrunken, a collapsed vessel that was in no condition to hold stuffing.

Recalling how salt is often used to rid vegetables of excess moisture, we cored and seeded a beefsteak tomato, rubbed salt into its interior, and placed it upside down on a stack of paper towels. Within 30 minutes, the paper towels had absorbed a tremendous amount of liquid. Besides draining the tomato of excess juice, the salt had the additional benefit of brightening and enhancing the tomato's flavor (especially important if you're working with supermarket tomatoes in January).

Now that we had the moisture problem under control, we moved on to the stuffing, baking times, and temperatures. We knew that two tomatoes made a good entrée-sized portion, but we needed a filling that would make enough for four tomatoes and could be easily prepared while the salted tomatoes drained. Bread crumbs are a common ingredient, but we found that even ultra-dry toasted bread crumbs tended to make a mushy stuffing, even when paired with our relatively dry tomatoes. We looked at other options, such as white rice, brown rice, and couscous. We liked couscous because it's quick and easy to cook in small amounts and we thought its pleasant, fluffy texture paired well with the other ingredients.

Lightly sautéing shallot (even a small onion added too much bulk) and garlic in olive oil made a good base for our filling. Next we added our zucchini, cut into ¼-inch pieces, to the mix. At this point, the filling was heading in the right direction—substantial and fresh-tasting—but we wanted more of a vegetable presence. Bell peppers and spinach got little more than a shrug from tasters, but cooking half a bulb of chopped fennel with the onion was a success.

After sautéing the vegetables, we added the couscous to the pan and toasted it until lightly browned (this step gives the couscous deeper flavor and ensures fluffy, distinct grains). Then we added some vegetable broth, brought it to a simmer, and let it sit off the heat until the couscous was tender, about five minutes.

Next we considered the cheese and nuts. We tried adding shredded mozzarella, but its flavor was too bland and its texture too stringy. Testing a few other cheeses, we liked the pairing of creamy goat cheese with the tangy saltiness of grated Parmesan. For the nuts, we sampled a variety of candidates in our filling, but settled on toasted, chopped walnuts, which contributed a nice meatiness and richness as well as a pleasant, lightly crunchy texture. Finally, we stirred in the basil, which brought an aromatic, herbal note.

Our previous oven-roasting tests ruled out a low and long baking period, but baking the tomatoes at an extremely high temperature (450 degrees) for a short time yielded burnt, crusty stuffing and raw tomatoes. With a more moderate approach—375 degrees for 20 minutes—the tomatoes were tender and topped with a lovely golden crust. The result: a sweet, savory, and filling stuffed tomato, a nice alternative to meaty main dishes any time of the year.

Stuffed Tomatoes with Goat Cheese and Zucchini
SERVES 2

Try to buy tomatoes with flat, sturdy bottoms so they will sit upright in the baking dish.

- **4** large tomatoes (8 ounces each)
- **Salt**
- **3** tablespoons extra-virgin olive oil
- **½** fennel bulb, trimmed of stalks, cored, and chopped fine (see page 18)
- **1** shallot, minced
- **1** small zucchini (about 6 ounces), cut into ¼-inch pieces (about 1½ cups)
- **2** garlic cloves, minced
- **¼** cup couscous
- **⅓** cup vegetable broth
- **1** ounce Parmesan cheese, grated (about ½ cup)
- **1** ounce goat cheese, crumbled (about ¼ cup)
- **¼** cup walnuts, toasted (see page 210) and chopped coarse
- **2** tablespoons chopped fresh basil
- **Pepper**

USE IT UP: FENNEL

Fennel, Olive, and Apricot Salad
SERVES 2

This salad makes a nice accompaniment to Pan-Roasted Halibut Steak with Chermoula (page 97).

- **½** fennel bulb, trimmed of stalks, cored, and sliced thin (see page 18)
- **2** tablespoons oil-cured black olives, pitted and sliced thin
- **2** tablespoons thinly sliced dried apricots
- **2** tablespoons minced fresh mint
- **1** tablespoon extra-virgin olive oil
- **2** teaspoons fresh lemon juice
- **Salt and pepper**

Combine the fennel, olives, apricots, and mint in a bowl. Whisk the oil and lemon juice together in a small bowl, pour over the fennel mixture, and toss to coat. Season with salt and pepper to taste and serve. (The salad can be refrigerated in an airtight container for up to 2 days.)

1. Following the photos, slice off ⅛ inch of the stem end of each tomato and remove the core and seeds. Sprinkle the inside of each tomato with ⅛ teaspoon salt. Place the tomatoes upside down on several layers of paper towels and let drain for 30 minutes.

2. Meanwhile, adjust an oven rack to the upper-middle position and heat the oven to 375 degrees. Heat 1 tablespoon of the oil in a medium saucepan over medium heat until shimmering. Add the fennel and shallot and cook until softened, 7 to 9 minutes. Add the zucchini and cook until tender, about 10 minutes. Stir in the garlic and cook until fragrant, about 30 seconds. Add the couscous and cook until lightly toasted, 1 to 2 minutes.

3. Stir in the broth and bring to a brief simmer, then remove from the heat, cover, and let the couscous steam for 5 minutes. Use a fork to gently stir in ¼ cup of the Parmesan, goat cheese, walnuts, and basil. Season with salt and pepper to taste.

4. Pat the inside of each tomato dry with paper towels. Line an 8-inch square baking dish with foil and spray with vegetable oil spray (or use nonstick foil). Brush the cut edges of the tomatoes with 2 teaspoons more oil. Mound about ½ cup of the couscous mixture in each tomato.

5. Arrange the tomatoes, cut-side up, in the prepared baking dish. Sprinkle the tops of the tomatoes evenly with the remaining ¼ cup Parmesan and drizzle with the remaining 4 teaspoons oil. Bake until the cheese is lightly browned and the tomatoes are tender, about 20 minutes. Serve.

SKILLET PIZZA

A CRISP, THIN, YET STURDY CRUST SIMPLY TOPPED with fresh tomato sauce and melted cheese is pizza at its finest. But making good thin-crust pizza at home requires a pizza stone (which in turn requires plenty of time to get good and hot in the oven), not to mention the agility to maneuver the dough onto the stone and the piping-hot pizza off it without burning fingers or arms. When you are cooking for two people, all this effort hardly seems worth it. We wanted to ditch the stone and come up with an easier, quicker way to make pizza in a home oven. We thought a skillet might help fill the role of a pizza stone. Our idea was to build the pizza in the skillet and give it a jump start with heat from the stovetop before transferring it to the oven.

First, we'd have to perfect the crust—we wanted a thin, crispy crust, not the thick, doughy crust of a pan pizza. We already had a handful of great pizza dough recipes in our library, but would any of these translate to a skillet? We started by halving our basic pizza dough recipe to yield 1 pound of dough (and one pizza). We then heated some oil in a skillet over medium-high heat, gently laid the pizza dough inside, and cooked it on the stovetop before piling on the toppings and baking it. The pizza looked perfect as it emerged from the oven, but once we cut into it, we could see that the crust was thick and gummy, not thin and crispy. Plus, dropping an 11-inch round of dough into a skillet full of hot oil was a bit challenging, to say the least.

We would need to test a slew of methods to get the dough right. First, we cut the dough recipe in

NOTES FROM THE TEST KITCHEN

PREPARING THE TOMATOES FOR STUFFING

1. Using a sharp knife, cut off the top ⅛ inch of the stem end of the tomato.

2. Using your fingers (or a paring knife), remove and discard the core and any seeds of the tomato.

3. Sprinkle the inside of the cored tomatoes with salt, then invert the tomatoes on paper towels to drain for 30 minutes before stuffing.

SKILLET PIZZA WITH RICOTTA, BACON, AND SCALLIONS

half again, making 8 ounces, so that we would have a thinner layer in the skillet. Also, we used bread flour instead of all-purpose flour to increase the chewiness in the finished crust (bread flour has a higher protein level and ensures strong gluten development). As for the cooking technique, we tried the simplest possible method—putting the dough into a cold skillet. We oiled a 12-inch skillet, transferred the dough to the pan, then set it over high heat until the crust turned brown. After three minutes, the crust was crisp with a chewy center. As for oven temperature, we knew that with pizza, the hotter, the better, so we cranked the oven up to 500 degrees.

NOTES FROM THE TEST KITCHEN

STORE-BOUGHT PIZZA DOUGH

The dough is probably the trickiest part of making pizza at home. While pizza dough is nothing more than bread dough with oil added for softness and suppleness, we have found that minor changes can yield dramatically different results. We think homemade dough is worth the modest effort, but we have to admit prepared dough can be a great time-saving option for a pizza night for two. Many supermarkets and pizzerias sell their dough for just a few dollars a pound, and the dough can be easily frozen. We found that store-bought dough, dough from a local pizzeria, and refrigerated pop-up canisters of pizza dough (such as Pillsbury) all worked well and tasted fine, but we recommend buying dough from a pizzeria where it is more likely to be fresh. Supermarket pizza dough is frequently unlabeled, so there's no way to know if the dough has been sitting in the refrigerated case for a long time, or how much dough is in the bag. Note that while most supermarket dough is sold in 1-pound bags, you will need only 8 ounces of dough for our pizza recipes.

THE BEST PIZZA CUTTER

A shoddy pizza cutter drags melted cheese out of place and fails to cut through crisp crust cleanly. A good pizza cutter gets the job done quickly, neatly, and safely (and also makes an excellent tool for trimming the edges of rolled-out pastry dough).

The basic wheel cutter is the most common variety, and we tested six of them—and ate our way through lots of pizzas—to find the best one. For its overall comfort, extreme sharpness, and helpful heft, we liked the **Italian Kitchen by Mario Batali Pizza Wheel**, $15.95. This extremely sharp stainless steel wheel kept cheese and toppings where they belonged. It has a comfortable soft-grip handle and large metal guard, which protects fingers from the blade.

The crust was ready for toppings, but we weren't sure when to add them. Should they go on just before the pizza went into the oven or before the dough was cooked on the stovetop? We tested both methods and found no difference between the two pizzas. For simplicity's sake, we decided to top the pizza before placing the skillet on the stovetop.

For the sauce, we determined that we needed about ½ cup for one pizza. Cooking such a small quantity of sauce seemed silly, so we gave no-cook pizza sauce a try, combining canned diced tomatoes, olive oil, garlic, and salt in the food processor. Tasters were happy with this fresh-flavored sauce. For the cheese, we used 1 cup of traditional shredded mozzarella along with 2 tablespoons of freshly grated Parmesan for a nice saltiness.

For those nights when we want something more festive than cheese pizza, we came up with a few variations. In our first one, we replaced the mozzarella with fontina cheese, then topped the fully cooked pizzas with arugula and prosciutto, which added nice textural and heat-level variations. For a vegetarian option, we made a pizza with goat cheese, olives, and spicy garlic oil. Saving the best for last, we created a pizza with ricotta, bacon, and scallions—tasters couldn't get enough of this addictive combination. For even more variety, we've included a whole wheat spin on our basic pizza dough.

Skillet Cheese Pizza
SERVES 2

We like to use our Basic Pizza Dough (page 103) and No-Cook Pizza Sauce (page 104) here; however, you can substitute premade pizza dough or sauce (or both) from the supermarket. Feel free to sprinkle simple toppings over the pizza before baking, such as pepperoni, sautéed mushrooms, or browned sausage, but keep the toppings light or they may weigh down the thin crust and make it soggy.

- 2 **tablespoons olive oil**
- 8 **ounces pizza dough (see note)**
- ½ **cup pizza sauce (see note)**
- 4 **ounces mozzarella cheese, shredded (about 1 cup)**
- 2 **tablespoons grated Parmesan cheese**

1. Adjust an oven rack to the upper-middle position and heat the oven to 500 degrees. Grease a 12-inch ovensafe skillet with the oil.

2. Turn the dough out onto a lightly floured counter and press and roll the dough into an 11-inch round. Transfer the dough to the prepared skillet.

3. Spread the pizza sauce over the dough, leaving a ½-inch border around the edge. Sprinkle the mozzarella and Parmesan over the top. Set the skillet over high heat and cook until the outside edge of the dough is set, the pizza is lightly puffed, and the bottom crust is spotty brown when gently lifted with a spatula, about 3 minutes.

4. Transfer the pizza to the oven and bake until the edges are brown and the cheese is golden in spots, 7 to 10 minutes. Using potholders (the skillet handle will be hot), transfer the pizza to a cutting board, slice into wedges, and serve.

VARIATIONS

Skillet Pizza with Fontina, Arugula, and Prosciutto

Toss 1 cup baby arugula with 2 teaspoons extra-virgin olive oil and salt and pepper to taste in a bowl. Follow the recipe for Skillet Cheese Pizza, omitting the Parmesan and substituting 1 cup shredded fontina cheese for the mozzarella. Immediately after baking, sprinkle 8 thin slices prosciutto (about 2 ounces), cut into ½-inch strips, and the dressed arugula over the top of the pizza before serving.

Skillet Pizza with Goat Cheese, Olives, and Spicy Garlic Oil

If your olives are particularly salty, be sure to rinse them.

Follow the recipe for Skillet Cheese Pizza, omitting the Parmesan. Mix 1 tablespoon olive oil, 1 minced small garlic clove, and ⅛ teaspoon red pepper flakes together in a small bowl. Brush the garlic-oil mixture over the top of the pizza before adding the sauce in step 3. Reduce the amount of shredded mozzarella to ¼ cup and sprinkle ½ cup crumbled goat cheese and ¼ cup pitted and halved kalamata olives on top of the mozzarella before baking.

Skillet Pizza with Ricotta, Bacon, and Scallions

See page 45 for a recipe to use up some of the leftover ricotta cheese.

Cook 2 slices bacon, cut into ¼-inch pieces, in an 8-inch skillet over medium heat until browned and most of the fat has rendered, about 7 minutes; transfer to a paper towel–lined plate. Mix ½ cup whole milk ricotta cheese, 1 thinly sliced scallion, ⅛ teaspoon salt, and a pinch of pepper together. Follow the recipe for Skillet Cheese Pizza, omitting the Parmesan. Reduce the amount of shredded mozzarella to ¼ cup. Dollop the ricotta mixture, 1 tablespoon at a time, on top of the mozzarella, then sprinkle with the bacon. Sprinkle the pizza with 1 more sliced scallion before serving.

Basic Pizza Dough
MAKES ½ POUND DOUGH

All-purpose flour can be substituted for the bread flour, but the resulting crust will be a little less chewy. If desired, you can slow down the dough's rising time by letting it rise in the refrigerator for 8 to 16 hours in step 2; let the refrigerated dough soften at room temperature for 30 minutes before using.

- 1 **cup (5½ ounces) bread flour,**
  plus extra as needed (see note)
- ¾ **teaspoon instant or rapid-rise yeast**
- ½ **teaspoon salt**
- 1½ **teaspoons olive oil, plus extra for the bowl**
- 7 **tablespoons warm water**

1. Pulse the flour, yeast, and salt together in a food processor (fitted with a dough blade if possible) to combine. With the processor running, slowly pour the oil, then water, through the feed tube and process until the dough forms a sticky ball that clears the side of the bowl, 1½ to 2 minutes. (If, after 1 minute, the dough is sticky and clings to the blade, add extra flour, 1 tablespoon at a time, as needed until it clears the side of the bowl.)

2. Turn out the dough onto a lightly floured counter and form it into a smooth, round ball. Place the dough in a lightly oiled bowl and cover tightly with greased plastic wrap. Let rise in a warm place until doubled in size, 1 to 1½ hours. (Once risen, the dough can be sealed in a zipper-lock bag and frozen for up to 1 month; let thaw on the counter for 2 to 3 hours, or overnight in the refrigerator, before using.)

VARIATION

Whole Wheat Pizza Dough

Follow the recipe for Basic Pizza Dough, substituting ½ cup whole wheat flour for ½ cup of the bread flour.

No-Cook Pizza Sauce

MAKES ½ CUP

See page 15 for a recipe to use up the leftover canned diced tomatoes.

- ½ cup drained canned diced tomatoes, juice reserved
- 2 teaspoons extra-virgin olive oil
- 1 small garlic clove, minced
- ⅛ teaspoon salt

Pulse the drained tomatoes, oil, garlic, and salt together in a food processor until coarsely ground and no large pieces remain, about 12 pulses. Transfer the mixture to a liquid measuring cup and add the reserved canned tomato juice until the sauce measures ½ cup.

STROMBOLI

WITH A CRUNCHY AND GOLDEN BROWN EXTERIOR and flavorful layered meat and cheese filling, stromboli, a close cousin to the calzone, pairs well with salad for a casual change-of-pace dinner. Stromboli often relies on a sturdy filling of deli meats and cheeses. We wanted a streamlined recipe that had flavorful fillings, crispy crust, and a properly cooked interior that was neither soggy nor gummy. And we wanted to cut our stromboli down to size—most recipes yield enough to feed at least four.

The first step was the dough. We had already developed a scaled-down dough recipe for Skillet Cheese Pizza (page 103), which was also perfect for stromboli. Though our basic pizza dough is easy to make, we know that premade pizza dough (readily available in most grocery stores and some pizzerias) can be a real time-saver on a busy weeknight, so we leave the decision of whether to make your own dough or purchase it up to you.

In our recipe search we were constantly reminded that a stromboli is a "rolled sandwich," so it seemed natural to include a variety of deli meats and cheese—which had the added benefit of streamlined prep, since our filling wouldn't need to be cooked beforehand. We settled on a combination of salami, capocollo, and provolone cheese. Two ounces of each produced a balanced filling-to-crust ratio and was a good portion for two. To boost the flavor of the meats and cheese, we included jarred roasted red peppers. To avoid any potential problems with these liquid-packed peppers, we thoroughly dried them with paper towels before slicing and adding them to the filling.

We next focused on developing some interesting flavor variations. First we tried pesto, but it was too oily; then we tried just fresh basil on its own, but the herb turned army green and lifeless after its stint in the oven. Chopped sun-dried tomatoes were up next, but their strong flavor overpowered the stromboli's other ingredients. It seemed as though the more we complicated the filling, the less successful we were. Returning to the "rolled sandwich" concept, we decided to take a simple flavor combination and use it in an unexpected way. A stromboli layered with ham and cheddar cheese, spread with mustard and dotted with slivers of pickle, surprised tasters and got a big thumbs-up.

NOTES FROM THE TEST KITCHEN

MAKING STROMBOLI

1. After rolling out the dough, arrange the meat and provolone over the dough, leaving a ¾-inch border along all of the edges. Top with the roasted peppers and Parmesan, then brush the edges with water.

2. Starting from a long side, roll the dough tightly into a long cylinder.

3. Pinch the seam and the ends of the dough to seal them securely. Transfer the stromboli, seam-side down, to an oiled baking sheet.

Switching gears now to the actual baking, we started at 450 degrees. We assumed that a high temperature would be the key to a crispy crust. The crust certainly got crispy, but the inside remained undercooked and doughy.

We next decided to reduce the oven temperature to 400 degrees and cover the stromboli with aluminum foil for the first half of the baking. This gave the interior a sufficient head start, and after 15 minutes we removed the foil to allow for proper browning on the outside. After pulling the stromboli from the oven, we allowed it to cool for at least five minutes before slicing. This allowed the cheese enough time to set up and kept it from oozing out when sliced. Tasters could hardly keep their hands off the slices as we served our stromboli in the kitchen—a good indication of how well this recipe will fit into your repertoire.

Salami, Capocollo, and Provolone Stromboli

SERVES 2

We like to use our Basic Pizza Dough (page 103) here; however, you can substitute premade pizza dough from the supermarket or a pizzeria. If desired, serve with our No-Cook Pizza Sauce (page 104), warmed, for dipping, or premade sauce from the supermarket.

  Vegetable oil
8 ounces pizza dough (see note)
2 ounces thinly sliced deli salami
2 ounces thinly sliced deli capocollo
2 ounces thinly sliced deli provolone cheese
2 ounces jarred roasted red peppers, drained, patted dry, and sliced thin (about ¼ cup)
¼ cup grated Parmesan cheese
1 large egg, lightly beaten
1 teaspoon sesame seeds
  Kosher salt (optional)

1. Adjust an oven rack to the middle position and heat the oven to 400 degrees. Brush a rimmed baking sheet lightly with oil. On a lightly floured counter, roll the dough into a 10 by 7½-inch rectangle, about ¼ inch thick. Place the meat and provolone slices over the dough, leaving a ¾-inch border along the edges. Top with the roasted peppers and Parmesan.

2. Brush the edges of the dough with water. Following the photos on page 104, and starting from a long side, roll the dough tightly into a long cylinder, pressing the edges to seal. Transfer the stromboli to the prepared baking sheet, seam-side down. Brush the egg over the top and sprinkle with the sesame seeds and kosher salt (if using).

3. Cover the stromboli lightly with foil that has been sprayed with vegetable oil spray (or use nonstick foil) and bake for 15 minutes. Remove the foil and continue to bake until the crust is golden, about 20 minutes longer. Transfer the stromboli to a wire rack and let cool for 5 minutes. Transfer to a cutting board and slice into 2-inch pieces. Serve.

VARIATION

Ham and Cheddar Stromboli
Swiss cheese also works well here.

Follow the recipe for Salami, Capocollo, and Provolone Stromboli, substituting 4 ounces thinly sliced deli ham for the salami and capocollo and 2 ounces thinly sliced deli cheddar cheese for the provolone. Before layering the cheese in step 1, spread 1 tablespoon yellow mustard evenly across the ham. Substitute 1 small dill pickle, cut into matchsticks and patted dry (about ¼ cup), for the roasted red peppers. Omit the Parmesan.

FILET MIGNON WITH PAN-SEARED ASPARAGUS AND GARLIC-HERB BUTTER

FILETS MIGNONS WITH PAN-SEARED ASPARAGUS

WHEN IT COMES TO PERFECTLY COOKED STEAK, Americans prize tenderness above all—and filet mignon is the most tender steak there is. But the mildly flavored filet mignon is also expensive, giving it a reputation as a grand, celebratory restaurant meal. We felt there was no reason to limit the decadence to restaurants. After all, filets are available in any supermarket, and when you're buying only two, they are not prohibitively expensive. We wanted to replicate the best restaurant filets in our own kitchen, which meant developing a deeply browned, rich crust on the steak's outside without overcooking the interior. We also wanted to pair our perfect filets with a classic steakhouse offering, asparagus, for a four-star meal at home.

Pan-searing over intense heat is typically the method of choice for cooking steak indoors, especially mild filet, because it develops a deep brown, caramelized crust on the meat. However, in our tests we found that by the time our steaks had developed a crust and reached medium-rare, the browned bits left in the pan after the steaks were cooked were often scorched, essentially ruining the pan for the asparagus. Attempting to avoid scorching the pan, we then tried lowering the temperature throughout the cooking process, but this only produced inferior crusts on the steaks.

Next we tried pan-roasting, which involves searing the steaks in a hot pan to achieve a crust, then transferring them—pan and all—to the oven to finish cooking. This method worked great, producing steaks with a beautiful crust and no scorched pan in sight. To avoid dirtying multiple skillets, we decided to transfer the steaks to a baking sheet so we could use our skillet to cook the asparagus. By preheating the baking sheet in the oven while the steaks seared in the skillet, we could achieve the same results as we had when using the skillet in the oven. Now we could start our asparagus.

We melted a tablespoon of butter in our now-empty skillet, then added the asparagus and waited for evenly cooked, crisp-tender stalks and lightly browned tips. That moment never came. The asparagus cooked unevenly; some stalks became soggy and army green and others remained practically raw. The only plus was that the nicely browned bits left behind from the steaks flavored the asparagus. But something was wrong with our technique. We needed to reevaluate.

In order for all the asparagus to cook at the same rate (and we found that one bunch was the right amount for two people), the heat would have to be evenly distributed among the spears. This meant putting a lid on the skillet, at least for part of the cooking time. Letting the asparagus steam for too long resulted in limp spears, but covering the asparagus at the onset of cooking allowed it to steam and just start to become tender. Five minutes was all it took. Then we uncovered the asparagus and continued to cook until we had achieved sufficient browning, about five minutes longer. And to ensure that all the asparagus fit evenly in the pan—we wanted each spear to come in contact with the hot pan—we pointed half the spears in one direction and half in the other.

In many steakhouses, filet mignon is often served with a compound butter—a simple combination of whipped butter and aromatics that forms a sauce for the steak as it melts. We thought this would be the perfect finishing touch to our dish and decided on garlic and herbs as our flavorings. We blended some softened butter with minced fresh tarragon and parsley, minced garlic, and a touch of salt and pepper. Placed on the steaks, the flavorful butter was the perfect finish to our steakhouse-at-home dinner.

Filets Mignons with Pan-Seared Asparagus and Garlic-Herb Butter
SERVES 2

We prefer these steaks cooked to medium-rare, but if you prefer them more or less done, see our guidelines in "Testing Meat for Doneness" on page 109. Thick asparagus (about ½ inch thick at the base) works best in this recipe; however, medium asparagus will also work. Do not use pencil-thin asparagus because it cannot withstand the heat and will overcook.

- 3 tablespoons unsalted butter, softened
- 2 teaspoons minced fresh tarragon
- 2 teaspoons minced fresh parsley
- 1 garlic clove, minced
  Salt and pepper
- 2 (7- to 8-ounce) center-cut beef tenderloin steaks, about 1½ inches thick
- 2 teaspoons vegetable oil
- 1 bunch thick asparagus (about 1 pound), tough ends trimmed (see note)

1. Adjust an oven rack to the lower-middle position, place a rimmed baking sheet on the rack, and heat the oven to 425 degrees. Mash 2 tablespoons of the butter, tarragon, parsley, garlic, ⅛ teaspoon salt, and ⅛ teaspoon pepper together in a bowl; set aside for serving.

2. Pat the steaks dry with paper towels and season with salt and pepper. Heat the oil in a 10-inch skillet over medium-high heat until just smoking. Carefully lay the steaks in the skillet and brown well on both sides, about 6 minutes, flipping them halfway through.

3. Transfer the steaks to the hot baking sheet and roast until the steaks register 125 degrees on an instant-read thermometer (for medium-rare), 10 to 15 minutes. Transfer the steaks to a plate, tent loosely with foil, and let rest for 5 minutes.

4. Meanwhile, add the remaining 1 tablespoon butter to the skillet and melt over medium heat. Add half of the asparagus to the skillet with the tips pointed in one direction and the other half with the tips pointed in the opposite direction. Cover and cook until the asparagus is bright green and still crisp, 3 to 5 minutes.

5. Uncover the asparagus and season with salt and pepper to taste. Increase the heat to medium-high and continue to cook, using tongs to occasionally move the asparagus around, until the spears are tender and well browned, 3 to 7 minutes. Transfer to a platter.

6. Spoon the garlic-herb butter over each steak and serve with the asparagus.

HERB-CRUSTED BEEF TENDERLOIN

THOUGH IT IS MILD IN FLAVOR, NOTHING BEATS THE extravagantly buttery texture of beef tenderloin. But this tender cut of meat has an extravagant price tag to match, which means that preparing a whole roast for a crowd is an expensive proposition. However, a small tenderloin roast (a center cut of the larger beef tenderloin) is just the right size for two people, so we thought it would make the perfect centerpiece for a scaled-down special-occasion meal.

The main challenge of this cut lies in expertly cooking the meat—typically the roast either emerges from the oven without the dark, caramelized crust that gives meat a deep roasted flavor or is marred by a thick gray band of overdone meat near the edge. Considering its steep price, overcooking this special-occasion roast is not an option.

To achieve a good crust on the meat, we could either sear it first in a skillet or simply crank up the oven as high as it would go, at the beginning or end of cooking. A few tests ruled out oven-searing. No matter what we tried—starting out high and dropping down much lower, or the reverse—the meat would not brown adequately. And worse still, by the time our small roast had developed any amount of browning on the exterior, it was overcooked all the way through.

Pan-searing it would have to be. We heated a couple of teaspoons of vegetable oil over medium-high heat in a skillet and then added our roast, browning it on all sides before transferring it to the oven. We placed it on a wire rack set inside a rimmed baking sheet to promote air circulation and more even cooking. After just half an hour in a 400-degree oven, our roast emerged with a well-browned exterior and a perfect rosy, medium-rare interior.

Our tenderloin was now perfectly cooked, but tasters thought this mild cut would benefit from an additional layer of flavor. An herb paste seemed like a simple yet elegant solution. After testing several combinations of herbs, we found that tasters preferred a blend of fresh parsley and thyme; other herbs such as sage and rosemary overpowered the delicate tenderloin, and dry herbs came out of the hot oven tasting dusty and stale. Some minced garlic and a little Parmesan provided another boost of flavor to the herb paste.

Pulsing the ingredients in a food processor with a little oil works great when creating thick pastes for larger cuts of meat, but our small roast had less surface area to cover, and we were having trouble processing the smaller amounts of ingredients. After some trial and error, we found a creative way to make a thick paste without the need for a food processor: We used mayonnaise. Mixed with the herbs, garlic, and Parmesan, the mayonnaise took the place of the oil and helped bind the mixture together to form a spreadable paste.

We spread our paste evenly over the roast before placing it in the oven and sprinkled some bread crumbs on top for a finishing touch. Our topping turned crisp and golden in the oven just as the tenderloin came up to temperature. With three distinct crusts on this premium roast—the pan-seared exterior, the herb paste coating, and the bread crumb crown—we had an entrée that was special enough for any occasion.

Herb-Crusted Beef Tenderloin
SERVES 2

We prefer this roast cooked to medium-rare, but if you prefer your meat more or less done, see our guidelines in "Testing Meat for Doneness" on page 109.

- 1 (1-pound) center-cut beef tenderloin roast, trimmed
  Salt and pepper
- 1 slice high-quality white sandwich bread, torn into pieces
- 3 tablespoons minced fresh parsley
- 1½ teaspoons minced fresh thyme
- ¼ cup grated Parmesan cheese
- 1 tablespoon olive oil
- 3 tablespoons mayonnaise
- 1 garlic clove, minced

1. Adjust an oven rack to the middle position and heat the oven to 400 degrees. Set a wire rack inside a foil-lined rimmed baking sheet. Pat the roast dry with paper towels and season with salt and pepper.

2. Pulse the bread in a food processor to fine crumbs, about 12 pulses. Transfer the bread crumbs to a bowl and toss with 1 tablespoon of the parsley, ½ teaspoon of the thyme, 1 tablespoon of the Parmesan, and 1 teaspoon of the oil. In a separate bowl, combine the mayonnaise, garlic, remaining 2 tablespoons parsley, remaining 1 teaspoon thyme, and remaining 3 tablespoons Parmesan.

NOTES FROM THE TEST KITCHEN

PREPARING HERB-CRUSTED BEEF TENDERLOIN

1. Using a spatula, spread the herb paste evenly over the top and sides of the tenderloin.

2. Press the bread crumb mixture evenly onto the roast with one hand, using the other hand to catch the crumbs and keep them from falling through the rack.

3. Heat the remaining 2 teaspoons oil in a 10-inch skillet over medium-high heat until just smoking. Carefully lay the roast in the skillet and brown lightly on all sides, 4 to 6 minutes.

4. Transfer the roast to the prepared wire rack and, following the photos on page 110, coat with the herb paste, then the bread crumb topping. Roast until the topping is golden and the roast registers 125 degrees on an instant-read thermometer (for medium-rare), 25 to 30 minutes. (If the topping browns before the meat is done, lightly cover with foil; remove the foil when resting the meat.)

5. Transfer the roast to a carving board and let rest for 15 minutes. Slice the roast into ½-inch-thick pieces and serve.

OSSO BUCO

OSSO BUCO, ITALIAN-STYLE BRAISED VEAL, IS AN elegant yet homey dish. The ingredients are simple: veal shanks (which are browned), aromatics (onions, carrots, and celery, all sautéed), and liquids (a blend of wine, broth, and tomatoes). The resulting dish should be rich in flavor and color and somewhat brothy but not stewy. We thought osso buco would make a refined meal for two; the challenge would lie in scaling back the ingredients of the braising liquid. We also hoped to shave some time off the preparation of this dish. Braises are slow-cooking by nature, but we hoped to make ours a recipe that wouldn't require an entire Sunday spent in the kitchen.

Researching several recipes, we found that settling on the type of cut was easy—almost all of them called for shanks from the upper portion of the hind leg, cut into pieces between 1 and 1½ inches thick. Purchasing them, however, was a different story. Because veal shanks can vary greatly in thickness and weight, we found it essential to shop carefully. Buying individual (rather than packaged) veal shanks allowed us to inspect them closely.

Preparing the meat for braising was the next challenge. Most recipes instruct you to tie the shanks before searing them to maintain their shape. We found that tying a piece of butcher's twine around each shank was unnecessary for our scaled-down braise for two, as the veal shanks fit snugly next to each other in a medium

saucepan (downsized from the traditional Dutch oven), preventing them from falling apart while cooking.

After searing the shanks right in the saucepan until a thick, golden brown crust formed, we removed them from the pan and began building the braising liquid. Traditionally, the braising liquid for osso buco begins with homemade stock, to which wine and tomatoes are added. To keep our recipe as streamlined as possible, we decided to see if store-bought chicken broth could be a reasonable substitute for the homemade stock. Indeed it was, and after testing several batches, we settled on ¾ cup as the proper amount for our small braise. To enrich the flavor of the broth, we added some onion, carrot, and celery, along with a little garlic. We also found adding a bit of flour at this point helped thicken the braising liquid to a sauce-like consistency.

Many recipes recommend a generous amount of wine—often more than the broth itself—but we found if we were not careful, the wine could quickly overpower the other flavors with its acidity. Equal amounts of broth and dry white wine provided the best balance of flavor.

Likewise, it was essential to use a light hand with the tomatoes. Diced tomatoes watered down the braising liquid, so we used tomato paste, which was easily incorporated into the dish and added rich but subtle flavor.

We still needed to determine the ideal braising time. Several sources suggested cooking the veal shanks until the meat was falling off the bone. Tasters loved the flavor of veal cooked this way, but we were after a more elegant presentation. We cooked the meat just until it was tender but still clinging to the bone. We found that two hours in a 325-degree oven produced veal that was meltingly soft but not falling apart. At this point, tasters were divided as to whether we should strain the braising liquid or leave the aromatics in the finished dish. In the end we decided a strained sauce made for a more refined osso buco.

Just before serving, osso buco is typically sprinkled with gremolata, a mixture of parsley, minced garlic, and lemon zest. In some recipes the gremolata is used as a garnish, and in others it is added to the braising liquid just before serving. We chose a compromise approach, stirring half of the gremolata into the pot so that the flavors permeated the dish, then sprinkling the remaining gremolata on individual servings for a hit of freshness.

SERVES 2

The zest in the gremolata should be fairly coarse; we like to use a vegetable peeler or paring knife to remove the zest from the lemon (without the bitter white pith), then mince it with a chef's knife. See page 10 for a recipe to use up the leftover celery.

GREMOLATA

- 2 tablespoons minced fresh parsley
- 1 garlic clove, minced
- ½ teaspoon minced lemon zest (see note)

OSSO BUCO

- 2 (8- to 10-ounce) veal shanks, about 1½ inches thick
- Salt and pepper
- 2 tablespoons vegetable oil
- ¾ cup dry white wine
- 1 small onion, minced
- 1 carrot, peeled and chopped fine
- 1 celery rib, minced
- 1 tablespoon tomato paste
- 2 garlic cloves, minced
- 2 teaspoons unbleached all-purpose flour
- ¾ cup low-sodium chicken broth
- 1 bay leaf

1. FOR THE GREMOLATA: Combine all of the ingredients in a small bowl and set aside.

2. FOR THE OSSO BUCO: Adjust an oven rack to the lower-middle position and heat the oven to 325 degrees. Pat the veal shanks dry with paper towels and season with salt and pepper.

3. Heat 1 tablespoon of the oil in a medium ovensafe saucepan over medium-high heat until shimmering. Brown the shanks well on all sides, about 10 minutes.

4. Transfer the shanks to a bowl. Off the heat, add ¼ cup of the wine to the saucepan, scraping up any browned bits, then pour into the bowl with the browned shanks.

5. Add the remaining 1 tablespoon oil to the saucepan and heat over medium heat until shimmering. Add the onion, carrot, and celery, and cook until the vegetables are softened and well browned, about 10 minutes. Stir in the tomato paste and garlic and cook until fragrant, about 30 seconds. Stir in the flour and cook for 30 seconds.

6. Whisk in the broth, remaining ½ cup wine, and bay leaf. Return the browned shanks to the pan, along with any accumulated juice and wine mixture, and bring to a simmer. Cover the pan, transfer to the oven, and cook until the meat is easily pierced with a fork but is not falling off the bone, about 2 hours.

7. Using potholders (the pan handle will be hot), remove the saucepan from the oven. Transfer the shanks to a plate and tent loosely with foil to keep warm. Strain the braising liquid through a fine-mesh strainer, discarding the solids. Return the braising liquid to the pan and simmer over medium heat until thickened and reduced to 1 cup, about 6 minutes.

8. Off the heat, stir in half of the gremolata and season the sauce with salt and pepper to taste. Place the veal shanks in individual bowls, ladle the braising liquid over the top, sprinkle with the remaining gremolata, and serve.

PAN-ROASTED LAMB CHOPS WITH MINT RELISH

THE WORD "MOUTHWATERING" MUST HAVE BEEN coined to describe lamb chops—the meat is ultra-tender and incomparably luscious. But like other premium cuts of meat, lamb can get expensive (even for just two people)—and there is nothing worse than investing in expensive meat, only to find you've improperly cooked it. The best lamb chops feature an intensely browned, crisp exterior, and rich, tender interior. We set out to determine the ideal cooking method for this cut of meat.

To achieve the proper exterior caramelization, we figured we could try cooking our lamb chops in one of two ways: pan-searing them entirely on the stovetop until they reached the proper internal temperature, or pan-roasting them by first browning the chops on the stovetop, then moving them to the oven to finish cooking. Pan-searing the chops on the stovetop in both instances created a crisp, brown exterior. But the chops that were cooked entirely on the stovetop quickly over-browned and developed a bitter crust before reaching the desired internal temperature; by contrast, the chops finished in the oven maintained their nice exterior and cooked to the perfect doneness.

With pan-roasting our method of choice, we needed to address oven temperature. We tried roasting the meat at temperatures as low as 200 degrees and all the way up to a blazing-hot 500 degrees. The slow-roast approach of the low oven temperature was a bust; the meat had a strange, murky taste and mushy texture. Meanwhile, at the high end of the spectrum the flavor was better but the margin of error was too small—these chops went from perfectly cooked to charred in the blink of an eye. In the end, a moderate temperature of 425 degrees proved best; the chops cooked in a reasonable amount of time and had no trace of the flavor or textural problems we had with the slow-cooked chops.

Satisfied with our roasting technique, we were ready to work on a sauce. We wanted a quick sauce that we could prepare ahead of time so it would be ready as soon as the lamb was done. Mint is a classic pairing with lamb, but we were after something more interesting than just a ho-hum mint jelly. Inspired by the parsley and garlic–based sauces we often put on grilled meats, we decided to incorporate those flavors into a mint relish. After experimenting with substituting different quantities of mint for some of the parsley, we settled on a 50–50 combination of the two herbs. Adding some minced garlic and shallot gave the sauce just the right amount of bite. Extra-virgin olive oil was favored over both regular olive oil and vegetable oil, since it stood up best to the boldness of the other ingredients. For the acid, we opted for red wine vinegar, which was smooth but not overshadowed by the other ingredients. As a final touch, a couple of teaspoons of honey kept things balanced. After 15 minutes, the flavors of the sauce had melded into a bold but balanced whole—an ideal match for our perfectly cooked lamb.

NOTES FROM THE TEST KITCHEN

BUYING LAMB

Shoppers typically have two choices when buying lamb: domestic meat or imported meat from Australia or New Zealand. Domestic lamb is distinguished by its larger size and milder flavor, while imported lamb features a far gamier taste. The reason for this difference boils down to diet—and the chemistry of lamb fat. Imported lamb is pasture-fed on mixed grasses, while lamb raised in the U.S. begins on a diet of grass but finish with grain, a switch that reduces the concentration of the fatty-acid chains that give any lamb its characteristic "lamb-y" flavor—and ultimately leading to sweeter-tasting meat. We prefer the milder taste of domestic lamb chops, but if you like strong-flavored lamb, choose imported.

Pan-Roasted Lamb Chops with Mint Relish
SERVES 2

We prefer the milder taste and bigger size of domestic lamb chops. If using lamb from New Zealand or Australia, the chops will probably be much smaller and cook more quickly. We prefer these lamb chops cooked to medium-rare, but if you prefer them more or less done, see our guidelines in "Testing Meat for Doneness" on page 109.

MINT RELISH
- 2 tablespoons extra-virgin olive oil
- 1 tablespoon minced fresh parsley
- 1 tablespoon minced fresh mint
- 1 small shallot, minced
- 2 teaspoons red wine vinegar
- 2 teaspoons honey
- 1 garlic clove, minced
- Salt and pepper

LAMB
- 4 (6- to 8-ounce) lamb loin chops, about 1½ inches thick (see note)
- Salt and pepper
- 2 teaspoons vegetable oil

1. FOR THE MINT RELISH: Combine the oil, parsley, mint, shallot, vinegar, honey, and garlic in a bowl, and season with salt and pepper to taste. Let stand at room temperature to allow the flavors to meld.

2. FOR THE LAMB: Adjust an oven rack to the middle position and heat the oven to 425 degrees. Pat the lamb chops dry with paper towels and season with salt and pepper.

3. Heat the oil in a 10-inch ovensafe skillet over medium-high heat until just smoking. Carefully lay the chops in the skillet and brown well on both sides, about 6 minutes, flipping them halfway through.

4. Transfer the skillet to the oven and roast until the chops register 125 degrees on an instant-read thermometer (for medium-rare), 6 to 8 minutes. Transfer the lamb chops to a plate, tent loosely with foil, and let rest for 5 minutes. Serve the lamb with the mint relish spooned over the top.

CHICKEN SALTIMBOCCA

CHICKEN SALTIMBOCCA

CHICKEN SALTIMBOCCA HAS LONG BEEN A STANDARD menu item in the trattorias of Italy as well as in fine Italian restaurants in this country. Made by sautéing chicken cutlets with prosciutto and sage, this simple but elegant dish is sure to impress with its distinctive blend of flavors. Yet many saltimbocca dishes we've seen hardly do that, with unnecessary elements, like stuffing or breading, or proportions that are way off, allowing a thick slab of prosciutto to outshine the chicken and knock the balance of flavors out of whack. Saltimbocca seemed like a perfect candidate for a makeover—especially since four chicken cutlets could easily fit in a large skillet and serve two for dinner. We intended to keep the dish simple, while still giving the chicken, prosciutto, and sage their due.

Most of the chicken saltimbocca recipes we came across followed the traditional practice of threading a toothpick through the prosciutto and a whole sage leaf to attach them to the cutlet, then dredging the entire package in flour before sautéing it on both sides. When we started cooking, we had a few problems with this method. Flour got trapped in the small gaps where the prosciutto bunched up around the toothpick, leaving sticky, uncooked spots. When we tried sautéing the chicken and prosciutto without any coating of flour, the prosciutto crisped nicely, but the chicken browned unevenly and stuck to the pan. Surprisingly, flouring only the cutlet before attaching the prosciutto proved to be the solution. And by sautéing the cutlet prosciutto-side down first, we were able to keep the flour under the prosciutto from turning gummy. Using a 12-inch skillet was key here, as it allowed all four cutlets plenty of room to brown properly.

With our flouring method under control, it was time to look at the prosciutto. High-quality prosciutto added rich flavor to the overall dish, but we needed to figure out the right slice thickness. If the prosciutto was too thick, it had trouble staying put and its flavor was overwhelming; if it was too thin, it fell apart easily. The ideal slice was just thick enough to hold its shape—about the thickness of two or three sheets of paper. Then we could trim the prosciutto to the size of the cutlet to make it fit.

While the prosciutto needed to be tamed, the sage flavor needed a boost. In the traditional dish, each cutlet features a single sage leaf—fried in oil before being attached—so that the herbal flavor imparted is very subtle. Tethering a leaf to the cutlet with a toothpick, however, was cumbersome and resulted in adding flavor only to bites that actually contained sage. We wanted a more even distribution of flavor. To infuse the cooking oil with sage, we tossed a handful of leaves into the oil before sautéing the cutlets, removing the herbs before they burned. Tasters, however, detected only a very slight flavor boost in the finished dish. The way to more intense and evenly distributed sage flavor turned out to be as simple as mincing the leaves and sprinkling them over the floured cutlet before adding the ham. The only thing missing was the attractive presentation of the fried sage leaf. While not necessary, frying just four sage leaves to place on the cooked cutlets is easy enough and adds an elegant finishing touch.

The only aspect of the dish we had not yet examined was the toothpick. After skewering prosciutto to more than 50 cutlets in the course of our testing, we decided enough was enough. What would happen if we just dropped the toothpick altogether? After flouring the cutlet, sprinkling it with sage, and placing the prosciutto on top, we carefully lifted the bundle and placed it as we had been doing, prosciutto-side down, in the hot oil. Once the edges of the chicken had browned, we flipped the cutlet, revealing prosciutto that seemed almost hermetically sealed to the chicken—no toothpick needed.

A quick pan sauce made from vermouth, lemon juice, butter, and parsley was all we needed to accentuate

---

NOTES FROM THE TEST KITCHEN

THE IMPORTANCE OF MISE EN PLACE

Before beginning any recipe, we always make sure to have each ingredient prepared and measured into its own bowl. This practice has a fancy French name—*mise en place*, which means "put in place"—but the concept is really quite simple: Prepare your ingredients before you start cooking. This approach is especially important when cooking for two; because you're using smaller amounts and fewer ingredients, cooking times are shorter and the recipe as a whole often moves faster. Having everything prepped and ready to go ensures that you're not left frantically chopping an ingredient when you should be adding it to the pan. It should be noted that some ingredients such as onions and garlic are best prepared just before cooking, but many can be prepared the night before—allowing you to put together a special-occasion meal with minimal last-minute fuss.

the perfect balance of flavors. We had taken chicken saltimbocca to a new level, and it was now both incredibly elegant and simple.

Chicken Saltimbocca

SERVES 2

We find the shape and size of store-bought cutlets to be inconsistent; consider making your own cutlets following the photo using two (6-ounce) boneless, skinless chicken breasts. Make sure to buy prosciutto that is thinly sliced, but not shaved. The prosciutto slices should be large enough to fully cover one side of each cutlet; if the slices are too large, simply cut them down to size.

¼ cup plus ½ teaspoon unbleached all-purpose flour

4 (3-ounce) boneless, skinless chicken cutlets,
    ¼ to ½ inch thick (see note)
    Pepper

2 teaspoons minced fresh sage,
    plus 4 large whole leaves (optional)

4 thin slices prosciutto (about 3 ounces) (see note)

2 tablespoons olive oil, plus extra as needed

1 small shallot, minced

⅓ cup low-sodium chicken broth

¼ cup dry vermouth or white wine

1 tablespoon unsalted butter, chilled

2 teaspoons minced fresh parsley

1 teaspoon fresh lemon juice
    Salt

1. Spread ¼ cup of the flour in a shallow dish. Pat the cutlets dry with paper towels and season with pepper. Following the photos, dredge the cutlets in the flour, shaking off the excess, and lay flat on a cutting board. Sprinkle the minced sage evenly over the top of the cutlets, top with a piece of the prosciutto, and press lightly on the prosciutto to help it adhere.

2. Heat the oil in a 12-inch skillet over medium-high heat until shimmering. Add the whole sage leaves (if using) and cook until the leaves begin to change color and are fragrant, 15 to 20 seconds. Using a slotted spoon, transfer the sage leaves to a paper towel–lined plate and set aside.

3. Carefully lay the chicken cutlets in the skillet, prosciutto-side down, and cook until lightly browned on the first side, about 2 minutes. Flip the cutlets and

continue to cook until no longer pink, about 1 minute longer. Transfer the cutlets to a plate and tent loosely with foil.

4. Pour off all but 1 teaspoon of the oil left in the skillet (or add more oil if necessary). Add the shallot and cook over medium heat until softened, 2 to 3 minutes. Stir in the remaining ½ teaspoon flour. Whisk in the broth and vermouth, scraping up any browned bits. Bring to a simmer and cook until the sauce is slightly thickened and has reduced to ⅓ cup, 3 to 5 minutes.

NOTES FROM THE TEST KITCHEN

MAKING CHICKEN CUTLETS

Place each chicken breast, smooth-side up, on a cutting board. Holding one hand on top of the breast, carefully slice the breast in half horizontally to yield two pieces, each between ¼ and ½ inch thick.

MAKING CHICKEN SALTIMBOCCA

1. Dredge the chicken in the flour, then shake off the excess.

2. Sprinkle the tops of the cutlets with the minced sage, then top each with a slice of prosciutto.

3. Cook the cutlets, prosciutto-side down, to fuse the prosciutto and cutlet together.

5. Return the chicken cutlets to the skillet, prosciutto-side up, along with any accumulated juice, and simmer until heated through, about 30 seconds. Transfer the cutlets to a platter.

6. Off the heat, whisk the butter, parsley, and lemon juice into the sauce, and season with salt and pepper to taste. Spoon the sauce over the cutlets, garnish with the fried sage leaves (if using), and serve.

STUFFED CHICKEN BREASTS

THOUGH CHICKEN BREASTS ARE TYPICALLY THOUGHT of as weeknight fare, they take on a whole new character when breaded and stuffed. When stuffed chicken breasts are sliced, the filling oozes out into a creamy, tasty sauce, and the crust provides a crunchy counterpoint. We wanted to create the ultimate stuffed chicken breast recipe, with a couple of flavor variations to add to our cooking-for-two repertoire.

Stuffed chicken breasts have three distinct parts: the chicken, the filling, and the coating. Typically, the stuffed chicken breast is rolled in a coating, then fried until crisp. However, getting the filling to survive cooking without leaking is key. So we started there.

Some recipes call for cutting a slit in the thickest part of the breast and inserting the filling. This approach was easy in theory, but it was impossible to get the pocket deep enough to accommodate more than a paltry amount of filling, and it became evident that giving the filling any path of egress (even the smallest opening) wasn't a good idea. One false move, and the hot filling came streaming out during cooking, leaving us with a hollow chicken breast.

We needed to find a way to encase the filling completely. In some recipes we came across in our research, the chicken was pounded thin, the filling was put on top, then the chicken was rolled around it to form a compact package. This method worked much better, but it was hard to pound the chicken thin and wide enough to encase the filling without accidentally tearing the flesh—or leaving awkward ragged edges in the process. Borrowing a trick the test kitchen has used for other recipes, we butterflied the breasts lengthwise first (giving us cutlets twice as wide but half as thick as the original), then pounded them just enough to make them even. Much better—less pounding meant less damage. Experimenting with various thicknesses, we settled on ¼ inch as optimal.

Flattened, our chicken cutlets resembled large teardrops. Following the rolling-and-folding technique, we placed the filling just above the tapered end of the "teardrop" and proceeded as if wrapping a burrito: rolling the tapered end completely over the filling (tasters preferred a simple cream cheese filling rather than butter), folding in the sides toward the center, then continuing to roll until we had a fairly tight bundle.

Now, with our two chicken bundles at the ready, we could focus on the crispy exterior. We quickly committed to making our own bread crumbs—boxed crumbs tasted stale—and toasting them ourselves. To keep their flavor and lightness and prevent a greasy exterior, we decided to forgo the traditional deep-frying technique in favor of baking in the oven. (Pan-frying was out because it often led to unraveled chicken breasts.) To ensure that the crumbs adhered to the breasts, we first dredged the stuffed breasts in flour (a modest ½ cup was plenty) and dipped them in egg before coating them with the toasted bread crumbs. We also found that when the stuffed breasts were refrigerated for an hour before being coated, the edges of the chicken stuck together and formed a much sturdier package that was easier to coat. Baked at 350 degrees for about 45 minutes, our chicken breasts had a perfectly crisp crust with a filling that didn't stray.

All we had left to do was to perk up the cream cheese filling. A sprinkling of fresh herbs offered a fragrant note, and sautéed onion and garlic provided a savory contrast to the rich cheese. Once we had the basics down, we used this mixture as a base to host three flavor combinations: cheddar cheese and ham; prosciutto, sage, and Gorgonzola; and goat cheese and thyme. Last, a teaspoon of Dijon mustard whisked into the egg wash (for coating the chicken) provided another layer of flavor to our chicken bundles.

After batches and batches of mediocre stuffed chicken breasts we had finally reached an impressive outcome—beautifully browned, crisp, stuffed chicken breasts with fragrant, herb-speckled filling.

BUILDING STUFFED CHICKEN BREASTS

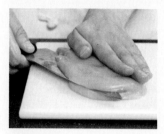

1. Butterfly the chicken breast by starting on the thinnest side and slicing lengthwise almost in half; do not cut all the way through the chicken.

2. Open up the chicken like a book, cover with plastic wrap, and pound lightly to an even ¼-inch thickness.

3. Lay a slice of ham on each chicken breast, then place half of the filling (about 3 tablespoons) near the tapered end of each cutlet.

4. Roll the tapered end of the chicken over the filling, then fold in the sides and continue rolling the chicken around the filling to form a tidy package, pressing on the seam to seal.

BUYING PRECRUMBLED CHEESE

How do the precrumbled cheeses found in the deli section of the supermarket stack up to the same brands sold in solid block or log form? We tasted blue cheese, goat cheese, and feta side by side in their crumbled and solid forms (comparing the same brand of each type) both plain and added to various recipes, including blue cheese dressing, polenta with Gorgonzola, spinach dip with feta, and our stuffed chicken breasts. Tasters found the precrumbled versions acceptable in all cases. What we found unacceptable, however, were the price differences. Stella blue cheese that sells for around $8 a pound in block form, for example, is $3.99 for a 5-ounce package in a precrumbled state. That's a price increase of over 160 percent! At prices like that, we'll gladly take 30 extra seconds to crumble our own cheese.

Stuffed Chicken Breasts with Ham and Cheddar
SERVES 2

Note that you need to plan ahead for this dish—the chicken needs to be chilled for an hour to set in step 4, otherwise it will unravel when being breaded in step 6.

FILLING

- 1 tablespoon unsalted butter
- ¼ cup minced onion
- 1 small garlic clove, minced
- ½ teaspoon minced fresh thyme
- 2 ounces cheddar cheese, shredded (about ½ cup)
- 1 ounce cream cheese, softened (about ¼ cup)
- Salt and pepper

CHICKEN

- 3 slices high-quality white sandwich bread, torn into pieces
- 1 tablespoon vegetable oil
- Salt and pepper
- 2 (7- to 8-ounce) boneless, skinless chicken breasts, trimmed
- 2 thin slices deli ham (about 2 ounces)
- ½ cup unbleached all-purpose flour
- 2 large eggs, lightly beaten
- 1 teaspoon Dijon mustard
- Lemon wedges, for serving

1. FOR THE FILLING: Melt the butter in an 8-inch skillet over medium heat. Add the onion and cook until softened and lightly browned, 5 to 7 minutes. Stir in the garlic and thyme and cook until fragrant, about 30 seconds. Transfer to a medium bowl and let cool.

2. Add the cheddar, cream cheese, ⅛ teaspoon salt, and ⅛ teaspoon pepper to the cooled onion mixture, mash together until uniform, and refrigerate until needed.

3. FOR THE CHICKEN: Adjust an oven rack to the lower-middle position and heat the oven to 300 degrees. Pulse the bread in a food processor to coarse crumbs, about 16 pulses. Toss the crumbs with the oil, ⅛ teaspoon salt, and ⅛ teaspoon pepper, then spread out on a rimmed baking sheet. Bake, stirring occasionally, until the crumbs are golden and dry, about 25 minutes. Let cool to room temperature.

4. Following the photos, butterfly and pound each chicken breast into a large ¼-inch-thick cutlet and season with salt and pepper. Lay a slice of ham on top of each chicken breast, then place half of the filling (about 3 tablespoons) near the tapered end of each cutlet. Roll the cutlet around the filling to form a tidy package, pressing on the seam to seal. Lay the chicken on a plate, cover with plastic wrap, and refrigerate until set, about 1 hour.

5. Adjust an oven rack to the middle position and heat the oven to 350 degrees. Set a wire rack inside a rimmed baking sheet. Combine the flour, ⅛ teaspoon salt, and a pinch of pepper in a shallow dish. In a second shallow dish, whisk the eggs and mustard together. Transfer the cooled bread crumbs to a third shallow dish.

6. Dredge the chicken in the flour, shaking off the excess. Using tongs, coat the chicken with the egg mixture, allowing the excess to drip off. Coat all sides of the chicken with a thick layer of bread crumbs, pressing to help them adhere. Transfer the breaded chicken to the prepared wire rack. (The unbaked, breaded chicken breasts can be covered and refrigerated for up to 24 hours, or wrapped tightly and frozen for up to 1 month.)

7. Bake the chicken until the centers register 160 to 165 degrees on an instant-read thermometer, 45 to 50 minutes. (If refrigerated, bake as directed, or if frozen, do not thaw and increase the baking time to about 1 hour.) Let the chicken rest on the wire rack for 5 minutes before serving with the lemon wedges.

VARIATIONS

Stuffed Chicken Breasts with Prosciutto and Gorgonzola

The prosciutto slices should be large enough to fully cover each cutlet; if the slices are too large, simply cut them down to size.

Follow the recipe for Stuffed Chicken Breasts with Ham and Cheddar, substituting 1 teaspoon minced fresh sage for the thyme, ½ cup crumbled Gorgonzola cheese for the cheddar, and 2 thin prosciutto slices (about 1½ ounces) for the ham.

Stuffed Chicken Breasts with Goat Cheese and Thyme

Follow the recipe for Stuffed Chicken Breasts with Ham and Cheddar, increasing the amount of thyme to 1 teaspoon and substituting ½ cup softened goat cheese for the cheddar.

ROAST DUCK À L'ORANGE

OF ALL THE CLASSIC FRENCH DISHES THAT HAVE MADE it across the Atlantic, duck à l'orange is one of our favorites. But we can see why it has remained largely in the realm of restaurants: Duck is notoriously fatty—a 4½-pound bird at the grocery store may weigh less than 2 pounds after roasting—which can make it tricky to cook. When prepared right, duck à l'orange features moist, flavorful meat and crisp, golden skin, with a brightly flavored orange sauce that is the perfect complement to the rich meat. Since one duck yields about two servings, and since we didn't think this dish should be out of reach for the home cook, we hoped to bring this bistro classic into our own kitchen.

We started with the roasting method. Every source we consulted agreed that placing the duck on a rack was necessary to keep it elevated above its own rendered fat. After that, there were varying philosophies. Several recipes we found suggested pricking the skin to provide an escape route for the fat as it rendered. Giving this a shot, we used a skewer to prick the duck all over and found this worked moderately well. Taking this concept a step further, we tried separating the skin from the meat over much of the duck to allow even more space for the fat to escape. We also cut a few holes in the skin near the back of the duck to provide additional channels for the rendering fat to drip down.

As for roasting temperature, some recipes swear by roasting the duck entirely in a hot oven, but we found this approach to be problematic—the fat typically burned before it had a chance to render and the meat was inevitably dry. Instead, we found that a combination of moderate and high heat worked best. We started the duck in a 350-degree oven until the breast meat reached 160 degrees. This prevented the duck from drying out and gave the fat plenty of time to render. We then cranked the heat up to 500 degrees and continued roasting until the skin was crisp. This duck was juicy and the fat was well rendered, producing the crispest skin so far. But could we get it even crisper?

A fellow test cook suggested an interesting technique he had used for crisping the skin of duck's more ubiquitous relative, chicken. The method involved rubbing a mixture of baking powder, salt, and pepper over the entire bird before allowing it to sit overnight—uncovered—in the refrigerator. Some research revealed the effects this method had on chicken skin: The salt allowed the surface moisture on the skin to evaporate—leading to crispier skin—and the alkalinity of the baking powder reinforced this dehydration process, enhancing the effects of the air-drying.

We eagerly tried this technique with our duck, combining baking powder with salt and pepper, rubbing the mixture evenly over the bird, and letting it rest overnight—uncovered—in the fridge. The next day we put the duck in the oven and roasted it using our established method. Success! Tasters devoured this duck with its thin, golden, crisp skin and moist, tender meat.

Now all we needed was the classic orange sauce to complement our rich roast duck. We started by creating a caramel with sugar and a little vinegar for an acidic note—a standard step for this sauce that we found to be crucial for developing deep, balanced flavor. Next we added the requisite orange juice and some chicken broth and reduced the mixture until thickened. Finally, we stirred in a little orange liqueur and a bit more vinegar for brightness, then finished our sauce with a couple of tablespoons of butter. Drizzled over the crisp duck, our sauce was the perfect finishing touch, and tasters gave this dish a standing ovation.

NOTES FROM THE TEST KITCHEN

PREPARING A DUCK FOR ROASTING

1. After removing the neck and giblets and trimming away excess skin and fat, tuck the wing tips back behind the bird—they should stay in place by themselves.

2. Cut five 1-inch-long shallow slashes along the back of the duck to create openings for the fat to escape.

3. Using your fingers, carefully separate the skin covering the thighs and breast.

4. Poke 25 to 30 holes through the skin covering the breast and thighs with a metal skewer, focusing on the large fat pockets.

CARVING A WHOLE DUCK

1. Cut the duck where the leg meets the breast, pulling the leg quarter away from the carcass.

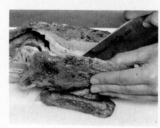

2. Pull the leg quarter out to the side and carefully cut through the joint to remove.

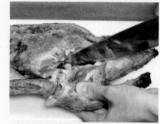

3. Cut down along the side of the breastbone, pulling the breast meat away from you as you cut.

4. Remove the wing from the breast meat by cutting through the wing joint.

Roast Duck à l'Orange

SERVES 2

A whole duck might seem like too much for two people, but once carved and plated, it will look appropriate. Refrigerating the duck for at least 12 hours before roasting is important for crisp skin. You can omit this step, but the skin will not be very crisp.

DUCK

- 1 (4½- to 5-pound) whole duck
- 1½ teaspoons salt
- 1 teaspoon baking powder
- ½ teaspoon pepper

SAUCE

- 2 tablespoons water
- 4 teaspoons white wine vinegar
- 1 tablespoon sugar
- ½ cup fresh orange juice
- ½ cup low-sodium chicken broth
- 1 tablespoon orange-flavored liqueur
- 2 tablespoons unsalted butter, cut into ½-inch pieces and chilled
  Salt and pepper

1. FOR THE DUCK: Set a wire rack inside a foil-lined rimmed baking sheet. Following the photos on page 120, discard the duck neck and giblets, trim away any excess skin and fat, and tuck the wings. Cut five 1-inch-long shallow slashes along the back of the duck. Using your fingers, carefully separate the skin covering the thighs and breast, then poke 25 to 30 holes through the skin covering the breast and thighs with a metal skewer, focusing on the large fat pockets.

2. Pat the duck dry with paper towels. Combine the salt, baking powder, and pepper in a small bowl, then rub the mixture evenly over the outside of the entire duck. Set the duck, breast-side up, on the prepared wire rack and refrigerate, uncovered, for 12 to 24 hours.

3. Adjust an oven rack to the middle position and heat the oven to 350 degrees. Transfer the duck (on the wire rack and baking sheet) to the oven and roast until the breast registers 160 to 165 degrees on an instant-read thermometer, about 1 hour.

4. Increase the oven temperature to 500 degrees and continue to roast the duck until the skin is golden and crisp and the thickest part of the breast registers 180 degrees, about 15 minutes longer.

5. FOR THE SAUCE: Meanwhile, pour the water and 1 tablespoon of the vinegar into a small saucepan, then pour the sugar into the center of the pan. Gently stir the sugar with a clean spatula to wet it thoroughly. Bring to a boil over medium-high heat and cook, without stirring, until the sugar has dissolved completely and the liquid is a faint golden color, 3 to 5 minutes.

6. Reduce the heat to medium and continue to cook until the caramel is a dark amber color, about 30 seconds longer. Carefully, slowly stir in the orange juice and broth (the mixture will bubble wildly), then continue to simmer until the mixture is thickened and has reduced to ¼ cup, 12 to 15 minutes. Cover to keep warm and set aside.

7. Transfer the duck to a carving board and let rest, uncovered, for 10 minutes. Return the sauce to a simmer over medium heat, then add the liqueur and remaining 1 teaspoon vinegar. Off the heat, whisk in the butter and season with salt and pepper to taste. Following the photos on page 120, carve the duck and serve, passing the sauce separately.

SMOKED SALMON AND LEEK TART

SMOKED SALMON REQUIRES LITTLE IN THE WAY OF preparation but adds deep, smoky flavor and rich, silky texture to a dish, making it a simple ingredient that can turn any dinner into a refined affair. Smoked salmon and leek tart is a great example of this. Done right, the tart is similar to quiche in that the filling is built on a custard base, but it differs from quiche in the amount of custard—the tart contains just enough to bind the ingredients together, so the end result is a bit lighter than quiche, with the flavor of salmon at the forefront. Each bite contains flaky, buttery pastry, creamy custard, and rich, briny salmon. While most tart recipes produce a single large tart, we wanted to create two small tarts—one for each diner at the table.

We love the flavor of an all-butter crust, but getting an all-butter dough into a single tart shell in one piece is stressful enough—often requiring going in and out of the refrigerator to keep the dough from getting too soft. We figured two small tarts would be double the headache, so we turned to testing pat-in-the-pan-style crusts.

We tried several recipes, which included everything from shortening to eggs and even cream cheese, but they all produced crusts that were too cookie-like and crumbly—and, more important, the intense butter flavor we wanted in this tart was lost. We returned to a basic crust recipe that relied on butter for the dairy ingredient. We began our tests by cutting the butter into the flour, but quickly turned to a food processor to speed things up. This worked like a charm—the dough was firm enough to press into the pans and baked as evenly as a traditional rolled tart dough. Better yet, the butter was evenly distributed throughout the dough (thanks to our food processor), so we got big bites of crispy, buttery crust with each forkful.

Next we focused on getting our custard base just right. We started out by experimenting with various ratios of eggs and cream to yield a custard light enough to let the other ingredients shine through but still cohesive enough to bind them all together. We tried two eggs and ½ cup of cream, but that turned out to be too much custard for our two small crusts—and it was too rich as well. We finally settled on one egg and ¼ cup of half-and-half. With the addition of some fresh dill, the custard was flavorful and delicate.

Moving along, we shifted to the leeks. We found that a quick sauté in a hot pan left us with brown, bitter leeks that were stringy and tough. Experimenting with the opposite end of the spectrum, we tried cooking them slowly over medium-low heat. This was a marked improvement in both texture and taste, but some bits and pieces were still getting too brown, so we covered the pan to sweat the leeks. Sweating allowed the leeks to cook to a tender state and develop a sweet flavor.

Finally, we focused on incorporating the salmon into the tart. Many of the recipes we researched fold the salmon into the custard, but we found this disappointing. The once-subtle flavor of the salmon turned fishy, overwhelming the other flavors in the filling. Placing the salmon over the custard didn't work well either. The salmon sank into the custard, again throwing all the flavors off balance. We then baked up our tarts once more, this time setting the salmon aside until the tarts were finished. Once they had cooled, we spooned the chopped salmon over the custard filling. Tasters raved about the distinct flavorful contrast between the delicate custard and the rich, smoky salmon. As a final touch, we tossed the salmon with a bit of olive oil and thinly sliced chives for some fresh onion flavor. At last, we had individual tarts that were easy to prepare but fancy enough for any special occasion.

Smoked Salmon and Leek Tart
SERVES 2

Buy smoked salmon that looks bright and glossy and avoid salmon that looks milky and dry.

- 1 tablespoon unsalted butter
- 1 leek, white and light green parts only, halved lengthwise, sliced thin, and rinsed thoroughly (see page 124)
  Salt
- 1 large egg
- ¼ cup half-and-half
- 2 teaspoons minced fresh dill
  Pepper
- 1 recipe All-Butter Tart Shells (page 124), fully baked and cooled
- 3 ounces thinly sliced smoked salmon, cut into ¼-inch pieces
- 2 teaspoons extra-virgin olive oil
- 2 teaspoons thinly sliced fresh chives
  Lemon wedges, for serving

1. Adjust an oven rack to the middle position and heat the oven to 375 degrees. Melt the butter in an 8-inch skillet over medium-low heat. Add the leek and ½ teaspoon salt, cover, and cook until softened, 5 to 7 minutes. Remove the lid and set the mixture aside to cool for 5 minutes.

2. Whisk the egg, half-and-half, dill, and ⅛ teaspoon pepper together in a bowl, then stir in the cooled leek mixture. Divide the mixture evenly between the tart shells. Bake the tarts on a baking sheet until the fillings are mostly set but still feel soft and a little jiggly in the very center, 10 to 15 minutes. (Do not overbake.)

3. Let the tarts cool on a wire rack to room temperature, about 15 minutes. To serve, remove the outer metal ring of the tart pan, slide a thin metal spatula between the tart and the tart pan bottom, and carefully slide the tart onto a plate. Toss the salmon with the olive oil and chives and season with salt and pepper to taste. Sprinkle the salmon over the tarts; serve with the lemon wedges.

SMOKED SALMON AND LEEK TART

WASHING LEEKS

To remove sand and dirt, rinse the sliced leeks thoroughly in a bowl of water. Dirt will settle to the bottom and the clean leeks can be lifted out.

MAKING A TART SHELL

1. Tear each piece of dough into walnut-sized clumps and spread them evenly into one of the prepared tart pans.

2. Working outward from the center, press the dough into an even layer, then press it up the sides and into the fluted edges of each tart pan.

3. Use your thumb to level off the top edge. Use this excess dough to patch any holes.

4. Lay plastic wrap over the dough and smooth out any bumps using your fingertips before freezing the tart shells until firm.

All-Butter Tart Shells

MAKES TWO 4-INCH TART SHELLS

You will need two 4-inch fluted tart pans with a removable bottom for this recipe (see page 3). The baked and cooled tart shells can be stored at room temperature for up to 1 day.

- ½ cup plus 2 tablespoons (3⅛ ounces) unbleached all-purpose flour
- 1½ teaspoons sugar
- ¼ teaspoon salt
- 4 tablespoons (½ stick) unsalted butter, cut into ½-inch pieces and chilled
- 2 tablespoons ice water

1. Spray two 4-inch tart pans with removable bottoms with vegetable oil spray. Pulse the flour, sugar, and salt together in a food processor until combined, about 4 pulses. Scatter the butter pieces over the flour mixture and pulse until the mixture resembles coarse sand, about 15 pulses. Add 1 tablespoon of the ice water and continue to process until large clumps of dough form and no powdery bits remain, about 5 seconds. (If the dough doesn't clump, add the remaining 1 tablespoon water and pulse to incorporate, about 4 pulses.)

2. Divide the dough into 2 equal pieces. Following the photos, tear each piece of dough into walnut-sized clumps, then pat the dough into the prepared tart pans. Lay plastic wrap over the dough and smooth out any bumps or shallow areas using your fingertips. Place the tart shells on a large plate and freeze until firm, about 30 minutes, or up to 1 day.

3. Adjust an oven rack to the middle position and heat the oven to 375 degrees. Remove the plastic wrap and place the frozen tart shells on a baking sheet. Gently press a piece of heavy-duty aluminum foil that has been sprayed with vegetable oil spray against the dough and over the edges of each tart pan. Fill the shells with pie weights and bake until the top edges of the dough just start to color and the surface of the dough under the foil no longer looks wet, about 30 minutes.

4. Carefully remove the foil and weights from the tart shells and continue to bake until golden, 5 to 10 minutes longer. Let the tart shells cool on a wire rack.

PAN-SEARED SCALLOPS

SCALLOPS ARE A GREAT CHOICE FOR A SPECIAL MEAL that doesn't require spending all day in the kitchen; they cook quickly, and their delicate but rich texture is best complemented by nothing more than a simple sauce. Scallops can be prepared in myriad ways, but pan-searing is our favorite method. Cooking them over high heat caramelizes the exterior, forming a nutty-flavored crust that enhances their natural sweetness. And when cooking for two, scallops are a great choice, because you can buy just what you need.

The biggest challenge when cooking scallops is getting a good crust before the scallops overcook and toughen. We already knew from experience that moisture is the enemy of a crusty brown exterior. To make sure our scallops were as dry as possible going into the pan, we laid them in a single layer on a paper towel–lined plate, seasoned them with salt and pepper, and placed paper towels over the top. The paper towels absorbed any moisture that the scallops released, and as an extra precaution just before they went into the pan, we pressed the paper towel flush to the surface of the scallops to ensure that every bit of moisture was absorbed.

Cooking our first batch of scallops over high heat, we quickly found that achieving a good sear on both sides resulted in tough, rubbery scallops. Once browned on the first side, the scallops needed little time in the pan to finish cooking, so by the time they were seared on the second side, they were overcooked. Our solution was to brown just one side and then lower the heat to finish cooking on the second side. In addition to lowering the heat halfway through, we also found it was critical to place the scallops in the skillet one at a time, ensuring that the flat side had maximum contact with the pan, and to leave them undisturbed once they began cooking. Typically we would have to sear scallops in batches to avoid crowding the pan (which inhibits browning), so we were happy to discover that two servings fit perfectly in a 10-inch skillet all at once.

This solved the crust dilemma, but what about the interior of the scallops? As a scallop cooks, the soft flesh firms and you can see an opaqueness that starts at the bottom of the scallop, where it sits in the pan, and slowly creeps up toward the center. To preserve the creamy texture of our pan-seared scallops, we cooked them to medium-rare, so they were hot all the way through but the center still retained some translucence.

As for the type of fat in which to sear our scallops, we tried butter, olive oil, vegetable oil, and a combination of butter and oil. The high heat necessary to achieve a golden exterior burned the butter before the scallops had a chance to form a crust. The scallops browned best in the olive and vegetable oils. Since tasters didn't detect a flavor difference between the two, we went with vegetable oil, which has a slightly higher smoke point.

As for the sauce to accompany our perfectly cooked scallops, we settled on a beurre blanc—a warm butter sauce traditionally made with a wine reduction and shallots into which cold butter is slowly whisked to create a velvety consistency—and decided to jazz up the sauce with lemon and a fresh herb. We began by softening some shallot with a little butter in a small saucepan. Next, we added some white wine and lemon juice and allowed the liquid to reduce until almost completely evaporated. Lowering the heat, we then began slowly whisking in butter until we had a smooth and creamy sauce. Off the heat, we stirred in some minced fresh tarragon and seasoned the sauce with salt and pepper. Though not traditional in a beurre blanc, we also decided to add just a tablespoon of cream to help emulsify the sauce. When we paired our sauce with the golden brown scallops, we knew we had a simple but decadent dish that was guaranteed to impress.

Pan-Seared Scallops with Lemon and Herb Beurre Blanc
SERVES 2

Depending on the size of your scallops, the cooking times may vary slightly. Be ready to serve the scallops right away because they will cool quickly. See page 229 for a recipe to use up the leftover heavy cream.

5	tablespoons unsalted butter, cut into 5 pieces and chilled
1	small shallot, minced
¼	cup dry white wine
2	teaspoons fresh lemon juice
1	tablespoon heavy cream
1	tablespoon minced fresh tarragon or parsley
	Salt and pepper
	Warm water, as needed
12	ounces large sea scallops (about 8 scallops), tendons removed (see page 126)
1	tablespoon vegetable oil

1. Melt 1 tablespoon of the butter in a small saucepan over medium heat. Add the shallot and cook until softened, 2 to 3 minutes. Add the wine and lemon juice and simmer until the liquid has almost completely evaporated, 3 to 5 minutes.

2. Reduce the heat to low, add the cream, and slowly whisk in the remaining 4 tablespoons butter, one piece at a time, until incorporated. Off the heat, stir in the tarragon, season with salt and pepper to taste, and cover to keep warm. (If the sauce appears too thick, thin with warm water, 1 teaspoon at a time, as needed.)

3. Lay the scallops on a paper towel–lined plate and season with salt and pepper. Lay a sheet of paper towel on top of the scallops and set aside.

4. Heat the oil in a 10-inch skillet over high heat until just smoking. Meanwhile, press the paper towel flush to the scallops to dry them. Carefully lay the scallops in the skillet and cook until golden brown on the first side, 1 to 2 minutes.

5. Reduce the heat to medium, flip the scallops, and continue to cook until the sides of the scallops have firmed up and all but the very middle of each scallop is opaque, 30 to 60 seconds longer.

6. Transfer the scallops to individual plates. Drizzle with some of the sauce and serve, passing the remaining sauce separately.

VARIATION

**Pan-Seared Scallops with
Saffron Beurre Blanc**

Follow the recipe for Pan-Seared Scallops with Lemon and Herb Beurre Blanc, omitting the tarragon, reducing the amount of lemon juice to 1 teaspoon, and adding a pinch of saffron threads to the sauce with the cream.

NOTES FROM THE TEST KITCHEN

PREPARING SCALLOPS

The small crescent-shaped tendon that is sometimes attached to the scallop will be inedibly tough when cooked. Use your fingers to peel it away from the side of each scallop before cooking.

LAZY MAN'S LOBSTER

WHEN IT COMES TO LOBSTER, MOST PEOPLE BOIL AND serve the whole crustacean with a side of drawn butter. There's nothing wrong with tradition, but fumbling around with a cooked lobster isn't exactly a tidy affair. We wanted a refined lobster dinner that still delivered the sweet, rich flavor of lobster.

Searching for ideas, we came across "lazy man's lobster," which consists of lobster meat in a rich cream sauce baked under a bread crumb topping—in essence, a lobster gratin. The dish was a winner in theory, however, most recipes we tried were bland and too rich. So we set out to create our own version of lazy man's lobster, one that was full of flavor but wasn't too heavy—and was perfect for just two.

We started by examining ways to get the most lobster flavor into the finished dish. A few of the recipes we found called for homemade lobster stock, which was then added to cream and reduced. While we were willing to put in extra time for a special dinner, making our own stock was an all-day project to which we didn't want to commit. In other recipes, precooked lobster meat was added to reduced cream that had been flavored with aromatics. We decided to take this streamlined approach.

Early tests helped us determine that 12 ounces of cooked lobster meat was the right amount for two people. We liked the flavor of freshly steamed lobster meat (see page 128), and steaming and shelling two lobsters is a simple procedure that can be completed up to two days ahead of time. Alternatively, you could purchase precooked lobster meat, which, depending on where you live, can be found at a good fish market or even a local supermarket; we leave the choice up to you.

We began by creating a basic but flavorful sauce using ½ cup heavy cream, ¼ cup sherry, a shallot, some thyme, and a bit of flour before stirring in our precooked lobster meat. For a stronger herbal presence, we added minced tarragon, a classic pairing with shellfish. Some tasters thought the generous dose of heavy cream created the leaden sauce we were trying to avoid, but cutting the heavy cream down to ¼ cup gave us a sauce with less richness than we expected from a lobster dish. In the end, we compromised and settled on ⅓ cup, which pleased everyone. Tasters also thought the filling could use some zing; a pinch of cayenne added a little heat that contrasted nicely with the sauce's creaminess.

LAZY MAN'S LOBSTER

Now all we needed to do was portion the lobster filling into individual gratin dishes and sprinkle them with a simple bread crumb topping. For flavor, we mixed Parmesan cheese, a little oil, more minced tarragon, and paprika into our bread crumbs before sprinkling them on top. With our filling already cooked, our lobster gratins needed only 15 minutes in a 400-degree oven to become bubbling hot and achieve a golden crown.

Lazy Man's Lobster

SERVES 2

You can either buy cooked lobster meat or cook 2 (1¼- to 1½-pound) lobsters and shell the meat (see below). You will need two shallow 2-cup gratin dishes (measuring approximately 9 by 6 inches; see page 3), or you can substitute one 8-inch square baking dish. See page 229 for a recipe to use up the leftover heavy cream.

NOTES FROM THE TEST KITCHEN

HARD-SHELL VERSUS SOFT-SHELL LOBSTERS

During the year, lobsters go through a molting stage in order to grow into a larger shell. If caught during this stage, the lobsters are called soft-shell. You can tell they are soft-shell just by squeezing them—if squeezed, their soft sides will yield to pressure. Does this matter? Yes and no. Soft-shell lobsters have less meat and are considered to be less flavorful. For most of us, though, soft-shell lobsters taste just fine. The only thing to keep in mind is that they cook faster than hard-shell lobsters do.

HOW TO COOK LOBSTER

We found that the best way to cook a lobster, hands down, is steaming. There is no difference in taste between boiled and steamed lobsters, but you'll eliminate waterlogged lobsters if you simply steam them. Here's how we steam live lobsters. For our Lazy Man's Lobster, you will need 12 ounces of cooked lobster meat, which is equivalent to two (1¼- to 1½-pound) lobsters (see the chart below for meat yields from different-sized lobsters).

Fit a large Dutch oven with a steamer basket and add water to the pot until it just touches the bottom of the basket. Bring the water to a boil over high heat, then add the lobsters to the steamer basket. Following the times in the chart, cover and steam the lobsters until they are bright red and fully cooked. Be sure to check the pot periodically to make sure the water has not boiled dry; add more water as needed. Remove the lobsters from the steamer basket and let them cool slightly before shelling. (The cooked lobster meat can be refrigerated in an airtight container for up to two days.)

SHELLING A LOBSTER

1. After the lobster is cooked and slightly cooled, remove the tail and claw appendages by twisting them off the body over a large bowl to prevent a mess. Discard the lobster body.

2. Use scissors to cut the tail shell open and pull the meat out with a fork.

3. Twist the claw from the connecting joint. Use lobster crackers or a mallet to break open the connecting joint and claw, and remove the meat from both with a cocktail fork if necessary.

ALL ABOUT SHERRY

We use sherry to add sweetness and offset richness in some dishes, such as our Lazy Man's Lobster. A fortified wine, sherry originated in the Andalusia region of southern Spain. Dry sherry is made from Palomino grapes, and cream (also called sweet) sherry comes from Pedro Ximénez grapes. They sound similar, but they can't be used interchangeably. If you try to substitute cream sherry for dry sherry, you'll need to add a squeeze of lemon juice to balance the additional sweetness from the cream sherry.

While cream sherry may be a fine stand-in for dry sherry in most instances, always avoid cooking sherry. Loaded with salt and artificial caramel flavoring, this sherry will ruin the flavor of most dishes.

LOBSTER	STEAMING TIME	MEAT YIELD
Soft-Shell		
1 lb	8 to 9 minutes	about 3 oz
1¼ lbs	11 to 12 minutes	3½ to 4 oz
1½ lbs	13 to 14 minutes	5½ to 6 oz
1¾–2 lbs	17 to 18 minutes	6¼ to 6½ oz
Hard-Shell		
1 lb	10 to 11 minutes	4 to 4½ oz
1¼ lbs	13 to 14 minutes	5½ to 6 oz
1½ lbs	15 to 16 minutes	7½ to 8 oz
1¾–2 lbs	about 19 minutes	8½ to 9 oz

LOBSTER

- 1 tablespoon vegetable oil
- 1 shallot, minced
- 1 teaspoon minced fresh thyme
-   Pinch cayenne pepper
- 4 teaspoons unbleached all-purpose flour
- ¼ cup dry sherry
- 1 cup low-sodium chicken broth
- ⅓ cup heavy cream
- 12 ounces cooked lobster meat (see note), chopped coarse
- 1 tablespoon minced fresh tarragon
-   Salt and pepper

TOPPING

- 1 slice high-quality white sandwich bread, torn into pieces
- 2 tablespoons grated Parmesan cheese
- 1 tablespoon minced fresh tarragon
- 1 teaspoon vegetable oil
- ⅛ teaspoon paprika

1. FOR THE LOBSTER: Heat the oil in a 10-inch skillet over medium heat until shimmering. Add the shallot, thyme, and cayenne, and cook until the shallot is softened, 2 to 3 minutes. Stir in the flour and cook for 30 seconds. Stir in the sherry and simmer until it has nearly evaporated, about 2 minutes. Whisk in the chicken broth and cream and simmer until the liquid has thickened and reduced to ¾ cup, 10 to 12 minutes.

2. Off the heat, add the cooked lobster meat and tarragon; season with salt and pepper to taste. Divide the mixture evenly between two shallow 2-cup gratin dishes. (The gratins can be covered tightly with plastic wrap and refrigerated for up to 24 hours. Remove the plastic wrap and microwave briefly on medium until warm, 2 to 4 minutes, before topping and baking.)

3. FOR THE TOPPING: Adjust an oven rack to the middle position and heat the oven to 400 degrees. Pulse the bread in a food processor to coarse crumbs, about 10 pulses. Combine the bread crumbs, Parmesan, tarragon, oil, and paprika in a bowl. (The topping can be stored in an airtight container at room temperature for up to 24 hours.)

4. Sprinkle the topping evenly over the gratins. Bake until the sauce is bubbling and the topping is golden brown, about 15 minutes. Let cool for 10 minutes before serving.

BOUILLABAISSE

FIND A COUNTRY WITH A COASTLINE, AND YOU WILL find fish stew in the culinary repertoire. Probably the best-known example of this is France's bouillabaisse—the celebrated stew chock-full of tender shellfish in a briny-sweet broth with tomatoes, wine, garlic, and saffron, topped with garlic croutons and a thick red pepper sauce called *rouille*. But while this stew is a culinary delight when ordered at a restaurant, when made at home it can be a kitchen disaster, requiring precise maneuvering through a laundry list of steps. We thought it was a shame for such an appealing dish to remain only in the realm of restaurants and sought to create our own simplified version of this famed classic made just for two.

We broke the recipe down into its different components: the broth, the fish, and the garnishes. For the broth, most recipes call for a homemade fish stock to serve as the base, but even for a special dinner for two, we didn't think it was worth investing the extra time and labor. And since we were planning on cooking the shellfish directly in the pot with the broth—in some of the recipes we found the two are cooked separately—we were confident that their rich liquors would release flavor into the broth and make up for the absence of stock.

We started making the broth in the typical fashion, by sautéing aromatics—we used onion, garlic, and red bell pepper—until they had softened. Saffron, red pepper flakes, and a bay leaf were then added to form the distinct flavor base; a half-teaspoon of sweet paprika added some warmth.

Tomatoes and dry white wine were then added to the pot to finish the liquid base. Fresh tomatoes are available for such a brief time during the year that we immediately reached for canned. We considered both whole and diced tomatoes. Although we had to chop the whole tomatoes, their flavor and texture were preferred to canned diced tomatoes in this dish. Some recipes also include brandy in addition to white wine. After making the broth with and without, tasters favored the depth of flavor that brandy lent to the dish.

With our broth settled, it was now time to turn our attention to the shellfish. When it comes to bouillabaisse, almost any type of shellfish is fair game, but since we were preparing our stew for only two people we didn't want to go overboard. After much discussion, we settled on including shrimp, scallops, mussels, and clams—plenty of variety but still manageable. Each shellfish requires a different cooking time, so we knew we'd have to stagger their additions to the pot. After some trial and error, we determined that the clams should be added to the stew first, followed by the mussels and scallops, and finally the shrimp.

Up until this point, we had been using shell-on shrimp, but some tasters felt this made eating the stew a bit challenging and somewhat messy for what was supposed to be an elegant dinner. Knowing that the shrimp shells were contributing significant flavor to the broth, we couldn't just dump them into the trash can. So we began testing ways to use the shells to enrich the broth's flavor. In the end we sautéed the shells in a touch of olive oil and then steeped them in the wine we had been adding to the broth. After a quick strain of the wine to remove the shells, we had a terrific flavor boost for our broth.

With a flavorful broth and perfectly cooked shellfish, all that was left to do was to work on the rouille and croutons. Traditionally, rouille is made by emulsifying olive oil into a mixture of freshly roasted red pepper, bread, and garlic. While we liked the flavor of this rouille, jarred roasted red peppers were much easier and provided ample flavor. For the croutons, we found the broiler made easy work of toasting slices of French bread, and we simply rubbed them with garlic and brushed them with oil. Topping our bouillabaisse with some croutons and a dollop of rouille, we had found what we were looking for: a simplified recipe that still brought the clean, briny taste of the ocean to the home table.

NOTES FROM THE TEST KITCHEN

DEBEARDING MUSSELS

Mussels contain a small weedy beard that can be difficult to tug out of place. The easiest way to perform this task is to trap the beard between the side of a small paring knife and your thumb and pull to remove it.

Bouillabaisse
SERVES 2

Be sure to reserve the shrimp shells when cleaning the shrimp; they add important flavor to the sauce. Any small clams, such as littlenecks, will work well, but avoid large clams because they exude extra liquid that dilutes the broth. The cooking time of the scallops will depend on their size; we used large sea scallops, but if your scallops are smaller, they will cook more quickly and should be added to the pot with the shrimp. See page 131 for a recipe to use up the leftover red bell pepper.

- 2 **tablespoons olive oil**
- 8 **extra-large shrimp (21 to 25 per pound), peeled and deveined (see page 31), shells reserved**
- ¾ **cup dry white wine**
- 1 **small onion, minced**
- ½ **red bell pepper, stemmed, seeded, and chopped fine**
  Salt
- 2 **garlic cloves, minced**
- ½ **teaspoon paprika**
- ⅛ **teaspoon saffron threads**
  Pinch red pepper flakes
- 1 **bay leaf**
- 2 **tablespoons brandy**
- 1 **(14.5-ounce) can whole peeled tomatoes, drained, juice reserved, and chopped medium**
- 8 **small clams (about 12 ounces), scrubbed (see note)**
- 8 **mussels (about 4 ounces), scrubbed, beards removed (see photo)**
- 4 **large sea scallops (about 6 ounces), tendons removed (see page 126) (see note)**
  Pepper
- 1 **recipe Garlic Croutons (page 131)**
- 1 **recipe Rouille (page 131)**

1. Heat 1 tablespoon of the oil in a small saucepan over medium heat until shimmering. Add the reserved shrimp shells and cook until pink, about 3 minutes. Off the heat, stir in the wine, cover, and let steep until ready to use.

2. Heat the remaining 1 tablespoon oil in a large saucepan over medium heat until shimmering. Add the onion, bell pepper, and ¼ teaspoon salt, and cook until the onion is softened and lightly browned, 5 to 7 minutes. Stir in the garlic, paprika, saffron, red pepper flakes, and bay leaf, and cook until fragrant, about 30 seconds. Stir in the brandy and simmer for

30 seconds. Stir in the tomatoes and juice and cook until slightly thickened, 3 to 5 minutes.

3. Strain the wine mixture into the tomato sauce through a fine-mesh strainer, pressing on the shrimp shells to extract as much liquid as possible; discard the shells. Continue to simmer the sauce until the flavors have melded, 3 to 5 minutes longer.

4. Increase the heat to medium-high, add the clams, cover, and cook, stirring occasionally, until the first few clams begin to open, about 4 minutes. Add the mussels and scallops, cover, and continue to cook until most of the clams have opened, about 2 minutes longer. Add the shrimp, cover, and continue to cook until the shrimp are pink and cooked through and the clams and mussels have opened, about 2 minutes longer.

5. Discard the bay leaf and any clams or mussels that have not opened. Season with salt and pepper to taste. Ladle the stew into individual bowls, top with the croutons and a dollop of rouille, and serve.

Garlic Croutons
MAKES 4 CROUTONS

For an attractive presentation, slice the bread on the bias.

- **4 (½-inch-thick) slices French bread (about 1 ounce)**
- **1 garlic clove, peeled**
- **2 teaspoons olive oil**

Adjust an oven rack to the upper-middle position and heat the broiler. Arrange the bread slices in a single layer on a baking sheet and broil until lightly toasted on both sides, 2 to 4 minutes, flipping them halfway through. Rub the garlic clove over one side of each piece of toast and brush with the oil. (The croutons can be kept at room temperature for up to 4 hours before serving.)

Rouille
MAKES ABOUT ½ CUP

Though this sauce is typically made with freshly roasted peppers, we found that good-quality jarred roasted red peppers work just fine.

- **½ cup jarred roasted red peppers (about 4 ounces), patted dry and coarsely chopped**
- **6 (½-inch-thick) slices French bread (about 1½ ounces), crusts discarded, torn into pieces**

USE IT UP: BELL PEPPER

Pepper Relish
MAKES ABOUT ⅓ CUP

Serve this relish over cream cheese and with crackers for a lively appetizer or use it as a spread on sandwiches. To make the relish spicier, increase the amount of red pepper flakes.

- **1 tablespoon vegetable oil**
- **1 small onion, minced**
- **½ red or green bell pepper, stemmed, seeded, and chopped fine**
- **1 garlic clove, minced**
- **⅛ teaspoon red pepper flakes**
- **½ cup water**
- **3 tablespoons cider vinegar**
- **3 tablespoons sugar**
- **⅛ teaspoon salt**

1. Heat the oil in a small saucepan over medium heat until shimmering. Add the onion and bell pepper and cook until softened and lightly browned, 5 to 7 minutes. Stir in the garlic and pepper flakes and cook until fragrant, about 30 seconds.

2. Stir in the water, vinegar, sugar, and salt, and bring to a boil. Reduce the heat to medium-low and simmer, stirring occasionally, until the mixture thickens to a jam-like consistency, about 30 minutes. Cool to room temperature before serving. (The relish can be refrigerated in an airtight container for up to 2 weeks.)

- **1 tablespoon water**
- **1 small garlic clove, minced**
- **Pinch cayenne pepper**
- **2 tablespoons olive oil**
- **Salt**

Process the roasted peppers, bread, water, garlic, and cayenne in a food processor until smooth, about 1 minute, scraping down the sides of the bowl as needed. With the machine running, gradually add the oil through the feed tube in a slow, steady stream and process until the rouille has a thick, mayonnaise-like consistency, 1 to 2 minutes. Season with salt to taste. (The rouille can be refrigerated in an airtight container for up to 24 hours.)

GAZPACHO WITH SHRIMP

ON THE LIGHTER SIDE

GAZPACHO

POPULAR ON BOTH SIDES OF THE ATLANTIC, gazpacho is a Spanish soup made of tomatoes (both whole and juice), cucumbers, bell peppers, and onions. The vegetables are seasoned with olive oil and vinegar, then the soup is chilled before being served. The most time-consuming part of the recipe is the chopping—with all the vegetables to prepare, this step can take a good chunk of time. Perhaps the level of effort and the time required are why this soup is traditionally made in large quantities. So we set out to develop a recipe for gazpacho for two, and we knew that scaling back the components in just the right ratio would be key to keeping the flavors balanced and lightening the workload.

Before we addressed ingredients and quantities, we needed to establish what type of gazpacho we were after. Traditionally, gazpacho is thickened with water-soaked bread for extra body, but modern recipes often skip the bread altogether. In addition to determining thickness, we had to decide whether we would puree the soup, as in some recipes, or leave it chunky. After testing examples of each, we came to the conclusion that bread-free, chunky gazpacho was a better candidate for our small-scale recipe. It would be simpler to prepare than the fussier bread-thickened and pureed soups.

With our preference for a chunky-style soup established, we set out to nail down the details and quantities of our vegetables. While many recipes called for several pounds of tomatoes, we found that one large, 8-ounce tomato was a good amount for two. We considered skinning and seeding the tomato, but not a single taster complained when we didn't, so we skipped the extra steps.

We found that half a bell pepper and half a cucumber provided the right vegetable balance with the tomato. Red bell pepper was preferred over green for its sweeter flavor. Tasters also favored sweeter shallot or red onion over yellow and white onion. For the sake of convenience, we went with a single shallot.

Next we looked at the best method for preparing the vegetables. Before we got out the cutting board, we gave our small appliances a shot. Even when processed for a short time, the vegetables broke down beyond recognition in the blender. They fared only somewhat better in the food processor—no matter how we finessed the pulse feature, the vegetable pieces were neither neatly chopped nor consistently sized, resulting in a soup more along the lines of a vegetable slushy. We ultimately chopped the vegetables by hand, knowing that with the smaller quantity, the work would go swiftly. The benefits to the gazpacho's texture were significant. Because the vegetable pieces were consistent in size and shape, they not only retained their individual flavors but also set off the tomato broth nicely.

To draw out the flavor of the vegetables and to ensure thorough seasoning, we marinated the vegetables in garlic, salt, pepper, and sherry vinegar before adding the liquid. Spain is a noted producer of sherry, so it follows that sherry vinegar is a popular choice for gazpacho. When we tasted it, along with champagne, red wine, and white wine vinegars, the sherry vinegar was our favorite by far, adding not only acidity but also richness and depth.

For the liquid component, most recipes called for tomato juice, which we sampled both straight and mixed in various amounts with water. The winning ratio was 1 cup of tomato juice thinned with ⅓ cup of water. The water cut the viscosity of the juice just enough to make it brothy and light, but not downright thin. Since we prefer ice-cold gazpacho, we decided to add ice cubes instead of water. The ice helped chill the soup while providing water as it melted. We refrigerated the soup for four hours (but it can be refrigerated for up to two days) to allow it to chill and the flavors to blossom.

NOTES FROM THE TEST KITCHEN

PREPARING TOMATO FOR GAZPACHO

1. After coring and halving the tomato lengthwise, scoop out the pulp and chop it finely. Then cut the tomato halves into ¼-inch-thick slices.

2. Cut the tomato slices into ¼-inch pieces.

To round out the individual bowls of soup, we made some easy garlic croutons and sprinkled them on top. A final dash of fresh parsley (or cilantro) enhanced the garden-fresh flavor of the soup, and a drizzle of extra-virgin olive oil added lushness. Cooked shrimp also made an excellent garnish, so we included it for a more substantial variation.

Gazpacho

SERVES 2

Cutting the vegetables into small (¼-inch) pieces is important for the texture of this soup; don't hesitate to pull out a ruler when preparing the vegetables. See page 131 for a recipe to use up the leftover red bell pepper.

 1 large tomato (about 8 ounces)
 ½ red bell pepper, stemmed and seeded
 ½ cucumber, seeded
 1 shallot, minced
 1 small garlic clove, minced
 2 tablespoons sherry vinegar
   Salt and pepper
 1 cup low-sodium tomato juice
 ¼ teaspoon hot sauce (optional)
 3 ice cubes
 2 teaspoons extra-virgin olive oil
 2 tablespoons minced fresh parsley
   or cilantro
 1 recipe Garlic Croutons (see page 136)

1. Following the photos, cut the tomato, bell pepper, and cucumber into ¼-inch pieces. Combine the tomato with its juice, bell pepper, cucumber, shallot, garlic, vinegar, ¼ teaspoon salt, and ¼ teaspoon pepper in a medium bowl, and let sit at room temperature for 5 minutes.

2. Stir in the tomato juice, hot sauce (if using), and ice cubes. Cover and refrigerate until the flavors blend, at least 4 hours or up to 2 days.

3. Remove and discard any unmelted ice cubes. Season with salt and pepper to taste. Serve chilled, drizzling each portion with the olive oil, sprinkling with the parsley, and topping with the croutons.

PER SERVING: Cal 200; Fat 6g; Sat fat 0.5g; Chol 0mg; Carb 30g; Protein 4g; Fiber 4g; Sodium 760mg

VARIATION

Gazpacho with Shrimp

Follow the recipe for Gazpacho, adding 4 ounces cooked, peeled, and deveined small shrimp (51 to 60 per pound) to the soup before topping with the olive oil, parsley, and croutons in step 3.

PER SERVING: Cal 310; Fat 7g; Sat fat 1g; Chol 220mg; Carb 30g; Protein 29g; Fiber 4g; Sodium 1020mg

NOTES FROM THE TEST KITCHEN

PREPARING BELL PEPPER FOR GAZPACHO

1. After stemming and seeding half of a bell pepper, slice it into ¼-inch-thick strips.

2. Cut the thin strips of pepper into ¼-inch pieces.

PREPARING CUCUMBER FOR GAZPACHO

1. After seeding the cucumber, slice it lengthwise into long, ¼-inch-thick strips.

2. Cut the thin strips of cucumber into ¼-inch pieces.

Garlic Croutons

MAKES 1 CUP

We prefer to use Italian or French bread to make these croutons, but any type of bread will work fine. Olive oil spray can be substituted for the vegetable oil spray.

- **1 cup ½-inch bread cubes (about 2 ounces)**
  Vegetable oil spray (see note)
- **⅛ teaspoon salt**
- **⅛ teaspoon garlic powder**

Adjust an oven rack to the middle position and heat the oven to 350 degrees. Spray the bread cubes generously with vegetable oil spray, then toss with the salt and garlic powder. Spread the bread cubes on a rimmed baking sheet and bake until golden brown, 20 to 25 minutes, stirring halfway through baking. Let cool to room temperature before using.

PER ½-CUP SERVING: Cal 70; Fat 0.5g; Sat fat 0g; Chol 0mg; Carb 14g; Protein 2g; Fiber 1g; Sodium 380mg

MEDITERRANEAN TUNA SALAD

WHILE WE LOVE TRADITIONAL TUNA SALAD, IT CAN make a sandwich so high in calories that it is on a par with a greasy burger. The culprit? The mayonnaise. We wanted to rethink tuna salad—after all, canned tuna is healthy and incredibly convenient, and it can be the perfect basis for a last-minute lunch or supper. To give the classic tuna salad a much-needed facelift, we would swap mayonnaise for olive oil and create a fresh Mediterranean-style tuna salad with a healthier, boldly flavored profile.

We knew that the kind of tuna we used would be crucial, so we started there. A side-by-side tasting showed that tasters preferred solid white albacore tuna packed in water, the mildest variety of processed tuna, over chunk light tuna in water; the chunk light tuna had unappealing strong flavors. We sampled pouched tuna as well but found the tuna to be mushy (pouched tuna is broken down more to fit into the narrow opening of the pouch), so we stuck with canned. Water-packed solid white tuna was praised for its meaty flavor and delicate texture. One 5-ounce can provided the right amount of meat for two diners.

A few small details made a huge difference in the finished salad. We found that the common practice of removing excess water in the can simply by pressing the detached lid down on the tuna for a few seconds makes for a watery tuna salad. Instead, we took an extra minute to drain the tuna thoroughly in a colander before mixing it. This gave the salad a toothsome, less watery texture and also got rid of any metallic flavors from the canning liquid. We also decided to ditch the fork when breaking apart the tuna, preferring to use our fingers to achieve a uniform, flaky texture that evenly absorbed dressing and seasonings.

Now that we had our tuna the way we wanted it, we tested other additions to the salad. Tasters liked the traditional chopped celery and onion, particularly milder onion flavor, such as that of red onion. Since we needed only a few tablespoons of onion, a shallot achieved the same delicate sweetness as a red onion with nothing left over. In keeping with the Mediterranean theme, chopped kalamata olives gave the salad a briny, rich pungency, and red bell pepper added a bright, sweet accent.

We wanted a dressing that was simple and clean-tasting but had some depth. Looking for an acid to pair with the olive oil, we tried a few different vinegars (balsamic vinegar, red wine vinegar, and rice vinegar), but none of them was quite right. In the end, simple, fresh lemon juice was the winner, brightening the salad without overwhelming it. We found that the combination of 1½ tablespoons of olive oil and 2 teaspoons of lemon juice was well balanced and the right quantity to coat

NOTES FROM THE TEST KITCHEN

THE BEST INEXPENSIVE SAFETY CAN OPENER
Traditional can openers cut through can lids from the top, leaving sharp edges on the lids (which sit atop the contents and must be fished out). Safety can openers, on the other hand, cut from the side and remove the entire top part of the can (lid and all), leaving dull, "safe" edges behind. We rounded up six safety openers as well as two traditional openers boasting "safer" operation, all priced under $20, to find out which one worked best. The surprise favorite was the traditional-style **OXO Good Grips i-Series Can Opener**, $19.95. It features a lid-catching magnet that made disposing of the lid easy and safe; it was also intuitive, comfortable to use, and very efficient.

the salad nicely. The addition of a small amount of garlic and Dijon mustard added dimension and tang. We marinated the shallot and garlic in the dressing for five minutes to mellow their flavor and incorporate them throughout the dish. A final sprinkling of parsley finished the dish.

For an interesting variation, we traded out the red pepper and celery for sweet shredded carrot and peppery radish; we also substituted minced cilantro for the parsley. In just minutes, we had two mayo-free takes on tuna salads. And best of all, our salads are fresh-tasting and flavorful.

Mediterranean Tuna Salad

SERVES 2

High-quality olive oil and canned tuna (solid white albacore packed in water) are crucial to the success of this recipe. Serve over mixed salad greens or in a sandwich. See page 131 for a recipe to use up the leftover red bell pepper and page 10 for a recipe to use up the leftover celery.

1½ tablespoons extra-virgin olive oil
2 teaspoons fresh lemon juice
1 small garlic clove, minced
¼ teaspoon Dijon mustard
   Salt and pepper
1 small shallot, minced
1 (5-ounce) can solid white tuna in water
1 celery rib, chopped fine
½ red bell pepper, stemmed, seeded, and chopped fine
1 tablespoon chopped pitted kalamata olives
1 tablespoon minced fresh parsley

1. Whisk the oil, lemon juice, garlic, mustard, ¼ teaspoon salt, and ⅛ teaspoon pepper together in a medium bowl. Stir in the shallot and let sit at room temperature for 5 minutes.

2. Meanwhile, drain the tuna in a colander. Using your fingers, shred the tuna to a fine texture until no clumps remain.

3. Add the shredded tuna, celery, bell pepper, olives, and parsley to the dressing, and toss to combine. Season with salt and pepper to taste and serve.

PER SERVING: Cal 200; Fat 14g; Sat fat 2g; Chol 20mg; Carb 6g; Protein 12g; Fiber 1g; Sodium 610mg

VARIATION

Mediterranean Tuna Salad with Carrot, Radishes, and Cilantro

Follow the recipe for Mediterranean Tuna Salad, substituting 3 minced radishes for the celery, ½ peeled and shredded carrot for the bell pepper, and 1 tablespoon minced fresh cilantro for the parsley.

PER SERVING: Cal 200; Fat 14g; Sat fat 2g; Chol 20mg; Carb 6g; Protein 12g; Fiber 1g; Sodium 610mg

GREEK CHOPPED SALAD

THE BEST CHOPPED SALADS ARE LIVELY COMBINATIONS of lettuce and other vegetables, cut into bite-sized pieces, with supporting players like cheese contributing hearty flavors and textures. Unfortunately, we've had more experience with the mediocre kind. These are little better than a random collection of cut-up produce from the crisper drawer, exuding moisture that blends in with the copious amounts of heavy dressing, turning the salad watery and bland. We wanted a salad with complementary flavors and textures in every bite. It should also be healthy and have a modest fat content (under 15 grams per serving seemed reasonable for a substantial salad like this one) but hearty enough for a light dinner for two. And while the salad should have variety, we wanted to keep the shopping list at a reasonable length since we were preparing only two servings.

Having just developed a tuna salad with Mediterranean flavors that was very successful, we decided to expand on that flavor profile with a Greek-style chopped salad. We started out with the usual suspects: cucumber, tomatoes (bite-sized cherry tomatoes fit the bill here), crumbled feta, a few kalamata olives, and mild, crisp romaine. A generous handful of parsley supplemented the romaine. Next we added creamy chickpeas, which contrasted well with the vegetal components and gave the salad heartiness. Red onion was a natural addition, but as we'd found when scaling other salads for two, a shallot was a better fit as it minimized the pile of leftover vegetables.

Salad ingredients selected, we were ready to address the issue of sogginess that was prevalent in the recipes we researched and tested. Salting some of the vegetables to remove excess moisture was an obvious first step.

We singled out the two worst offenders: cucumbers and tomatoes. We halved a cucumber and scooped out its watery seeds before dicing it, tossing it with salt, and allowing it to drain in a colander. After 15 minutes, the cucumber had shed more than a teaspoon of water. As for the cherry tomatoes, seeding them was out of the question; much of the tomato flavor is concentrated in the seeds and surrounding jelly. But we did cut them into quarters to expose more surface area to the salt, which released 1 tablespoon of liquid from ⅔ cup of tomatoes.

Next we looked at the dressing. After some initial testing, it became clear that most of the dressings weren't doing anything for the chopped salads except weighing them down. Most recipes for chopped salads called for a

ratio of 3 parts oil to 1 part vinegar. This proportion is optimal for dressing tender, subtly flavored leafy greens. A more assertive blend of equal parts oil and vinegar was far better at delivering the bright, acidic kick needed in our hearty, chunky salad. We found that not much more than 2 tablespoons of dressing—a tablespoon each of extra-virgin olive oil and red wine vinegar, plus a small clove of garlic—was enough to coat our ingredients. As an added bonus, the reduction in oil cut down on the fat and calories in our salad.

Looking to enhance our salad further, we wondered if we could use the dressing to even greater advantage. Tossing a green salad just before serving prevents the tender leaves from absorbing too much dressing and turning soggy. But a little flavor absorption by some of the sturdier components of a chopped salad would actually be a good thing. We found that marinating the heartier ingredients in the dressing for just five minutes before adding the feta and romaine brought a welcome flavor boost to our salad while still keeping it fresh and light.

NOTES FROM THE TEST KITCHEN

THE BEST PARING KNIFE

A short, nimble paring knife can accomplish all of the small, close jobs that a chef's knife can't, such as quartering cherry tomatoes, cutting citrus segments, and slivering garlic. In our tests, we found that the way a paring knife feels in your hand makes a big difference. Also, the blade should be somewhat flexible for easy maneuvering into tight spots and for handling curves when peeling and paring. Our preferred paring knife is the **Victorinox Fibrox Paring Knife** (formerly Victorinox Forschner), $12.95, which has a slightly flexible blade that holds a sharp edge for days.

WHAT'S IN YOUR VINEGAR?

Many people know that vinegar will keep for a long time if stored in a dark pantry at room temperature, which is good news when you're cooking for two and not using a lot of vinegar at any one time. Most vinegars, in fact, will last indefinitely because they contain about 5 percent acetic acid, which (along with pasteurization) prevents the growth of harmful bacteria. So then what's up with the sediment or particles seen floating in some vinegars that have been properly stored? Once a bottle of vinegar has been opened and the contents exposed to air, harmless "vinegar bacteria" may start to grow. These bacteria cause the formation of that cloudy sediment, which is nothing more than harmless cellulose, a complex carbohydrate that does not affect the quality of the vinegar or its flavor. But if the unsightly sediment bothers you, simply strain the vinegar through a coffee filter set inside a fine-mesh strainer before using it.

Greek Chopped Salad

SERVES 2

See page 140 for a recipe to use up the leftover chickpeas and page 131 for a recipe to use up the leftover red bell pepper.

- ½ cucumber, peeled, halved lengthwise, seeded, and cut into ½-inch pieces
- 4 ounces cherry tomatoes (about ⅔ cup), quartered
  Salt
- 1 tablespoon extra-virgin olive oil
- 1 tablespoon red wine vinegar
- 1 small garlic clove, minced
- ¾ cup drained and rinsed canned chickpeas
- 2 tablespoons chopped pitted kalamata olives
- ¼ cup minced fresh parsley
- 1 shallot, minced
- ½ romaine lettuce heart, cut into ½-inch pieces (about 1½ cups)
- 1 ounce feta cheese, crumbled (about ¼ cup)
  Pepper

GREEK CHOPPED SALAD

1. Toss the cucumber and tomatoes with ¼ teaspoon salt and let drain in a colander for 15 minutes.

2. Whisk the oil, vinegar, and garlic together in a medium bowl. Add the drained cucumber and tomatoes, chickpeas, olives, parsley, and shallot, and toss to combine. Let sit at room temperature for 5 minutes.

3. Add the romaine and feta and toss to combine. Season with salt and pepper to taste and serve.

PER SERVING: Cal 230; Fat 14g; Sat fat 3g; Chol 10mg; Carb 18g; Protein 8g; Fiber 5g; Sodium 750mg

---

USE IT UP: CHICKPEAS

Curried Chickpeas
SERVES 2

Serve as a side dish to grilled chicken. To make this dish vegetarian, substitute vegetable broth for the chicken broth.

- 1 **teaspoon vegetable oil**
- 1 **shallot, minced**
- 1 **garlic clove, minced**
- ¼ **teaspoon curry powder**
- ¾ **cup drained and rinsed canned chickpeas**
- ½ **cup low-sodium chicken broth (see note)**
- 2 **tablespoons raisins**
- ½ **teaspoon fresh lime juice or lemon juice**
- 1 **tablespoon minced fresh cilantro, parsley, or chives**
  Salt and pepper

1. Heat the oil in an 8-inch skillet over medium heat until shimmering. Add the shallot and cook until softened and lightly browned, 3 to 5 minutes. Stir in the garlic and curry powder and cook until fragrant, about 30 seconds.

2. Stir in the chickpeas, broth, and raisins, and bring to a simmer. Reduce the heat to medium-low, cover, and cook until the chickpeas have softened, about 5 minutes. Uncover, increase the heat to medium-high, and simmer until the liquid thickens slightly, about 2 minutes.

3. Off the heat, stir in the lime juice and cilantro and season with salt and pepper to taste. Serve.

PER SERVING: Cal 130; Fat 3.5g; Sat fat 0g; Chol 0mg; Carb 22g; Protein 4g; Fiber 4g; Sodium 360mg

ASIAN CABBAGE SALAD WITH CHICKEN

ASIAN CABBAGE SALAD CAN BE A WELCOME alternative to both mayonnaise-rich coleslaw and the monotony of limp green lettuce salads. Typically composed of shredded cabbage studded with a few bright vegetables, tossed in vinaigrette, and topped with a crunchy garnish of nuts, Asian cabbage salad offers bold flavor, textural contrast, and visual appeal. Add some shredded chicken to the mix and you have an easy and satisfying healthy supper for two. Research of existing recipes, however, revealed that this salad can go bad fast, with cabbage buried in a frenzy of garnishes, such as bean sprouts, bamboo shoots, and fried noodles. When cooking for two, these epic-long ingredient lists often result in numerous leftovers that don't lend themselves easily to other uses. Furthermore, many recipes have oily dressings that mute the freshness of the ingredients. Intent on eliminating the clutter and excess ingredients, we headed to the test kitchen. Our goal was to create a simple cabbage salad that was light, featuring crisp cabbage and moist chicken tossed in a bright, well-balanced vinaigrette.

First we wanted to nail down the vegetables, starting with the cabbage. Thinly sliced napa cabbage was a natural choice, and we determined that half a head was a good amount for two diners. Rather than throw in everything but the kitchen sink, we chose a few flavorful additions to complement the crisp, subtly mustard-flavored napa. The sweetness of a shredded carrot worked well, as did a couple of thinly sliced scallions. A generous handful of both cilantro and mint added a bold, aromatic brightness. The only thing missing now was some textural contrast, a situation we remedied with a small sprinkle of crunchy peanuts.

As for the chicken, we wanted it to be fresh and moist, so leftover roast or grilled chicken was not an option. At the same time, we didn't want to make preparing the chicken a production, especially since we had determined that a single boneless, skinless breast—both lean and quick-cooking—was the right amount for a salad serving two. Considering cooking technique, we wanted the flavor and color of browning, but browning both sides of the chicken breast required more oil than we wanted to use. We found our answer in a half-sautéing, half-poaching method that required very little fat. First we browned the chicken on one side in a single teaspoon of oil, then we flipped the chicken over, added a small amount of water to the skillet, reduced the heat, and covered the skillet until the chicken was cooked through. This method yielded moist, flavorful chicken.

With the salad components in place, we tackled the dressing. Many recipes we found used ½ cup of oil for a head of cabbage. Not surprisingly, tasters thought that scaled-down versions of these dressings (using ¼ cup of oil) were heavy and dull. With 2 tablespoons of oil the dressing was reasonably light, but tasters were convinced we could go lower still. We settled on only 2 teaspoons of oil, which added the perfect richness but ensured that the brighter flavors in the dressing would shine through.

Next we needed an acid to balance the oil. We found that rice vinegar was the most commonly used acid, though some recipes called for other vinegars. We tested a variety, and in the end rice vinegar proved best; its mild acidity and slight sweetness (enhanced by a tablespoon of sugar) were ideal for keeping this salad fresh and light. A small amount of minced ginger and a clove of garlic were natural additions. For a salty element we tried soy sauce, but the dressing tasted flat and predictable. A tablespoon of fish sauce, however, was successful, adding briny, savory depth to the salad. A small amount of Asian chili-garlic sauce added heat and brightened the other flavors.

While the overall flavor of the dressing was spot-on, tasters found it to be a little raw and harsh. Looking for a solution, we thought of a coleslaw recipe where we'd cooked the dressing to meld the flavors and poured it—still hot—over the salad. It seemed worth a shot—plus we could use the same skillet we'd used to cook the chicken. As it turned out, not only did a short exposure

to heat round out the flavor of the dressing, but the hot vinaigrette was more readily absorbed by the salad, and it wilted the vegetables just enough to unify the salad without losing the crunchiness of the cabbage.

Warm Asian Cabbage Salad with Chicken
SERVES 2

Be careful not to simmer the dressing for very long before adding the chicken in step 5 or it will reduce too much. To make the salad spicy, use the greater amount of Asian chili-garlic sauce. See page 142 for a recipe to use up the leftover napa cabbage.

SALAD
- ½ small head napa cabbage (about ½ pound), cored and sliced thin (about 2 cups)
- 1 carrot, peeled and shredded
- ¼ cup minced fresh mint
- ¼ cup fresh cilantro
- 2 scallions, sliced thin on the bias (optional)
- 1½ tablespoons coarsely chopped peanuts

CHICKEN AND DRESSING
- 1 (8-ounce) boneless, skinless chicken breast, trimmed
- ⅛ teaspoon salt
- ⅛ teaspoon pepper
- 1 tablespoon vegetable oil
- 1 garlic clove, minced
- 1½ teaspoons grated or minced fresh ginger
- 2½ tablespoons rice vinegar
- 1 tablespoon fish sauce
- 1 tablespoon sugar
- ½-1 teaspoon Asian chili-garlic sauce (see note)

1. FOR THE SALAD: Combine all of the ingredients in a medium bowl and set aside.

2. FOR THE CHICKEN AND DRESSING: Pat the chicken dry with paper towels and season with the salt and pepper. Heat 1 teaspoon of the oil in an 8-inch non-stick skillet over medium-high heat until just smoking. Carefully lay the chicken breast in the skillet and cook until lightly browned on the first side, about 3 minutes.

3. Flip the chicken, add ⅓ cup water, and cover. Reduce the heat to medium and continue to cook until the chicken registers 160 to 165 degrees on an instant-read thermometer, 6 to 8 minutes longer.

4. Transfer the chicken to a carving board, let cool slightly, then shred into bite-sized pieces.

5. Discard any water left in the skillet and wipe clean with paper towels. Heat the remaining 2 teaspoons oil in the skillet over medium heat until shimmering. Add the garlic and ginger and cook until fragrant, about 30 seconds. Whisk in the vinegar, fish sauce, sugar, and chili-garlic sauce, and bring to a simmer. Stir in the shredded chicken and cook until warmed through, about 30 seconds.

6. Pour the chicken and dressing over the cabbage mixture, toss to combine, and serve.

PER SERVING: **Cal** 310; **Fat** 12g; **Sat fat** 1.5g; **Chol** 65mg; **Carb** 19g; **Protein** 31g; **Fiber** 4g; **Sodium** 650mg

---

USE IT UP: NAPA CABBAGE

Quick Kimchi
SERVES 2

Kimchi is a pickled vegetable condiment that can be served as a side dish for Asian rice dishes or grilled meats. This kimchi is fairly spicy; use the lesser amount of red pepper flakes for a milder flavor. The kimchi can be refrigerated in an airtight container for up to 4 days.

- ½ **small head napa cabbage (about ½ pound), cored and cut into ¾-inch pieces (about 2 cups)**
- ½ **teaspoon salt**
- 2 **scallions, sliced thin**
- 1 **tablespoon rice vinegar**
- 2 **teaspoons fish sauce**
- 1½ **teaspoons sugar**
- ½–1 **teaspoon red pepper flakes (see note)**
- 1 **garlic clove, minced**
- 1 **teaspoon grated or minced fresh ginger**

1. Toss the cabbage with the salt in a colander and let sit until wilted, about 1 hour. Rinse the cabbage with cold water, then drain and dry well with paper towels. Transfer to a small bowl and add the scallions.

2. In another bowl, whisk the remaining ingredients together until the sugar is dissolved. Pour over the cabbage mixture and toss to coat. Cover and refrigerate for at least 1 hour before serving.

PER SERVING: **Cal** 50; **Fat** 0g; **Sat fat** 0g; **Chol** 0mg; **Carb** 9g; **Protein** 3g; **Fiber** 2g; **Sodium** 540mg

CURRIED CHICKEN SKEWERS

BONELESS, SKINLESS CHICKEN BREASTS ARE PACKED with protein, virtually fat-free, and frequently sold in convenient packages of two. The challenge comes when looking for alternatives to simple baked, pan-roasted, or poached (see page 144) chicken breasts—dishes that are fairly light and lean. Popular at parties and restaurants, chicken skewers came to mind. Good chicken skewers boast ultra-juicy and well-seasoned meat, but they're usually accompanied by a rich, creamy dipping sauce that can tip the fat scales fairly high. We knew that if we could lighten up the sauce and create a foolproof recipe for tender, well-seasoned strips of chicken, we'd have the makings of a light yet flavorful supper for two.

First we needed to pick a flavor profile for our chicken and decide how we would incorporate it. Since chicken has a mild flavor, it is usually soaked in a zesty marinade or coated with a highly spiced glaze before skewering. We decided to combine both methods: We could marinate the chicken in a thick, sweet, spiced marinade that would also act as a glaze and promote browning during cooking. In terms of thickness and sugar content, honey fit the bill perfectly. For the dominant flavor, we selected curry, a common ingredient in skewer marinades. Starting with a moderate amount of honey (1½ tablespoons), we stirred in the curry powder, along with some paprika, salt, and garlic powder, until we had achieved a good balance of sweet and savory.

After slicing two chicken breasts into long strips that would easily slide onto skewers and coating the strips with the spice mixture, we tested a range of marinating times, from one hour up to 24 hours. While the cooked chicken that was marinated for one hour was good, we found that a longer marinating time resulted in better flavor. However, after 24 hours the texture of the chicken began to deteriorate and turn mushy.

For the cooking method, grilling is an obvious choice when serving up skewers for a crowd, but it didn't seem worth it to heat the grill to cook skewers for two. Broiling was a better option; the broiler heats up quickly and is easy to monitor.

Because these skewers would be eaten out of hand, tasters preferred wooden to metal skewers; the metal skewers were incredibly hot straight from the oven and didn't look as attractive on the plate. The only downside to wooden skewers is that they run the risk of smoldering under the broiler. To combat this issue, after sliding our chicken strips onto the skewers, we lined up the meat side of the skewers on the same side of the broiler pan and protected the exposed wood with a strip of aluminum foil. Arranged about 6 inches below the broiler element, the chicken cooked through in 10 minutes and the skewers themselves remained unharmed.

Finally, it was time to make over the dipping sauce, which is usually made with full-fat yogurt. We tried swapping in low-fat yogurt, but it was too runny unless we took the extra step of draining it (see below). Then we turned to low-fat Greek yogurt, which is thicker than regular yogurt; it made a sauce that was tangy and rich. Some mint, a chopped scallion, and a small clove of garlic enhanced the savory notes of the sauce and paired well with the curry flavor in our skewers.

At last, our chicken was tender, the sauce bright (and lighter), and we didn't have to spend the next day cleaning up after a party.

Curried Chicken Skewers with Yogurt-Mint Dipping Sauce

SERVES 2

You will need six 10-inch wooden skewers for this recipe. To make it easier to cut the chicken into thin, neat strips, place it in the freezer for 15 minutes. We prefer the flavor and richness of 2 percent Greek yogurt to that of nonfat Greek yogurt.

CHICKEN

- 1½ tablespoons honey
- 1 teaspoon curry powder
- ¼ teaspoon salt
- ¼ teaspoon paprika
- ⅛ teaspoon red pepper flakes
- ⅛ teaspoon garlic powder
- 2 (6-ounce) boneless, skinless chicken breasts, trimmed (see note)

SAUCE

- ½ cup 2 percent Greek yogurt
- 2 tablespoons minced fresh mint
- 1 tablespoon water
- 1 scallion, sliced thin (optional)
- 1 small garlic clove, minced
  Salt and pepper

NOTES FROM THE TEST KITCHEN

MAKING CHICKEN SKEWERS

1. Using a chef's knife, slice the partially frozen chicken on the bias into ½-inch-thick strips.

2. Weave the marinated chicken securely onto six 10-inch wooden skewers. You will be able to fit two or three pieces of chicken per skewer.

3. To keep the exposed portions of the skewers from burning, cover the ends of the skewers with a piece of foil.

ALL ABOUT GREEK YOGURT

We use low-fat Greek yogurt in the sauce for our Curried Chicken Skewers because it adds richness and creaminess without adding too much fat. Greek yogurt is thicker and creamier than American-style yogurts; much of the whey (the watery liquid that separates from the solids) is strained out of Greek yogurt, giving it a rich, smooth texture that is slightly thicker than that of sour cream. In terms of flavor, Greek yogurt is fairly mild, with a slight tang. Greek yogurt is available in many supermarkets, but there's an easy way to improvise with regular low-fat yogurt. Simply strain plain low-fat yogurt in a fine-mesh strainer lined with a coffee filter and set over a bowl to catch the whey. After one hour (in the refrigerator, covered with plastic wrap), the yogurt will have reduced in volume by one-third, achieving a thick, rich consistency and flavor closely resembling that of Greek yogurt.

1. FOR THE CHICKEN: Combine the honey, curry powder, salt, paprika, red pepper flakes, and garlic powder in a large bowl. Following the photo on page 143, slice the chicken on the bias into ½-inch-thick strips. Add the chicken to the spice mixture and toss to coat. Cover the bowl and refrigerate for at least 1 hour, or up to 24 hours.

2. FOR THE SAUCE: Meanwhile, combine the yogurt, mint, water, scallion (if using), and garlic in a small bowl, and season with salt and pepper to taste. Cover and refrigerate until needed.

3. Position an oven rack 6 inches from the broiler element and heat the broiler. Line a rimmed baking sheet with foil and spray with vegetable oil spray. Following the photos on page 143, weave the chicken evenly onto six 10-inch wooden skewers. Lay the skewers on the prepared baking sheet and cover the skewer ends with foil.

4. Broil the skewers until the chicken is fully cooked and beginning to brown, about 10 minutes, flipping the skewers halfway through. Transfer the skewers to a serving platter and serve with the sauce.

PER SERVING: **Cal** 280; **Fat** 3.5g; **Sat fat** 1.5g; **Chol** 100mg; **Carb** 18g; **Protein** 45g; **Fiber** 1g; **Sodium** 420mg

SPA CHICKEN

WHEN COOKING FOR TWO, POACHING IS AN EASY way to get a healthy dinner on the table in half an hour using a minimum of ingredients. And when prepared correctly, poached chicken breasts boast such tender meat that few other cooking methods can compete. But because the method relies on moist heat—and no oil or butter—a careful hand is required to prevent the meat from turning dry or chalky. We set out to develop a reliable poaching technique that would consistently deliver moist, flavorful chicken—without added fat.

Our first consideration was the cooking liquid. Traditional poaching liquids consist of water, wine, herbs, vegetables, and aromatics that are boiled briefly and then strained. This method produces flavorful results, but since we were cooking dinner for two, we'd have to purchase and prepare a slew of ingredients, only to dump them down the drain at the end. This waste isn't bothersome when you're preparing dinner to feed a group, but it's hardly worth it for a simple Tuesday night supper.

Starting from scratch, we decided to compose a flavorful poaching liquid with just a few ingredients that required minimal prep and were likely to be on hand. For the liquid component, we decided to use the minimal quantity of water that we would need to cook two chicken breasts in order to get the most concentrated flavor. A few cloves of garlic, smashed, and some sprigs of thyme briefly simmered in a cup of water gave us a good start. But the flavor was missing something. Scouring the pantry, we fell upon soy sauce, which we've often used in the test kitchen in small quantities to add meaty flavor to non-Asian dishes. Just 2 teaspoons were enough to give the chicken a complex, savory flavor that tasters noticed but couldn't identify as soy sauce.

We had nailed the flavor issue, but tasters complained that the meat was dry and the texture rubbery. We'd been adding the chicken breasts to the simmering liquid and removing them as soon as they hit 160 to 165 degrees on an instant-read thermometer, which took about 20 minutes. Since we weren't overcooking them according to the chicken's internal temperature, the most obvious solution was to lower the cooking temperature. For the next test, we didn't preheat the poaching liquid. Instead, we placed the chicken in the pan with the water and aromatics, slowly brought the liquid to a simmer over medium-low heat, and covered the pan until the chicken cooked through. This slow, gentle technique took an extra few minutes, but it was worth it—the chicken was now juicy, tender, and flavorful.

With a streamlined method and shopping list, we decided we had time to develop a couple of simple sauces to accompany the chicken. Since our poached chicken produced no fond (browned bits) to use for a pan sauce, we chose combinations of flavorful ingredients that would give our sauces intensity without ingredients that were high in fat. Dried apricots, fresh orange, and smoky chipotle produced a sauce with a bright, sweet-spicy flavor. For a deeper, more savory flavor profile, we paired the sweet richness of caramelized onion with the pungency of whole grain mustard. This chicken is great served with one of these easy sauces on the side, but it is flavorful enough to be served spa-style—with merely a spritz of lemon and a sprinkling of fresh herbs.

Spa Chicken

SERVES 2

Do not let the poaching liquid boil or else the chicken will be tough. The chicken can be served on its own or with Apricot-Orange Chipotle Sauce or Caramelized Onion and Whole Grain Mustard Sauce (recipes follow).

2 **(6-ounce) boneless, skinless chicken breasts, trimmed and pounded ½ inch thick**
⅛ **teaspoon salt**
⅛ **teaspoon pepper**
1 **cup water**
3 **garlic cloves, peeled and smashed**
3 **sprigs fresh thyme**
2 **teaspoons soy sauce**
1 **tablespoon minced fresh chives, parsley, cilantro, or tarragon**
   Lemon wedges, for serving

1. Pat the chicken dry with paper towels and season with the salt and pepper. Combine the water, garlic, thyme, and soy sauce in a 10-inch skillet. Add the chicken and bring to a simmer over medium-low heat, 10 to 15 minutes.

2. When the water is simmering, flip the chicken, cover, and continue to cook until the chicken registers 160 to 165 degrees on an instant-read thermometer, 10 to 15 minutes longer.

3. Transfer the chicken to a carving board, tent loosely with foil, and let rest for 5 minutes. Cut on the bias into ½-inch-thick slices, sprinkle with the chives, and serve with the lemon wedges.

PER SERVING: Cal 190; Fat 2g; Sat fat 0.5g; Chol 100mg; Carb 1g; Protein 39g; Fiber 0g; Sodium 260mg

Apricot-Orange Chipotle Sauce

MAKES ABOUT ½ CUP

Cut the orange over a bowl to reserve the juice.

1 **teaspoon extra-virgin olive oil**
1 **small shallot, minced**
1 **garlic clove, minced**
¼ **teaspoon minced canned chipotle chile in adobo sauce**
½ **cup fresh orange juice**
2 **tablespoons finely chopped dried apricots**
½ **orange, peeled and cut into ½-inch pieces (see note)**
1 **tablespoon minced fresh cilantro**
   Salt and pepper

Heat the oil in an 8-inch nonstick skillet over medium heat until shimmering. Add the shallot and cook until softened, 2 to 3 minutes. Stir in the garlic and chipotle and cook until fragrant, about 30 seconds. Stir in the orange juice and apricots and simmer until the apricots are plump and the sauce has reduced to ⅓ cup, 3 to 5 minutes. Off the heat, stir in the orange pieces and cilantro. Season with salt and pepper to taste and serve.

PER ¼-CUP SERVING: Cal 110; Fat 2.5g; Sat fat 0g; Chol 0mg; Carb 21g; Protein 2g; Fiber 2g; Sodium 0mg

Caramelized Onion and Whole Grain Mustard Sauce

MAKES ABOUT ½ CUP

While we prefer whole grain mustard, Dijon mustard works well, too.

2 **teaspoons extra-virgin olive oil**
1 **small onion, halved and sliced thin**
1 **teaspoon brown sugar**
1 **small garlic clove, minced**
1 **teaspoon unbleached all-purpose flour**
¾ **cup low-sodium chicken broth**
1 **tablespoon whole grain mustard**
1 **teaspoon fresh lemon juice**
   Salt and pepper

Heat the oil in an 8-inch nonstick skillet over medium-high heat until shimmering. Add the onion and brown sugar and cook until the onion is softened, about 5 minutes. Reduce the heat to medium-low and continue to cook, stirring often, until the onion is dark golden and caramelized, 15 to 20 minutes longer. Stir in the garlic and flour and cook until fragrant, about 30 seconds. Whisk in the broth and mustard, scraping up any browned bits. Simmer until the sauce has thickened and measures ½ cup, about 5 minutes. Off the heat, stir in the lemon juice. Season with salt and pepper to taste and serve.

PER ¼-CUP SERVING: Cal 90; Fat 6g; Sat fat 0.5g; Chol 0mg; Carb 7g; Protein 1g; Fiber 1g; Sodium 370mg

PAN-ROASTED CHICKEN BREASTS WITH RUBY RED GRAPEFRUIT–TARRAGON SAUCE

PAN-ROASTED CHICKEN

THERE ARE MYRIAD WAYS TO COOK CHICKEN, BUT pan-roasting is one of the test kitchen's favorites. Pan-roasting yields a deeply browned, flavorful exterior from starting the chicken on the stovetop, and extra-juicy, evenly cooked meat from finishing the chicken in the oven. The problem is that the skin, as flavorful and attractive as it is, is also loaded with fat. Could we come up with a lighter version that had just as much flavor and was as appealing on a plate?

The first decision we made was to use only chicken breasts, not the fattier dark meat pieces. In addition to being lower in fat, bone-in chicken breasts are great when cooking for two because they are frequently packaged by the pair. We decided to remove the skin at the outset and pan-roast the breasts, following our go-to method. They emerged from the oven an attractive golden brown, but they tasted like worn leather. Skin normally protects the meat from the hot pan and seals in the moisture, and it was clear that the sizzling skillet was too much for the vulnerable, lean breast meat. Our chicken breasts were missing that protective barrier. What if we gave the breasts a faux skin, a coating to protect them from the hot pan?

Flour, cornstarch, and cornmeal all seemed like good candidates for a coating. We removed the skin from several chicken breasts, pressed the coating onto the skinned side, and left a few bare for comparison. After browning the chicken in a hot skillet, we transferred the breasts, skinned-side down, to a 450-degree oven to finish cooking. All of the coatings resulted in more even browning and a better texture than we got on the chicken without any coating, but the cornmeal was the clear winner. Its coarse texture created a substantial coating without making the chicken seem "battered." The cornstarch fared the worst, as it was gummy and didn't create a distinct layer. However, the one bonus of the cornstarch coating was that the heat of the pan caramelized it to an attractive, deep mahogany brown.

Hoping to incorporate this browning characteristic into our cornmeal coating, we experimented with adding different amounts of cornstarch to the cornmeal base. We found that 1½ teaspoons of cornstarch and ¼ cup of cornmeal made the perfect coating and gave the crust the beautiful mahogany color we were after. The cornstarch also held on to some of the juice from the chicken, moistening the coating just enough that it started to bubble up in some places, looking just like real skin. Tasters in the test kitchen did a double take when we told them the breasts were skinless!

Since we were working with faux skin, there was little desirable fond to save, so we developed sauces with bright, bold flavors that we could cook while the chicken was in the oven. For a bright citrus sauce, we paired tart grapefruit with fresh tarragon. We started with a sautéed shallot, then whisked in chicken broth and grapefruit juice, reducing the mixture to concentrate the flavor and slightly thicken the sauce. Finally, we stirred in grapefruit pieces, honey, minced tarragon, and a touch of butter. For a sweet and spicy variation, we reduced chicken broth with a mixture of brown sugar, lime juice, fish sauce, garlic, and Thai curry paste. A small amount of cornstarch thickened the sauce, and before serving, we stirred in cilantro and another hit of fresh lime juice.

Pan-Roasted Chicken Breasts with Ruby Red Grapefruit-Tarragon Sauce
SERVES 2

You will need a 10-inch ovensafe skillet for this recipe. If using kosher chicken, do not brine. If brining the chicken, do not season with salt in step 1. Be sure to trim away the bitter white pith and any tough membranes from the grapefruit.

CHICKEN
- ¼ cup yellow cornmeal
- 1½ teaspoons cornstarch
- 2 (12-ounce) bone-in, skin-on split chicken breasts, trimmed (see page 148), skin removed, brined if desired (see note; see page 162)
- ⅛ teaspoon salt
- ⅛ teaspoon pepper
- 1 tablespoon vegetable oil

SAUCE
- 1 tablespoon unsalted butter, cut into 2 equal pieces
- 1 shallot, minced
- ¾ cup low-sodium chicken broth
- ¼ cup grapefruit juice
- ½ pink grapefruit, peeled and cut into ½-inch pieces
- 1 tablespoon honey
- 1 tablespoon minced fresh tarragon
- Salt and pepper

TRIMMING SPLIT CHICKEN BREASTS

Using kitchen shears, trim off the rib sections from each breast, following the vertical line of fat from the tapered end of the breast up to the socket where the wing was attached. Trimming the rib sections helps ensure even cooking.

1. FOR THE CHICKEN: Adjust an oven rack to the lower-middle position and heat the oven to 450 degrees. Whisk the cornmeal and cornstarch together in a shallow dish. Pat the chicken dry with paper towels and season with the salt and pepper. Press the skinned side of the chicken into the cornmeal mixture to coat.

2. Heat the oil in a 10-inch ovensafe skillet over medium-high heat until just smoking. Carefully lay the chicken breasts in the skillet, skinned-side down, and cook until well browned, about 4 minutes. Flip the chicken and cook until well browned on the second side, about 4 minutes longer. Flip the chicken skinned-side down, transfer the skillet to the oven, and cook until the chicken registers 160 to 165 degrees on an instant-read thermometer, 15 to 18 minutes.

3. Using potholders (the handle will be hot), remove the skillet from the oven. Transfer the chicken to a platter, tent loosely with foil, and let rest while making the sauce.

4. FOR THE SAUCE: Meanwhile, melt one piece of the butter in a small saucepan over medium heat. Add the shallot and cook until softened, 2 to 3 minutes. Stir in the broth and grapefruit juice and bring to a simmer. Cook until the sauce has reduced to ¼ cup, about 15 minutes.

5. Stir in the grapefruit pieces and honey and simmer for 30 seconds. Off the heat, stir in the tarragon and remaining piece of butter and season with salt and pepper to taste. Spoon the sauce over the chicken and serve.

PER SERVING: **Cal** 470; **Fat** 16g; **Sat fat** 6g; **Chol** 145mg; **Carb** 28g; **Protein** 53g; **Fiber** 1g; **Sodium** 510mg

VARIATION

Pan-Roasted Chicken Breasts with Spicy Thai Sauce

Follow the recipe for Pan-Roasted Chicken Breasts with Ruby Red Grapefruit-Tarragon Sauce, substituting the following sauce. Cook ¼ cup brown sugar, 2 tablespoons fresh lime juice, 1 tablespoon fish sauce, 2 minced garlic cloves, and 1 teaspoon Thai red curry paste together in a small saucepan over medium heat until thickened, about 3 minutes. Whisk in ¾ cup low-sodium chicken broth and simmer until it has reduced to ½ cup, about 5 minutes. Whisk 1 teaspoon water and ½ teaspoon cornstarch together in a bowl, then whisk into the simmering sauce. Continue to simmer until thickened, about 45 seconds longer. Off the heat, stir in 1 tablespoon fresh lime juice and 2 tablespoons minced fresh cilantro.

PER SERVING: **Cal** 470; **Fat** 10g; **Sat fat** 2g; **Chol** 130mg; **Carb** 41g; **Protein** 54g; **Fiber** 1g; **Sodium** 930mg

PORK CUTLETS WITH CHUTNEY

FOR A HEALTHY PORK DISH FOR TWO, SAUTÉED PORK cutlets are your best bet. They're leaner than larger cuts of pork, they cook quickly, and you won't have tons of leftovers to contend with. The problem is that because they are so lean, pork cutlets have a tendency to dry out. Many recipes compensate for this by including a sauce rich with cream and butter—certainly not what we would consider light fare. Our goal was twofold: First off, we wanted perfectly cooked, juicy pork cutlets. Second, we wanted to pair them with a flavorful—but not fattening—sauce. In the past we've found that sauces made with fresh or dried fruit can add a lot of flavor but few calories and almost no fat to sautéed meat. Since apples pair naturally with pork, we decided a chunky apple relish would make a perfect accompaniment.

First we focused on the pork. From past testing, we knew that pork chops make for dry cutlets and that prepackaged pork cutlets are fatty and sinewy. Cutlets from pork tenderloin, however, are easy to make, lean, and extremely tender. We found it best to cut the tenderloin crosswise at an angle into two equal chunks that we then pounded to ensure even thickness.

Now we were ready to cook our cutlets. First we needed to choose what pan we would use. A 10-inch skillet was exactly the right size to fit our cutlets; a 12-inch skillet tended to scorch because there was a lot of uncovered surface area that simply burned, and an 8-inch skillet crowded the cutlets, causing them to steam and turn flabby. Then we turned to testing traditional and nonstick skillets. Normally, one outperforms the other, but in this case we were surprised to see that the two performed similarly well. We opted to use a nonstick skillet because it would allow us to cook with less fat than a traditional skillet. In this case, vegetable oil was preferred to olive oil for its higher smoke point and neutral flavor.

We also experimented with various heat levels. When we sautéed the pork over the highest level of heat, it quickly became too dark on the outside while remaining underdone on the inside. On the other hand, cutlets cooked slowly over low heat failed to develop sufficient browning. Working between these two ranges, we determined that the optimal heat level was a combination of medium-high and medium heat. First, we achieved a brown crust on one side of the cutlets by cooking them for three minutes over medium-high heat. Then we flipped the cutlets, lowered the heat to medium, and continued to cook the pork through for another eight minutes. This way, the cutlets achieved an attractive brown crust while remaining juicy and tender inside.

While the pork rested, we sautéed a chopped apple with some sugar to jump-start browning (brown sugar trumped white for its deep caramel notes). Adding two quartered shallots to the sauce not only helped offset the sweetness of the dish but also gave an appealing contrast of texture to the mixture. The addition of ¼ cup of dried cranberries was also well received, lending the sauce a tart punch and some bright color; to soften the cranberries, we heated them in the microwave with chicken broth. Thyme and allspice provided spicy, herbal depth. We deglazed the pan with the chicken broth and 1 teaspoon of cider vinegar, which both enhanced the apple flavor and provided a welcome acidity. Barely 10 minutes had passed and we had a rustic, chunky apple chutney to accompany our juicy, flavorful pork.

Pork Cutlets with Sautéed Apple and Cranberry Chutney

SERVES 2

We like the flavor of Granny Smith and Golden Delicious apples here; however, any type of apple will work fine.

- ¼ cup dried cranberries
- ½ cup low-sodium chicken broth
- 1 (12-ounce) pork tenderloin, trimmed and cut on the bias into 2 equal pieces (see page 86)
  Salt and pepper
- 1 tablespoon vegetable oil
- 2 shallots, peeled and quartered
- 1½ teaspoons minced fresh thyme or ½ teaspoon dried
- ⅛ teaspoon ground allspice
- 1 apple, peeled, cored, and cut into ½-inch pieces
- 2 teaspoons brown sugar
- 1 teaspoon cider vinegar

1. Combine the cranberries and broth in a small bowl, cover, and microwave on high until hot, about 1 minute. Set aside.

2. Place each piece of pork between 2 sheets of plastic wrap and pound to an even ½-inch thickness. Season the pork with ⅛ teaspoon salt and ⅛ teaspoon pepper.

3. Heat 2 teaspoons of the oil in a 10-inch nonstick skillet over medium-high heat until just smoking. Carefully lay the cutlets in the skillet and cook until browned on the first side, about 3 minutes. Flip the pork, reduce the heat to medium, and continue to cook until the pork registers 140 to 145 degrees on an instant-read thermometer, 5 to 10 minutes longer. Transfer the pork to a platter and tent loosely with foil. (Do not wipe out the skillet.)

4. Add the remaining 1 teaspoon oil to the skillet and heat over medium heat until shimmering. Add the shallots and cook until softened and lightly browned, 3 to 5 minutes. Stir in the thyme and allspice and cook until fragrant, about 30 seconds.

5. Stir in the apple and sugar and cook, stirring occasionally, until the apple is softened and golden brown, 5 to 7 minutes. Stir in the cranberry-broth mixture and vinegar, scraping up any browned bits. Bring to a simmer and cook until thickened, about 2 minutes.

6. Off the heat, season the chutney with salt and pepper to taste and serve with the pork.

PER SERVING: **Cal** 380; **Fat** 11g; **Sat fat** 2g; **Chol** 110mg; **Carb** 34g; **Protein** 37g; **Fiber** 3g; **Sodium** 380mg

LEMON-STEAMED SOLE

STEAMED DISHES ARE OFTEN FROWNED UPON, WITH diners presuming that they will be washed out and watered down and have as much flavor as a piece of cardboard. But when done correctly, steaming is not only healthy and quick, but it keeps the food moist and the flavor pure. We set out to apply this technique to a popular, mild white fish—sole. We decided to first perfect our steaming technique and then incorporate some interesting flavors in a sauce that would enhance the clean, mild flavor of this fish. We aimed to develop a recipe for steamed fish for two that would impress anyone, whether counting calories or not.

We thought back to our Baked Sole with Garlicky Spinach (page 24), in which the fillets were rolled into bundles before being baked, making for an attractive presentation. In addition to the aesthetic appeal, rolling the fillets had multiple advantages. Sole fillets can be as thin as ⅛ inch thick and quite long. The long, thin fillets were easy to overcook, especially at the tapered ends of the fillet, which were often thinner than the center. Rolled into tight cylinders, the fillets were thicker and more uniform, resulting in more gentle and even cooking. The bundles were also less likely to break apart, both raw and cooked. We found that the smaller fillets (3 ounces) were easy to roll, and two per person were an ample serving.

However, even with the rolling technique, we were having trouble with the fish sticking to the steamer basket. Lining the steamer basket with parchment paper inhibited the steam, and the fish cooked unevenly. Our solution was to line the basket with lemon slices. This worked like a charm, and it had the added benefit of imparting a light citrus aroma to the fish. Tasters liked this flavor so much that we topped the fish with another lemon slice before steaming. Keeping the water underneath the basket at a simmer, rather than a boil, was key to ensuring slower, more even cooking.

Finally, we wanted a vibrant, bright sauce that would come together quickly and complement the fish. We thought a fresh sauce reminiscent of spring would suit the fish nicely, and green peas were perfect for the job. We used frozen peas; aside from being convenient, peas are one of the few vegetables that are often better frozen because they are processed right after being picked. After sautéing a minced shallot and a clove of garlic, we stirred in some white wine and chicken broth before adding ½ cup of peas. We knew they would need just a couple of minutes of cooking to warm through and maintain their fresh, vibrant flavor. After pureeing the sauce until smooth, we finished it with lemon juice for further punch. Topped with the sauce and sprinkled with a handful of chopped fresh basil, these fish bundles were so packed with the bright flavor of spring, no one missed the fat.

Lemon-Steamed Sole with Green Pea Sauce
SERVES 2

Try to purchase fillets that are similar in size so that they cook at the same rate. If the sole fillets are very large (6 ounces each), serve just 1 fillet per person and increase the steaming time to 6 to 10 minutes in step 4. If the sauce cools off while the fish is cooking, reheat it briefly over medium-low heat before serving.

- 1 **lemon, sliced into ¼-inch-thick rounds**
- 1 **teaspoon extra-virgin olive oil**
- 1 **small shallot, minced**
- 1 **garlic clove, minced**
- ⅓ **cup low-sodium chicken broth**
- 2 **tablespoons dry white wine**
- ½ **cup frozen peas**
- ½ **teaspoon fresh lemon juice**
  Salt and pepper
- 4 **(3-ounce) boneless, skinless sole fillets,**
  ⅛ to ¼ inch thick (see note)
- 1 **tablespoon chopped fresh basil**

NOTES FROM THE TEST KITCHEN

BUYING AND STORING FISH
Buying top-quality fish is just as important as cooking it right. We recommend buying your fish from a trusted source (preferably one with high volume to help ensure freshness). The store, and the fish in it, should smell like the sea, not fishy or sour, and all of the fish should be on ice or properly refrigerated. Be sure to examine the fish before you buy it— the flesh should look bright, shiny, and firm, not dull or mushy. When possible, have your fishmonger slice steaks and fillets to order rather than buying precut pieces that may have been sitting around. To keep the fish fresh, keep it cold, especially if you have a long ride home; just ask your fishmonger for a plastic bag of ice to lay the fish on. At home, store the fish at the back of your refrigerator, which is the coldest part; in a sealed bag over a bowl of ice is best. And try to cook your fish the day you buy it.

LEMON-STEAMED SOLE WITH GREEN PEA SAUCE

1. Fit a large Dutch oven with a steamer basket. Add water to the pot until it just touches the bottom of the basket. Line the basket with 4 lemon slices, cover, and bring to a boil.

2. Meanwhile, heat the oil in a small saucepan over medium heat until shimmering. Add the shallot and cook until softened, 2 to 3 minutes. Stir in the garlic and cook until fragrant, about 30 seconds. Stir in the broth and wine and bring to a boil over high heat. Stir in the peas and cook until tender, about 2 minutes. Transfer to a blender and puree until completely smooth, about 30 seconds. Return the sauce to the pan, stir in the lemon juice, and season with salt and pepper to taste. Cover to keep warm.

3. Pat the fish dry with paper towels and season with ⅛ teaspoon salt and ⅛ teaspoon pepper. Following the photo on page 25, roll the fillets into tight bundles.

4. Reduce the heat under the Dutch oven so that the water is at a simmer. Lay a fish bundle, seam-side down, on top of each lemon slice. Top the bundles with the remaining lemon slices. Cover the pot and steam until the fish flakes apart when gently prodded with a paring knife, 4 to 6 minutes.

5. Gently transfer the fish to individual plates, top with the sauce, sprinkle with the basil, and serve.

PER SERVING: **Cal** 220; **Fat** 4.5g; **Sat fat** 1g; **Chol** 80mg; **Carb** 7g; **Protein** 34g; **Fiber** 1g; **Sodium** 380mg

BAKED COD WITH CHERRY TOMATOES AND ARTICHOKES

FOR MANY, BAKING IS THE MOST FUSS-FREE COOKING method for white fish. A common preparation involves dipping the fillets into a coating of buttery bread crumbs before baking, but we had something more imaginative and healthier in mind. We imagined the simplest of baked fish dishes: one where we could arrange the fish on a bed of vegetables. Once baked, the fillets would turn tender and flaky and the vegetables would cook down into a chunky sauce, lending flavor and additional moisture to the fish.

To start, we turned to our choice of fish and quickly settled on cod. Its mild flavor pairs well with a variety of other flavors, and we knew the thick fillets—one fillet per person—would hold up well during baking. For our vegetables, we wanted bold flavor but

minimal prep. We selected cherry tomatoes; we decided to quarter them, thinking they would then easily break down in the oven and create the juicy sauce we were after. Although we are often skeptical of frozen vegetables, after some experimentation with frozen artichoke hearts, we were impressed by their flavor, especially when combined with other ingredients.

To keep our dish streamlined, we decided to combine the seasonings with the vegetables and cook them alongside the fish in the oven. Looking to imbue the fish with bold character, we chose heady, aromatic ingredients. We tossed the artichoke hearts and tomatoes with a minced shallot, olives, white wine, and a teaspoon of extra-virgin olive oil. We needed an herb as well and settled on thyme, which imparted a subtle depth.

We layered our vegetable mixture in the bottom of a baking dish, nestled the fish into the vegetables, and transferred the dish to a 450-degree oven. An 8-inch square baking dish was the right size to hold the vegetables and two cod fillets; anything larger and the vegetables were spread too thinly over the increased surface area, which caused them to scorch and the juices to evaporate too quickly.

Hedging our bets on the tomatoes and artichokes paid off; the tomatoes cooked down, releasing their sweet juice into a thick, chunky sauce, and the artichokes remained firm and created a nice textural counterpoint to the soft tomatoes. With everything cooked together, the flavors of the seasonings and vegetables mingled and developed in the oven. Tasters approved of the flavorful vegetables, which straddled the line between sauce and side dish.

We stopped short of patting ourselves on the back when we got feedback on the fish—tasters found it lean and dry. To impart more moisture, we decided to brush the top of the fish with extra-virgin olive oil—just 1 teaspoon did the trick. This move had the added bonus of bringing a slight richness to the flavor of the fish. Then, we covered the dish with foil for the first 10 minutes of cooking, removing it at the end to concentrate the juices in the sauce. We sprinkled the top with some basil, and after one bite, we knew our dish was a success. The fish was now as flavorful and moist as our sauce, making for a light but satisfying dish. For such little work, the dish tasted complex, with a sauce offering a variety of textures and concentrated flavor that played beautifully against the tender and mild cod.

Artichoke Relish

MAKES ABOUT ¾ CUP

Be sure to pat the artichokes dry with paper towels before using. The relish can be refrigerated in an airtight container for up to 2 days. Serve with bread or crackers.

½ (9-ounce) package frozen artichoke hearts (about 1 cup), thawed, patted dry, and chopped fine

2 tablespoons capers, rinsed

2 teaspoons light mayonnaise

1½ teaspoons fresh lemon juice plus ¼ teaspoon grated lemon zest

1 teaspoon extra-virgin olive oil

1 small garlic clove, minced

Salt and pepper

Combine the artichokes, capers, mayonnaise, lemon juice, lemon zest, oil, and garlic in a small bowl. Cover and refrigerate until the flavors blend, about 15 minutes. Season with salt and pepper to taste and serve.

PER SERVING: Cal 70; Fat 4.5g; Sat fat 0.5g; Chol 0mg; Carb 7g; Protein 2g; Fiber 4g; Sodium 340mg

Baked Cod with Cherry Tomatoes and Artichokes

SERVES 2

You can substitute haddock or halibut for the cod. To thaw the frozen artichokes quickly, microwave them on high, covered, for about 3 minutes. Be sure to pat the artichokes dry with paper towels before using.

6 ounces cherry tomatoes (about 1 cup), quartered

½ (9-ounce) package frozen artichoke hearts (about 1 cup), thawed and patted dry (see note)

¼ cup pitted kalamata olives, chopped coarse

2 tablespoons dry white wine

1 shallot, minced

2 teaspoons extra-virgin olive oil

1 garlic clove, minced

½ teaspoon minced fresh thyme or ⅛ teaspoon dried

¼ teaspoon salt

¼ teaspoon pepper

2 (6-ounce) skinless cod fillets, 1 to 1½ inches thick (see note)

1 tablespoon chopped fresh basil

Lemon wedges, for serving

1. Adjust an oven rack to the middle position and heat the oven to 450 degrees. Toss the tomatoes, artichokes, olives, wine, shallot, 1 teaspoon of the oil, garlic, thyme, ⅛ teaspoon of the salt, and ⅛ teaspoon of the pepper together in a medium bowl, then spread in an 8-inch square baking dish.

2. Pat the cod dry with paper towels and nestle into the tomato mixture. Brush the top of the fish with the remaining 1 teaspoon oil and season with the remaining ⅛ teaspoon salt and remaining ⅛ teaspoon pepper. Cover the dish tightly with foil and bake for 10 minutes.

3. Remove the foil and continue to bake until the fish flakes apart when gently prodded with a paring knife, 5 to 10 minutes longer. Sprinkle with the basil and serve with the lemon wedges.

PER SERVING: Cal 290; Fat 11g; Sat fat 1.5g; Chol 75mg; Carb 14g; Protein 33g; Fiber 5g; Sodium 660mg

CHICKPEA CAKES

JUST BECAUSE A DISH IS VEGETARIAN DOESN'T MEAN it's low in fat. Case in point: falafel. These savory patties may be made with little more than ground chickpeas, onion, spices, and fresh herbs. But after being deep-fried in oil, these fritters enter not-so-healthy territory. We set out to develop a recipe for falafel-inspired chickpea cakes. Our chickpea cakes would boast the same moist, light interior and well-browned crust so characteristic of good falafel, but they would be lighter and easier to make.

With our goals established, we headed to the test kitchen. We dealt with the chickpeas first. Although we generally prefer the flavor of dried beans to canned, soaking and simmering beans is time-consuming and didn't seem practical when we needed just enough beans for two. And because we'd be mashing the chickpeas and mixing in other flavorings, canned would work just fine. We estimated that a 15-ounce can of chickpeas would serve two, but after some preliminary testing, we quickly realized that this was far too much.

Half a can of chickpeas was plenty and gave us two good-sized cakes.

Next we had to figure out how to prepare the chickpeas. We started with a food processor and started pureeing. Chickpeas that were pureed until smooth resulted in chickpea cakes that were unappealingly pasty. When the chickpeas were minimally processed, and still very chunky, the resulting patties were dry and difficult to keep together. Chickpeas that were pulsed until they were nearly smooth turned out to make the best cakes, offering good textural contrast.

For a binder, we had been using one egg, but the cakes still weren't holding together and tasted dry. Tasters thought that chickpea cakes made with two eggs were unpleasantly eggy, so we experimented with other low-fat binders. We tried low-fat sour cream and low-fat mayonnaise, but it was 2 percent Greek yogurt, which is thicker than regular yogurt, that was the winner, imparting a subtle tang and good moisture.

Next we turned to seasoning. While tasters welcomed the flavor of onion, using anything more than a tablespoon released too much moisture. We achieved deeper allium flavor (and avoided leftover vegetables) by replacing the onion with a small shallot and some scallions, which also added some color. Minced cilantro brought its trademark bright flavor. In addition to salt and pepper, tasters liked the warm notes of garam masala and a pinch of cayenne. Because garam masala is a mixture of spices, we were able to get complex flavor without having to mix minuscule amounts of multiple spices. A little olive oil brought our cakes' richness to just the right level without increasing the fat count significantly. To further ensure stability, we incorporated a small amount of bread crumbs—a binding ingredient often used in meatloaf and meatball recipes—to help absorb any excess moisture.

Pan-frying was the most obvious method to cook the patties, and it was quite successful. A 10-inch nonstick skillet worked best, allowing both patties to fit comfortably. With the nonstick surface, we needed just 2 teaspoons of oil to cook the patties. After 10 minutes in the skillet, our patties were nicely browned, with a crust that contrasted pleasantly with the creamy, moist interior.

The chickpea cakes were good at this point, but like falafel, they needed a sauce. Instead of tahini sauce, we craved something cool and creamy for our slightly spicy cakes. Our initial thought was to make a cucumber-yogurt sauce, and tasters loved the idea. As an added bonus, the tangy sauce used a few of the ingredients already in the chickpea cakes—Greek yogurt, scallions, cilantro—which kept our shopping list short, something we can appreciate no matter how many people we're cooking for.

Chickpea Cakes with Cucumber-Yogurt Sauce
SERVES 2

Be careful not to overprocess the chickpeas in step 3, or else the cakes will have a mushy texture. Serve the cakes with salad. See page 140 for a recipe to use up the leftover chickpeas.

- 1 slice high-quality white sandwich bread, crusts removed, torn into pieces
- ½ cucumber, peeled, halved lengthwise, seeded, and shredded
  Salt
- ½ cup plus 2 tablespoons 2 percent Greek yogurt
- 3 scallions, sliced thin
- 3 tablespoons minced fresh cilantro
  Pepper
- ¾ cup drained and rinsed canned chickpeas
- 1 large egg
- 4 teaspoons olive oil
- ¼ teaspoon garam masala
  Pinch cayenne pepper
- 1 small shallot, minced
  Lime wedges, for serving

1. Adjust an oven rack to the middle position and heat the oven to 350 degrees. Pulse the bread in a food processor to coarse crumbs, about 10 pulses. Spread the crumbs on a rimmed baking sheet and bake, stirring occasionally, until golden brown and dry, 10 to 12 minutes. Let cool to room temperature.

2. Meanwhile, toss the cucumber with ¼ teaspoon salt in a colander and let drain for 15 minutes. Combine the drained cucumber, ½ cup of the yogurt, 1 tablespoon of the scallions, and 1 tablespoon of the cilantro in a bowl, and season with salt and pepper to taste.

3. Pulse the chickpeas in the food processor to a coarse puree with large pieces remaining, 5 to 8 pulses. In a medium bowl, whisk the egg, 2 teaspoons of the oil, garam masala, cayenne, and ⅛ teaspoon salt together. Add the bread crumbs, processed chickpeas, remaining 2 tablespoons yogurt, remaining scallions, remaining

CHICKPEA CAKES WITH CUCUMBER-YOGURT SAUCE

2 tablespoons cilantro, and shallot until just combined. Divide the chickpea mixture into 2 equal portions, about ½ cup each, and lightly pack into 1-inch-thick patties.

4. Heat the remaining 2 teaspoons oil in a 10-inch nonstick skillet over medium heat until shimmering. Carefully lay the patties in the skillet and cook until well browned on both sides, 8 to 10 minutes, flipping them halfway through. Transfer the chickpea cakes to a platter and serve with the cucumber-yogurt sauce and lime wedges.

PER SERVING: **Cal** 280; **Fat** 15g; **Sat fat** 3.5g; **Chol** 110mg; **Carb** 25g; **Protein** 15g; **Fiber** 5g; **Sodium** 780mg

ASIAN BRAISED TOFU

LONG A STAPLE OF MEAT-FREE DIETS, PROTEIN-RICH tofu with its creamy, mild flavor makes an ideal canvas for a variety of flavors. Braising is particularly effective in that tofu will literally soak up the flavors of the liquid in which it is cooked. We particularly like Asian tofu braises that include coconut milk (we'd use light coconut milk to cut back on fat) and lemon grass. With a few hearty vegetables added to the mix, this new take on tofu had the potential to join the weeknight dinner rotation as an easy yet exciting meatless offering.

The technique of braising, or slowly simmering food in a small amount of liquid in a tightly covered vessel, is most often used for tough cuts of meat that need to cook gently until tender. Because tofu is already cooked, it would need to simmer just long enough to absorb the flavors of the sauce. Our first order of business was to determine what type of tofu to use and how to prepare it for braising; we could settle on braising time later.

Starting with whole blocks of tofu, we cut wide planks, thin fingers, and cubes of tofu and simmered them in a 10-inch skillet in soy sauce, which would give us an easy visual indicator of the rate of absorption. The first thing we noticed was that the tofu picked up the most flavor in the first 10 minutes; prolonged simmering didn't help the soy sauce penetrate much beyond the outer surface of the tofu. We settled on cutting the tofu into cubes, which maximized the surface area to absorb sauce but they weren't so small they would crumble over the heat. After testing soft, medium-firm, firm, and extra-firm tofu, we were impressed with how the cubes of extra-firm tofu held their shape in the pan.

Considering that we would be adding other vegetables to the mix, we cut our 14-ounce block of tofu in half and put the rest back in the fridge.

As for the rest of the ingredients, we wanted to add a couple of hearty, earthy vegetables that would be good candidates for a short braise. We tried a variety of combinations, ultimately hitting upon the duo of butternut squash and eggplant. The sweet creaminess of the squash played well against the smoky, slightly meaty flavor of the eggplant. About 8 ounces of butternut squash seemed sufficient. For the eggplant, we preferred baby eggplant to the more common globe eggplant because, at about 7 ounces, it was just the right amount for two servings when combined with the tofu and squash.

We peeled the thick inedible skin off the squash but left the eggplant's skin untouched. In addition to being tasty and visually appealing, the skin helps the eggplant stay intact during cooking. We then cut the vegetables into ½-inch cubes. We found that browning the vegetables before combining them with the other ingredients had an important impact on both flavor and texture. The dry heat of the pan drove off the vegetables' excess moisture, concentrating their flavor and preventing them from becoming mushy when simmered.

After sautéing the squash and eggplant (separate batches fit better in the pan), we set them aside to build the sauce. We browned some minced onion, then tossed in four cloves of garlic, a tablespoon of grated ginger, and half a stalk of lemon grass. Next came the liquid. We didn't need much—just ¾ cup of vegetable broth, ½ cup of light coconut milk, and a splash of fish sauce. Then we returned the browned vegetables to the pan and added the tofu. Once the liquid was gently simmering, we covered the skillet, removing the lid only in the last few minutes of cooking to thicken the sauce slightly.

NOTES FROM THE TEST KITCHEN

SMASHING LEMON GRASS

Smashing lemon grass helps release its flavorful oils. To smash lemon grass, set the stalk on a cutting board and smash it with a meat pounder. This keeps the stalk intact so it can be easily removed from the pan.

With a sprinkle of fresh cilantro and a dash of tart lime juice, our new take on tofu was so flavorful and exciting, we didn't even miss the meat.

Asian Braised Tofu with Butternut Squash and Eggplant

SERVES 2

If you can't find baby eggplant, you can use ½ globe eggplant (about 8 ounces) instead. If using prepeeled and seeded squash from the supermarket, you will need 8 ounces for this recipe. The tofu and vegetables are delicate and can break apart easily, so be gentle when stirring. See page 54 for a recipe to use up the leftover butternut squash and page 72 for a recipe to use up the leftover tofu.

- 1 tablespoon vegetable oil
- ⅓ medium butternut squash, peeled, seeded, and cut into ½-inch cubes (about 1½ cups) (see note)
- 1 baby eggplant (about 7 ounces), cut into ½-inch cubes (see note)
- 1 small onion, minced
- 4 garlic cloves, minced
- 1 tablespoon grated or minced fresh ginger
- ½ stalk lemon grass, smashed (see page 156)
- ½ (14-ounce) block extra-firm tofu, patted dry and cut into ¾-inch cubes
- ¾ cup vegetable broth
- ½ cup light coconut milk
- 2½ teaspoons fish sauce
- ¼ cup minced fresh cilantro
- 2 teaspoons fresh lime juice
  Salt and pepper

1. Heat 1 teaspoon of the oil in a 10-inch nonstick skillet over medium-high heat until shimmering. Add the squash and cook until spotty brown and tender, 7 to 10 minutes. Transfer the squash to a bowl.

2. Add 1 teaspoon more oil to the skillet and heat over medium-high heat until shimmering. Add the eggplant and cook until golden brown, 5 to 7 minutes. Transfer to the bowl with the squash.

3. Add the remaining 1 teaspoon oil to the skillet and heat over medium heat until shimmering. Add the onion and cook until softened and lightly browned, 5 to 7 minutes. Stir in the garlic, ginger, and lemon grass, and cook until fragrant, about 30 seconds.

4. Stir in the tofu, broth, coconut milk, fish sauce, and sautéed squash and eggplant. Bring to a simmer, cover, and reduce the heat to medium-low. Cook, stirring occasionally, until the vegetables are softened, about 10 minutes. Uncover and continue to simmer until the sauce is slightly thickened, about 2 minutes.

5. Off the heat, remove and discard the lemon grass. Stir in the cilantro and lime juice, season with salt and pepper to taste, and serve.

PER SERVING: Cal 300; Fat 15g; Sat fat 3g; Chol 0mg; Carb 32g; Protein 12g; Fiber 8g; Sodium 540mg

---

USE IT UP: LIGHT COCONUT MILK

Coconut Pudding

SERVES 2

For a smooth pudding, strain the pudding through a fine-mesh strainer to remove any bits of cooked egg. The pudding can be refrigerated in an airtight container for up to 2 days; gently stir before serving. You can use regular coconut milk in this recipe if desired.

- 3 tablespoons sugar
- 1½ tablespoons cornstarch
  Pinch salt
- 1¼ cups light coconut milk (see note)
- 1 large egg

1. Whisk the sugar, cornstarch, and salt together in a small saucepan. Slowly whisk in the coconut milk, then the egg.

2. Bring the mixture to a simmer over medium-high heat, whisking gently but constantly and scraping the bottom and sides of the pan. Reduce the heat to medium and continue to cook, stirring constantly, until the pudding is thick and coats the back of a spoon, 1 to 2 minutes longer.

3. Strain the pudding through a fine-mesh strainer into a bowl, scraping the inside of the strainer with a rubber spatula to pass the pudding through. Serve warm or cover with plastic wrap, pressing the plastic wrap directly onto the surface of the pudding, and refrigerate until cool, about 3 hours; gently stir before serving.

PER SERVING: Cal 220; Fat 10g; Sat fat 6g; Chol 105mg; Carb 30g; Protein 3g; Fiber 0g; Sodium 160mg

RUSTIC TURKEY TART

ONE BIG ROAST, THREE GREAT MEALS

ROAST TURKEY BREAST

WE CAN'T IMAGINE OUR THANKSGIVING WITHOUT a 15-pound bird on the table—and all the turkey dinners we enjoy the following week. But when you're cooking for two, even when you want some leftovers, a whole bird results in a daunting amount of food. For a more sensible alternative, we set our sights on a whole turkey breast, widely available year-round in supermarkets. The challenge when roasting turkey breast, as with all white meat, is that it can quickly dry out. It can also be tough to get crisp, golden brown skin—more often than not, the skin on roasted turkey breast is pallid and flabby. We wanted a foolproof technique for both tasty, crispy skin and moist, flavorful meat—and plenty of it, so we could pack up the leftovers and make two more turkey-based meals that were more exciting than the standard day-after-Thanksgiving sandwich.

Starting with the turkey breast, we reviewed our options. Turkey breasts are available bone-in and boneless. Bones keep meat moist, especially during longer cooking times, so bone-in was the clear choice for roasting. We found that bone-in turkey breasts are sold in a few varieties—natural (untreated), self-basted (injected with a brine solution), and kosher (salted and rinsed). Although the test kitchen prefers the taste of natural turkey, which we most often brine ourselves, we found after a few basic tests that any of the options would work here, and that brining is optional. (Kosher and self-basting birds should not be brined since they have already been salted; for more on brining, see page 162.) As for weight, a 6- to 7-pound breast gave us two substantial dinner portions, along with enough meat for two more meals. But choosing the right turkey breast is not enough. The proper roasting technique is essential, too.

To get crisp skin, we followed the test kitchen method of loosening the skin and rubbing the meat with softened butter. Loosening the skin helps it to lift and separate from the meat, which promotes even browning and creates crisper skin. The fat in the butter also keeps the breast meat moist and adds flavor. We prepared the turkey breast this way and set it, skin-side up, in a V-rack inside a roasting pan. We then roasted at various high and low temperatures; at 450 degrees, the turkey skin scorched and the meat was much too dry, but at 325 degrees, the turkey breast emerged with flabby, straw-colored skin. At 325 degrees, however, the meat was tender and flavorful.

Ultimately, a combination of high heat and low heat worked best. We started the turkey breast in a 425-degree oven for the first half hour of cooking, then reduced the heat to 325 degrees for the remaining hour. The initial blast of heat kick-starts the browning, ensuring the skin is beautifully golden by the end of the cooking time. And the low temperature gently finishes the turkey meat, helping it stay moist and tender.

However, there was one minor problem: During the high-heat roasting, the minimal drippings in the pan burned, smoking up the oven. A quick solution was to add water to the roasting pan before cooking. A cup was the perfect amount; any more and too much steam formed, preventing the skin from browning properly.

With the smoke problem settled, and our skin nicely browned and crisp, we set out to create a simple relish to pair with our turkey. Instead of the typical cranberry relish, we opted to make a warm apricot relish by simmering dried apricots with orange juice and minced shallot. When spooned over slices of tender white breast meat, this simple relish was the perfect complement to our roast turkey dinner. Now happily full, and with over a pound of cooked meat reserved, we were ready to tackle our next recipes.

For our first entrée, we wanted an elegant dish and thought an easy gratin—a French-style casserole topped with seasoned bread crumbs and baked until golden—would fit the bill. For the filling, we constructed a sauce with aromatics, white wine, chicken broth, and a bit of rosemary. Flour thickened the liquid to the proper consistency, and heavy cream added richness and a velvety texture. When the sauce was properly thickened, all that was left to do was stir in the turkey and frozen peas, which added color and freshness. Tasters wanted the topping to be more substantial than just bread crumbs and to provide some contrast with the creamy filling, so we cut French bread into ½-inch cubes and seasoned them with olive oil, minced garlic, salt, and pepper. Once baked (an 8-inch square baking dish was the perfect vessel), this casserole boasted a crispy, golden topping and richly flavored turkey filling.

Next, we looked south of the border to the bold, spicy flavors of enchiladas. For the filling, we sautéed sliced onion with garlic, cumin, and chili powder, then stirred in our shredded cooked turkey, corn, green chiles, Monterey Jack cheese, and canned enchilada sauce (we felt homemade enchilada sauce would negate the time we were saving by using precooked meat).

Fresh cilantro brought an herbal note to the sauce. We wrapped the filling in corn tortillas (three enchiladas per person seemed a good portion) and arranged them in an 8-inch square baking dish. To keep the tortillas from drying out and cracking, we lightly coated them with vegetable oil spray, poured more enchilada sauce over the top, and sprinkled on more cheese. After just 10 minutes in the oven, our enchiladas were piping hot and the cheese was gooey and bubbling.

For our last recipe, we put a spin on the classic turkey pot pie. Free-form tarts are easy to make, as far as tarts go, and retain the contrast of crisp, buttery pie pastry with creamy, savory filling, so we decided to transform some of our turkey into a rustic tart. Focusing first on the pastry dough, we preferred our basic test kitchen dough recipe, using butter and shortening as the fat, to store-bought dough in terms of flavor and texture; however, store-bought pie crust gave us acceptable results and allowed us to speed this dish to the table. For the filling, we started by sautéing sliced mushrooms with thyme, then sprinkled a bit of flour over the mushrooms and stirred in chicken broth and heavy cream. Finally, we folded in the cooked turkey along with a scallion for color and oniony flavor. We placed the filling in the center of the dough round, folded in the sides, and, for a finishing touch, scattered crumbled goat cheese on top before baking. Our homey turkey tart was so good no one could believe it was made from leftovers.

NOTES FROM THE TEST KITCHEN

THE BEST ROASTING PAN

Even if you're cooking for two most of the time, a good-quality roasting pan is a key piece of kitchen equipment and useful to have on hand. The pan must be sturdy enough to support the weight of a large bird or a heavy roast and must have handles that are easily accessible and a bottom that is heavy and thick enough to prevent burning. We tested models ranging in price from $8.99 to $180. Our favorite was the **Calphalon Contemporary Stainless Steel Roasting Pan**, $129.99. It had all the features of more expensive pans (including its own V-rack), was hefty enough for even the biggest bird, was easy to get into and out of the oven, and is widely available.

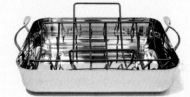

Roast Turkey Breast with Warm Apricot Relish
SERVES 2, WITH LEFTOVERS

You can use the leftovers to make two of the following recipes: Turkey Gratin (page 162); Turkey and Green Chile Enchiladas (page 163); and/or Rustic Turkey Tart (page 163). If using a kosher or self-basting turkey breast, do not brine. If brining the turkey breast, do not season with salt in step 2.

TURKEY
- 1 **(6- to 7-pound) whole bone-in, skin-on turkey breast, trimmed, brined if desired (see note; see page 162)**
- 4 **tablespoons (½ stick) unsalted butter, softened**
- 1 **tablespoon olive oil**
- **Salt and pepper**
- 1 **cup water**

RELISH
- ½ **cup water**
- ¼ **cup dried apricots, chopped**
- 2 **tablespoons fresh orange juice**
- 1 **small shallot, minced**
- 1½ **teaspoons fresh lemon juice**
- 1 **teaspoon minced fresh parsley**
- **Salt and pepper**

1. FOR THE TURKEY: Adjust an oven rack to the middle position and heat the oven to 425 degrees. Coat a V-rack with vegetable oil spray and set inside a large roasting pan.

2. Use your fingers to carefully separate the skin covering each breast from the meat. Place the butter under the skin, then gently press on the skin to evenly distribute the butter. Pat the turkey dry with paper towels. Rub the turkey with the oil, season with salt and pepper, and place on the prepared V-rack. Pour the water into the roasting pan and roast the turkey breast for 30 minutes.

3. Reduce the oven temperature to 325 degrees and continue to roast until the turkey registers 160 to 165 degrees on an instant-read thermometer, about 1 hour longer. Transfer the turkey to a carving board and let rest while making the relish. *To make any two of the recipes on pages 162–163, reserve 1¼ pounds of the turkey breast and refrigerate in an airtight container for up to 3 days.*

4. FOR THE RELISH: Meanwhile, bring the water, apricots, orange juice, and shallot to a simmer in a medium saucepan over medium heat. Reduce the heat to low, cover, and simmer, stirring often, until the apricots are plump and very soft, about 10 minutes.

5. Uncover and continue to simmer until the sauce is slightly thickened, 3 to 5 minutes longer. Off the heat, stir in the lemon juice and parsley and season with salt and pepper to taste. Carve the turkey breast and serve with the relish.

NOTES FROM THE TEST KITCHEN

BRINING 101

Both poultry and pork are lean, and in some preparations they can cook up dry. The salt in a brine changes the structure of the muscle proteins and allows them to hold on to more moisture when exposed to heat. In a sample test, tasters had no trouble picking out brined pork chops versus chops left untreated. Though we leave brining optional, if you have the time it will give you juicier meat in recipes like our Pan-Fried Pork Chops and Dirty Rice (page 9) and Roast Turkey Breast with Warm Apricot Relish (page 161).

To brine: Follow the amounts in the chart and dissolve the salt (we use table salt) in the water in a container or bowl large enough to hold the brine and meat. Submerge the meat completely in the brine. Cover and refrigerate, following the times in the chart (do not overbrine or the meat will taste too salty). Remove the meat from the brine, rinse, and pat dry with paper towels. The meat is now ready to be cooked.

Note that kosher poultry, frozen injected turkey, and enhanced pork (see page 10) should not be brined because they've already been treated with salt. Brining will only make the meat unpalatably salty.

POULTRY OR MEAT	COLD WATER	SALT	TIME
Chicken			
1 (1½-pound) whole bone-in, skin-on chicken breast	2 quarts	½ cup	30 minutes to 1 hour
2 (12-ounce) bone-in, skin-on split chicken breasts	2 quarts	½ cup	30 minutes to 1 hour
1 (6- to 8-pound) whole chicken	2 quarts	½ cup	1 hour
Turkey			
1 (6- to 7-pound) whole bone-in, skin-on turkey breast	4 quarts	½ cup	3 to 6 hours
Pork			
2 (12- to 14-ounce) bone-in pork rib chops	2 quarts	¼ cup	30 minutes to 1 hour

Turkey Gratin

SERVES 2

The cooked turkey in this recipe is from Roast Turkey Breast with Warm Apricot Relish on page 161. See page 10 for a recipe to use up the leftover celery and page 229 for a recipe to use up the leftover heavy cream.

- 2 **tablespoons olive oil**
- 1 **small onion, minced**
- 1 **carrot, peeled and sliced ¼ inch thick**
- 1 **celery rib, sliced ¼ inch thick**
- 1 **teaspoon minced fresh rosemary or ¼ teaspoon dried**
- 2 **tablespoons unbleached all-purpose flour**
- ¼ **cup dry white wine**
- 1½ **cups low-sodium chicken broth**
- ¼ **cup heavy cream**
- 10 **ounces cooked turkey (see note), shredded (about 2 cups)**
- ½ **cup frozen peas**
  Salt and pepper
- 4 **ounces French or Italian bread, cut or torn into ½-inch cubes (about 2 cups)**
- 1 **garlic clove, minced**

1. Adjust an oven rack to the middle position and heat the oven to 450 degrees. Heat 1 tablespoon of the oil in a 10-inch skillet over medium heat until shimmering. Add the onion, carrot, and celery, and cook until the vegetables are softened and well browned, about 10 minutes.

2. Stir in the rosemary and cook until fragrant, about 30 seconds. Stir in the flour and cook for 1 minute. Stir in the wine, scraping up any browned bits, and simmer until the wine has almost completely evaporated, about 2 minutes.

3. Whisk in the broth and cream, bring to a simmer, and cook until the liquid has thickened slightly and measures about 2 cups, about 5 minutes. Off the heat, stir in the turkey and peas and season with salt and pepper to taste.

4. Transfer the turkey mixture to an 8-inch square baking dish. Toss the bread with the remaining 1 tablespoon oil, garlic, ⅛ teaspoon salt, and ⅛ teaspoon pepper, then sprinkle over the top. Bake until the filling is bubbling and the bread topping is toasted and golden brown, about 15 minutes. Let cool for 10 minutes before serving.

Turkey and Green Chile Enchiladas

SERVES 2

The cooked turkey in this recipe is from Roast Turkey Breast with Warm Apricot Relish on page 161. Serve with sour cream, thinly sliced scallion, and hot sauce.

- 1 tablespoon vegetable oil
- 1 small onion, halved and sliced thin
- 2 garlic cloves, minced
- ½ teaspoon ground cumin
- ¼ teaspoon chili powder
- 10 ounces cooked turkey (see note), shredded (about 2 cups)
- 6 ounces Monterey Jack cheese, shredded (about 1½ cups)
- ¼ cup frozen corn
- 1 (10-ounce) can enchilada sauce
- 1 (4-ounce) can chopped green chiles, drained
- ½ cup minced fresh cilantro
- 6 (6-inch) corn tortillas, warmed (see page 81)
  Vegetable oil spray
  Lime wedges, for serving

1. Adjust an oven rack to the middle position and heat the oven to 450 degrees. Lightly coat an 8-inch square baking dish with vegetable oil spray.

2. Heat the oil in a 10-inch skillet over medium heat until shimmering. Add the onion and cook until softened and lightly browned, 5 to 7 minutes. Stir in the garlic, cumin, and chili powder, and cook until fragrant, about 30 seconds. Off the heat, stir in the turkey, ¾ cup of the cheese, corn, ¼ cup of the enchilada sauce, chiles, and cilantro.

3. Spread the tortillas on a clean counter. Spoon ½ cup of the filling down the center of each tortilla. Tightly roll the tortillas around the filling and lay them, seam-side down, in the prepared baking dish.

4. Lightly coat the tops of the enchiladas with vegetable oil spray. Pour the remaining enchilada sauce over the top. Sprinkle the remaining ¾ cup cheese down the center of the enchiladas.

5. Cover the baking dish tightly with foil and bake until the enchiladas are heated through, about 10 minutes. Remove the foil and continue to bake until the cheese is completely melted, about 5 minutes longer. Serve with the lime wedges.

USE IT UP: TORTILLAS

Homemade Tortilla Chips

MAKES 36 CHIPS

If using tortillas larger than 6 inches, you will be able to cut more than 6 wedges out of each tortilla.

- 6 (6-inch) corn tortillas or flour tortillas, each cut into 6 wedges (see note)
  Vegetable oil spray
  Salt

1. Adjust an oven rack to the middle position and heat the oven to 350 degrees. Spread the tortilla wedges on a rimmed baking sheet. Coat both sides with vegetable oil spray and sprinkle with salt.

2. Bake the tortilla wedges until they begin to crisp and are lightly browned, about 10 minutes. Flip the wedges and continue to bake until they are fully toasted, about 10 minutes longer. Let cool before serving.

Rustic Turkey Tart

SERVES 2

The cooked turkey in this recipe is from Roast Turkey Breast with Warm Apricot Relish on page 161. If desired, you can substitute 1 round of store-bought pie dough, such as Pillsbury Just Unroll!, for the homemade pie dough. See page 229 for a recipe to use up the leftover heavy cream.

- 1 tablespoon unsalted butter
- 4 ounces white mushrooms, trimmed and sliced thin
- 1 teaspoon minced fresh thyme or ¼ teaspoon dried
- 1 tablespoon unbleached all-purpose flour
- ¼ cup low-sodium chicken broth
- ¼ cup heavy cream
- 10 ounces cooked turkey (see note), shredded (about 2 cups)
- 1 scallion, sliced thin
  Salt and pepper
- 1 recipe Homemade Pie Dough (page 263; see note)
- 2 ounces goat cheese, crumbled (about ½ cup)
- 1 egg white, lightly beaten

1. Adjust an oven rack to the middle position and heat the oven to 400 degrees.

2. Melt the butter in a 10-inch skillet over medium heat. Add the mushrooms and thyme and cook until the mushrooms release their liquid and begin to brown, 5 to 7 minutes. Stir in the flour and cook for 1 minute. Whisk in the broth and cream, bring to a simmer, and cook until thickened, about 1 minute. Off the heat, stir in the turkey and scallion and season with salt and pepper to taste.

3. Roll out the dough into a 10-inch round, about ⅜ inch thick, on a lightly floured counter. Transfer the dough to a rimmed baking sheet lined with parchment paper and reshape as needed. Following the photos, spread the turkey filling in the center of the dough, leaving a 1½-inch border, and sprinkle with the cheese. Fold the edge of the dough in over the filling, pleating it every 1 to 2 inches as needed, and lightly brush with the egg white.

4. Bake the tart until the crust is golden and crisp and the filling is heated through, 35 to 40 minutes. Let the tart cool slightly on the baking sheet for 5 minutes before serving.

NOTES FROM THE TEST KITCHEN

MAKING RUSTIC TURKEY TART

1. After spreading the turkey filling in the center of the dough, leaving a 1½-inch border, sprinkle with the cheese.

2. Fold the edge of the dough in over the filling, pleating it every 1 to 2 inches as needed, and lightly brush with the egg white.

SIMPLE ROAST CHICKEN

WITH ITS CRISP, GOLDEN SKIN AND TENDER, JUICY meat, roast chicken is an incredibly satisfying dish. But what if you're cooking for two? You might assume that preparing a whole bird will be too much work and result in way too much food. But the great thing is that those leftovers can easily be transformed into a host of other dinners. And while roasting a bird can take a good chunk of time in the oven (from 1 to 2 hours, depending on size), it isn't really labor-intensive. Sure, you could take a shortcut and pick up a rotisserie chicken at the supermarket, but chances are it's been sitting under heat lamps, resulting in desiccated skin that's flaked off and flavorless meat that's dried out. We set our sights on developing the perfect simple roast chicken for two—it would provide enough meat for today's meal as well as for two more easy weeknight meals. And we wouldn't be just morphing our cooked chicken into plain old chicken salad—we aimed to come up with appealing, lively dinner options.

We first chose our chicken. The largest birds in our supermarket, the big oven roasters, typically weigh in at between 6 and 8 pounds and can easily provide enough meat for three meals for two.

We next turned to the basic test kitchen method for roasting chicken. Our method cuts out the superfluous steps of trussing the bird, which makes it more difficult for the inner thigh to cook since it's not exposed to the heat, and the fussy step of basting the bird multiple times, which results in chewy, greasy skin. Instead, before the chicken went into the oven, we distributed some butter under the skin for flavor and moisture, as we did for our Roast Turkey Breast with Warm Apricot Relish (page 161), then we rubbed the exterior with oil for crispy skin. For evenly cooked meat, we started by roasting the bird on its side, then rotated it so the other side was facing up. Finally, we finished roasting the bird breast-side up. This way, all portions of the bird were directly exposed to the oven heat at some point. Over the years, we've learned that a large roasting pan fitted with a V-rack is essential because it allows the air to circulate, resulting in crispy, not soggy, skin. Our simple method of roasting in a 400-degree oven for an hour and a half yielded a fully cooked, juicy chicken with golden brown, crisp skin—exactly what a roast chicken should be.

Having set our chicken aside to rest, we were now ready to make a pan sauce or jus (literally "juice" in French) to accompany the moist but mildly flavored meat. Typically, a pan sauce is made by sautéing aromatics with the browned bits left in the pan from cooking the meat. Then broth and wine are added to the pan and the mixture is simmered until it has reduced and intensified in flavor. Usually this is done in a skillet, but now we were working with a whole chicken in a large roasting pan, and we found it awkward to maneuver the pan on the stovetop once the bird was done. We decided to streamline our method and add a few cloves of garlic and some chicken broth, white wine, and water directly to the roasting pan before the chicken was done, using the heat from the oven (not the stovetop) to reduce the liquid for our sauce. Less than an hour later, we had both tender, moist chicken and, once we defatted the pan juices, a light, garlicky jus to drizzle over it.

With our main recipe set, we turned to the secondary recipes. Armed with 10 ounces (about 2 cups) of reserved shredded cooked chicken for each recipe, we decided first to make a simple calzone. We combined the cooked chicken with a cup of shredded mozzarella, some chopped kalamata olives, and minced fresh basil for a tasty filling. We rolled out our Basic Pizza Dough (page 103; store-bought works fine, too) to a 12-inch round, spread the filling on half the dough, and folded the other half over the filling. Ensuring that the calzone was sealed properly was the secret to this recipe—in one test, a burst seam left a gooey, burnt mess on the baking sheet. For a sufficiently tight seal, we found we had to brush the exposed edges with water, then press them together, leaving a slight overhang, which we could then fold over and crimp together. With our super-seal set and a piping-hot oven ready to go, we had a pizzeria-style calzone on the dinner table in under 20 minutes.

Next, we thought of making chicken soup, but instead of classic chicken and noodle, we turned to chicken and tortellini. Fresh tortellini are sold in 9-ounce packages found in the refrigerated section at the supermarket (about half of a package was perfect for two). We sautéed onion, carrot, and celery, added a little minced garlic and thyme, and then stirred in some chicken broth. With the soup base established, we added our tortellini along with a single diced plum tomato, which tasters preferred to other vegetables because it rounded out the flavors and added a fresh note. When the tortellini were tender, we added the shredded chicken and kept the pot on the stovetop until the meat was just heated through. Garnished with some shredded basil, our chicken soup was almost as comforting as Grandma's, but it didn't take all day to make.

Finally, we created an Asian-style soba noodle salad. Because we wouldn't be serving the noodles hot but at room temperature, we rinsed them immediately after cooking—this washes away excess starch that can cause the noodles to stick as they're waiting to be dressed. Tossing the rinsed noodles with sesame oil also ensured that they wouldn't clump together and added flavor to the dish. For the dressing, we relied on potent ingredients such as ginger and a hefty amount of soy sauce; some sugar and mirin balanced the saltiness and pungency of the ginger and soy. Tasters liked this simple dressing, but a few thought it could use some spiciness. A little wasabi—a mere ¼ teaspoon—added just enough heat. With our noodles and dressing ready to go, we sliced a few radishes and some cucumber, shredded a carrot, and combined all the components with our shredded chicken for a fresh and brightly flavored salad.

NOTES FROM THE TEST KITCHEN

PREPARING A CHICKEN FOR ROASTING

1. After removing the neck and giblets and trimming away excess skin and fat, twist the wingtips back behind the bird—they should stay in place by themselves.

2. After separating the skin covering each breast from the meat, spoon 1 tablespoon of the butter under the skin on each side, then use your fingers to distribute the butter evenly over the breast.

Simple Roast Chicken with Garlic Jus

SERVES 2, WITH LEFTOVERS

You can use the leftovers to make two of the following recipes: Chicken Calzone (page 167); Chicken and Tortellini Soup (page 169); and/or Chicken and Soba Noodle Salad (page 169). You will need a V-rack for this recipe. If using a kosher chicken, do not brine. If brining the chicken, do not season with salt in step 3. Serve the roast chicken with mashed or roasted potatoes.

> 1 (6- to 8-pound) whole chicken, brined if desired (see note; see page 162)
>
> 2 tablespoons unsalted butter, softened
>
> 1 tablespoon olive oil
>
> Salt and pepper
>
> ½ cup low-sodium chicken broth
>
> ½ cup dry white wine
>
> ½ cup water
>
> 4 garlic cloves, minced

1. Adjust an oven rack to the lower-middle position, place a large roasting pan on the rack, and heat the oven to 400 degrees. Coat a V-rack with vegetable oil spray.

2. Discard the chicken giblets, trim the excess skin and fat, and tuck the wings, following the photos on page 165. Using your fingers, carefully separate the skin covering each breast from the meat and place the butter under the skin. Gently press on the skin to evenly distribute the butter.

3. Pat the chicken dry with paper towels. Rub the chicken with the oil, season with salt and pepper, and place, wing-side up, on the prepared V-rack. Place the V-rack in the preheated roasting pan and roast for 30 minutes.

4. Remove the roasting pan from the oven and, using 2 large wads of paper towels, rotate the chicken so that the opposite wing side is facing up. Continue to roast for another 30 minutes.

5. Using 2 large wads of paper towels, rotate the chicken again so that the breast side is facing up. Combine the chicken broth, wine, water, and garlic, then add to the roasting pan. Continue to roast until the breast registers 160 to 165 degrees and the thighs register 175 degrees on an instant-read thermometer, 30 to 40 minutes longer.

6. Tip the chicken to let the juice flow from the cavity into the roasting pan, then transfer the chicken to a carving board and let rest for 10 minutes. *To make any two of the recipes on pages 167–169, reserve 1¼ pounds of the chicken and refrigerate in an airtight container for up to 3 days.*

7. Meanwhile, using a wooden spoon, scrape up any browned bits on the bottom of the roasting pan and pour the jus into a fat separator. Let the jus settle for 5 minutes, then defat and season with salt and pepper to taste. Following the photos, carve the chicken and serve with the jus.

NOTES FROM THE TEST KITCHEN

CARVING A WHOLE CHICKEN

1. Cut the chicken where the leg meets the breast, then pull the leg quarter away. Push up on the joint, then carefully cut through it to remove the leg quarter.

2. Cut through the joint that connects the drumstick to the thigh. Repeat on the second side to remove the other leg.

3. Cut down along one side of the breastbone, pulling the breast meat away from the bone.

4. Remove the wing from the breast by cutting through the wing joint. Slice the breast into attractive slices.

Chicken Calzone

SERVES 2

The cooked chicken in this recipe is from Simple Roast Chicken with Garlic Jus on page 166. We like to use our Basic Pizza Dough (page 103) here; however, you can substitute pre-made pizza dough from the supermarket or a pizzeria. An equal amount of oil-packed sun-dried tomatoes or roasted red peppers can be substituted for the olives. Serve with warm tomato sauce, such as our No-Cook Pizza Sauce (page 104), for dipping.

10 ounces cooked chicken (see note),
    shredded (about 2 cups)
 4 ounces mozzarella cheese, shredded
    (about 1 cup)
⅓ cup pitted kalamata olives, chopped
    (see note)
 1 teaspoon chopped fresh basil or parsley
    Pepper
 8 ounces pizza dough (see note)
    Water, for brushing the dough
 1 tablespoon olive oil

1. Adjust an oven rack to the lower-middle position and heat the oven to 450 degrees. Combine the chicken, cheese, olives, basil, and ⅛ teaspoon pepper in a bowl.

2. On a lightly floured counter, roll out the dough into a 12-inch round. Transfer the dough to a baking sheet lined with parchment paper and reshape as needed.

3. Following the photos, spread the filling evenly over half of the dough, leaving a 1-inch border along the edge. Gently press on the filling to compact it, then brush the edge of the dough lightly with water. Fold the other half of the dough over the filling, leaving ½ inch of the edge uncovered. Press and crimp the edge to seal.

4. Using a sharp knife, score the top of the calzone and brush with the oil. Bake until golden brown, about 15 minutes. Transfer the calzone to a cutting board, slice into wedges, and serve.

MAKING CHICKEN CALZONE

1. Spread the filling evenly over half of the dough, leaving a 1-inch border along the edge. Gently press on the filling to compact it, then brush the edge of the dough with water.

2. Fold the other half of the dough over the filling, leaving ½ inch of the edge uncovered.

3. With your fingers, press firmly on the edge of the top layer of dough to seal, leaving the bottom edge exposed.

4. Gently pull the exposed portion of the dough over the tip of an index finger to crimp and seal the edge.

5. Using a sharp knife, cut five slits, about 2½ inches long, diagonally across the top of the calzone, cutting through the top layer of dough only and not completely through the calzone.

BUYING KALAMATA OLIVES

When shopping for kalamata olives, pass up the jarred, shelf-stable specimens; they are bland and mushy. We prefer the fresher kalamatas from the refrigerator section of the grocery store. If you can't find kalamatas in the refrigerator section, look for them at the salad bar or the olive bar.

CHICKEN AND SOBA NOODLE SALAD

Chicken and Tortellini Soup

SERVES 2

The cooked chicken in this recipe is from Simple Roast Chicken with Garlic Jus on page 166. Fresh tortellini can be found in the refrigerator section of most supermarkets. Although we prefer the flavor and delicate texture of fresh tortellini here, frozen tortellini can be substituted; note that frozen tortellini may require a longer cooking time. See page 10 for a recipe to use up the leftover celery.

- 1 tablespoon olive oil
- 1 small onion, minced
- 1 carrot, peeled and sliced ¼ inch thick
- 1 celery rib, sliced ¼ inch thick
- 2 garlic cloves, minced
- ½ teaspoon minced fresh thyme or ⅛ teaspoon dried
- 3 cups low-sodium chicken broth
- 1 cup fresh cheese tortellini (about 5 ounces) (see note)
- 1 plum tomato, cored and cut into ½-inch pieces
  Salt
- 10 ounces cooked chicken (see note), shredded (about 2 cups)
- 2 tablespoons shredded fresh basil (see page 57)
  Pepper

1. Heat the oil in a large saucepan over medium heat until shimmering. Add the onion, carrot, and celery, and cook until the vegetables are softened and lightly browned, 5 to 7 minutes. Stir in the garlic and thyme and cook until fragrant, about 30 seconds.

NOTES FROM THE TEST KITCHEN

REVIVING CELERY

Celery is at the top of the list when it comes to foods that go to waste in the cooking-for-two kitchen, since most recipes for two include one or maybe two ribs at most. If you've got a few ribs left in the crisper drawer (and yes, celery should be stored in the crisper drawer in its original plastic wrapping or a partially open plastic bag) that are starting to turn limp, here's a quick tip for bringing them back to life. Simply trim off an inch from the ends of the stalks and submerge the stalks in a bowl of ice water for 30 minutes.

2. Stir in the broth, bring to a simmer, and cook until the vegetables are tender, 7 to 10 minutes. Stir in the tortellini, tomato, and ½ teaspoon salt, and simmer until the tortellini are tender, about 5 minutes.

3. Stir in the chicken and cook until just heated through, about 2 minutes. Off the heat, stir in the basil, season with salt and pepper to taste, and serve.

Chicken and Soba Noodle Salad

SERVES 2

The cooked chicken in this recipe is from Simple Roast Chicken with Garlic Jus on page 166. To make this salad spicier, add additional wasabi paste or powder to taste. See page 43 for tips on how to measure out long strands of pasta without using a scale.

- ⅓ pound soba noodles
  Salt
- 1 teaspoon toasted sesame oil
- ¼ cup soy sauce
- 3 tablespoons mirin
- ½ teaspoon sugar
- ½ teaspoon grated or minced fresh ginger
- ¼ teaspoon wasabi paste or powder (see note)
- 10 ounces cooked chicken (see note), shredded (about 2 cups)
- 3 large radishes, trimmed, halved, and sliced thin
- 1 small carrot, peeled and shredded
- ½ cucumber, halved lengthwise, seeded, and sliced thin
- 2 scallions, sliced thin on the bias
  Pepper

1. Bring 4 quarts water to a boil in a large pot. Add the noodles and 1 tablespoon salt and cook, stirring often, until tender, about 8 minutes. Drain the noodles and rinse under cold running water until cool. Transfer the noodles to a large bowl and toss with the sesame oil.

2. Whisk the soy sauce, mirin, sugar, ginger, and wasabi together, then pour over the noodles. Add the chicken, radishes, carrot, cucumber, and 1 of the scallions, and toss to combine. Season with salt and pepper to taste. Sprinkle with the remaining scallion before serving.

CUBAN-STYLE OVEN-ROASTED PORK

CUBAN ROAST PORK—PORK THAT'S BEEN MARINATED in a mixture of citrus, garlic, olive oil, and spices prior to grilling or roasting—makes a welcome change of pace from the same old roast ham or roast pork loin. When prepared right, the meat is fork-tender, juicy, and infused with robust flavor. And even better, the flavorful leftovers can be the starting point for a host of weeknight meals. We wanted to create a foolproof recipe for this dish, complete with rich, tender, flavorful meat, along with appealing ways to reinvent the leftovers into entirely new meals.

Cuban-style roast pork should have a texture somewhere between that of sliceable American pork roast and pulled pork—the meat should be tender but not fall apart. The best recipes we sampled all followed the basic sequence of using a marinade or wet paste to flavor the raw meat, roasting the pork for several hours, then cutting it into small pieces before tossing it with a traditional garlicky mojo sauce. A whole pig is the traditional choice of meat, but we went with a modern-day substitution—picnic shoulder, which is an inexpensive, fatty, bone-in cut with a good amount of skin attached. A 7- to 8-pound roast provided the right amount of meat for three meals for two people.

Off the bat, we chose slow-roasting the pork over grilling, so we could enjoy this dish year-round. Slow-roasting involves roasting meat at a low temperature for a long duration, so that the meat cooks through gently and evenly, preserving moisture and flavor. After following the traditional method of marinating the pork overnight, we proceeded to roast it in the oven on a wire rack set inside a rimmed baking sheet (this allowed air to circulate around the entire roast). After testing various oven temperatures, we found 325 degrees was best—the gentle heat produced pork that was evenly cooked throughout. It took the interior of the roast a total of six hours to reach our target of 190 degrees (at which point the fat and collagen had mostly broken down and rendered but not quite disintegrated). To ensure crisp skin that didn't burn, we started the pork in the oven skin-side down and flipped it halfway through cooking.

Our marinade had penetrated the pork with flavor, but an overnight marinade, combined with a six-hour roasting time, seemed just too long. There was no way

of speeding up the roasting time without drying out the meat, so we decided to try using a more potent wet paste to flavor the pork in less time. We combined garlic, oregano, cumin, olive oil, and orange juice, plus a shot of white vinegar for kick, then rubbed it over the pork and allowed it to sit at room temperature for an hour. This technique produced a roast with well-seasoned meat in a fraction of the time. Looking to improve our method, we also tried cutting fairly wide slits all over the pork to help trap some of the paste; this proved to be the most effective method for infusing the meat with flavor.

We now had a solid cooking method and great flavor. The only problem remaining was inconsistent moisture. The sections of the meat closest to the fat cap and skin always came out moist, but the leaner interior was noticeably drier. In the test kitchen, we often rest large cuts of meat after cooking to allow the juice to redistribute. We decided our Cuban pork roast was no exception. Compared side by side, a roast rested for 30 minutes was much juicier than one we sliced after 15 minutes of resting. Resting the roast for an entire hour was even better: The exterior and the portions next to the fatty pockets were not only delicious, but now the lean interior was every bit as moist. All the pork slices needed now was a dip in mojo sauce. Made with many of the same ingredients used in the paste, the mojo provided another bright, fresh hit of flavor that was the perfect finishing touch to our rich, tender pork.

Now ready to create our follow-up recipes, we first developed a recipe for pork empanadas. In these Spanish-style turnovers, a savory meat filling is encased in a tender, flaky crust. We found that homemade dough was the best way to guarantee a great crust, but store-bought pie dough works well for a quick weeknight meal. Focusing on the filling, we stuck with a standard combination of pork, raisins, olives, and onion. To keep the filling moist in the oven, we added some chicken broth and shredded Monterey Jack cheese. Our empanadas made for a tasty dinner, whether served warm right out of the oven or at room temperature.

Next, we looked to a simple dish that would showcase the complex flavors of the pork. We decided to make tostadas, which are basically open-faced tacos and are even easier to assemble when making just two portions. We began by toasting corn tortillas in the oven until crisp. Next, we spread refried beans over the crisp tortillas and topped them with the cooked pork, which we shredded, along with some crumbled queso fresco—a slightly salty fresh cheese typically found in this dish (but easy-to-find feta can be substituted). We baked the tostadas until the cheese was melted and the pork was hot and served them with a tangy sour cream sauce. Our tostadas were on the table in less than 30 minutes—and were lively and satisfying, too.

Finally, we created a streamlined version of an Italian meat sauce. The roasted pork was so richly flavored that in just 15 minutes we had a sauce that tasted as if it had simmered all day. We cooked the leftover pork with onion, diced tomatoes, garlic, and oregano to form the base of the sauce. In early tests, the sauce was too chunky, with the tomatoes and pork fighting for center stage. We decided to replace the tomatoes with a can of tomato sauce, then rounded out the flavors with red wine, chicken broth, and tomato paste. Now our tender pork was the star of this simple but hearty meat sauce—the perfect partner to a big bowl of ziti and just one more easy way to showcase the juicy pork from our Cuban-style roast.

Cuban-Style Oven-Roasted Pork
SERVES 2, WITH LEFTOVERS

You can use the leftovers to make two of the following recipes: Pork Empanadas (page 172); Pork Tostadas (page 173); and/or Ziti with Hearty Meat Sauce (page 173). Letting the cooked roast rest for a full hour before serving is crucial for tender and juicy meat. This roast has a crispy skin that should be served along with the meat.

PORK

- 12 garlic cloves, peeled and chopped coarse
- 2 tablespoons ground cumin
- 2 tablespoons dried oregano
- 1 tablespoon salt
- 1½ teaspoons pepper
- 6 tablespoons fresh orange juice
- 2 tablespoons white vinegar
- 2 tablespoons olive oil
- 1 (7- to 8-pound) bone-in, skin-on pork picnic shoulder

MOJO SAUCE

- 2 garlic cloves, minced
- ¼ teaspoon salt
- ¼ cup olive oil
- ¼ teaspoon ground cumin
- 2 tablespoons white vinegar
- 2 tablespoons fresh orange juice
- ⅛ teaspoon dried oregano
- Pinch pepper

1. FOR THE PORK: Pulse the garlic, cumin, oregano, salt, and pepper together in a food processor to a coarse paste, about 10 pulses. With the machine running, add the orange juice, vinegar, and oil through the feed tube, and process until smooth, about 20 seconds.

2. Pat the pork dry with paper towels and cut 1-inch-deep slits, about 1 inch long, all over the pork, spaced about 2 inches apart. Rub the paste all over the pork and into the slits. Cover the pork loosely with plastic wrap and let sit at room temperature for 1 to 2 hours.

3. Adjust an oven rack to the lower-middle position and heat the oven to 325 degrees. Set a wire rack inside a foil-lined rimmed baking sheet. Transfer the pork to the prepared wire rack, skin-side down, and roast for 3 hours.

4. Flip the pork skin-side up and continue to cook until the roast registers 190 degrees on an instant-read thermometer, about 3 hours longer. (If the pork skin begins to get too dark, lightly cover with foil.)

5. Transfer the pork to a carving board, tent loosely with foil, and let rest for 1 hour. *To make any two of the recipes on pages 172–173, reserve 1¼ pounds of the pork and refrigerate in an airtight container for up to 3 days.*

6. FOR THE MOJO SAUCE: Following the photo on page 43, mince the garlic and salt to a smooth paste. Heat the oil in a small saucepan over medium heat until shimmering. Add the garlic paste and cumin and cook until fragrant, about 30 seconds. Off the heat, whisk in the vinegar, orange juice, oregano, and pepper. Transfer the sauce to a bowl and cool to room temperature.

7. Remove the skin from the roast in one large piece. To serve the skin, scrape the excess fat from the underside and cut into strips. Scrape off and discard the top layer of fat from the pork, then cut the meat away from the bone in 3 or 4 large pieces. Slice the meat against the grain into ¼-inch-thick slices and serve with the sauce.

Pork Empanadas

SERVES 2

The cooked pork in this recipe is from Cuban-Style Oven-Roasted Pork on page 171. If desired, you can substitute 2 rounds of store-bought pie dough, such as Pillsbury Just Unroll!, for the empanada dough.

- 1 tablespoon unsalted butter
- 1 small onion, minced
- 1 garlic clove, minced
- 1 teaspoon minced fresh thyme or ¼ teaspoon dried
- 1 teaspoon chili powder
- ¼ cup low-sodium chicken broth
- 1 ounce Monterey Jack cheese, shredded (about ¼ cup)
- 10 ounces cooked pork (see note), chopped fine (about 2 cups)
- ¼ cup raisins, chopped fine
- ¼ cup green olives, chopped fine
  Salt and pepper
- 1 recipe Empanada Dough (recipe follows; see note)
- 1 large egg, lightly beaten

1. Adjust an oven rack to the middle position and heat the oven to 400 degrees. Line a rimmed baking sheet with parchment paper.

2. Melt the butter in a 10-inch skillet over medium heat. Add the onion and cook until softened and lightly browned, 5 to 7 minutes. Stir in the garlic, thyme, and chili powder, and cook until fragrant, about 30 seconds. Stir in the broth and cheese and cook until slightly thickened, about 1 minute. Off the heat, stir in the pork, raisins, and olives, and season with salt and pepper to taste.

3. Working with one piece of dough at a time, roll each out into a 10-inch round, about ⅜ inch thick, on a lightly floured counter and cut each in half. Following the photos, spread ½ cup of the pork filling over half of each piece of dough, leaving a ½-inch border along the edge. Gently press on the filling to compact it, then brush the edge of the dough with water. Fold the other half of the dough over the filling, press the edges to seal, and crimp with a fork.

4. Transfer the empanadas to the prepared baking sheet. Brush with the egg and bake until golden brown, 25 to 30 minutes, rotating the baking sheet halfway through. Let cool for 5 minutes before serving.

NOTES FROM THE TEST KITCHEN

MAKING EMPANADAS

1. Spread ½ cup filling over half of each piece of dough, gently pressing on the filling to compact it; brush the edge of the dough with water.

2. Fold the other half of the dough over the filling, then press the edges with your finger to seal.

3. Crimp the edges with a fork to secure.

Empanada Dough

MAKES 2 (10-INCH) ROUNDS

If you don't have a food processor, see the hand mixing instructions on page 264.

- 2 cups (10 ounces) unbleached all-purpose flour
- 2 teaspoons sugar
- 1 teaspoon salt
- 8 tablespoons (1 stick) unsalted butter, cut into ¼-inch pieces and chilled
- ¾ cup ice water

1. Process the flour, sugar, and salt together in a food processor until combined. Scatter the butter over the top and pulse until the mixture resembles coarse crumbs, about 10 pulses. Transfer the mixture to a medium bowl.

2. Sprinkle ½ cup of the water over the flour mixture and stir it in with a stiff rubber spatula. Stir in the remaining water, 1 tablespoon at a time, pressing the dough against the side of the bowl until it sticks together.

3. Turn the dough out onto a clean counter. Divide the dough into 2 even pieces. Shape each one into a ball and flatten into a 5-inch disk; wrap each piece with plastic wrap and refrigerate for 1 hour. Before rolling out the dough, let it sit on the counter to soften slightly, about 10 minutes. (The wrapped dough can be refrigerated for up to 2 days or frozen for up to 1 month. If frozen, let the dough thaw completely on the counter before rolling it out.)

Pork Tostadas

SERVES 2

The cooked pork in this recipe is from Cuban-Style Oven-Roasted Pork on page 171. To make this dish spicier, use the higher amount of chipotle. Serve with shredded lettuce, guacamole, and salsa. See page 163 for a recipe to use up the leftover tortillas and page 249 for a recipe to use up the leftover sour cream. See page 178 for a recipe for refried beans, or you could use store-bought refried beans.

6	(6-inch) corn tortillas
	Vegetable oil spray
½	cup refried beans (see note)
10	ounces cooked pork (see note), shredded (about 2 cups)
2	ounces queso fresco or feta cheese, crumbled (about ½ cup)
⅓	cup sour cream
3	tablespoons minced fresh cilantro
1-2	teaspoons minced canned chipotle chile in adobo sauce (see note)
1	small garlic clove, minced
1	teaspoon fresh lime juice
⅛	teaspoon salt
⅛	teaspoon pepper
	Lime wedges, for serving

1. Adjust an oven rack to the middle position and heat the oven to 450 degrees. Spray both sides of the tortillas with vegetable oil spray and spread out on a

rimmed baking sheet. Bake until lightly browned and crisp, about 10 minutes, rotating the baking sheet halfway through. (Do not turn the oven off.)

2. Spread the refried beans evenly over the tortillas and top with the pork and cheese. Bake until the meat is heated through and the cheese is melted, about 10 minutes.

3. Stir the sour cream, cilantro, chipotle, garlic, lime juice, salt, and pepper together in a bowl, then drizzle over the tostadas. Serve with the lime wedges.

Ziti with Hearty Meat Sauce

SERVES 2

The cooked pork in this recipe is from Cuban-Style Oven-Roasted Pork on page 171. Other pasta shapes can be substituted for the ziti; however, their cup measurements may vary (see page 43).

1	tablespoon olive oil
1	small onion, minced
1	tablespoon tomato paste
2	garlic cloves, minced
1	teaspoon minced fresh oregano or ¼ teaspoon dried
½	cup dry red wine
1	(15-ounce) can tomato sauce
1	cup low-sodium chicken broth
10	ounces cooked pork (see note), shredded (about 2 cups)
	Salt and pepper
½	pound ziti (about 2½ cups; see note)
2	tablespoons shredded fresh basil (see page 57)
	Grated Parmesan cheese, for serving

1. Heat the oil in a medium saucepan over medium heat until shimmering. Add the onion and cook until softened and lightly browned, 5 to 7 minutes. Stir in the tomato paste, garlic, and oregano, and cook until fragrant, about 30 seconds.

2. Stir in the wine and cook until it has nearly evaporated, 3 to 5 minutes. Stir in the tomato sauce, broth, and pork, and simmer until thickened, stirring often, about 15 minutes. Season with salt and pepper to taste.

3. Meanwhile, bring 4 quarts water to a boil in a large pot. Stir in the pasta and 1 tablespoon salt and cook, stirring often, until al dente. Reserve ½ cup of the cooking water, then drain the pasta and return it to the pot.

4. Add the sauce to the pasta and toss to combine, adjusting the sauce consistency with the reserved cooking water as desired. Stir in the basil and serve with the Parmesan.

SLOW-ROASTED BEEF

FOR MOST PEOPLE, ROAST BEEF DOESN'T MEAN FANCY and pricey prime rib or beef tenderloin—it's a more affordable (read: inexpensive) cut that, after a few hours in the oven's heat, is turned into something tender, juicy, and delicious. The drawback of using a cheaper cut, however, is that sometimes the resulting dish is meaty and tender, but other times it's dry and bland. Our goal was to transform a bargain cut into something that was always juicy, rosy, and beefy-tasting. After that, we wanted to come up with flavorful ways to turn our extra meat into two more dinners.

First we searched for the most promising kind of roast. The eye round roast won us over with its good beefy flavor and uniform shape from front to back that would roast evenly.

We were pretty sure this tougher cut would benefit from low-and-slow cooking, which would allow the connective tissue to break down, making the roast more tender. Some recipes we found insisted that the most tender roast is obtained by roasting at temperatures around 130 degrees for up to 30 hours. Tossing aside practicality and food safety issues, we tested this; 24 hours later, our roast was juicy and meltingly tender.

Looking into the science, we discovered that as the temperature of beef rises, enzymes within the meat begin to break down its connective tissues and act as natural tenderizers—but just until it reaches 122 degrees, at which point all action stops. Roasting the eye round in an oven set to 130 degrees allowed it to stay below 122 degrees far longer than when roasted in the typical low-temperature range of 250 to 325 degrees, transforming this unassuming cut into something great. But who really wants to run the oven for several hours? We decided to take a more reasonable approach.

After browning the roast to obtain color and a flavorful crust, we cooked it in a 225-degree oven for about two hours. This roast was tender, but nothing like the eye round cooked at 130 degrees; the beef was still reaching the 122-degree mark too quickly. We wondered what we could do to keep the meat below 122 degrees longer. Someone suggested shutting off the oven just before the roast reached the threshold, so that the roast could continue to cook slowly as the oven cooled.

We tried again, this time shutting off the oven when the meat reached 115 degrees. Sure enough, the meat stayed below 122 degrees for 30 minutes longer than before, allowing its enzymes to continue tenderizing the interior before creeping to 130 degrees for medium-rare. Tasters were definitely happy; this roast was remarkably tender and very juicy, particularly for such a lean roast.

With the tenderness problem solved, it was time to tackle taste. So far we'd simply sprinkled salt and pepper on the roast before searing it. Maybe the flavor would improve if the meat was salted for a period of time. We tried salting the meat for first four, then 12, and finally 24 hours. As might be expected, the roast benefited most from the longest salting. As an added bonus, salt breaks down proteins to further improve texture but without the negative effects of water absorption. Clearly, salting was essential.

Finally, we had arrived at a tender and flavorful roast beef. When paired with a simple horseradish sauce, our rosy slices of roast beef could easily pass as a fancy entrée in the best restaurant in town.

Now we eagerly looked ahead to our spin-off recipes. Working with 10 ounces of tender, thinly sliced beef

SLOW-ROASTED BEEF

(5 ounces per serving), we couldn't help but think of a Tex-Mex favorite—burritos. We set out to make a fresher-tasting filling than the usual canned refried beans, jarred salsa, and rice. Simmering pinto beans and a tomato with onion, garlic, and chipotle chile gave us a filling with authentic (not canned) flavors. Then we combined cooked rice with our thinly sliced beef, a generous amount of shredded cheddar, and cilantro. We mashed the bean mixture lightly and spread it over the tortillas. After mounding the beef mixture on top, we rolled up our tortillas. While other recipes call it quits at this point, we sprinkled our burritos with more cheddar and baked them in a 450-degree oven until the cheese melted and the filling was piping hot throughout.

For our next recipe, we decided to revisit a classic: the French dip sandwich. A key component of a great French dip sandwich is the dipping sauce, or jus, that accompanies it. While traditional French dip sauces are simmered for several hours to develop rich flavor, we wanted a faster approach for our weeknight sandwich. By simmering store-bought beef broth with a sautéed onion and thyme, we were able to create a boldly flavorful broth in just 10 minutes. Adding a little flour also helped to mimic the viscosity of a long-simmered broth. With the sauce ready, we began building the sandwiches. We stuck with convention here—layering slices of beef on a toasted sub roll, then topping the meat with caramelized onions and cheese (we liked provolone or Swiss cheese), then broiling the sandwiches in the oven until the cheese was melted. And to ensure that our sandwiches were perfectly juicy, we quickly dipped the slices of beef into the warmed sauce before placing them on the rolls. To stay true to the name, we served the sandwiches with the extra sauce on the side so diners could dip as they wished.

For our last option, we changed gears and developed a Vietnamese rice noodle soup with the leftover beef. We started by fortifying store-bought chicken broth with garlic, lemon grass, fish sauce, soy sauce, star anise, and cloves. We quickly cooked our rice noodles in hot water and placed them in individual bowls before ladling the broth and sliced beef (heated briefly in the broth) over the noodles. To add a fresh note to our dish, we topped the bowls with bean sprouts and whole basil and cilantro leaves (both classic accompaniments).

Our one big affordable roast had provided us with three very different, satisfying, and hearty meals.

Slow-Roasted Beef with Horseradish Sauce
SERVES 2, WITH LEFTOVERS

You can use the leftovers to make two of the following recipes: Beef Burritos (page 177); French Dip Sandwiches (page 178); and/or Vietnamese Rice Noodle Soup with Beef (page 179). We prefer this roast cooked to medium-rare, but if you prefer it more or less done, see our guidelines in "Testing Meat for Doneness" on page 109. Open the oven door as little as possible in step 4 and remove the roast from the oven when taking its temperature. See page 249 for a recipe to use up the leftover sour cream.

BEEF

- 2 teaspoons salt
- 1 (3½- to 4½-pound) boneless eye round roast
- 2 tablespoons vegetable oil
- Pepper

HORSERADISH SAUCE

- ⅓ cup sour cream
- 1 tablespoon mayonnaise
- 1 tablespoon horseradish
- 2 teaspoons fresh lemon juice
- ¼ teaspoon garlic powder
- Salt and pepper
- Water, as needed

NOTES FROM THE TEST KITCHEN

THE BEST SLICING KNIFE
Even if you're cooking for two, you will occasionally need a good slicing knife, whether you're cooking a big roast, like our Slow-Roasted Beef, or a holiday bird. Specially designed to cut neatly through meat's muscle fibers and connective tissues, this knife can cut with incredible precision in a single stroke. We already knew the key attributes to look for: an extra-long, sturdy, tapered blade with a round tip, which allows for easy, trouble-free strokes; a granton edge (which means there are oval scallops carved into both sides of the blade), making for a thinner edge on the blade without sacrificing the heft or rigidity carried by the top of the blade (perfect for producing thin slices with little effort); and, finally, a comfortable handle. After we tested nine knives that fit these criteria, the **Victorinox Fibrox 12-Inch Granton Edge Slicing Knife** (formerly Victorinox Forschner), $44.95, came out in front, scoring more points than the competition. Testers liked its thin, long, razor-sharp blade, which could draw through a large roast in one stroke.

1. FOR THE BEEF: Sprinkle the salt evenly over the roast. Transfer the roast to a plate, cover with plastic wrap, and refrigerate for at least 4 hours, or up to 24 hours.

2. Adjust an oven rack to the middle position and heat the oven to 225 degrees. Set a wire rack inside a foil-lined rimmed baking sheet. Pat the roast dry with paper towels, rub with 1 tablespoon of the oil, and season with pepper.

3. Heat the remaining 1 tablespoon oil in a 12-inch skillet over medium-high heat until just smoking. Carefully lay the roast in the skillet and cook until well browned on all sides, 12 to 14 minutes, reducing the heat if the pan begins to scorch. Transfer the roast, fat-side up, to the prepared wire rack and roast until the center registers 115 degrees on an instant-read thermometer, 1¼ to 1¾ hours.

4. Turn the oven off and let the roast continue to cook in the oven, opening the door as little as possible, until the beef registers 130 degrees (for medium-rare), 30 to 35 minutes longer. If the roast has not reached the desired temperature in the time specified, heat the oven to 225 degrees for 5 minutes, shut it off, and continue to cook the roast to the desired temperature.

5. Transfer the roast to a carving board, tent loosely with foil, and let rest for 30 minutes. *To make any two of the recipes on pages 177–179, reserve 1¼ pounds of the roast and refrigerate in an airtight container for up to 3 days.*

6. FOR THE HORSERADISH SAUCE: Meanwhile, combine the sour cream, mayonnaise, horseradish, lemon juice, and garlic powder in a small bowl, season with salt and pepper to taste, and add water as needed to thin the sauce to the desired consistency. Cover and refrigerate until needed. Slice the roast very thinly and serve, passing the sauce separately.

Beef Burritos

SERVES 2

The cooked roast beef in this recipe is from Slow-Roasted Beef with Horseradish Sauce on page 176. You will need ½ cup cooked rice for this recipe. Serve with guacamole, sour cream, shredded lettuce, and hot sauce. See page 178 for a recipe to use up the leftover canned beans and page 163 for a recipe to use up the leftover tortillas.

1 tablespoon vegetable oil

1 small onion, minced

2 garlic cloves, minced

1 teaspoon minced canned chipotle chile in adobo sauce

¾ cup drained and rinsed canned pinto, red kidney, or black beans

1 plum tomato, cored and cut into ½-inch pieces

¼ cup water

   Salt and pepper

½ cup cooked rice

10 ounces cooked roast beef (see note), sliced thin and cut into ½-inch pieces (about 2 cups)

4 ounces cheddar cheese, shredded (about 1 cup)

2 tablespoons minced fresh cilantro

2 (10-inch) flour tortillas, warmed (see page 81)

   Lime wedges, for serving

1. Adjust an oven rack to the middle position and heat the oven to 450 degrees. Heat the oil in a 10-inch skillet over medium heat until shimmering. Add the onion and cook until softened and lightly browned, 5 to 7 minutes.

2. Stir in the garlic and chile and cook until fragrant, about 30 seconds. Stir in the beans, tomato, and water, and cook until the liquid has evaporated and the beans

---

NOTES FROM THE TEST KITCHEN

ASSEMBLING BEEF BURRITOS

1. After spreading some bean mixture on half of the tortilla, leaving a 1½-inch border along the bottom and a 2-inch border on the sides, mound half of the beef mixture on top.

2. Then fold the sides of the tortilla over the filling, tightly roll the bottom edge of the tortilla up over the filling, and continue to roll into a burrito.

are softened, about 8 minutes. Off the heat, use the back of a wooden spoon to mash some of the beans against the side of the pot. Season with salt and pepper to taste.

3. Place the rice in a medium microwave-safe bowl and microwave on high until hot, 1 to 2 minutes. Stir in the beef, ½ cup of the cheese, and cilantro.

4. Following the photos on page 177, lay the tortillas on a clean counter and spread the bean mixture over half of each tortilla, leaving a 1½-inch border along the bottom and a 2-inch border on the sides. Mound half of the beef mixture on top of the bean mixture on each tortilla, then tightly roll the tortillas into burritos. Transfer the burritos, seam-side down, to a foil-lined rimmed baking sheet and sprinkle with the remaining ½ cup cheese.

5. Cover the burritos with greased foil and bake until the burritos are heated through, about 10 minutes. Uncover and continue to bake until the cheese is completely melted, about 5 minutes. Serve with the lime wedges.

USE IT UP: CANNED BEANS

Refried Beans
MAKES ½ CUP

Serve these beans on Pork Tostadas (page 173), tacos, and nachos.

- ¾ cup drained and rinsed canned pinto, red kidney, or black beans
- ¼ cup low-sodium chicken broth
- 2 tablespoons olive oil
- ¼ cup minced onion
- 1 garlic clove, minced
- ⅛ teaspoon ground cumin
- Pinch cayenne pepper
- Salt and pepper

1. Process the beans and broth in a food processor until smooth, about 30 seconds. Heat the oil in a 10-inch nonstick skillet over medium heat until shimmering. Add the onion and cook until softened, 2 to 4 minutes.

2. Stir in the garlic, cumin, and cayenne, and cook until fragrant, about 30 seconds. Stir in the processed beans and cook until thickened, about 5 minutes. Season with salt and pepper to taste and serve.

French Dip Sandwiches
SERVES 2

The cooked roast beef in this recipe is from Slow-Roasted Beef with Horseradish Sauce on page 176.

- 2 tablespoons vegetable oil
- 1 onion, halved and sliced thin
- 2 sprigs fresh thyme
- 1 teaspoon unbleached all-purpose flour
- 2 cups beef broth
- 2 (6-inch) sub rolls, sliced in half lengthwise
- 1 tablespoon unsalted butter, softened
- 10 ounces cooked roast beef (see note), sliced thin (about 2 cups)
- 2 slices provolone or Swiss cheese, cut in half

1. Heat 1 tablespoon of the oil in a small saucepan over medium heat until shimmering. Add half of the onion and cook until softened and lightly browned, 5 to 7 minutes. Add the thyme and cook until fragrant, about 30 seconds. Stir in the flour and cook for 1 minute.

2. Whisk in the broth, scraping up any browned bits. Bring to a simmer and cook until the mixture is slightly thickened and has reduced to 1 cup, about 10 minutes. Strain the liquid through a fine-mesh strainer, discarding the solids. Return the sauce to the pan, cover, and keep warm.

3. Meanwhile, heat the remaining 1 tablespoon oil in a 10-inch skillet over medium heat until shimmering. Add the remaining onion and cook until softened and lightly browned, 5 to 7 minutes; set aside.

4. Position an oven rack 6 inches from the broiler element and heat the broiler. Spread the cut sides of the rolls with the butter. Transfer the rolls to a rimmed baking sheet, buttered-side up, and broil until golden brown, 1 to 3 minutes. (Do not turn the broiler off.)

5. Remove the rolls from the oven and set the top halves aside. Using tongs, dip the beef slices into the sauce and lay over the bottoms of the rolls. Spread the onions evenly over the beef and top with the cheese. Broil until the cheese has melted, 1 to 2 minutes.

6. Pour the remaining sauce into two small bowls. Set the tops of the rolls on the sandwiches and serve with the sauce.

Vietnamese Rice Noodle Soup with Beef

SERVES 2

The cooked roast beef in this recipe is from Slow-Roasted Beef with Horseradish Sauce on page 176. Flat rice noodles come in a variety of widths, but the thinner (¼-inch-wide) noodles are traditional for this recipe. Be ready to serve the soup immediately after adding the beef in step 5; if the beef sits in the hot broth for too long it will become tough. If you can't find Thai basil, regular basil will work fine.

BROTH

- 1 teaspoon vegetable oil
- 1 small onion, minced
- 2 garlic cloves, minced
- 1 stalk lemon grass, trimmed and sliced thin (see photos)
- 3 tablespoons fish sauce
- 4 cups low-sodium chicken broth
- 1 cup water
- 1 tablespoon soy sauce
- 1 tablespoon sugar
- 2 star anise pods
- 2 whole cloves

NOODLES, MEAT, AND GARNISH

- 4 ounces flat rice noodles (¼ inch wide; see note)
- 1 cup bean sprouts
- ½ cup fresh basil, preferably Thai basil
- ½ cup fresh cilantro
- 1 fresh Thai, serrano, or jalapeño chile, stemmed, seeded, and sliced thin
  Lime wedges, for serving
- 10 ounces cooked roast beef (see note), sliced thin and cut into 1-inch-wide strips

1. FOR THE BROTH: Heat the oil in a large saucepan over medium heat until shimmering. Add the onion, garlic, lemon grass, and 1 tablespoon of the fish sauce, and cook, stirring often, until the onion is softened but not browned, 2 to 4 minutes.

2. Stir in the remaining 2 tablespoons fish sauce, chicken broth, water, soy sauce, sugar, star anise, and cloves, and bring to a simmer. Cover, reduce the heat to low, and simmer until the flavors have blended, about 10 minutes. Strain the broth, discarding the solids.

3. FOR THE NOODLES, MEAT, AND GARNISH: Bring 4 quarts water to a boil in a large pot. Remove the boiling water from the heat, add the rice noodles, and let sit, stirring occasionally, until the noodles are tender, about 10 minutes.

4. Drain the noodles, divide them evenly between 2 individual serving bowls, and top with the bean sprouts. Arrange the basil, cilantro, chile, and lime wedges attractively on a serving platter.

5. Transfer the broth to a clean saucepan and bring to a simmer over medium-high heat. Reduce the heat to low, add the beef, and cook until just warmed through, about 1 minute (do not overcook). Ladle the soup over the noodles and serve, passing the platter of garnishes separately.

NOTES FROM THE TEST KITCHEN

SLICING LEMON GRASS

1. Trim and discard all but the bottom 5 inches of the lemon grass stalk.

2. Remove the tough outer sheath. If the lemon grass is particularly thick or tough, you may need to remove several layers to reveal the tender inner stalk.

3. Cut the trimmed and peeled lemon grass in half lengthwise, then slice it thin crosswise.

WHAT IS FISH SAUCE?

Fish sauce is a salty, amber-colored liquid made from salted, fermented fish. When used in small amounts, it adds a well-rounded, salty flavor to sauces, soups, and marinades.

Because most supermarkets don't carry a wide selection of fish sauce, we recommend buying whatever is available. Fish sauce will keep indefinitely without refrigeration.

GRILLED PORK TENDERLOIN WITH RADICCHIO AND GORGONZOLA SALAD

DINNER OFF THE GRILL

GRILLED CHICKEN AND VEGETABLE KEBABS

CHICKEN AND VEGETABLE KEBABS ARE AN OBVIOUS choice when cooking for two—they cook quickly and are a snap to assemble. The problem is that it's easy to overcook poultry on the grill—especially boneless chicken that has been cut small so it can slide onto a skewer. We wanted chicken kebabs that were moist and well seasoned, and we wanted to balance our kebab dinner with a good mix of vegetables that wouldn't leave us with a pile of leftover halvsies.

We started with the chicken. With its extra fat, dark meat was juicier than white meat (although chicken breasts would work, too), but it would still need a considerable flavor boost. We determined that 1 pound of boneless, skinless thighs was just the right amount of meat for two. We cut the thighs into 1½-inch chunks—just large enough to make good contact with the grill. Next we looked at how to season the chicken.

Since we wanted to add not just flavor but additional moisture as well, we decided to use a marinade. From experience we knew that acid-based marinades (containing citrus juice or vinegar) add flavor to meat but can also turn it mushy. Was there a way to season the chicken all the way through and keep it moist on the grill without the acid? We ruled out brining because it would make the small, skinless chicken pieces too salty. But we wanted to get the juiciness and flavor that brining imparts. We figured that soaking the chicken in an acid-free but lightly salted marinade might work. We whisked together a marinade of minced garlic, chopped herbs, salt, and pepper combined with a few tablespoons of olive oil, then we added the chunks of chicken for a one-hour soak before grilling. The results were what we had hoped for: The salted marinade produced plump, well-seasoned chunks of tender, but not mushy, chicken.

Although the flavor of the chicken was good, we thought it could be even better. After making the marinade, we reserved a portion before adding the chicken, spiked it with a little lemon juice, and poured the mixture over the kebabs as they came off the grill. This gave the kebabs the final boost of fresh, bright flavor that we were after.

After 10 minutes over a hot fire, the chicken was nicely browned and tasted great; now we just had to pick the right veggies to go with it. Onions, peppers, and zucchini were good candidates; they cooked at the same rate, plus we were able to use whole vegetables— one red bell pepper, one zucchini, and one small onion—so we didn't have to deal with any leftovers. To boost their flavor, we tossed the vegetables with some extra marinade before skewering them. By the time the chicken was done, the vegetables were perfectly cooked and grill-marked without being incinerated, giving us a moist, tender, and flavorful kebab dinner for two.

Herbed Grilled Chicken and Vegetable Kebabs
SERVES 2

You can substitute chicken breasts for the thighs in this recipe; the cooking time in step 4 should be 7 to 11 minutes. Whichever you choose, do not mix the white and dark meat on the same skewer as they cook at different rates. You will need four 12-inch metal skewers for this recipe. If the chicken pieces are smaller than 1½ inches, thread two small pieces together.

- ¼ cup olive oil
- 2 tablespoons minced fresh parsley, chives, basil, tarragon, or oregano
- 3 garlic cloves, minced
- ¾ teaspoon salt
- ½ teaspoon pepper
- 2 teaspoons fresh lemon juice
- 1 pound boneless, skinless chicken thighs, trimmed and cut into 1½-inch pieces (see note)
- 1 red bell pepper, stemmed, seeded, and cut into 1½-inch pieces
- 1 small red onion, cut into 1½-inch pieces
- 1 zucchini, cut into ½-inch rounds

1. Whisk the oil, parsley, garlic, salt, and pepper together in a large bowl. Measure out 1½ tablespoons of the marinade and transfer to another bowl; stir in the lemon juice and reserve for serving. Measure out 2 tablespoons more of the marinade, transfer to a large zipper-lock bag, and add the chicken. Seal the bag tightly, toss to coat, and marinate in the refrigerator for at least 1 hour, or up to 24 hours.

2. Add the bell pepper, onion, and zucchini to the large bowl with the remaining marinade, and toss to coat. Thread the chicken and vegetables evenly onto four 12-inch metal skewers, starting and ending with the meat.

3A. FOR A CHARCOAL GRILL: Open the bottom grill vents completely. Light a large chimney starter filled with charcoal briquettes (100 briquettes; 6 quarts). When the coals are hot, pour them in an even layer over the grill. Set the cooking grate in place, cover, and heat the grill until hot, about 5 minutes.

3B. FOR A GAS GRILL: Turn all the burners to high, cover, and heat the grill until hot, about 15 minutes. (Adjust the burners as needed to maintain a hot fire; see below.)

4. Clean and oil the cooking grate. Place the kebabs on the grill and cook (covered if using gas) until the chicken is well browned on all sides and the vegetables are tender, 8 to 12 minutes, turning as needed.

5. Transfer the kebabs to a platter, tent loosely with foil, and let rest for 5 minutes. Drizzle with the reserved marinade mixture and serve.

VARIATIONS

Curried Grilled Chicken and Vegetable Kebabs
Follow the recipe for Herbed Grilled Chicken and Vegetable Kebabs, substituting 2 tablespoons minced fresh cilantro or mint for the parsley and 2 teaspoons fresh lime juice for the lemon juice. In step 1, whisk 1 teaspoon curry powder into the oil mixture before reserving some for serving.

NOTES FROM THE TEST KITCHEN

HOW HOT IS YOUR FIRE?
To determine the heat level of the cooking grate itself, heat up the grill and hold your hand 5 inches above the grate, counting how long you can comfortably keep it there. Note that this works with both charcoal and gas grills.

Hot fire	2 seconds
Medium-hot fire	3 to 4 seconds
Medium fire	5 to 6 seconds
Medium-low fire	7 seconds

Southwestern Grilled Chicken and Vegetable Kebabs
Follow the recipe for Herbed Grilled Chicken and Vegetable Kebabs, substituting 2 tablespoons minced fresh cilantro for the parsley and 2 teaspoons fresh lime juice for the lemon juice. In step 1, whisk 1 tablespoon minced canned chipotle chile in adobo sauce and 1 teaspoon chili powder into the oil mixture before reserving some for serving.

GRILLED JERK CHICKEN WITH CORN

SMOKY, SPICY "JERK" COOKING CAN BE TRACED BACK to Jamaica's native inhabitants, who cooked meat over green wood to give it a distinctive smoky flavor and "jerked" the meat before cooking, which involves making deep slashes in the flesh and stuffing the cuts with herbs and spices. We wanted to bring the jerk flavors—hot chiles, warm spices, and grilled meat—into our own backyard. To turn this dish into a meal, we needed a simple but worthy accompaniment to the complex flavor of the jerk sauce; corn on the cob offered a clean sweetness that would provide a welcome contrast. We gathered some recipes from a variety of cookbooks and headed into the test kitchen.

Most recipes for jerk chicken start with a whole chicken, which is then broken down into pieces. This didn't make sense for two portions, so we opted for bone-in chicken breasts. Some recipes we gathered used dried spices to infuse the meat with flavor, and others relied on a paste. While Jamaican jerk seasoning (both rubs and pastes) can be found in almost any supermarket spice aisle, it often tastes dusty and stale. Besides, we would be using such a small amount that it seemed wasteful to spend money on yet another jar that would take up space in the pantry. To incorporate some fresh notes, we decided to make a paste, not a spice rub; our paste had to be well balanced and flavor the tender meat of the chicken, not just the skin.

We began making our paste with habanero chiles, which are hotter than jalapeños and offer a slow, steady burn. A single habanero was enough to lace two chicken breasts with bold heat. We then added some allspice, a traditional jerk ingredient, along with garlic and scallions, for their subtler punch, and thyme for an herbal touch. To temper the heat and spice, we added vegetable oil and molasses (a fairly common ingredient in recipes we found), both of which had the added benefit of making the paste smoother and more cohesive.

We knew that to instill our chicken with the most flavor possible, we'd have to replicate the traditional "jerk" technique. To flavor both the meat and the skin, we loosened the skin on the chicken breasts and rubbed the paste underneath, then coated the skin with the rest of the paste. We then tested different ranges of time to find out how long the chicken would need to marinate to absorb the flavors. After an hour, the flavor was barely there, but at the two-hour mark, the chicken was well seasoned. After more testing, we found that the chicken could rest in the marinade for up to 24 hours, making this recipe a good candidate for a make-ahead dinner.

To keep the skin from burning before the meat near the bone was cooked through, we set up our charcoal grill with briquettes piled on one half of the grill, leaving the other half empty. This way, the meat could cook through and the skin could render its fat over indirect heat on the cooler side without any fear of burning or flare-ups. We could then finish it over a hotter fire toward the end of grilling to get the skin browned and allow the jerk paste on the exterior to char slightly— just enough to create an authentic smoky flavor. To promote even cooking, we covered the meat with a piece of foil while it cooked on the cooler side; the foil traps a layer of heat against the meat that maintains a consistent temperature. After 30 minutes of cooking, the meat was moist and flavorful and boasted perfectly charred skin. All that was left was the corn.

While grilling husk-on corn delivers great pure corn flavor, it lacks the smokiness of the grill; essentially, the corn is steamed in its protective husk. But grilling with the husk off is too much heat for the unprotected corn. We compromised by leaving only the innermost layer of husk in place and trimming the silk (to prevent it from catching fire). After 10 minutes, we were rewarded with perfectly tender corn infused with the grill's flavor. All our cobs needed to enhance them was a brush of butter and a sprinkling of salt and pepper. Accompanied with lime wedges, our jerk chicken cookout had all the robust, spicy, well-balanced flavor we were looking for.

Grilled Jerk Chicken Breasts with Corn on the Cob

SERVES 2

This dish is very spicy; to tone down the spice level, remove the habanero seeds and ribs before processing. Be careful when handling the habanero as its oils can cause your skin to burn; be sure to use latex gloves when handling the pureed mixture in step 2. If you cannot find a habanero, substitute 2 jalapeño chiles. Eight bone-in, skin-on chicken thighs or drumsticks can be substituted for the breasts; you will need to cook them until they register 175 degrees on an instant-read thermometer in step 5.

- 4 scallions, chopped
- 2 tablespoons vegetable oil
- 1 tablespoon light or mild molasses
- 1 habanero chile, stemmed (see note)
- 2 garlic cloves, peeled
- 1½ teaspoons dried thyme
- 1 teaspoon ground allspice
   Salt
- 2 (12-ounce) bone-in, skin-on split chicken breasts (see note), trimmed (see page 148)
- 2 ears fresh corn, all but innermost layer of husk removed, silk trimmed (see page 185)
- 1 tablespoon unsalted butter, softened
   Pepper
   Lime wedges, for serving

1. Process the scallions, oil, molasses, habanero, garlic, thyme, allspice, and 1 teaspoon salt together in a food processor (or blender) until almost smooth, about 15 seconds.

2. Carefully loosen the skin on the chicken breasts by sliding your fingers between the skin and the meat. Wearing latex gloves, rub 1 tablespoon of the pureed scallion mixture underneath the skin of each breast. Transfer the chicken to a large zipper-lock bag and add the remaining scallion mixture. Seal the bag tightly, toss to coat, and marinate in the refrigerator for at least 2 hours, or up to 24 hours.

3A. FOR A CHARCOAL GRILL: Open the bottom grill vents completely. Light a large chimney starter filled with charcoal briquettes (100 briquettes; 6 quarts). When the coals are hot, pour them in an even layer over half the grill, leaving the other half empty. Set the cooking grate in place, cover, and open the lid vents completely. Heat the grill until hot, about 5 minutes.

3B. FOR A GAS GRILL: Turn all the burners to high, cover, and heat the grill until hot, about 15 minutes. Leave the primary burner on high and turn off the other burner(s). (Adjust the burners as needed to maintain a temperature of 350 degrees.)

4. Clean and oil the cooking grate. Remove the chicken breasts from the marinade and place them, skin-side down, on the cooler part of the grill, with the thicker sides of the breasts facing the hotter part of the grill. Tent the chicken breasts loosely with foil, cover the grill, and cook until the chicken registers 150 degrees on an instant-read thermometer, 25 to 35 minutes.

5. Slide the chicken breasts to the hotter part of the grill and cook (covered if using gas) until well browned on both sides and the chicken registers 160 to 165 degrees on an instant-read thermometer, 6 to 10 minutes longer, flipping the breasts halfway through. (If flare-ups occur, slide the chicken breasts to the cooler part of the grill and mist the fire with water from a spray bottle.) Transfer the chicken breasts to a serving platter, tent loosely with foil, and let rest.

6. While the chicken cooks on the hotter part of the grill, place the corn on the hotter part of the grill and cook until the husks are charred and the kernels are tender, 8 to 10 minutes, turning as needed. Transfer the corn to the platter with the chicken and carefully remove and discard the charred husks and silk. Brush the corn with the butter and season with salt and pepper to taste. Serve the chicken with the corn and lime wedges.

NOTES FROM THE TEST KITCHEN

PREPARING CORN FOR THE GRILL

1. Remove all but the innermost layer of the husk so the kernels are covered by, but visible through, this layer of the husk.

2. Use scissors to snip off the tassel, or long silk ends, at the tip of the ear.

KEEPING CORN SWEET

Generally, it's best to eat corn on the cob the same day you buy it, as its sugars start converting to starches as soon as it is harvested, causing the corn to lose sweetness. But if you buy corn and don't plan to cook it the same day, it should be stored in the refrigerator until you're ready to use it. We recommend storing corn unshucked and wrapped in a wet paper bag to slow down the conversion from sugar to starch, then placing the wet paper bag in a plastic bag (any shopping bag will do). Because corn on the cob is sensitive to chill injury, it should be placed in the front of the fridge, where the temperatures tend to be higher.

GRILLED GAME HENS WITH CHERRY TOMATO SALAD

BUTTERFLIED CHICKEN GRILLED UNDER A BRICK is an Italian specialty, and one that looks much more impressive than standard grill fare. But the brick isn't just for show—its weight compresses the bird for more even, quicker cooking and also produces perfectly golden, crisp skin by maximizing contact with the grill. Since a whole chicken provides enough meat for about six diners, we decided to substitute two smaller birds—Cornish game hens—for a fancy weekend dinner off the grill.

Like other poultry, Cornish game hens need all the help they can get to keep the breast meat from drying out on the grill before the dark meat is cooked through. We tried brining our birds (soaking them in salted water), but preliminary tests revealed that when the brined birds were compressed with a brick, the excess moisture was pushed out and soaked the skin, preventing it from becoming crispy. We nixed the brining and instead opted to salt the meat under the skin; this step draws out moisture from inside the bird that, over time, gets reabsorbed with the salt, helping the meat retain its juice during cooking. A quick test proved that the salted hens could be grilled under a brick with none of the problems of brining. While an hour of salting sufficed, double that was better yet. The only problem was that the thin skin on the legs and thighs had a tendency to tear when we loosened it to apply the salt. Since it is the white meat that needs the boost anyway, we limited our salting to the breast.

While the salt worked to retain moisture, it did nothing for the flavor of the meat. For traditional Mediterranean flavor, we rubbed some aromatics under the skin. Raw garlic, lemon zest, and herbs tasted too harsh, but these same ingredients sautéed in olive oil, which we then strained off, infused the hens with rich flavor. We used a combination of thyme and rosemary for the herbs and added a bit of heat with red pepper flakes.

We were ready to move on to the cooking method. The most obvious method—grilling our hens over a single-level fire—flopped miserably, resulting in flare-ups that charred the skin. It became clear that we needed to render some of the juice and fat before the birds could be set directly over the hot fire. We made a half-grill fire (spreading the coals over half of the grill and leaving the other half empty) and plopped the hens, skin-side down, over the cooler side—without coals. We then balanced the bricks (which we had preheated, right on the grill, to provide heat from above) on top, covered the grill, and left the birds alone long enough to firm the flesh, about 25 minutes. We then removed the bricks and slid the hens to the hot side of the grill to brown and crisp. Not only had we eliminated the flare-ups, but the meat was now incredibly juicy and the skin crispy and golden.

For a salad in keeping with the Italian tone of our dish, we started by grilling cherry tomatoes. Their sweetness is a perfect complement to just about anything smoky from the grill, and they don't take long to cook. We tossed the tomatoes with a little extra-virgin olive oil and skewered them. We wanted to serve them warm, so we waited until the hens were resting to grill them. After about six minutes over the coals, the tomatoes were pleasantly blistered but still plump. We combined the warm tomatoes with some baby spinach and Parmesan shavings and realized we needed a dressing. What about that olive oil we'd used to sauté our herbs and then discarded? In the next test, we reserved the flavored oil and mixed it with some lemon juice and more fresh herbs. Now we had the perfect vinaigrette for our salad, as well as a bright drizzling oil for our crispy grilled birds.

Italian-Style Grilled Cornish Game Hens with Cherry Tomato and Spinach Salad
SERVES 2

You will need two standard-sized bricks for this recipe. Use an oven mitt or dish towel to safely grip and maneuver the hot bricks. Don't skip the step of placing the bricks on the game hens while they cook; this ensures that the skin will be evenly browned and well rendered. A cast-iron skillet or other heavy pan can be used in place of the bricks. You will need two to three 12-inch metal skewers for this recipe, depending on the size of your tomatoes. Use a vegetable peeler to shave the Parmesan. Note that the seasoned game hens need to be refrigerated for at least 1 hour prior to grilling.

¼ cup extra-virgin olive oil
4 medium garlic cloves, minced
½ teaspoon grated lemon zest plus
 1 tablespoon fresh lemon juice
 Pinch red pepper flakes
1½ teaspoons minced fresh thyme
1 teaspoon minced fresh rosemary
 Salt and pepper
2 (1¼- to 1½-pound) Cornish game hens, giblets removed
12 ounces cherry tomatoes (about 2 cups)
2 ounces baby spinach (about 2 cups)
¼ cup thinly shaved Parmesan cheese (see note)

1. Bring 3 tablespoons of the oil, garlic, lemon zest, and red pepper flakes to a simmer in a small saucepan over medium-low heat. Stir in 1 teaspoon of the thyme and ¾ teaspoon of the rosemary and cook until fragrant, about 30 seconds.

2. Pour the mixture through a fine-mesh strainer into a bowl, pressing on the solids to extract the oil. Transfer the solids to another bowl, cool to room temperature, then stir in ½ teaspoon salt and ¼ teaspoon pepper. Stir the lemon juice, remaining ½ teaspoon thyme, and remaining ¼ teaspoon rosemary into the strained oil. Season with salt and pepper to taste and set aside for serving.

3. Pat the game hens dry with paper towels. Following the photos on page 188, butterfly the game hens and

ITALIAN-STYLE GRILLED CORNISH GAME HEN WITH CHERRY TOMATO AND SPINACH SALAD

NOTES FROM THE TEST KITCHEN

PREPARING CORNISH GAME HENS FOR THE GRILL

1. Cut through the bones on either side of the backbone, then discard the backbone.

2. Flip the hen, then gently flatten the breastbone.

3. Tuck the wings behind the back, then carefully separate the skin covering the breast from the meat and remove any excess fat.

4. Spread the garlic-salt mixture under the skin of the breast, then season the meat on the bone side with salt and pepper.

FIGHTING FLARE-UPS

Flare-ups from the grill are a not-so-rare occurrence, caused primarily by fats melting into the fire. They are much more problematic with charcoal grills since the burners on gas grills often have covers to protect them. Regardless, sometimes there's just no avoiding them, so it's important to make sure a little flare-up doesn't turn into an out-of-control grease fire that ruins your meal. We recommend keeping a squirt bottle or plant mister filled with water near the grill. At the first sign of flames, pull foods to a cool part of the grill and douse the flames with water.

tuck the wings. Using your fingers, carefully separate the skin covering each breast from the meat and remove any excess fat. Gently spread the garlic-salt mixture evenly under the skin over the breasts. Flip the game hens and season the meat on the bone side with salt and pepper. Place the hens, skin-side up, on a wire rack set inside a rimmed baking sheet and refrigerate for at least 1 hour, or up to 2 hours.

4. Meanwhile, wrap 2 bricks tightly with foil. Toss the tomatoes with the remaining 1 tablespoon oil, then thread them through the stem ends onto two or three 12-inch metal skewers.

5A. FOR A CHARCOAL GRILL: Open the bottom grill vents completely. Light a large chimney starter filled three-quarters with charcoal briquettes (75 briquettes; 4½ quarts). When the coals are hot, pour them in an even layer over half the grill, leaving the other half empty. Set the cooking grate in place, place the bricks on the grate over the coals, cover, and open the lid vents completely. Heat the grill until hot, about 5 minutes.

5B. FOR A GAS GRILL: Turn all the burners to high, place the bricks on the cooking grate, cover, and heat the grill until hot, about 15 minutes. Leave the primary burner on high and turn the other burner(s) off. (Adjust the burners as needed to maintain a temperature of 325 degrees.)

6. Clean and oil the cooking grate. Place the hens, skin-side down, on the cooler part of the grill, with the legs facing the hotter part of the grill. Place a hot brick widthwise on each hen, cover, and cook until the skin just begins to turn golden brown and faint grill marks appear, 22 to 25 minutes.

7. Remove the bricks from the hens. Slide the hens to the hotter part of the grill with the breasts facing the cooler part of the grill. Cook (covered if using gas) until the hens are well browned on the skin side, 8 to 12 minutes. (If flare-ups occur, slide the hens to the cooler part of the grill and mist the fire with water from a spray bottle.)

8. Using two spatulas, gently flip the hens skin-side up and continue to cook until lightly browned on the bone side and the breasts register 160 to 165 degrees and the thighs register 175 degrees on an instant-read thermometer, 3 to 6 minutes longer. Transfer the hens to a serving platter and let rest.

9. Meanwhile, place the skewered tomatoes on the hotter part of the grill and cook until the skins begin to blister and wrinkle, 3 to 6 minutes, turning as needed. Remove the skewers from the grill and carefully slide the tomatoes off the skewers into a medium bowl. Add the spinach and 2 tablespoons of the reserved vinaigrette; toss to coat. Season with salt and pepper to taste and transfer to the serving platter. Sprinkle the cheese over the top of the salad and serve, passing the remaining reserved vinaigrette separately.

GRILLED PORK TENDERLOIN WITH RADICCHIO SALAD

BECAUSE OF THE COMPACT SIZE AND SHAPE OF pork tenderloin, it's a good candidate for both the grill and dinner for two. But the leanness of pork tenderloin can make it a challenge to cook: Little fat translates to little flavor and meat that easily dries out. We needed a grilling technique that would consistently yield pork with an attractive, well-browned crust and a juicy, perfectly cooked interior. We also wanted to figure out the best way to incorporate some potent flavorings—rosemary and garlic came to mind—that would enhance the mild flavor of the pork. And finally, we wanted a complementary side dish that would turn our recipe into a satisfying dinner.

We focused first on cooking technique. We knew we needed to set up two cooking zones: a hotter area of the grill to brown the pork and a cooler area where it could cook through. When the grill was hot, we put the pork on the grill, directly above the coals, and seared the meat on each of the four sides; the internal temperature at this point hovered around 125 degrees. We then moved the tenderloin to the cooler part of the grill and waited for the internal temperature to climb. It took about 15 minutes, and countless temperature checks, for the meat to arrive at 140 degrees. Looking for a quicker way to bring the pork up to temperature, we decided to cover the tenderloin loosely with foil to trap the heat. In just five minutes, the tenderloin reached an internal temperature between 140 and 145 degrees without picking up additional char on the crust. After it rested for a short time on a carving board, we sliced the tenderloin and found juicy, moist meat surrounded by a nice circle of crust. We now needed to find the best way to incorporate our chosen seasonings. Up until now, we'd been sprinkling the pork with salt, pepper, and brown sugar to encourage browning, but we wanted more flavor.

Our first thought was to smear the tenderloin with a paste made of rosemary, garlic, and oil, but the paste burned over the hot fire before the meat had a chance to brown. Instead, we decided to flavor our salt rub with a complementary spice and finish our pork with a drizzling oil enhanced with fresh herbs. After testing a variety of spices in our salt rub, we settled on a small amount of citrusy coriander, which added a rich brightness to the tenderloin's crust. For our drizzling oil, we set our sights on something akin to a South American chimichurri sauce, a traditional accompaniment to grilled meats. We combined minced garlic, rosemary, and parsley with olive oil, salt, and pepper. After the pork had rested, we sliced it thin and

---

NOTES FROM THE TEST KITCHEN

THE BEST CHIMNEY STARTER
A chimney starter is the safest, most effective way to start a fire. These cylindrical canisters quickly ignite quarts of briquettes without lighter fluid. To use a chimney starter, simply add briquettes to the large top chamber, place a crumpled sheet of newspaper in the smaller chamber under the coals, and light it. In about 20 minutes, the coals are red-hot, covered with a fine gray ash, and ready to pour into your grill. Our favorite is the **Weber RapidFire Chimney Starter**, $14.95, for its sturdy construction, generous capacity, heat-resistant handle, and second handle for better leverage. It also has plenty of ventilation holes in its canister, maximizing airflow and allowing coals to ignite quickly.

spooned our herb oil on top. The result: browned, juicy pork with a robust yet balanced hit of garlic and herbs.

With the pork and sauce ready to go, we decided to take advantage of our still-hot coals to grill a vegetable. We chose slightly bitter radicchio, which would make a lively partner to the slices of tenderloin. We quartered a head of radicchio—a single head was plenty for two people—and brushed it with oil. Leaving the core intact kept the wedges together on the grill, as the leaves tend to separate as they cook. After five minutes, the radicchio was browned and lightly charred. We sliced the grilled radicchio into thin strips before tossing it with balsamic vinegar, olive oil, and crumbled Gorgonzola cheese. The interplay of sweet, creamy, and bitter won tasters over.

In about 30 minutes, we had created a complexly flavored dinner of tender grilled pork tenderloin, a garlicky herb oil, and a balsamic radicchio and Gorgonzola salad—not too shabby for a simple dinner off the grill.

Grilled Pork Tenderloin with Radicchio and Gorgonzola Salad

SERVES 2

Do not remove the core from the radicchio; it will help keep the leaves together on the grill.

- 5 tablespoons extra-virgin olive oil
- 1 tablespoon minced fresh parsley
- 1 small garlic clove, minced
- ½ teaspoon minced fresh rosemary
  Salt and pepper
- ¾ teaspoon brown sugar
- ½ teaspoon ground coriander
- 1 (12-ounce) pork tenderloin, trimmed
- 1 head radicchio (about 8 ounces), quartered lengthwise through the core (see note)
- 1 ounce Gorgonzola cheese, crumbled (about ¼ cup)
- 1 tablespoon balsamic vinegar

1. Whisk 2 tablespoons of the oil, parsley, garlic, rosemary, ⅛ teaspoon salt, and ⅛ teaspoon pepper together in a bowl, and set aside for serving.

2. Combine the sugar, coriander, ½ teaspoon salt, and ¼ teaspoon pepper in another bowl. Pat the tenderloin dry with paper towels and rub with 1 tablespoon more oil, followed by the sugar mixture. Brush the radicchio with 1 tablespoon more oil and season with salt and pepper.

3A. FOR A CHARCOAL GRILL: Open the bottom grill vents completely. Light a large chimney starter filled with charcoal briquettes (100 briquettes; 6 quarts). When the coals are hot, pour them in an even layer over half the grill. Set the cooking grate in place, cover, and open the lid vents completely. Heat the grill until hot, about 5 minutes.

3B. FOR A GAS GRILL: Turn all the burners to high, cover, and heat the grill until hot, about 15 minutes. Leave the primary burner on high and turn off the other burner(s). (Adjust the burners as needed to maintain the grill temperature around 350 degrees.)

4. Clean and oil the cooking grate. Place the pork on the hotter part of the grill and cook (covered if using gas) until well browned on all sides, 10 to 12 minutes, turning as needed. Slide the pork to the cooler part of the grill, tent loosely with foil, and continue to cook until the pork registers 140 to 145 degrees on an instant-read thermometer, 5 to 8 minutes longer. Transfer the pork to a carving board, tent loosely with foil, and let rest.

5. While the pork cooks on the cooler part of the grill, place the radicchio, cut-side down, on the hotter part of the grill and cook until slightly wilted and browned on all sides, about 5 minutes, turning as needed.

6. Transfer the radicchio to a cutting board and slice into thin strips, discarding the core. Toss the sliced radicchio, remaining 1 tablespoon oil, cheese, and vinegar together in a bowl. Season with salt and pepper to taste. Cut the pork into ¼-inch-thick slices, drizzle with the reserved herb-oil mixture, and serve with the radicchio salad.

GRILL-SMOKED PORK CHOPS WITH APPLE SALAD

THE THING ABOUT BARBECUING PORK IS THAT IT takes a decent chunk of time to get good smoke flavor in every bite. If we're grilling a pork roast for a backyard get-together, we don't mind tending a hot fire all day, but when we're cooking for two, the daylong grill fest just doesn't make sense. That's when we turn to pork chops. But grilling them for hours over low heat, a method that keeps big roasts moist, just dries pork chops out. Slathering the chops with barbecue sauce and setting them over a super-hot fire doesn't pan out either—it provides a nicely browned crust, but the only flavor is in the sauce, not the meat. We set out to develop a recipe that would give us everything we wanted: pork chops that boasted a deep smoky flavor, stayed moist, and also developed the crusty glaze that forms from being quickly cooked over intense heat. And because two chops wouldn't take up a lot of room on the grill, we aimed to use the available space on the grate to prepare an interesting and fresh accompaniment at the same time.

For grilling, we knew bone-in thick-cut chops were the best choice. We like center-cut chops and rib chops, both of which are cut from the middle of the pig's loin. Both are tender and flavorful, but tasters preferred the rib chops, which were juicy and well marbled with fat. To ensure that they could withstand a hot grill without overcooking, we opted for chops about 1½ inches thick. For the barbecue sauce, we kept things simple, briefly simmering a mix of sweet and tangy ingredients— ketchup, molasses, brown sugar, onion, Worcestershire sauce, mustard, and cider vinegar—until thickened.

Armed with the right cut of meat and a tasty sauce, we focused on the grilling technique. To reap the benefits of both high and low heat, we made a half-grill fire; for good smoke flavor, we put a handful of soaked wood chips (sealed in a foil packet) over the coals. We started with the simplest method: We seared the chops on the hot side, then slid them to the cool side until they reached 140 to 145 degrees, which took less than 10 minutes. To prevent burning, we slathered on the barbecue sauce in the last few minutes of cooking. When pulled off the grill, these chops had a decent crust, but they were dry in the interior and their smoke flavor was weak. We needed to try a different approach.

Past research had taught us that the enzymes that break down collagen, which helps to tenderize meat, are active only at temperatures below 122 degrees— hence the effectiveness of low-and-slow cooking when it comes to big roasts. If we wanted optimally tender chops, we had to keep the pork at a low temperature for as long as possible. We decided to reverse the order of cooking and started the chops under cover on the cooler side of the grill (with an aluminum roasting pan positioned underneath to catch the dripping fat), allowing the smoke to do its job for about 15 minutes. We then applied a few coats of sauce and finished by browning the chops, uncovered, over the hot coals. The results were a huge improvement, by far the smokiest and most tender yet, but we wondered if there was an even better way to slow down the cooking.

We reasoned that if we could somehow support the chops so the bone was facing down, the heat from below would penetrate the meat more slowly. We speared the chops with skewers to keep them from toppling over, making sure to leave some space between them to allow smoke to circulate. With bone, not meat, now touching the grill, we could leave the chops standing for a full 20 minutes to maximize the meat's exposure to the smoke. When the meat reached an internal temperature of 120 degrees, we removed the skewers, applied the glaze, and finished the chops over the hot coals, flipping the chops so that both sides had a chance to brown. These chops had it all—a charred crust, rosy, ultra-moist meat, and true smoke flavor throughout.

Since pork pairs naturally with fruit, we decided to come up with a salad featuring grilled apples. Cutting the apple into slices maximized contact with the grill and achieved the most caramelization on the surface. After 10 minutes on the grill, the apple was ready to be cut into thin batons, which we tossed with tender Bibb lettuce and a simple vinaigrette. Our salad was good, but tasters felt it was missing something. A small red onion, cut into rounds and grilled on a skewer to keep it from falling through the cooking grate, did the trick, providing a crunchy and pungent contrast to the sweet, tender apple.

GRILL-SMOKED PORK CHOPS WITH APPLE AND BIBB LETTUCE SALAD

Grill-Smoked Pork Chops with Apple and Bibb Lettuce Salad

SERVES 2

If the pork is "enhanced" (see page 10 for more information), do not brine. If brining the pork, do not season with salt in step 2. Use the large holes of a box grater to grate the onion for the sauce. You will need three 12-inch metal skewers for this recipe. Do not core the apple before slicing; it holds up better on the grill with the core intact. Although we prefer hickory wood chips, any variety of chip, except mesquite, will work.

SAUCE

¼ cup ketchup

2 tablespoons light or mild molasses

1 tablespoon grated onion (see note)

1 tablespoon Worcestershire sauce

1 tablespoon Dijon mustard

1 tablespoon cider vinegar

1½ teaspoons brown sugar

Salt and pepper

PORK CHOPS AND SALAD

3 tablespoons extra-virgin olive oil

1 tablespoon cider vinegar

2 (12- to 14-ounce) bone-in pork rib chops, about 1½ inches thick, trimmed, sides slit (see page 10), brined if desired (see note; see page 162)
Salt and pepper

1 small red onion, sliced into ¾-inch-thick rounds

1 large, firm, crisp apple, such as Granny Smith, Cortland, or Empire, sliced into ¾-inch-thick rounds (see note)

1 (13 by 9-inch) disposable aluminum roasting pan (if using charcoal)

1 cup wood chips (see note), soaked, drained, and sealed in a foil packet (see page 194)

1 head Bibb lettuce, torn into bite-sized pieces (about 4 cups)

1. FOR THE SAUCE: Bring the ketchup, molasses, onion, Worcestershire sauce, mustard, vinegar, and sugar to a simmer in a small saucepan over medium heat, and cook, stirring occasionally, until thickened and reduced to about ½ cup, 3 to 5 minutes. Season with salt and pepper to taste. Measure out and reserve ¼ cup of the sauce for serving.

2. FOR THE PORK CHOPS AND SALAD: Whisk the oil and vinegar together in a medium bowl. Pat the pork chops dry with paper towels and season with salt and pepper. Stand the pork chops on their rib bones on a cutting board, side by side and facing in the same direction. Following the photo on page 194, pass two skewers through the loin muscle of each chop, close to the bone, about 1 inch from each end. Once the chops have been threaded onto the skewers, pull them apart to create a 2-inch space between them. Thread the onion rounds, from side to side, onto another metal skewer. Brush the skewered onion and the apple with 1 tablespoon of the vinaigrette and season with salt and pepper.

3A. FOR A CHARCOAL GRILL: Open the bottom grill vents completely and place the roasting pan on one side of the grill. Light a large chimney starter filled with charcoal briquettes (100 briquettes; 6 quarts). When the coals are hot, pour them in an even layer over half the grill, opposite the roasting pan. Place the wood chip packet on top of the coals. Set the cooking grate in place, cover, and open the lid vents halfway. Heat the grill until hot and the wood chips begin to smoke heavily, about 5 minutes.

3B. FOR A GAS GRILL: Place the wood chip packet directly on the primary burner. Turn all the burners to high, cover, and heat the grill until hot and the wood chips begin to smoke heavily, about 15 minutes. Leave the primary burner on high and turn off the other burner(s). (Adjust the burners as needed to maintain the grill temperature around 350 degrees.)

4. Clean and oil the cooking grate. Stand the pork chops, bone-side down, on the cooler part of the grill. Cover (positioning the lid vents over the pork chops if using charcoal) and cook until the chops register 120 degrees on an instant-read thermometer, 20 to 25 minutes.

5. Carefully remove the pork chops from the skewers and brush one side with half of the remaining sauce. Transfer the chops, sauce-side down, to the hotter part of the grill and cook (covered if using gas) until browned on the first side, 3 to 6 minutes. Brush the tops of the chops with the remaining sauce, flip, and continue to cook until the second side is browned and the chops register 140 to 145 degrees on an instant-read thermometer, 3 to 6 minutes longer. Transfer the pork chops to a serving platter, tent loosely with foil, and let rest.

6. While the pork chops cook on the hotter part of the grill, place the onion and apple on the hotter part of the grill and cook until spottily charred on both sides, 8 to 12 minutes, flipping them halfway through. Transfer the onion and apple to a cutting board, remove the onion from the skewer, and cut the onion into 1-inch pieces and the apple into ½-inch-thick batons, discarding the apple core.

7. Add the apple, onion, and lettuce to the bowl with the remaining vinaigrette, and toss to combine. Season with salt and pepper to taste. Serve the salad with the pork, passing the reserved barbecue sauce separately.

NOTES FROM THE TEST KITCHEN

GRILLING PORK CHOPS

1. To provide stability when standing the pork chops on the grill, pass two skewers through the loin muscle of each chop. Then pull the chops apart to create space to allow smoke to circulate.

2. Stand the skewered chops, bone-side down, on the cooking grate, on the cooler part of the grill.

HOW TO MAKE A FOIL PACKET

After soaking the wood chips in water for 15 minutes, drain and spread them in the center of a 15 by 12-inch piece of heavy-duty foil. Fold to seal the edges, then cut three or four slits to allow smoke to escape.

GRILLED RACK OF LAMB WITH ZUCCHINI

WHEN YOU COOK AN EXPENSIVE CUT OF MEAT LIKE rack of lamb, you want it to be spectacular. The meat should be pink and juicy, surrounded by a well-caramelized crust that provides a textural contrast to the rich, tender meat. We decided this pricey cut of meat had the makings to be a great special-occasion dinner off the grill—the intense heat of the coals would produce a dark brown crust and melt away the lamb's fat, distributing flavor and tenderness throughout. Even though we were grilling only one rack, we'd still have to figure out how to keep all the rendering fat from creating the scorching flare-ups and sooty flavors that are guaranteed to ruin this cut. We set out to come up with a foolproof technique for grilling rack of lamb—one that would deliver a well-browned crust and flavorful, tender meat, every time.

The key to lamb's unique flavor and tenderness is its high proportion of fat, most of which covers one side of the rack like a cap. We knew from experience that leaving the fat in place would lead to aggressive flare-ups virtually as soon as we put the lamb over the coals. But removing all of the cap wasn't the solution either. When we did this, the rack ended up dry, with very little distinctive lamb flavor. As a compromise, we left a thin layer of fat over the loin and removed most of the fat between the bones.

Even when we trimmed the lamb of fat, we knew we couldn't cook it directly over the coals the entire time. Lamb still has enough interior fat that it would be only a matter of minutes before the flare-ups started. When grilling fattier meat, we often build a half-grill fire (all the coals are on one side of the grill to create hot and cool areas) and place a foil pan on the cool side to act as a drip tray to catch rendering fat. We then brown the meat over the hot coals, sliding it to the cooler side of the grill to finish. When we tried this method, the rack cooked to medium-rare at the center and had decent grilled flavor. However, many tasters found the outer layers of the meat to be overdone and tough. Plus, starting the rack on the hot side of the grill still led to flare-ups if we weren't paying close attention.

We thought back to our Grill-Smoked Pork Chops (page 193) and decided to switch the order of cooking. We started the lamb over indirect heat to allow the fat to render, then moved the rack over to the hot side for just a short while to brown the exterior without fear of flare-ups. The lamb now had a crispy, well-browned exterior while boasting tender, rosy meat on the inside.

Our biggest challenge met, we set out to flavor the lamb. Because lamb tastes so good on its own, we wanted to enhance the meat's flavor without overwhelming it. A wet rub consisting of garlic and a couple of robust herbs (rosemary and thyme) mixed with a little oil (just enough to adhere the flavorings to the lamb without causing flare-ups) was the best way to flavor the meat—marinades turned the lamb mushy, and dry rubs simply charred with our grilling method. For a rich crust that wasn't burned, we applied the wet rub during the last few minutes of grilling, keeping the surface crisp.

Having pulled off great-tasting grilled rack of lamb, we set our sights on a simple side dish. Tasters liked the idea of grilled zucchini, and we had the perfect opening to cook it while the lamb was resting, as the slightly cooled coals provided the moderate blast of heat the zucchini required. To round out our side, we tossed chunks of the grilled zucchini with cooked couscous, which is often paired with lamb. Crumbled feta, fresh lemon juice, and fresh mint echoed the Mediterranean flavor profile and helped to make a bright and fresh salad that was the perfect counterpoint to the rich lamb.

NOTES FROM THE TEST KITCHEN

THE BEST GRILL TONGS

For the most part, we pass on the new models of tongs that appear each grilling season and just rely on a traditional and effective pair. But to make sure that we weren't missing anything, we picked up a few of the latest on the market. Unfortunately, most looked and performed like medieval torture devices, with sharp, serrated edges that nicked the surface of steaks and shredded fish into flakes. Our overall winner was a plain pair of **OXO Good Grips 16-Inch Locking Tongs**, $14.95. Not only do they grip, turn, and move food around the grill easily, but they are also long enough to keep hands a safe distance from the grill.

Grilled Rack of Lamb with Zucchini and Couscous Salad
SERVES 2

We prefer the milder taste and bigger size of domestic lamb, but you may substitute imported lamb from New Zealand or Australia. Since imported racks are generally smaller, follow the shorter cooking times given in the recipe. While most lamb is sold frenched (meaning part of each rib bone is exposed), chances are there will still be some extra fat between the bones. Remove the majority of this fat, leaving an inch at the top of the small eye of meat. Also, make sure that the chine bone (along the bottom of the rack) has been removed to ensure easy cutting between the ribs after cooking. Ask the butcher to do this; it's very hard to cut off at home. We prefer the lamb cooked to medium-rare, but if you prefer it more or less done, see the guidelines in "Testing Meat for Doneness" on page 109.

½ cup boiling water

½ cup couscous

2 tablespoons olive oil

2 teaspoons minced fresh rosemary

1 teaspoon minced fresh thyme

1 garlic clove, minced

1 (1½- to 1¾-pound) rack of lamb,
    rib bones frenched and meat trimmed
    of all excess fat (see page 196; see note)
    Salt and pepper

1 zucchini, halved lengthwise

1 (13 by 9-inch) disposable aluminum roasting pan
    (if using charcoal)

2 ounces feta cheese, crumbled (about ½ cup)

2 tablespoons minced fresh mint or basil

1 tablespoon fresh lemon juice

1. Combine the boiling water and couscous in a medium bowl, cover, and let sit until the liquid is absorbed and the couscous is tender, about 5 minutes. Fluff with a fork and set aside.

2. Combine 2½ teaspoons of the oil, rosemary, thyme, and garlic in a bowl, and set aside. Pat the lamb dry with paper towels, rub with ½ teaspoon more oil, and season with salt and pepper. Brush the zucchini with 1 teaspoon more oil and season with salt and pepper.

3A. FOR A CHARCOAL GRILL: Open the bottom grill vents completely and place the roasting pan on one side of the grill. Light a large chimney starter filled with charcoal briquettes (100 briquettes; 6 quarts). When the coals are hot, pour them in an even layer over half the grill, opposite the roasting pan. Set the cooking grate in place, cover, and open the lid vents completely. Heat the grill until hot, about 5 minutes.

3B. FOR A GAS GRILL: Turn all the burners to high, cover, and heat the grill until hot, about 15 minutes. Leave the primary burner on high and turn off the other burner(s). (Adjust the burners as needed to maintain the grill temperature around 350 degrees.)

TRIMMING FAT FROM RACK OF LAMB

1. If the rack has a thick outer layer of fat, peel it back and cut any tissue connecting the fat cap to the rack.

2. Trim the remaining thin layer of fat that covers the loin, leaving the thin strip of fat between the loin and the bone.

3. Make a straight cut along the top side of the bones, an inch up from the small eye of meat.

4. Remove any fat above this line and scrape any remaining meat or fat from the exposed bones.

4. Clean and oil the cooking grate. Place the rack, bone-side up, on the cooler part of the grill, with the meaty side of the rack facing the hotter part of the grill. Cover and cook until the meat is lightly browned and the fat has begun to render, 8 to 10 minutes.

5. Flip the rack bone-side down, slide to the hotter part of the grill, and cook until well browned on both sides, 6 to 8 minutes, flipping and brushing with the garlic-herb mixture halfway through. Using tongs, hold the rack upright on the hotter part of the grill and continue to cook until the bottom is well browned and the lamb registers 125 degrees on an instant-read thermometer (for medium-rare), 3 to 8 minutes longer. (Alternatively, you can use a tight ball of foil, about 3 inches in diameter, to prop up the rack.) Transfer the lamb to a carving board, tent loosely with foil, and let rest.

6. While the lamb rests, place the zucchini on the hotter part of the grill and cook (covered if using gas) until spottily charred on both sides, 10 to 15 minutes, flipping the zucchini halves halfway through. Transfer the zucchini to the carving board with the lamb.

7. Cut the zucchini into ½-inch pieces. Gently fold the zucchini, remaining 2 teaspoons oil, feta, mint, and lemon juice into the couscous, and season with salt and pepper to taste. Cut the lamb between the ribs to separate the chops and serve with the couscous.

CHILE CHEESEBURGERS WITH SWEET POTATOES

TO LIVEN UP BURGER NIGHT, WE DECIDED TO TRY our hand at a special tradition from the Southwest: the green chile burger. At roadside restaurants all over New Mexico, ground beef patties are grilled to a crusty brown and topped with fire-roasted, chopped chiles and a slice of cheese. The chiles add an intense heat and sweet, smoky flavor to the burger. The authentic chile burger relies on chile varieties that are abundant in New Mexico but hard to find outside the region. We set out to make our own burgers (just two) that would pack the same heat and flavor, but we wanted to use conventional ingredients so we could skip the plane ticket.

Starting with the meat, tasters preferred the flavor and fat of 85 percent lean ground beef. After a few trial runs, we settled on 6-ounce patties, which could

GRILLED GREEN CHILE CHEESEBURGERS WITH SWEET POTATOES

accommodate a generous portion of chile topping. To shape the burgers, we used a proven test kitchen technique—making a small indentation in the patties to keep them from buckling and dislodging the topping. Grilled for about 10 minutes over medium-high heat, these patties were juicy and meaty.

With the burger in place, we considered the chiles. Most recipes suggest canned chiles as a substitute for the heat-packing New Mexican varieties, but we found them tinny and so mild we could eat them with a spoon. Casting about for an alternative, we spied Anaheim chiles at the supermarket. We roasted the supermarket Anaheims under the broiler and found them somewhat mild. To fix that, we added a jalapeño. To round out the flavor, we borrowed from recipes we'd seen that included sautéed onion in addition to the chiles. Rather than dirtying a pan, we simply broiled the onion with the chiles, then chopped them all. Minced garlic rounded out the chile mixture's flavors.

Now ready to combine the two components, we spooned the chile mixture on top of the burgers while they were finishing on the grill. We were disappointed when tasters complained that the chiles were being upstaged. The obvious solution was extra topping, but any more would just fall into the grill. What if we put the chile mixture into the burgers themselves? We reserved the majority of the chile mixture for the topping, but we minced 2 tablespoons of it and mixed it into the ground meat before we formed our patties. These burgers packed a pleasurable hot punch. Finally, we tried topping the burgers alternately with cheddar, Monterey Jack, and American cheese. Tasters preferred mild American cheese, which melted well. We flipped a final batch of burgers and topped them with spoonfuls of the reserved chile mixture and a slice of cheese; the cheese melted as the burgers finished cooking, which helped the topping stay put.

With only two burgers on the grill, we had plenty of room to add a side. Potatoes are a natural partner for burgers; to play up the sweet-and-spicy aspect of our meal, we went with sweet potatoes. We sliced two small sweet potatoes into ½-inch-thick rounds, brushed them with oil to prevent sticking, and seasoned them with salt and pepper. So that the potatoes would be done at the same time as the burgers, we gave them a head start by parcooking them in the microwave. We placed the potatoes on the grill next to the burgers, flipping them

after a few minutes when dark grill marks had appeared on the first side. By the time the cheese was melted on the burgers, the potatoes were nicely browned on both sides. Now we could enjoy the sweet flavor and heat of this Southwestern favorite in our own backyard.

Grilled Green Chile Cheeseburgers with Sweet Potatoes
SERVES 2

Pressing a shallow divot in the center of each burger patty keeps the burgers flat during grilling.

- 1 small onion, sliced into ½-inch-thick rounds
- 2 Anaheim chiles, stemmed, seeded, and halved lengthwise
- 1 jalapeño chile, stemmed, seeded, and halved lengthwise
- 1 small garlic clove, minced
  Salt and pepper
- 12 ounces 85 percent lean ground beef
- 1 pound sweet potatoes (about 2 small), cut crosswise into ½-inch-thick rounds
- 1 tablespoon olive oil
- 2 slices deli American cheese
- 1 (13 by 9-inch) disposable aluminum roasting pan
- 2 buns, toasted

1. Position an oven rack 2½ to 3½ inches from the broiler element and heat the broiler. Arrange the onion and chiles in a single layer on a foil-lined baking sheet. Broil the vegetables until lightly charred and tender, 8 to 10 minutes, flipping them halfway through. Transfer the vegetables to a bowl, cover, and let cool for 5 minutes. Remove the skins from the chiles and discard.

2. Coarsely chop the onion and chiles, transfer to a bowl, and stir in the garlic. Measure out 2 tablespoons of the chile mixture and chop finely. Season the remaining chile mixture with salt and pepper to taste and set aside.

3. Combine the finely chopped chile mixture, beef, ¼ teaspoon salt, and ¼ teaspoon pepper in a bowl, and knead gently until well incorporated. Shape the beef mixture into two ¾-inch-thick patties and press a shallow divot in the center of each.

4. Meanwhile, place the sweet potatoes in a single layer on a large microwave-safe plate, brush with the oil, and season with salt and pepper. Microwave on high until the sweet potatoes just begin to soften but still hold their shape, 6 to 8 minutes, flipping them halfway through.

5A. FOR A CHARCOAL GRILL: Open the bottom grill vents completely. Light a large chimney starter filled three-quarters with charcoal briquettes (75 briquettes; 4½ quarts). When the coals are hot, spread them in an even layer over the grill. Set the cooking grate in place, cover, and heat the grill until hot, about 5 minutes.

5B. FOR A GAS GRILL: Turn all the burners to high, cover, and heat the grill until hot, about 15 minutes. Turn all the burners to medium-high. (Adjust the burners as needed to maintain a medium-hot fire; see page 183.)

6. Clean and oil the cooking grate. Place the burgers on one side of the grill and cook until well browned on the first side, 5 to 7 minutes. Flip the burgers, top with the reserved chile mixture and cheese, and cover with the roasting pan. Continue to cook until the cheese is melted and the burgers are cooked through, 5 to 7 minutes longer. Transfer the burgers to a platter, tent loosely with foil, and let rest.

7. While the burgers cook, place the sweet potatoes on the grill, opposite the burgers, and cook until spottily charred and tender, 8 to 12 minutes, flipping them halfway through. Set the burgers on the buns and serve with the sweet potatoes.

NOTES FROM THE TEST KITCHEN

FREEZING EXTRA MEAT
When you're shopping for two, inevitably you'll sometimes buy more food than you need. Case in point: meat. Poultry and ground beef are frequently sold in larger, family-sized packages that are priced more affordably than smaller packages. If you purchase one of these and find yourself with a surplus of meat, we've found an easy way to freeze the rest so that you can remove just what you need when you're ready to use it. Wrap two pieces of meat, whether it's chicken breasts, portions of ground meat, or small steaks, in plastic wrap and place them in the opposite corners of a large zipper-lock freezer bag. Flatten the bag, forcing the air out in the process, so that the meat portions do not touch. Then fold the bag over in the center and freeze it. This way, you have the choice of using one or both frozen meat portions.

BLACKENED RED SNAPPER WITH PINEAPPLE

WITH A SWEET-SMOKY, TOASTED-SPICE EXTERIOR AND a moist, flaky interior, blackened fish offers unique flavor and texture. Famed Cajun chef Paul Prudhomme popularized blackened redfish in the 1980s; now blackened anything is synonymous with nouvelle Cajun cookery. Though Prudhomme first blackened fish in a ripping-hot cast-iron skillet, he later moved it to the grill, since cooking a fish coated in spices and butter creates an inordinate amount of smoke. Switching out redfish for the more readily available red snapper made this recipe the perfect addition to our grilling roster.

First, we had to determine the best way to cook our fillets (two small fillets would be easier to maneuver on the grill than one larger fillet). We began by coating our fish with a little oil and a traditional spice rub of paprika, cayenne pepper, onion powder, garlic powder, coriander, salt, and pepper, then grilled the fillets over a basic single-level fire. Time and again, we found that the fish fused to the cooking grate, and because the skin on the thin fillets shrank as the fish cooked, the fillets were curling midway through, leading to burnt edges and barely blackened centers. Even worse was the flavor—the spices tasted either raw or charred. After trying every grill setup in the book, we ultimately settled on a half-grill fire using three-quarters of a chimney of coals; this concentrated the heat enough to cook the fish through and give it a dark crust without charring it. Addressing the curling problem turned out to be a quick fix—scoring the skin ensured that the fillets stayed flat. Next up, we needed to address the pesky sticking problem.

Because preheating the grate is what keeps food from sticking, we realized that what we needed to do was get it super-hot and incredibly clean. Covering the grate with a large piece of foil while it preheated allowed it to reach almost 900 degrees, incinerating any nasty gunk left from previous grilling. After brushing the charred remnants off the grate, we oiled the grate several times so the surface was well lubricated. At last, we could cook our fillets without any fear of sticking.

To address the blackened-spice issue, we took a step back and revisited the traditional indoor method of preparing blackened fish. In past recipe development, we've learned that "blooming," a technique to rid spices of their raw flavor, works well. To bloom the spices, we sautéed them in melted butter until they turned several shades darker and emitted a fragrant aroma. But when applied to the fish, this mixture slid right off. Instead, we allowed the mixture to cool, then broke up any large clumps and applied it to the fish in a thin layer. By the time the fillets were fully cooked, they were also well blackened (but not burnt), and the spice crust had finally acquired the depth and richness we were after.

Thinking about the hot and steamy environs of Cajun country, we decided to make a refreshing salad based on grilled pineapple. Grilling caramelizes the sugars on the exterior of the pineapple, intensifying its sweetness as well as giving it an appealing brown crust. We paired the pineapple with a single red bell pepper, which we also grilled. We chopped the pepper and pineapple into bite-sized pieces and tossed them with fresh, clean cilantro. At last, we had an authentic blackened fish dinner that made us feel like we were down on the bayou.

Grilled Blackened Red Snapper with Pineapple and Red Bell Pepper Salad

SERVES 2

Striped bass, halibut, or grouper can be substituted for the snapper; if the fish fillets are thicker or thinner, they will have slightly different cooking times. Instead of purchasing a whole pineapple, you can often find prepackaged pineapple halves at the grocery store, ready to be cut and used in a recipe. Be sure to oil the grate well in step 4; fish is delicate and tends to stick. See page 30 for a recipe to use up some of the leftover pineapple.

- 1   tablespoon paprika
- 1   teaspoon onion powder
- 1   teaspoon garlic powder
- ½   teaspoon ground coriander
- ⅛   teaspoon cayenne pepper
-     Salt and pepper
- 4   tablespoons (½ stick) unsalted butter
- 2   (6- to 8-ounce) red snapper fillets, about ¾ inch thick (see note)

- ½   medium pineapple, peeled, cored, and cut into ½-inch-thick half-moons (see note)
- 1   red bell pepper, stemmed, seeded, and quartered
- 1   tablespoon minced fresh cilantro or scallions
-     Lime wedges, for serving

1. Combine the paprika, onion powder, garlic powder, coriander, cayenne, ½ teaspoon salt, and ¼ teaspoon pepper in a bowl. Melt 2 tablespoons of the butter in an 8-inch skillet over medium heat. Stir in the spice mixture and cook, stirring constantly, until fragrant and the spices turn a dark rust color, about 2 minutes. Transfer the mixture to a pie plate and cool to room temperature, then use a fork to break up any large clumps.

2. Pat the fish fillets dry with paper towels. Using a serrated knife, score the skin side of the fillets with 3 or 4 parallel slashes, being careful not to cut into the flesh. Rub the spice mixture evenly over both sides of the fillets. Lay the fish on a wire rack set over a baking sheet and refrigerate until the grill is ready. Microwave the remaining 2 tablespoons butter in a bowl on high until melted, about 40 seconds. Brush the pineapple and bell pepper with the melted butter and season with salt and pepper.

3A. FOR A CHARCOAL GRILL: Open the bottom grill vents completely. Light a large chimney starter three-quarters full with charcoal briquettes (75 briquettes; 4½ quarts). When the coals are hot, pour them in an even layer over half the grill. Set the cooking grate in place and loosely cover the grate with a large piece of heavy-duty aluminum foil. Cover and heat the grill until hot, about 5 minutes.

3B. FOR A GAS GRILL: Turn all the burners to high and loosely cover the cooking grate with a large piece of heavy-duty aluminum foil. Cover and heat the grill until hot, about 15 minutes. (Adjust the burners as needed to maintain a hot fire; see page 183.)

4. Remove the foil with tongs and discard, then clean the cooking grate. Dip a wad of paper towels in oil; holding the wad with tongs, oil the cooking grate. Continue to wipe the grate with oiled paper towels, redipping the towels in the oil between applications, until the cooking grate is black and glossy, 5 to 10 times.

Lay the snapper on the hotter part of the grill, skin-side down and perpendicular to the bars of the cooking grate. Cook until the exterior is dark brown and the fish is opaque and flakes apart when gently prodded with a paring knife, 10 to 14 minutes, gently flipping the fish halfway through with two spatulas. Transfer the fish to a wire rack, tent loosely with foil, and let rest.

5. While the fish cooks, place the pineapple and bell pepper on the hotter part of the grill and cook until spottily charred on both sides, 6 to 12 minutes. Transfer the pineapple and bell pepper to a cutting board and cut into 1-inch pieces. Transfer to a bowl, toss with the cilantro, and season with salt and pepper to taste. Serve the salad with the snapper and lime wedges.

NOTES FROM THE TEST KITCHEN

PREVENTING FISH FROM STICKING TO THE GRILL

We always recommend cleaning and oiling the cooking grate before placing any food on the grill, but this step is especially important when it comes to fish, which is particularly prone to sticking to the grate. Before grilling fish, we super-heat the grill by setting a piece of heavy-duty aluminum foil on the grate while the grill is heating; this traps heat and incinerates any stuck-on gunk from previous grilling, so what's left is a clean, smooth surface. We also apply oil to the grate several times prior to cooking, coating the grate until it's black, glossy, and well lubricated. (One note of caution: While vegetable oil spray might seem like a shortcut, it's not; if you spray it on a hot cooking grate, you risk having a flare-up on your hands.)

THE BEST GRILL BRUSH

We set out to find a grill brush that could make the tedious task of cleaning a gunked-up cooking grate more efficient. What did we find? Brushes with stiffer bristles fared better than their softer counterparts, but none of them worked very well. The bristles on most bent after a few strokes and trapped large quantities of gunk, thereby decreasing their efficiency. Our favorite—the **Tool Wizard BBQ Brush**, $9.99—has no brass bristles to bend, break, or clog with unwanted grease and grime. Instead, this brush has one large woven-mesh stainless steel scrubbing pad, which is able to conform to any cooking grate's spacing, size, and material. Best of all, the pad is detachable, washable, and replaceable (a spare is included).

NEW ENGLAND CLAMBAKE

A CLAMBAKE IS A RITE OF SUMMER ALL ALONG THE East Coast. Loads of shellfish and vegetables are layered with seaweed and piled on top of white-hot rocks in a wide sandpit. After a wet tarp is laid on top, the food steams beneath until it's done. This feast usually takes a day or more to prepare—digging the pit is no small chore—and hours to cook. All this preparation may be worth it if you are feeding a crowd, but it would be impractical (to say the least) for two people. Rather than dig a huge pit in the backyard, what if we just used the grill? It seemed as if it would be a simple and efficient way to prepare a great shellfish dinner for two.

Hitting our research library, we unearthed lots of recipes. We learned that while the cooking methods vary dramatically, the ingredient list is pretty consistent: clams, lobsters, potatoes, corn, and sausage. In some recipes each ingredient is partially cooked separately, then everything is finished together on the grill. Other recipes start and end on the grill, with the ingredients layered between beds of seaweed or corn husks. The common goal of all these recipes is to have everything cooked and ready to serve at the same time.

Before we started cooking, we pared down our shopping list. To feed two, we decided we would need one lobster and 1 pound of clams. This quantity of shellfish, when combined with three small potatoes, 4 ounces of sausage, and two ears of corn, gave us a good balance of all the components of the clambake. Plus, the grill was big enough to fit all of our ingredients in one round, so we didn't have to worry about the food sitting and getting cold.

We quickly decided that layering with corn husks or seaweed was troublesome at best. Eliminating this step, we prepared our ingredients for the grill one by one, starting with the shellfish. We split the lobster in half, head to tail, and brushed the tail meat with butter. To help the claws cook at the same rate as the exposed tail meat, we cracked them with the back of a chef's knife. We started the lobster halves meat-side down, which gave them some smoky flavor, and brushed the tail again with butter (after flipping the halves) to keep it moist.

The clams needed less attention; we just placed them on the grill and waited for them to open.

The potatoes were the only component that needed partial cooking, since they take longer to cook. We found that microwaving them until just tender before transferring them to the grill sped things up, and halving and skewering them made them more manageable. Poking the potatoes with a skewer before brushing them with butter and sprinkling them with salt and pepper ensured that both the interior and exterior were well seasoned.

To grill the corn, we employed the same method we used in our Grilled Jerk Chicken Breasts with Corn on the Cob (page 184), removing all but the innermost husk, which kept the kernels from burning but allowed the smoky flavor to penetrate. The sausage was more straightforward. We stuck with the traditional choice, kielbasa, and grilled it whole, then sliced it into chunks just before serving.

When everything was cooked and hot, we arranged it all on a platter and dug in. Our grilled clambake captured all the smoky flavor of the traditional version—in a lot less time and with no shovel necessary.

New England Clambake
SERVES 2

You will need one or two 12-inch wooden skewers for this recipe. We prefer to use small red potatoes that are 1 to 2 inches in diameter; if your potatoes are larger, you may need to quarter them and increase the microwaving time as needed in step 1. Don't move the lobster and clams around too much when grilling or you'll risk spilling the flavorful juices that collect inside the shells.

    8 ounces small red potatoes (about 3), halved and
       skewered (see page 203)
    4 tablespoons (½ stick) unsalted butter, melted,
       plus extra for serving
       Salt and pepper
    1 (1¼- to 1½-pound) live lobster
    2 ears fresh corn, all but innermost layer of husk
       removed, silk trimmed (see page 185)
    4 ounces kielbasa
    1 pound littleneck clams (about 10), scrubbed
       Lemon wedges, for serving

1. Place the skewered potatoes on a large microwave-safe plate and poke each potato several times with a skewer. Brush the potatoes with 1 tablespoon of the melted butter and season with salt and pepper. Microwave on high until the potatoes begin to soften, 6 to 8 minutes, flipping them halfway through.

2. Following the photos on page 203, split the lobster in half lengthwise and remove and discard the internal organs. Using the back of a chef's knife, whack one side of each claw to crack the shell. Brush the exposed lobster tail meat with 1 tablespoon more melted butter and season with salt and pepper.

3A. FOR A CHARCOAL GRILL: Open the bottom grill vents completely. Light a large chimney starter filled with charcoal briquettes (100 briquettes; 6 quarts). When the coals are hot, pour them in an even layer over the grill. Set the cooking grate in place, cover, and heat the grill until hot, about 5 minutes.

3B. FOR A GAS GRILL: Turn all the burners to high, cover, and heat the grill until hot, about 15 minutes. (Adjust the burners as needed to maintain a hot fire; see page 183.)

4. Clean and oil the cooking grate. Place the skewered potatoes, corn, and kielbasa on half of the grill. Cook (covered if using gas) until the potatoes are brown and tender, the kielbasa is seared and hot throughout, and the husk of the corn is charred and the kernels are tender, 10 to 16 minutes, turning as needed. Transfer the vegetables and sausage as they finish cooking to a serving platter and tent loosely with foil.

5. While the vegetables and sausage cook, place the lobster, cut-side down, and clams on the grill, opposite the vegetables and sausage. Cook (covered if using gas) until the clams have popped wide open and the lobster is cooked through, 8 to 14 minutes, flipping the lobster and brushing the exposed lobster meat with 1 tablespoon more melted butter halfway through. As the lobsters and clams finish cooking, transfer them to the platter with the vegetables and sausage, trying to preserve any juices that have accumulated inside their shells. Discard any clams that have not opened.

6. Carefully remove and discard the charred husks and silk from the corn, brush with the remaining 1 tablespoon melted butter, and season with salt and pepper to taste. Slice the sausage into 1-inch chunks and remove the skewers from the potatoes. Serve with the lemon wedges and extra melted butter.

PREPARING LOBSTER FOR THE GRILL

1. Plunge a chef's knife into the body at the point where the shell forms a T to kill the lobster. Move the blade straight down through the head. (Freezing the lobster for 5 to 10 minutes first will sedate it.)

2. Turn the lobster around and, while holding the upper body with one hand, cut through the body toward the tail.

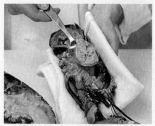

3. Remove and discard the stomach, intestinal tract, and green tomalley. Remove the rubber bands, then crack the claw shells slightly by whacking them with the back of the chef's knife.

SKEWERING POTATOES FOR THE GRILL

Place a potato half cut-side down on the counter and pierce it through the center with a skewer. Repeat, holding the already-skewered potatoes for better leverage.

BUYING AND STORING CLAMS

Most clams nowadays are farmed and virtually free of grit. Occasionally, you may come across "wild" clams, which may be full of grit, at your local fish store. And despite the common folklore, this grit is impossible to purge. Look for tightly closed clams (some shells may gape slightly, but should close when they are tapped) and avoid any that are cracked, broken, or sitting in a puddle of water. They should smell clean, not sour or sulfurous, and the shells should appear moist. The best way to store them is in the refrigerator in a colander of ice set over a bowl; discard any water that accumulates so that the shellfish are never submerged.

GRILLED VEGETABLE AND BREAD SALAD

GRILLED VEGETABLES ARE THE PERFECT BASIS FOR A summer supper, when produce is at the height of its ripeness. However, a few challenges lie in the seemingly simple task of grilling vegetables. First, there is the challenge of grilling them to just the right point— gently charred on the outside and tender within—while avoiding blackened and mushy vegetables. Then there's the issue of flavor: Usually there's just not enough of it. Finally, there's the question of how to make a handful of vegetables into a filling entrée. We were mulling over these issues when the idea for an Italian-style vegetable and bread salad came to mind. Pair grilled vegetable chunks with cubes of rustic bread, fresh herbs, and a bright vinaigrette, and little else is needed. With a little testing, we figured we'd have a surefire winner that was a light and flavorful lunch or supper for two.

We began by determining the vegetables to use, focusing on Mediterranean flavors. Mindful of complementary cooking times, we matched zucchini with sweet red onion and red bell pepper. Cutting the zucchini lengthwise and the bell pepper into quarters gave us large pieces that were easy to handle on the grill, and threading the onion slices onto a metal skewer ensured that not an onion ring was lost through the cooking grate. Once cooked, our vegetables would be easy enough to cut up into bite-sized chunks. After 10 minutes on the grill, the zucchini, onion, and pepper were perfectly browned and tender and full of smoky flavor.

The bread was up next. We knew the quality of the bread would be fundamental to the success of this dish, so we tried several varieties. Sliced white bread was out. Its overly smooth texture meant it turned to mush when tossed with the vinaigrette (at this point a simple combination of lemon juice and extra-virgin olive oil), and its surprisingly sweet flavor conflicted with the savory flavors of the salad. A high-quality rustic loaf or baguette worked best. Its sturdy texture and strong wheaty flavor paired well with the bolder grilled flavor of the vegetables, and it held up reasonably well once dressed. To make the bread a little sturdier and add appealing crunch, we decided to toast it on the grill. As we did with our vegetables, we grilled the bread in larger pieces for easier handling, then cubed it once cooked. Before grilling, we brushed the slices with olive oil and seasoned them with salt and pepper for flavor.

GRILLED VEGETABLE AND BREAD SALAD

Now all we needed to do was put the finishing touches on our vinaigrette and toss everything together. Keeping with our Mediterranean theme, we started with a basic combination of lemon juice and extra-virgin olive oil and added a touch of mustard and garlic for tanginess and chopped basil and lemon zest for freshness. Tasters were raving over our grilled vegetable salad with bread, but someone suggested adding a little goat cheese for a creamy contrast and a little richness. Just ½ cup, crumbled on top of the salad, put this simple summery dinner over the top.

Grilled Vegetable and Bread Salad

SERVES 2

A rustic round loaf, or a baguette sliced on the extreme bias, works best for this recipe. Be sure to use high-quality bread. You will need one 12-inch metal skewer for this recipe.

¼ cup extra-virgin olive oil

1 tablespoon chopped fresh basil

2 teaspoons fresh lemon juice plus
   ½ teaspoon grated lemon zest

1 small garlic clove, minced

½ teaspoon Dijon mustard
   Salt and pepper

1 small red onion, sliced into ¾-inch-thick rounds

1 red bell pepper, stemmed, seeded, and quartered

1 zucchini, halved lengthwise

3 ounces French or Italian bread,
   cut into 1-inch-thick slices (see note)

2 ounces goat cheese, crumbled (about ½ cup)

1. Whisk 2 tablespoons of the oil, basil, lemon juice, lemon zest, garlic, mustard, ⅛ teaspoon salt, and ⅛ teaspoon pepper together in a large bowl, and set aside.

2. Thread the onion rounds, from side to side, onto a metal skewer. Brush the skewered onion rounds, bell pepper, zucchini, and bread slices with the remaining 2 tablespoons oil, and season with salt and pepper.

3A. FOR A CHARCOAL GRILL: Open the bottom grill vents completely. Light a large chimney starter half full with charcoal briquettes (50 briquettes; 3 quarts). When the coals are hot, spread them in an even layer over the grill. Set the cooking grate in place, cover, and heat the grill until hot, about 5 minutes.

3B. FOR A GAS GRILL: Turn all the burners to high, cover, and heat the grill until hot, about 15 minutes. Turn all the burners to medium. (Adjust the burners as needed to maintain a medium fire; see page 183.)

4. Clean and oil the cooking grate. Place the vegetables on one side of the grill and cook (covered if using gas) until spottily charred on both sides, 10 to 15 minutes, flipping them halfway through. Transfer the vegetables to a cutting board and remove the onion from the skewer.

5. While the vegetables cook, place the bread slices on the grill, opposite the vegetables, and cook (covered if using gas) until golden brown on both sides, about 4 minutes, flipping them halfway through. Transfer the bread to the cutting board with the vegetables.

6. Cut the vegetables into 1-inch pieces and the bread slices into 1-inch cubes. Add the vegetables and bread to the bowl with the vinaigrette and toss to coat. Divide the salad evenly between two plates, sprinkle evenly with the cheese, and serve.

EASY QUICHE LORRAINE

OVERNIGHT SOUR CREAM COFFEE CAKE

SERVED WITH A STRONG CUP OF COFFEE OR A TALL glass of cold milk, coffee cake is a breakfast classic. But standard coffee cakes yield enough to serve a lot more than two—and leftovers don't hold up all that well after a day or two. We wanted a scaled-down recipe for a tender, moist, richly flavored coffee cake that would provide enough for breakfast, with maybe a snack-sized piece left over to satisfy that afternoon craving. To up the ante, we also wanted to be able to mix the batter the night before and refrigerate it, so that all we'd have to do in the morning was bake it off and enjoy.

We started with our own recipe for overnight sour cream coffee cake (made with all-purpose flour, white and light brown sugar, eggs, butter, sour cream, baking powder, and baking soda). This cake boasts a moist crumb and sweet, buttery streusel, but when we scaled back the ingredient amounts to accommodate a 6-inch round cake pan (from the original 9-inch cake pan), the results were not as we had hoped. Tasters were quick to point out the flaws: The streusel sank into the cake and the crumb was dry, not moist. Because of baking's chemical nature, simply cutting a recipe by half, one-third, three-quarters, and so on doesn't always work so smoothly, and we were seeing that effect here. We'd need to let go of the cake's original ratios and rethink each ingredient amount through good old-fashioned trial and error.

At this point we had been making our coffee cake with one egg and decided to try two eggs, thinking that another egg would add moisture and contribute additional protein for a heartier batter that would hold up the streusel. We were disappointed to find that rather than adding richness and structure, the extra egg made the batter too eggy. What if we adjusted the batter by backing down on the amount of flour instead of upping the number of eggs? Cutting back on the flour slightly—from ¾ cup to ⅔ cup—worked perfectly; the batter was just dense enough to hold up the topping while the cake baked, and the cake came out of the oven moister than before.

We then decided to look at the fat content, thinking that increasing the amount of sour cream would add more moisture and enable us to refrigerate the cake batter without loss of flavor or texture. We were working with ¼ cup of sour cream and decided to try ⅓ cup, but found that this increase added too much tanginess to the finished cake. We wondered how the cake would turn out if we tinkered with the quantity of butter instead. We had been using 1 tablespoon of melted butter, so we tested cakes made with 2 and 3 tablespoons of butter. The batter made with 3 tablespoons of butter baked up into a cake that was too greasy and rich; however, the batter made with 2 tablespoons of butter had just enough fat to bake up to a perfectly tender, moist cake after an overnight stay in the fridge.

Our cake was nearly finished—it just needed the streusel topping. A simple combination of light brown sugar, granulated sugar, flour, and butter spiced with cinnamon and enriched with crunchy walnuts did the trick. Fresh out of the oven—with no dirty dishes left to do—this tender coffee cake is the perfect start to any day.

NOTES FROM THE TEST KITCHEN

THE BEST CINNAMON
Not too long ago, cinnamon was just a basic spice in your cupboard. These days, however, it's anything but a standardized commodity. Labels advertise various origins and make claims such as "extra fancy" or "gourmet." But once the spice is mixed into batter, does all the pageantry really amount to anything? We gathered 10 supermarket and mail-order brands and tested them in applesauce, cinnamon buns, and rice pudding. In the end, we found that while our tasters had their favorites—many of the top-rated cinnamons contained complex floral and spicy notes—most brands of cinnamon rated reasonably well as long as they were used before their expiration date (if you can't remember when you bought it, it's probably time for a new jar). Our favorite was a mail-order cinnamon, **Penzeys Extra Fancy Vietnamese Cassia Cinnamon** (left), which exhibited "warm clove" and "fruity" notes that tasters loved.

But if you don't want to spend the money ($5.45 for 1.7 ounces) or wait for it to show up in the mail, our supermarket best buy, **Durkee Ground Cinnamon** (right), scored almost as well with tasters, who praised its unique complex and woodsy flavor, but cost about $2 less.

Overnight Sour Cream Coffee Cake

MAKES ONE 6-INCH COFFEE CAKE

You will need one 6-inch round cake pan for this recipe (see page 3). The unbaked coffee cake can be refrigerated for up to 24 hours, frozen for up to 1 month, or baked right away. See page 249 for a recipe to use up the leftover sour cream.

STREUSEL

- 1 tablespoon light brown sugar
- 1 tablespoon granulated sugar
- 1 tablespoon unbleached all-purpose flour
- 1 tablespoon unsalted butter,
   cut into ½-inch pieces and chilled
- ¼ teaspoon ground cinnamon
- 2 tablespoons chopped walnuts, pecans,
   or almonds

CAKE

- ⅔ cup (3⅓ ounces) unbleached all-purpose flour
- ½ teaspoon baking powder
- ¼ teaspoon baking soda
- ⅛ teaspoon ground cinnamon
- ⅛ teaspoon salt
- ¼ cup sour cream
- 3 tablespoons light brown sugar
- 2 tablespoons unsalted butter,
   melted and cooled
- 1 tablespoon granulated sugar
- 1 large egg, room temperature

1. FOR THE STREUSEL: Using your fingers, combine the brown sugar, granulated sugar, flour, butter, and cinnamon in a bowl until the mixture resembles coarse meal. Stir in the nuts and set aside.

2. FOR THE CAKE: Grease a 6-inch round cake pan, then line the bottom with parchment paper. Whisk the flour, baking powder, baking soda, cinnamon, and salt together in a medium bowl. Whisk the sour cream, brown sugar, melted butter, granulated sugar, and egg together in another bowl until smooth. Gently fold the sour cream mixture into the flour mixture with a rubber spatula until just combined. (The batter will be lumpy with a few spots of dry flour; do not overmix.)

3. Scrape the batter into the prepared pan and smooth the top. Sprinkle the streusel evenly over the top of the cake. Wrap the pan tightly with plastic wrap and refrigerate for up to 24 hours, or freeze for up to 1 month (do not thaw the frozen cake before baking). (To bake the cake right away, do not wrap the pan with plastic wrap. Bake the cake as directed in step 4, reducing the baking time to 25 to 30 minutes.)

4. When ready to bake, adjust an oven rack to the lower-middle position and heat the oven to 350 degrees. Unwrap the cake and bake until the top is golden and a toothpick inserted into the center comes out with a few crumbs attached, 30 to 35 minutes if refrigerated, or 40 to 45 minutes if frozen, rotating the pan halfway through.

5. Let the cake cool in the pan for 10 minutes. Run a small knife around the edge of the cake, then flip it out onto a wire rack. Peel off the parchment paper, flip the cake right-side up, and let cool completely before serving.

VARIATIONS

Overnight Lemon-Blueberry Sour Cream Coffee Cake

You can substitute frozen blueberries for the fresh; they must be thawed, rinsed, and dried, but they do not need to be tossed with flour.

Toss ¼ cup fresh blueberries with ½ teaspoon unbleached all-purpose flour. Follow the recipe for Overnight Sour Cream Coffee Cake, adding ¼ teaspoon grated lemon zest to the dry ingredients and the floured berries to the finished batter in step 2.

Overnight Cranberry-Orange Sour Cream Coffee Cake

Follow the recipe for Overnight Sour Cream Coffee Cake, adding ¼ teaspoon grated orange zest to the dry ingredients and 3 tablespoons dried cranberries to the finished batter in step 2.

BANANA BREAD

GREAT BANANA BREAD IS SOFT AND TENDER WITH plenty of banana flavor. It should be moist and light, something so delicious that you look forward to the bananas on the counter turning soft and mushy so you can pull a loaf out of the oven that afternoon. But recipes typically make a 9 by 5-inch loaf, which is almost too much for a family of four. We set out to scale down traditional banana bread, using a mini loaf pan, but to keep all the flavor and moisture intact.

We began with our established banana bread recipe, which yielded a loaf with a moist and delicate crumb with the help of a little yogurt. With this recipe as our starting point, and with a 5½ by 3-inch loaf pan ready to go, we adjusted the dry ingredients to one-quarter of the original recipe—so we had ½ cup flour, ¼ cup sugar, ½ teaspoon baking soda, and a sprinkling of salt—but scaled down the eggs from two to one. Our full-size banana bread called for three bananas, but quartering that amount would have been silly, leaving us with a small portion of leftover banana. So we opted to use a more sensible amount—a whole banana—and made sure it was an ultra-ripe, darkly speckled one so it would infuse the bread with the most banana flavor possible. For the fat in our loaf, a single tablespoon each of butter and yogurt provided the right amount of moisture and richness without making the bread greasy or obscuring the banana flavor. For crunch, we added ¼ cup toasted walnuts; a splash of vanilla enhanced the overall flavor of the bread.

While many banana bread recipes rely on creaming the butter and sugar (beating them together) first before mixing in the other wet ingredients and folding in the flour, salt, baking soda, and walnuts, we had learned in the past that this method often results in dense banana bread—and we found this also applied to our scaled-down version. The quick-bread method, which calls for the dry ingredients to be mixed in one bowl, liquids in another, and the two then gently folded together, produced a far superior bread with an impressively delicate texture.

As for oven temperatures, we baked our mini loaf at 325, 350, and 375 degrees. At the highest temperature, the bread developed a thick crust and uneven crumb. Finding little difference in the breads baked at the other two temperatures, we opted for 350 degrees (and a slightly faster baking time) and pulled out the perfect loaf half an hour later. Not wanting to stop there, we also created a rich chocolate version. Now we had two petite loaves of banana bread that would satisfy any midmorning craving and were just as tender and moist as their full-size siblings.

Banana Bread

MAKES ONE 5½ BY 3-INCH LOAF

The key to this recipe is using a very ripe, soft, darkly speckled banana. You will need a 5½ by 3-inch loaf pan or a pan of similar size for this recipe (see page 3).

- ½ cup (2½ ounces) unbleached all-purpose flour
- ¼ cup walnuts, toasted (see below) and chopped coarse
- ¼ cup sugar
- ½ teaspoon baking soda
- ⅛ teaspoon salt
- 1 small ripe banana (see note), mashed well (about ¼ cup)
- 1 large egg, room temperature
- 1 tablespoon unsalted butter, melted and cooled
- 1 tablespoon plain yogurt
- ½ teaspoon vanilla extract

NOTES FROM THE TEST KITCHEN

HOW TO TOAST NUTS AND SEEDS

In order for nuts and seeds to contribute the most flavor, they need to be toasted. To toast a small amount (under 1 cup) of nuts or seeds, put them in a dry skillet over medium heat. Simply shake the skillet occasionally to prevent scorching and toast until they are lightly browned and fragrant, 3 to 8 minutes. Watch the nuts and seeds closely because they can go from golden to burnt very quickly.

STORING FLOUR

Even if you're cooking only for yourself and another, all-purpose flour is one ingredient that can be worthwhile to purchase in a larger package (such as a 5-pound bag). Flour is essential for a variety of kitchen tasks, not just baking, such as breading chicken breasts or pork cutlets and thickening soups. To keep our flour fresh, we transfer it from the paper bag in which it was sold to a wide-mouth container, which makes it easy to dip in a measuring cup and level off the excess back into the container. The container can go right into your pantry, where it can be stored for up to a year. Note that whole grain flour, such as whole wheat and rye, is more perishable and should be stored in the freezer.

1. Adjust an oven rack to the middle position and heat the oven to 350 degrees. Grease a 5½ by 3-inch loaf pan.

2. Whisk the flour, walnuts, sugar, baking soda, and salt together in a medium bowl. Whisk the mashed banana, egg, melted butter, yogurt, and vanilla together in another bowl until smooth. Gently fold the banana mixture into the flour mixture with a rubber spatula until just combined. (The batter will be lumpy with a few spots of dry flour; do not overmix.) Scrape the batter into the prepared pan and smooth the top.

3. Bake until the loaf is golden brown and a toothpick inserted into the center comes out clean, 30 to 40 minutes, rotating the pan halfway through. Cool the bread in the pan for 5 minutes, then flip it out onto a wire rack and let cool for at least 1 hour before serving.

VARIATION

Banana-Chocolate Bread

Follow the recipe for Banana Bread, adding ¾ ounce grated bittersweet chocolate to the dry ingredients in step 2.

GERMAN APPLE PANCAKE

WE'VE SAMPLED GERMAN APPLE PANCAKE AT MANY a pancake house (often found on the menu under the name "Dutch baby"). This breakfast treat is basically a crisp, puffy, skillet-baked pancake packed with caramelized apples. But when we've seen it at pancake houses, the plate is overflowing with a massive floppy pancake that looks as if it would serve six hungry diners. We wanted to make a German apple pancake for two but retain the crisp top, rich cake, and well-caramelized apples that are the hallmarks of this dish. So with an 8-inch skillet in hand—instead of the usual 10-incher that's used—we headed into the test kitchen.

German apple pancake batter is relatively simple, close in composition and consistency to thin crepe batter. It should be a loose mixture of eggs, milk or cream, flour, and a pinch of salt. The secret to perfecting this batter is balancing the amount of egg with the milk or cream. Many of the batters we tested yielded pancakes

that were way too eggy. Tasters agreed that one egg was enough for structure and flavor; two eggs made a dense, gummy pancake.

As for the dairy component of the batter, we found that ⅓ cup provided the right consistency, but we needed to zero in on the right dairy. We tried milk, cream, and half-and-half. Milk alone made for a flavorless pancake dominated by the eggs, and cream produced an over-the-top custardy pancake. Half-and-half proved a great compromise between milk and cream, giving the pancake body and depth without being overly rich.

To round out the pancake's flavors, we added salt, vanilla extract, and a small amount of granulated sugar. The apple would provide sweetness in the pancake, but 1½ teaspoons of sugar helped the flavors meld.

We moved on to the apple—we had already determined that we'd need only one. We wanted the slices of apple to become well-caramelized but still retain some bite for contrast against the soft and creamy pancake. We knew that firm Granny Smiths hold up well under baking, so that became our choice of apple. Starting with the simplest method for cooking the apple, we peeled, cored, and sliced our apple, then tried cooking it in some butter in the skillet until it turned golden brown and its natural sugars caramelized. Our first few attempts were frustrating—the apple morphed into chunky applesauce before it caramelized. Since Granny Smiths are as firm as they come, we needed to look for another solution. We found it with brown sugar. Adding some brown sugar to the pan with the apple encouraged quicker caramelization; now the apple slices were golden and still had some bite.

Now that we'd brought the right flavoring elements together, we focused on our cooking method. Unlike stovetop pancakes, which use chemical leaveners to promote height, oven-baked pancakes rely on heat and eggs for rising power. The pancake gets its first burst of heat from the hot skillet, then the heat from the oven takes over the rest of the cooking. In our tests, a very hot oven—500 degrees—guaranteed a dramatic rise and golden crust, but it failed to fully cook the pancake's interior before the crust was ready. On the other hand, we discovered that if the oven temperature is brought too low, the pancake needs to bake too long and the exterior dries out by the time the interior is set. After several tests, we found it best to preheat the oven to 500 degrees, then lower the temperature to 425 degrees when the pancake goes into the oven. After pouring the batter over the cooked apples, we moved our skillet to the oven; it took only 10 minutes for our pancake to puff right up.

Straight from the oven and with a sprinkling of powdered sugar, our German apple pancake is both dramatic and homey at the same time. But note that, like a soufflé, it needs to be served immediately, because it sinks after a few minutes out of the oven.

German Apple Pancake

SERVES 2

Using an 8-inch skillet is essential to getting the right texture and height in the pancake. Be sure to reduce the oven temperature in step 3; otherwise the pancake will burn. Serve the pancake as soon as it comes out of the oven as its puffy texture sinks within just a few minutes.

⅓ cup half-and-half
1 large egg
1½ teaspoons granulated sugar
½ teaspoon vanilla extract
¼ teaspoon salt
¼ cup (1¼ ounces) unbleached all-purpose flour
1 tablespoon unsalted butter
1 Granny Smith apple, peeled, cored, and sliced ¼ inch thick
2 tablespoons light brown sugar
1 tablespoon confectioners' sugar

1. Adjust an oven rack to the middle position and heat the oven to 500 degrees. Vigorously whisk the half-and-half, egg, granulated sugar, vanilla, and salt together in a medium bowl until well combined and frothy. Whisk in the flour until thoroughly combined and free of lumps.

2. Melt the butter in an 8-inch ovenproof non-stick skillet over medium-high heat. Add the apple slices and sprinkle with the brown sugar. Cook, stirring

NOTES FROM THE TEST KITCHEN

PREPARING GERMAN APPLE PANCAKE

1. Pour the batter around the edge of the pan, then over the apple slices before placing the skillet in the oven to bake.

2. To remove the pancake from the skillet, loosen the edge with a rubber spatula, then slide the pancake onto a cutting board.

STORING BUTTER

When cooking for two, chances are that unless you're a frequent baker, it will take you a while to run through a pound of butter. And when stored in the refrigerator, butter (even when wrapped) can pick up odors and turn rancid within just a few weeks. To avoid bad butter, keep it in the freezer and transfer it, one stick at a time, to the fridge.

occasionally, until the apple slices are tender and golden brown, 8 to 10 minutes. Remove the skillet from the heat.

3. Whisk the batter to recombine. Following the photo, quickly pour the batter around the edge of the pan, then over the apple slices. Immediately transfer the skillet to the oven, reduce the oven temperature to 425 degrees, and bake until browned and puffed, 8 to 10 minutes.

4. Using a potholder (the skillet handle will be hot), remove the skillet from the oven. Use a rubber spatula to loosen the pancake from the skillet, then slide it onto a cutting board. Dust the pancake with the confectioners' sugar and serve.

BUTTERMILK PANCAKES

A PLATE OF FLUFFY BUTTERMILK PANCAKES IS HARD to beat, no matter what time of day it is. But how often are they really memorable? Most attempts only result in a tall stack of pancake pitfalls. Some are thick and cottony; others are dense and gummy. We wanted to create a foolproof recipe for buttermilk pancakes with a crispy, golden crust and light, tender, and tangy interior. And our pancakes had to have just enough structure to withstand a good dousing of maple syrup.

First up was the flour. We experimented with cake flour, thinking its refined texture and high starch content would keep our pancakes tender, but it only turned our pancakes into thin crepes. We stuck with all-purpose flour, which provided just enough structure. A single cup of flour was ample for eight pancakes.

Sugar was next, and since most recipes include about 1½ tablespoons of sugar for 16 pancakes, we thought 2 teaspoons of sugar might work. We started there, but found tasters preferred pancakes that were a touch sweeter, so we settled on 1 tablespoon. As for leavener, most pancake recipes call for only baking powder, but we found the addition of baking soda to provide the best rise. While the baking powder reacted to the heat in the skillet to produce gas and aerate our pancakes, the baking soda reacted to the acid in the batter to release additional gas. In the end we opted to use slightly more baking powder (½ teaspoon to ¼ teaspoon baking soda) because too much baking soda made our pancakes taste bitter. Finally, a little salt went in to enhance the whole mix.

With the dry ingredients set, we were ready for some moisture. Like flour, eggs play a key role in the texture of pancakes by adding structure-reinforcing proteins. They also add moisture, which evaporates as the pancakes cook, creating bubbles that help it rise. Most pancake recipes call for two eggs, but since we were scaling down, we began by incorporating one egg with the other wet ingredients; tasters thought the texture of this pancake was spot-on. Next we looked at the amount of butter; 2 tablespoons were all we needed to maintain the structure of the pancake and keep the buttery flavor.

As for the namesake ingredient—the buttermilk—other pancake recipes we came across used anywhere from 1½ to 2 cups of buttermilk for 16 pancakes, so we tried a range of buttermilk amounts for our smaller batch. Tasters couldn't get enough of its tangy flavor, but when we tried increasing the amount of buttermilk—from 1 to 1½ cups—the pancakes spread out too thin. Considering other tangy options, we tried dehydrated buttermilk powder (basically pure buttermilk with just the liquid component removed), but tasters complained that these pancakes tasted soapy. Yogurt also produced disappointing results, adding too much moisture and not enough tang. Finally we tried sour cream. Cultured with the same bacteria as buttermilk, it has many of the same flavor compounds, but with far less moisture. Just 2 tablespoons added along with 1 cup of buttermilk gave our pancakes the rich tang we were after, without diluting the batter.

With our pancake ingredients set, we whisked up our final batch. While testing we had found that less is more when it comes to whisking. When we whisked the batter until no lumps of flour could be seen, the pancakes were tough. Instead we just folded the wet ingredients into the flour mixture until a few lumps of flour were still visible. For cooking, we found the traditional method was best and portioned some batter onto a warm nonstick skillet coated with a light film of vegetable oil. Moderate heat was essential; if the pan got too hot, the pancakes scorched before they had time to cook through. After 10 minutes (5 minutes per batch) and a drizzling of maple syrup, we had two stacks of light, fluffy pancakes that would not be easily forgotten.

NOTES FROM THE TEST KITCHEN

THE BEST MAPLE SYRUP

Sold side by side at the supermarket, genuine maple syrup and so-called pancake syrup (made with high-fructose corn syrup) can range from more than $1 per ounce for the real deal to a mere 14 cents per ounce for an imitation. But price aside, which tastes best? To find out, we pitted four top-selling national brands of maple syrup against five popular pancake syrups. The pancake syrups were universally disliked for their artificial flavor and unnaturally thick texture. Of the maple syrups, those with a good balance of sweetness and maple flavor rose to the top of the pack (tasters downgraded some maple syrups for being too sweet). With its clean, intense maple flavor, moderate sweetness, and just the right consistency, our favorite was **Maple Grove Farms Grade A Dark Amber Syrup**.

BUTTERMILK PANCAKES

Buttermilk Pancakes

MAKES 8 PANCAKES

The pancakes can be cooked on a countertop griddle. Set the griddle temperature to 350 degrees and cook as directed. See page 249 for a recipe to use up some of the leftover sour cream.

- 1 cup (5 ounces) unbleached all-purpose flour
- 1 tablespoon sugar
- ½ teaspoon baking powder
- ¼ teaspoon baking soda
- ¼ teaspoon salt
- 1 cup buttermilk
- 2 tablespoons sour cream
- 2 tablespoons unsalted butter, melted and cooled
- 1 large egg
- 1 teaspoon vegetable oil, plus more as needed

USE IT UP: BUTTERMILK

Very Berry Smoothie

SERVES 2

Fresh berries can be substituted for the frozen berries in this recipe; simply add ½ cup ice cubes to the blender with the berries.

- 1½ cups buttermilk
- 1½ cups frozen berries (see note)
- 1 banana, broken into chunks
- 1 tablespoon sugar, plus extra to taste
  Pinch salt
  Water, as needed

Pour the buttermilk into a blender, then add the berries, banana, sugar, and salt. Process on low speed until the mixture is combined but still coarse in texture, about 10 seconds. Increase the blender speed to high and continue to process until the mixture is completely smooth, 20 to 40 seconds longer. Season with additional sugar to taste and adjust the consistency with water as needed. Serve immediately.

1. Adjust an oven rack to the middle position and heat the oven to 200 degrees. Set a wire rack inside a rimmed baking sheet and set aside.

2. Whisk the flour, sugar, baking powder, baking soda, and salt together in a medium bowl. Whisk the buttermilk, sour cream, melted butter, and egg together in another bowl until smooth. Gently fold the buttermilk mixture into the flour mixture with a rubber spatula until just combined. (The batter will be lumpy with a few spots of dry flour; do not overmix.) Let the batter rest for 10 minutes before cooking.

3. While the batter rests, heat the oil in a 12-inch nonstick skillet over medium heat until shimmering. Use a wad of paper towels to carefully wipe out the oil, leaving a thin film of oil on the bottom and sides of the pan. Using ¼ cup of the batter per pancake, portion the batter into the pan in three places. Cook until the edges are set, the first side is golden brown, and bubbles on the surface are just beginning to break, 2 to 3 minutes.

4. Using a thin, wide spatula, flip the pancakes and continue to cook until the second side is golden brown, 1 to 2 minutes longer. Transfer the pancakes to the wire rack (don't overlap them) and keep warm in the oven. Repeat with the remaining batter, using more oil as needed. Serve.

CORN MUFFINS

WITH A MOIST CRUMB AND HEARTY CORN FLAVOR, corn muffins are the muffin of choice for those who prefer a not-too-sweet breakfast treat. Most muffin recipes, of course, make the standard 12, so we aimed to whittle our muffin yield down to just four—perfect for a breakfast for two, plus an extra for an afternoon snack.

Intense corn flavor was our top priority, so we began by focusing on our choice of cornmeal. Starting with a basic 12-muffin recipe (containing 2 cups of flour, 1 cup of cornmeal, ¾ cup of sugar, two eggs, and a stick of butter, along with varying amounts of baking powder, baking soda, and salt), we tested the two styles of cornmeal typically found in the grocery store: degerminated and whole ground. Comparing batches of the muffins made with each type of cornmeal, tasters noticed significant differences. The muffins made with degerminated cornmeal, from which the germ and husk have been removed, offered an unremarkable corn flavor. This is because the germ contains most of the flavor and natural oils; while removing it allows for a longer shelf life, it results in a less flavorful cornmeal. The muffins made with whole ground cornmeal, which still contained the germ, had a more complex corn flavor. The choice was obvious; now we had to tackle the scaling.

We knew that successfully cutting the recipe down would be a result of much trial and error. Numerous attempts failed, resulting in too much batter and overflowing muffin cups. After many tests, we finally reached the best combination of ingredients: ⅓ cup of cornmeal, ⅔ cup of flour, an egg, ¼ cup of sugar, a few pats of butter, and, of course, small amounts of the requisite salt, baking powder, and baking soda. The 1-to-2 ratio of cornmeal to flour provided plenty of corn flavor and also ensured that the crumb was substantial. Because we wanted a sturdy muffin, not an airy cake, we used the quick-bread method for mixing; we whisked the dry ingredients together, then gently folded in the wet ingredients. Tasters agreed that this method produced a hearty crumb that paired well with the corn flavor.

Our muffins now had the right texture and good flavor but were a little dry. We hoped the solution would be as simple as increasing the amount of butter and adding enough milk to hit the right consistency. When we tested this, however, the muffins were still lacking in moisture. Some recipes we found recommended using buttermilk in place of the milk, but since most buttermilk is packaged in 1-quart containers (we would need less than ½ cup), this seemed unreasonable. Sour cream was a better solution; combined with the milk and butter, it helped produce a moist, tender muffin.

We were ready to bake our sweet corn muffins but wondered what to bake the batter in; whether using a 6-cup or a 12-cup muffin tin, there would be empty muffin cups left after we filled 4 cups with our batter. Did it matter where the muffin batter was placed in the tin—on the inside or the outside? Our testing revealed that placement didn't matter at all; all the muffins, regardless of placement, rose and browned equally.

After 15 minutes in a 400-degree oven, our muffins were subtly sweet and had a crunchy, golden crust. Wanting to increase the flavor even more, we decided to pick two directions for flavor enhancement. For a

sweet version, we chose to include dried apricots and orange zest. Subtly sweet, apricots complemented the corn's hearty flavor, and orange zest lent some brightness. For a savory corn muffin, we cut the amount of sugar in half and added some shredded cheddar cheese and scallions—a perfect muffin partnered with eggs or later in the day with soup or chili. Now we had three satisfying, moist, and ultra-corny muffin recipes for breakfast time or anytime.

Corn Muffins

MAKES 4 MUFFINS

We prefer to use yellow whole grain cornmeal in this recipe for its strong flavor. Any size muffin tin will work well here, and the batter can be placed in any of the muffin cups. See page 249 for a recipe to use up the leftover sour cream.

- ⅔ cup (3⅓ ounces) unbleached all-purpose flour
- ⅓ cup (1⅔ ounces) yellow cornmeal (see note)
- ½ teaspoon baking powder
- ½ teaspoon baking soda
- ¼ teaspoon salt
- ⅓ cup sour cream
- ¼ cup (1¾ ounces) sugar
- 3 tablespoons unsalted butter, melted and cooled
- 2 tablespoons whole milk
- 1 large egg, lightly beaten

1. Adjust an oven rack to the middle position and heat the oven to 400 degrees. Grease 4 cups in a muffin tin.

2. Whisk the flour, cornmeal, baking powder, baking soda, and salt together in a medium bowl. Whisk the sour cream, sugar, melted butter, milk, and egg together in another bowl until smooth. Gently fold the sour cream mixture into the flour mixture with a rubber spatula until just combined. (The batter will be lumpy with a few spots of dry flour; do not overmix.)

3. Using an ice cream scoop or large spoon, divide the batter equally among the 4 prepared muffin cups (the batter should fill the cups and mound slightly). Bake until the muffin tops are golden and a toothpick inserted into the center of a muffin comes out with just a few crumbs attached, 12 to 17 minutes, rotating the pan halfway through. Cool the muffins in the muffin tin for 5 minutes, then flip them out onto a wire rack and let cool for 5 minutes longer before serving.

WHEN BAKING POWDER LOSES PUNCH

In the cooking-for-two kitchen, it can be hard to monitor baking ingredients for freshness. But it's important to check the date on a package when it comes to certain ingredients, like baking powder. Over time, baking powder (composed of baking soda, acid salt, and cornstarch) loses its ability to produce carbon dioxide and give baked goods their lift—sooner than many manufacturers claim. We compared biscuits made with a fresh can of baking powder to biscuits made with cans opened and stored for one month all the way up to a year. The rise of the biscuits began to decrease with the six-month-old powder. So for best results, replace your baking powder every six months.

VARIATIONS

Apricot-Orange Corn Muffins

Follow the recipe for Corn Muffins, adding ¼ teaspoon grated orange zest and ⅓ cup dried apricots, chopped fine, to the sour cream mixture in step 2.

Cheddar Cheese and Scallion Corn Muffins

Follow the recipe for Corn Muffins, reducing the amount of sugar to 2 tablespoons. Add 2 thinly sliced scallions and ½ cup shredded cheddar cheese to the sour cream mixture in step 2. Sprinkle 2 tablespoons more shredded cheddar cheese over the tops of the muffins before baking in step 3.

OPEN-FACED POACHED EGG SANDWICHES

MOST HOME COOKS SEEM TO HAVE WRITTEN OFF poached eggs, considering them finicky, difficult, and outdated, all at the same time. But really, poaching is a basic cooking method that requires very little work. There's no laundry list of ingredients to gather, and the whole process takes but a few minutes. Plus, you don't need to be a short-order cook when poaching eggs for two, since two servings can be cooked at the same time. We wanted to come up with a foolproof poaching technique that would guarantee evenly cooked eggs, with a slightly runny yolk and a tender white—and no stray strands of egg white. But we wondered how we should serve our eggs. We didn't want to make a fussy hollandaise, but we didn't want to just add a couple of slices of toast either. Instead, we thought an open-faced poached egg sandwich should be the order of the day—not as much work as eggs Benedict, but just as satisfying.

We suspected that part of the problem with many poached egg recipes was the pot. Instead of the traditional deep saucepan, we decided to try poaching in a 12-inch nonstick skillet, which we figured might make it easier to maneuver the eggs. Our assumptions were quickly validated: The shallower water enabled the eggs to reach the bottom of the skillet sooner than they would in a pot just a few inches taller. This gave the eggs a shallow floor on which to land gently. The sooner the eggs were on solid ground, the quicker the whites held together and the less likely they were to become stringy.

Even with these measures, however, our eggs were still a little ragged around the edges. At this point we had been cooking the eggs in simmering water, but the temperature wasn't constant. In the end we had success "cooking" the eggs off the heat. First, we brought water to a simmer in the skillet. While it was heating, we cracked the eggs into teacups, which we found helped us gently add all four eggs to the skillet at once. We added vinegar to the water to lower its pH, which helps stabilize the egg whites. The lower pH of the water lowers the temperature at which the whites and yolks set, which means that after the initial dunk into boiling water, the eggs can cook in water that's slightly cooler and, hence, calmer. We also added salt for flavor. We then slipped the eggs into the skillet and removed the pan from the heat. We covered the skillet and waited about five minutes before we removed the eggs with a slotted spoon. This method consistently produced restaurant-worthy poached eggs with soft, runny yolks and perfectly formed, round whites.

Now we turned to building our sandwich. Using a toasted English muffin as a base, we spread the muffin with goat cheese. Mixed with a little lemon juice and olive oil, the crumbly cheese was easy to spread and even more flavorful. Turning again to our skillet, we sautéed quick-cooking baby spinach with minced shallot and garlic before using the pan to poach the eggs. After layering the wilted spinach (and a sliced tomato for more flavor) on toasted English muffins, we topped each half with a poached egg. Tasters approved.

To ensure that all the components of our sandwich were piping hot by the time they made it to the breakfast table, we toasted the muffins, sautéed the spinach, and assembled the entire base of the sandwiches. We kept the partially assembled sandwiches warm in the oven while we poached the eggs. Once we were finished poaching, we simply brought out the warmed English muffins and placed the eggs on top. All that was left to do now was dig in.

Open-Faced Poached Egg Sandwiches

SERVES 2

You will need a 12-inch nonstick skillet with a tight-fitting lid for this recipe. The vinegar in the egg poaching water adds more than just flavor—it lowers the pH in the water, ensuring that the egg whites stay intact during cooking.

>   2 **ounces goat cheese, crumbled (about ½ cup) and softened**
>   4 **teaspoons olive oil**
>   1 **teaspoon fresh lemon juice**
>   **Salt and pepper**
>   2 **English muffins, split in half, toasted, and still warm**
>   1 **small tomato, cored and sliced thin (about 8 slices)**
>   1 **shallot, minced**
>   1 **small garlic clove, minced**
>   4 **ounces baby spinach (about 4 cups)**
>   2 **tablespoons white vinegar**
>   4 **large eggs**

1. Adjust an oven rack to the middle position and heat the oven to 300 degrees. Stir the goat cheese, 1 teaspoon of the oil, and lemon juice together in a bowl until smooth. Season with salt and pepper to taste.

2. Spread the goat cheese mixture evenly over the warm English muffin halves and top with 2 tomato slices each. Arrange the English muffins on a rimmed baking sheet and keep warm in the oven.

3. Heat the remaining 1 tablespoon oil in a 12-inch nonstick skillet over medium heat until shimmering. Add the shallot and ¼ teaspoon salt and cook until softened, 2 to 3 minutes. Stir in the garlic and cook until fragrant, about 30 seconds. Stir in the spinach,

a handful at a time, until wilted. Continue to cook, stirring frequently, until the spinach is uniformly wilted and glossy, about 30 seconds longer. Using tongs, squeeze out any excess moisture from the spinach, then divide evenly among the English muffins and return to the oven to keep warm.

4. Wipe out the skillet with a wad of paper towels, then fill it nearly to the rim with water. Add the vinegar and 1 teaspoon salt and bring to a boil over high heat.

5. Meanwhile, crack the eggs into two teacups (2 eggs in each). Reduce the heat so the water is simmering. Following the photo, lower the rims of the teacups into the water and gently tip the eggs into the skillet simultaneously. Remove the skillet from the heat, cover, and poach the eggs for 4 minutes (add 30 seconds for firm yolks).

6. When the eggs are cooked, gently lift them from the water using a slotted spoon and let drain before laying them on top of each English muffin. Season with salt and pepper to taste and serve.

NOTES FROM THE TEST KITCHEN

POURING EGGS INTO A SKILLET

To add eggs to the water at the same time for poaching, crack two eggs into each teacup and tip the cups, simultaneously, into the simmering water.

THE BEST ENGLISH MUFFINS

Are there any differences among the various national brands of English muffins? To find out, we purchased four brands, got out the toaster, and invited tasters to the table. We were looking for slightly yeasty, slightly sweet flavor and a texture—once the muffins were toasted—that was crisp and craggy on top and soft and chewy inside. Although Thomas' English Muffins indeed had the most "nooks and crannies," **Bays English Muffins** were declared the favorite. Interestingly, this brand had more salt than the competition, which brought forward the sweetness of the muffins.

24-HOUR "OMELET"

A 24-HOUR OMELET IS NOTHING LIKE OMELETS THAT you have ordered at your favorite breakfast spot. Nor does it take a day to bake. This large homey casserole consists of an eggy custard, bread, and cheese. It's usually assembled the night before serving, so the bread can soak up the richness of the eggs and milk, then popped into the oven the next morning while the coffee brews. At its best, the 24-hour omelet is lighter than the fluffiest scrambled eggs and practically melts in your mouth. Since it can be made the night before and baked off in the morning, this dish is ideal for a weekend breakfast. But with most recipes serving eight, we would definitely need to scale it down.

To convert this crowd-friendly dish to a smaller size, we began by trading our large casserole dish for a smaller baking dish. In the past, we've found that most recipes for 24-hour omelets are overloaded with custard and cheese, which lead to wet, sagging casseroles. To form a cohesive casserole perfect for two, we knew we had to get the proportions of bread, custard, and cheese just right.

The foundation of a 24-hour omelet is the bread, which basically melts into the custard. With that in mind, we quickly ruled out rustic breads with heavy crusts—these would never break down enough—and really soft loaves, which disintegrated and gave the dish an unpleasant raw, yeasty flavor. Ultimately, we found that a high-quality white sandwich bread provided the best texture. Two slices of bread gave us a good base; buttering the slices added richness and flavor to the omelet that tasters favored.

We then turned our attention to the tender custard. Recipes we found commonly called for a custard with 2 parts dairy to 1 part eggs. Keeping in mind the name of the dish, we felt a more pronounced egg flavor was needed and decided to reduce the ratio. In the end, we settled on a custard consisting of two eggs (about ½ cup) and ¾ cup of dairy. When it came to the type of dairy, we tested the recipe with milk, half-and-half, and heavy cream (both on their own and in combinations). Wanting to keep the emphasis on the eggs in the dish, we chose milk, as both the half-and-half and the cream obscured the egg flavor and made the dish too heavy.

For the additional flavors for our omelet, simpler was better. Shredded cheddar cheese was a standard among most recipes, and we found that ¾ cup was just enough to add rich flavor without weighing down the omelet. A small amount of onion provided some pungency, and a little dry mustard and hot sauce gave the dish a hint of spiciness and accentuated the flavor of the eggs.

Finally, we refined our process. After cutting the buttered slices of bread into 1-inch pieces, we layered them in the casserole dish with the cheese and poured the custard over the top. Gently pressing on the bread helped to ensure that it fully absorbed the custard and softened while sitting overnight. Finishing up the casserole in a 350-degree oven the next day produced a delicate texture, similar to that of a soufflé. After only an hour in the oven, our 24-hour omelet emerged boasting a beautiful golden brown crust and a perfectly set and supple custard.

24-Hour "Omelet"
SERVES 2

You will need a 3-cup baking dish (measuring approximately 7¼ by 5¼ inches) or a dish of a similar size for this recipe (see page 3). The omelet needs to sit in the refrigerator, well covered, for at least 8 hours in order to achieve the desired consistency, and it can be made up to 24 hours in advance.

- 1 tablespoon unsalted butter, softened
- 2 slices high-quality white sandwich bread
- 3 ounces cheddar cheese, shredded (about ¾ cup)
- ¾ cup whole milk
- 2 large eggs
- ¼ cup grated onion
- ¼ teaspoon salt
- ¼ teaspoon dry mustard
- ⅛ teaspoon pepper
- ⅛ teaspoon hot sauce

1. Grease a 3-cup baking dish. Spread the butter evenly over one side of each slice of bread, then cut the bread into 1-inch pieces. Scatter half of the bread evenly into the prepared dish and sprinkle with half of the cheese. Repeat with the remaining bread and cheese.

24-HOUR "OMELET"

2. Whisk the milk, eggs, onion, salt, mustard, pepper, and hot sauce together in a bowl, then pour evenly over the bread. Gently press down on the bread to help it soak up the egg mixture. Cover tightly with plastic wrap and refrigerate for at least 8 hours or up to 24 hours.

3. When ready to bake, adjust an oven rack to the middle position and heat the oven to 350 degrees. Unwrap the dish and bake until puffed and golden brown, about 1 hour. Let cool slightly before serving.

VARIATIONS

24-Hour "Omelet" with Pepper Jack and Chipotle Chiles

Follow the recipe for 24-Hour "Omelet," substituting pepper Jack cheese for the cheddar. Whisk 1 teaspoon minced canned chipotle chile in adobo sauce with the eggs in step 2, and sprinkle 1 tablespoon minced fresh cilantro over the top before serving.

24-Hour "Omelet" with Sun-Dried Tomatoes and Mozzarella

Follow the recipe for 24-Hour "Omelet," substituting mozzarella cheese for the cheddar. Sprinkle ¼ cup grated Parmesan cheese and 2 tablespoons drained oil-packed sun-dried tomatoes, patted dry and chopped coarse, over the bread with the mozzarella in step 1.

SPANISH TORTILLA

EGGS AND POTATOES ARE A CLASSIC BREAKFAST combination that always satisfies. And while the typical pairing of eggs and home fries or hash browns usually hits the spot, we wanted an alternative with a bit more flair. After we searched through our library of recipes, it was a recipe from across the ocean that we finally settled on: the Spanish tortilla, a frittata-like dish of eggs, potatoes, and onions, typically served as part of tapas, an evening snack served with drinks.

Traditionally, a Spanish tortilla is made by first cooking potatoes and onions in ample olive oil, which gives the dish both flavor and moisture, then mixing in beaten eggs. While the egg flavor is present, it's the rich, creamy flavor of the potatoes that dominates. However, after initial recipe tests, we realized the tortilla was no

simple undertaking. Recipes we sampled were greasy and the cooking instructions complicated. To create a successful recipe for tortilla for two, we would need to not only develop a streamlined cooking method, but also revisit the amount of oil required. We started with the potatoes.

Starchy, creamy potatoes would be key, and we narrowed our testing down to russets and Yukon golds. Though they share many common traits, the Yukon gold—only one was necessary—won out for its creamier texture. Typically, Spanish tortilla recipes call for thinly sliced potatoes, and in this case we stuck with tradition. After testing several thicknesses, we found that ⅛-inch-thick slices were essential in creating the proper distribution of egg and potato. For the onion, tasters favored the mellow flavor of standard yellow onion over shallots. Half of a small onion provided just the right amount of sweetness to balance the hearty potatoes.

Many recipes for Spanish tortilla start with gently simmering the potatoes and onions in quite a lot of olive oil—3 to 4 cups for a recipe serving four—to achieve a meltingly tender consistency, but even after scaling down this amount and draining off the excess oil, our tortilla was still extremely greasy. Looking for ways to reduce the amount of oil, we first tried simply sautéing the potatoes and onions in an 8-inch skillet with a few tablespoons of oil. These potatoes did soften eventually, but by that time they were also overly browned and tasted bitter. Trying a gentler approach, we sautéed the potatoes and onions, covered, until softened. This method produced tender potatoes that were light and fluffy. Best of all, we found that just a tablespoon of oil was all we needed to cook the potatoes and onions and still add the right amount of richness and flavor to the dish.

With the potatoes and onions done, all we needed to do was mix them with five beaten eggs—four eggs made for a loose pile of potatoes with some egg interspersed, and six eggs made the tortilla too eggy—and add them back to the skillet to finish cooking. Traditionally, the tortilla is flipped when the bottom has set but the top is still liquid. This might be easy for an experienced tortilla maker, but we were quickly cleaning up an egg-splattered floor. We tried skipping the flip and finishing the tortilla under a hot broiler, but this only puffed up the eggs like a soufflé—not the

FLIPPING A SPANISH TORTILLA

1. After browning the first side of the tortilla, loosen the sides with a rubber spatula and slide it onto a plate.

2. Place a second plate facedown over the tortilla; invert the tortilla, browned-side up, onto the second plate.

3. To brown the second side of the tortilla, slide it back into the skillet, browned-side up, and tuck the edges into the pan with a rubber spatula. Return to medium heat.

STORING LEFTOVER ONION

Although onions are relatively inexpensive, there's no reason to let extra sliced or chopped onions go to waste, especially when even a small portion can be used in so many ways. To make sure those extras don't dry out in the fridge, we tested two common storage methods—submerging the onion in water versus placing it in a zipper-lock bag—and had our answer. The sliced onions submerged in water were excessively odorous with a sharp flavor, but the sliced onions stored in a zipper-lock bag were much tamer. Looking into the science behind this, we found that water helps to distribute enzymes on the surface of the onion, which in turn leads to an increase in the pungent odor and flavor. If you find that you've chopped or sliced too much onion, simply store the extras in the fridge in a zipper-lock bag for up to 2 days and give them a quick rinse to remove any residual odor right before using.

cohesive texture we wanted. We then tried cooking another tortilla, this time placing a lid on the pan as soon as the bottom of the egg-and-potato mixture was set. This time the tortilla remained dense and the top was cooked just enough to make flipping less risky—but still not easy. Fed up, we ditched tradition. By sliding the partially cooked tortilla out of the pan and onto a large plate, then placing another plate upside-down over the tortilla, we could easily flip the whole thing and slide the tortilla back into the pan, making a once-messy task foolproof.

By this point our tortilla was nearing perfection, but some tasters wondered how it might taste with additional flavors. We tried preparing two tortillas with basic omelet ingredients (roasted red peppers for one and crispy bacon and scallions for the other) and served them with some garlic mayonnaise—a traditional accompaniment to tortillas in Spain. Tasters quickly finished their slices and came back for seconds, praising the exceptionally creamy potatoes and eggs. We had strayed from tradition, but our tortillas still delivered true Spanish flavor.

Spanish Tortilla with Roasted Red Peppers
SERVES 2

Prepare and assemble all of the ingredients before slicing the potatoes or the potatoes will begin to turn brown (do not store the sliced potatoes in water). Slicing the potatoes ⅛ inch thick is crucial for the success of this dish; use a mandoline or a food processor fitted with a ⅛-inch slicing blade. Be sure to use an 8-inch nonstick skillet for this recipe. Serve with Garlic Mayonnaise (page 223).

- 1 Yukon gold potato (about 8 ounces), peeled, quartered, and sliced ⅛ inch thick (see note)
- ½ small onion, sliced thin
- 2 tablespoons extra-virgin olive oil
  Salt and pepper
- 5 large eggs
- 2 ounces jarred roasted red peppers, drained, patted dry, and coarsely chopped (about ¼ cup)

1. Toss the potato, onion, 1 tablespoon of the oil, ¼ teaspoon salt, and ⅛ teaspoon pepper in a bowl.

2. Heat 2 teaspoons more oil in an 8-inch nonstick skillet over medium-low heat until shimmering. Add the potato mixture to the skillet, cover, and cook, stirring occasionally, until the potatoes are tender, about 10 minutes.

3. Meanwhile, whisk the eggs, ¼ teaspoon salt, and ⅛ teaspoon pepper together in a medium bowl until just combined. Using a rubber spatula, fold the hot potato mixture and red peppers into the eggs until combined, making sure to scrape all of the potato mixture out of the skillet.

4. Heat the remaining 1 teaspoon oil in the skillet over medium heat until shimmering. Add the egg mixture and cook, shaking the pan constantly, for 30 seconds. Smooth the top with a rubber spatula, folding down any of the egg mixture that has built up along the sides of the skillet. Cover and cook, gently shaking the pan every minute, until the bottom is golden brown and the top is lightly set, about 5 minutes.

5. Following the photos on page 222, use a rubber spatula to loosen the tortilla from the pan and slide it onto a plate. Invert the tortilla onto a second plate and slide it, browned-side up, back into the skillet. Tuck the edges of the tortilla into the skillet with a rubber spatula to form a disk shape.

6. Return the skillet to medium heat and continue to cook, gently shaking the pan every 30 seconds, until the second side is golden brown, about 2 minutes. Slide the tortilla onto a cutting board or serving plate and let cool for at least 15 minutes before serving.

VARIATION

Spanish Tortilla with Bacon and Scallions

Cook 4 slices bacon, cut into ¼-inch pieces, in an 8-inch nonstick skillet over medium-low heat until crisp, about 10 minutes. Using a slotted spoon, transfer the bacon to a paper towel–lined plate and pour off all but 2 teaspoons of the bacon fat. Follow the recipe for Spanish Tortilla with Roasted Red Peppers, substituting the reserved bacon fat for the oil in step 2. Substitute the crisp bacon and 2 thinly sliced scallions for the roasted peppers in step 3.

Garlic Mayonnaise
MAKES ABOUT ¼ CUP

This mayonnaise can be stored in an airtight container for up to 2 days. Serve with Spanish Tortilla (page 222) or Easier French Fries (page 251).

- ¼ cup mayonnaise
- 1 teaspoon fresh lemon juice
- ½ teaspoon Dijon mustard
- ½ small garlic clove, minced
- Salt and pepper

Combine all of the ingredients in a bowl and season with salt and pepper to taste. Refrigerate until the flavors have melded, about 15 minutes.

EASY QUICHE

ANYONE WHO HAS EVER EATEN BRUNCH HAS encountered quiche—and probably has been smitten by the combination of creamy custard and flaky crust. But recipes waver between serving a whole breakfast crowd (think a 9-inch quiche) or a party (think cocktail-hour minis). We wanted a quiche that was somewhere in between when it came to size, but still showcased the custard's silky texture and the crispiness of the buttery crust.

Our first challenge was to decide what size pie plate to use. After hunting around at local kitchen supply shops, we found a 6-inch pie plate that we thought would provide the right amount of quiche for two. We decided to use our Homemade Pie Dough (page 263), which uses both shortening and butter for the fat. After rolling out the dough and fitting it into the pie plate, we allowed the crust to chill (to prevent it from shrinking while it baked), then got a jump start on the baking and parbaked it in a 375-degree oven until dry and light in color.

Now we were ready to move on to the filling, which would be a combination of eggs, dairy, cheese, and herbs. Eggs contribute structure, moisture, and flavor to quiche, and recipes typically include anywhere from three to six eggs for a quiche serving six to eight people. Early on, we found that recipes with too many eggs resulted in a rubbery texture; with too few eggs, the quiche was too soft to cut neatly, and the flavor was too mild. After a number of tests, we settled on two whole eggs and ⅔ cup of dairy. Firm-textured and yet not rubbery, rich but not overly eggy, our quiche was progressing in the right direction.

As for the type of dairy, we tried milk and cream alone, as well as half-and-half. By itself, milk tasted too lean and cream was far too rich; half-and-half made the best quiche by far, rich-tasting and with a substantial—but not dense—texture.

When it came to the cheese, we didn't want to get carried away—some recipes we tasted seemed more like a cheese tart than a custardy quiche. For our easy quiche for two, we found that ½ cup of cheddar brought just enough rich cheese flavor without overwhelming the custard. For an herb, we wanted something mild but bright; a bit of minced chives worked perfectly.

After mixing the cheese and chives into our custard base, we poured the mixture into our prepared crust and allowed it to bake. Finally, we had just what we were looking for: a tender, flaky crust and a custard that was creamy but not overly rich. It puffed slightly while baking and settled neatly as it cooled.

Of course, taking the quiche out of the oven at just the right time was also essential to obtaining a perfectly creamy custard. To do this we found that watching the oven, not the clock, was the best method. Once the surface of the quiche was puffed and had a light golden brown color, we tested the doneness of the custard by inserting a knife blade about 1 inch from the edge. If the quiche was done, the knife blade came out clean; at this point the center still appeared slightly soft, but we found that the residual heat finished the baking while the quiche cooled on the rack.

Our easy quiche was good, but we thought the addition of ham or bacon would definitely please many diners (what doesn't go well with bacon?). So we created two just-as-easy variations designed to make the most of these breakfast meats—a ham and Swiss quiche and a classic quiche Lorraine (made with bacon and Gruyère). Served slightly warm or at room temperature, all three quiches were a piece of cake—or custard.

Easy Cheesy Quiche

SERVES 2

You will need a 6-inch pie plate for this recipe (see page 3). If desired, you can substitute 1 round of store-bought pie dough, such as Pillsbury Just Unroll!, for the homemade pie dough. If the pie dough becomes too soft to work with, simply refrigerate it until firm. It is important to add the custard to the pie shell while it is still warm; if the crust has cooled, rewarm it in the oven for 5 minutes before adding the custard.

1   **recipe Homemade Pie Dough (page 263; see note)**
⅔   **cup half-and-half**
2   **large eggs, lightly beaten**
2   **teaspoons minced fresh chives or parsley**
⅛   **teaspoon salt**
⅛   **teaspoon pepper**
2   **ounces cheddar cheese, shredded (about ½ cup)**

1. Roll out the dough into a 10-inch round, about ⅜ inch thick, on a lightly floured counter. Following the photos on page 264, fit the dough into a 6-inch pie plate and trim, fold, and crimp the edge. Cover loosely with plastic wrap and freeze for 20 minutes.

2. Adjust an oven rack to the lower-middle position and heat the oven to 375 degrees. Line the chilled crust with a sheet of lightly greased foil and fill with pie weights. Bake until the pie dough looks dry and is light in color, 25 to 30 minutes.

3. Meanwhile, whisk the half-and-half, eggs, chives, salt, and pepper together in a large measuring cup. Stir in the cheese until well combined.

4. Remove the pie shell from the oven and reduce the oven temperature to 350 degrees. Remove the pie weights and foil and transfer the pie shell to a foil-lined rimmed baking sheet. Return the pie shell to the oven. Carefully pour the egg mixture into the warm shell until it reaches about ½ inch from the top edge of the crust (you may have extra egg mixture).

5. Bake the quiche until the top is lightly browned, the very center still jiggles and looks slightly underdone, and a knife inserted about 1 inch from the edge comes out clean, 30 to 40 minutes.

6. Let the quiche cool for at least 30 minutes or up to 1 hour. Serve slightly warm or at room temperature.

VARIATIONS

Easy Quiche Lorraine

Cook 2 slices bacon, cut into ¼-inch pieces, in an 8-inch skillet over medium-low heat until crisp, about 10 minutes. Using a slotted spoon, transfer the bacon to a paper towel–lined plate and pour off all but 1 tablespoon of the bacon fat. Add ¼ cup minced onion to the skillet and cook over medium heat until softened and lightly browned, 5 to 7 minutes. Follow the recipe for Easy Cheesy Quiche, substituting Gruyère cheese for the cheddar and adding the cooked bacon and onion to the filling in step 3.

Easy Ham and Swiss Quiche

Follow the recipe for Easy Cheesy Quiche, substituting Swiss cheese for the cheddar and adding 2 thin slices deli ham (about 2 ounces), cut into ¼-inch pieces, to the filling in step 3.

SAVORY SPINACH STRUDEL

TRADITIONAL GREEK SPINACH PIE, ALSO KNOWN AS spanakopita, is a savory baked pie consisting of an aromatic mixture of spinach, onion, and feta cheese layered between sheets of phyllo dough. While we're certainly fans of all things eggs when it comes to breakfast and brunch, sometimes it's nice to have something different; spinach pie, we thought, could be easily transformed into a savory, alternative-to-eggs brunch dish. Rather than layering the sheets of phyllo dough in a baking dish, we could roll them up and bake them to form a crisp, flaky strudel that could easily be sliced and served. Instead of ending up with a whole pie, we'd have on our hands a petite strudel perfect for two.

We decided to focus first on perfecting the spinach filling before handling the phyllo dough, which is notorious for being difficult to work with. Wilted fresh spinach and frozen spinach both worked well once chopped, but we eventually settled on 5 ounces of frozen spinach, the more convenient option of the two as the only preparation required (in addition to

chopping) was thawing it and squeezing it dry. Feta cheese was a given, following the spinach pie theme; we crumbled about ½ cup of feta into small pieces before mixing it with the spinach so it would be evenly distributed throughout the filling. We found this amount added just enough tangy flavor without overwhelming the spinach.

For additional flavors, tasters liked the combination of scallions, garlic, and oregano the best. Grated nutmeg is commonly used in spinach pie, so we kept that spice in our strudel. Some toasted pine nuts provided a nice textural contrast to the mix, as did a handful of raisins, and fresh lemon juice added brightness and a clean flavor. However, at this point, some tasters were finding the filling a little dry and lacking richness. Although it's not traditional, we took the suggestion of a fellow test cook and folded in some ricotta cheese. Tasters agreed that the ricotta rounded out the flavors and gave the filling a moist, creamy texture.

Now ready to roll up our strudel, we prepared ourselves for working with the phyllo. Phyllo is notorious for drying out and cracking when briefly left sitting out; to prevent this from happening, we kept the layers of phyllo covered with damp towels while we worked. Coating each sheet of phyllo with olive oil before layering on the next—we found that five layers of phyllo formed an ample crust on our strudel—also provided additional moisture, helping the sheets adhere to each other, and promoted a crispy texture once baked.

NOTES FROM THE TEST KITCHEN

ALL ABOUT FETA CHEESE
Within the European Union, only cheese made in Greece from a mixture of sheep's and goat's milk can be legally called feta, but most of the feta in American supermarkets is made from pasteurized cow's milk that has been curdled, shaped into blocks, sliced, and steeped in brine. Feta can range from soft to semihard and has a tangy, salty flavor. Feta dries out quickly when removed from its brine, so always store it in the brine in which it is packed (we do not recommend buying precrumbled "dry" feta).

SAVORY SPINACH STRUDEL

Traditional strudels are formed by placing the filling in a strip on the pastry, folding in the two sides, then rolling the whole thing up into a tight package. Working with our delicate dough of just a few layers of phyllo was difficult enough, and folding in the sides seemed like an extra step we could do without. We found that the easiest method worked best: We left the sides of the phyllo open as we rolled up the strudel, securing the filling inside. Baked in a hot oven for 40 minutes, our strudel emerged with a beautiful golden and crisp exterior, but as it cooled on the rack, the outer layers curled and flaked like a bad sunburn. We thought the long baking time might be drying out the phyllo, so we tried baking the strudel at a higher temperature—400 degrees—for just 20 minutes. This crust was perfect: toothsome yet slightly yielding, with a golden exterior. Cut into attractive slices, our savory strudel is perfect when you're in the mood for something fresher and more flavorful than scrambled eggs.

Savory Spinach Strudel

SERVES 2

Make sure to thoroughly squeeze the spinach dry, or the filling will leak. Make sure that the phyllo is fully thawed before using. To thaw frozen phyllo, let it sit in the refrigerator overnight or on the counter for several hours; don't thaw it in the microwave or it will turn into an unusable, soggy mess. See page 45 for a recipe to use up some of the leftover ricotta cheese.

2 ounces feta cheese, crumbled (about ½ cup)
2 ounces whole milk ricotta cheese (about ¼ cup)
3 scallions, sliced thin
¼ cup golden raisins
1 tablespoon pine nuts, toasted (see page 210)
1 tablespoon minced fresh oregano
1 tablespoon fresh lemon juice
1 garlic clove, minced
¼ teaspoon ground nutmeg
5 ounces frozen spinach, thawed, squeezed dry (see note), and chopped coarse
Salt and pepper
5 (14 by 9-inch) sheets phyllo dough, thawed (see note)
Olive oil

MAKING SPINACH STRUDEL

1. On a clean counter, layer the phyllo sheets on top of one another, brushing each sheet with olive oil.

2. Mound the spinach mixture into a narrow log along the bottom edge of the phyllo, leaving a 2-inch border at the bottom and a ½-inch border on the sides.

3. Fold the bottom edge of the dough over the filling, then continue to roll the dough around the filling into a tight log, leaving the sides open.

4. After transferring the strudel, seam-side down, to the prepared baking sheet and brushing it with olive oil, cut four 1½-inch vents at a diagonal across the top of the strudel.

1. Adjust an oven rack to the middle position and heat the oven to 400 degrees. Mix the feta, ricotta, scallions, raisins, pine nuts, oregano, lemon juice, garlic, and nutmeg together in a medium bowl. Stir in the spinach until well combined. Season with salt and pepper to taste and set aside.

2. Line a rimmed baking sheet with parchment paper. Following the photos, lay 1 phyllo sheet on a clean counter and brush with oil, making sure to cover the entire surface. Repeat and layer with 4 more phyllo sheets, brushing each with oil.

3. Mound the spinach mixture evenly along the bottom edge of the phyllo (forming a 2-inch-wide log), leaving a 2-inch border at the bottom and a ½-inch border on the sides. Fold the dough on the bottom over the spinach mixture and continue to roll the dough around the filling into a tight log, leaving the sides open.

4. Gently transfer the strudel, seam-side down, to the prepared baking sheet and brush with oil. Cut four 1½-inch vents at a diagonal across the top of the strudel.

5. Bake the strudel until golden brown, 20 to 25 minutes, rotating the baking sheet halfway through. Let cool on the baking sheet for 10 minutes before serving.

SKILLET-BAKED GRITS

GO TO ANY SOUTHERN DINER AND YOU WILL BE sure to find grits on the menu. Cooked in a multitude of ways—from a porridge-style mixture sweetened with maple syrup or enriched with cheese to thicker cakes that are pan-fried until crispy—they are a staple addition to any good breakfast down South. One of our favorite ways to prepare grits is to mix in a pile of shredded cheese and bake the whole thing until it's brown on the top and creamy in the middle. Since baked grits are typically served up for a crowd, we needed our own recipe that cut back on ingredient amounts while still getting the ratio of grits to cooking liquid just right.

While baked grits are typically cooked in a pot and then transferred to a casserole dish to finish baking, we decided to use an ovensafe 8-inch skillet instead. The skillet provided just the right amount of space to cook the grits and enabled us to cut down on cleanup since it could go right into the oven to finish baking, replacing a separate baking dish. As for the grits, we found three different styles to work with: instant grits, which cook in five minutes; quick grits, which cook in seven to nine minutes; and old-fashioned grits, which cook in 15 minutes. In a side-by-side tasting, most tasters thought the instant grits were too loose and had a processed flavor. The old-fashioned grits were creamy yet retained a slightly coarse texture. Quick grits had a creamy yet substantial texture and didn't take long to cook, so they were our first choice.

To add richness without relying solely on butter, as many recipes do, we cooked the grits in milk rather than water—a technique we've used with success before. But because we were using such a small amount of grits—just ¼ cup—their flavor disappeared behind the dairy. Even when we diluted the milk with water, the grits tasted too heavily of cooked milk. We then tried a small amount of heavy cream and water mixed together. Tasters liked this batch—the grits were rich and clean-tasting, without an overwhelming dairy flavor. We were surprised to find that cooked cream does not develop the same strong "cooked" flavor as milk because the extra fat in cream keeps the milk proteins from breaking down when heated. After a few more batches of varying proportions, we found that 1 part cream to 3 parts water provided the best flavor.

To improve the flavor of our grits, we cooked some minced onion in the skillet before adding the liquid; the sautéed onion brought depth and a touch of sweetness. Hot sauce added piquancy that cut through the richness of the dish.

NOTES FROM THE TEST KITCHEN

THE BEST EXTRA-SHARP CHEDDAR

For our Skillet-Baked Grits, in which cheese plays a starring role, we turned to extra-sharp cheddar. As the cheddar ages, new flavor compounds are created, and the cheese gets firmer in texture and more concentrated in flavor—and it gets sharper. But there are numerous brands of extra-sharp cheddar available at the supermarket, all aged for different amounts of time (but usually in the range of nine to 18 months), so we set out to whittle the competition and find out which one was best. We purchased eight varieties and tried them plain and in grilled cheese sandwiches. Of the cheeses sampled, two rose above the pack, praised by tasters for both complex flavor and level of sharpness. The winners were **Cabot Private Stock** (left) and **Cabot Extra Sharp** (right), which are both aged for at least 12 months.

With the grits cooked, we had to choose our cheese, which we'd fold in before baking. Monterey Jack and pepper Jack cheeses made the grits taste sour; regular cheddar was good, but we wanted more flavor. Extra-sharp cheddar proved to be the winner. The flavor was assertive and complemented the subtle corn flavor.

Now we were ready to bake our grits. After 20 minutes in a 375-degree oven, the cheesy grits emerged with a beautiful golden top and tasted great, but when it came to texture, they were unpleasantly dense. Adding one lightly beaten egg to the grits before baking provided an airy, almost soufflé-like texture that tasters found appealing. And for a final touch, a sprinkle of sliced scallion gave our grits both a colorful contrast and a fresh burst of flavor. Finally, our baked grits were rich and flavorful, with a clear corn flavor and delicate texture—perfect for breakfast no matter where you live.

Skillet-Baked Grits

SERVES 2

Do not substitute instant grits or old-fashioned grits for the quick-cooking grits in this recipe, as they require different amounts of liquid for cooking. We like to serve these grits with eggs.

- 1 tablespoon unsalted butter
- ¼ cup minced onion
- ¾ cup water
- ¼ cup heavy cream
- ½ teaspoon salt
- ¼ teaspoon hot sauce
- ¼ cup quick grits (see note)
- 3 ounces extra-sharp cheddar cheese, shredded (about ¾ cup)
- 1 large egg, lightly beaten
- ⅛ teaspoon pepper
- 1 scallion, sliced thin

1. Adjust an oven rack to the middle position and heat the oven to 375 degrees.

USE IT UP: HEAVY CREAM

Homemade Butter

MAKES ABOUT 3 TABLESPOONS

You can use any amount of heavy cream for this recipe, with the yield increasing or decreasing accordingly; no matter the amount of heavy cream used, the whipping time in step 1 won't vary much. The butter can be stored in an airtight container in the refrigerator for up to 3 days.

- ½ cup heavy cream (see note)
  Pinch salt

1. Whip the heavy cream in a medium bowl with an electric mixer on medium-high speed until the cream separates and chunks of pale-yellow butter begin to form, 8 to 10 minutes, scraping down the bowl as needed.

2. Drain the butter mixture in a fine-mesh strainer and press on the butter with a rubber spatula to release any excess liquid. Transfer the butter to a bowl and stir in the salt.

2. Melt the butter in an 8-inch ovensafe nonstick skillet over medium heat. Add the onion and cook until softened and lightly browned, 5 to 7 minutes. Stir in the water, cream, salt, and hot sauce, and bring to a boil. Slowly whisk in the grits, reduce the heat to low, and cook, stirring often, until the grits are thick and creamy, 5 to 7 minutes.

3. Off the heat, stir in ½ cup of the cheese, egg, and pepper until combined. Smooth the grits into an even layer in the skillet and sprinkle with the remaining ¼ cup cheese. Transfer the skillet to the oven and bake until the cheese is melted and golden, 15 to 20 minutes.

4. Using a potholder (the skillet handle will be hot), remove the skillet from the oven and transfer to a wire rack. Let cool for 10 minutes, sprinkle with the scallion, and serve.

SOUR CREAM AND ONION SMASHED POTATOES

SIDE DISHES

PAN-ROASTED CARROTS

MOST HOME COOKS HAVE A BAG OF CARROTS stocked away in the fridge, making this vegetable the perfect basis for a last-minute side dish for two. Pan-roasting is a nice way to draw out the naturally sweet flavor of carrots, so we decided to use this method to create a simple and delicious side; we also thought the inclusion of some woodsy rosemary would provide a savory counterpoint to the carrots' sweetness.

We began with how to prepare the carrots for cooking. Matchsticks were out from the get-go—we were looking for simplicity, not to improve our knife skills. Bagged "baby" carrots offered convenience, but once cooked, these carrots were shy on both carrot flavor and good looks. Instead, we peeled regular bagged carrots and cut them on the bias into ovals; this elegant shape, we thought, would help to dress up any main course.

Some recipes begin with steaming or blanching the carrots, but we wanted a more streamlined approach. First, we browned the carrots in a little vegetable oil (olive oil imparted too much flavor) over medium-high heat for about 10 minutes. Then we gently simmered them, covered, with some chicken broth for richness and a bit of brown sugar to accentuate their sweetness. (Brown sugar gave the carrots more depth than white.) Ten minutes later, the carrots were handsomely browned as well as cooked through and tender.

As for the rosemary, we figured we'd simply throw in a handful of the chopped herb at the end, but when we did that, the carrots tasted medicinal, and the rosemary speckled them like grass clippings. While we frequently finish vegetable dishes with delicate fresh herbs such as chives or basil, we quickly discovered that assertively flavored rosemary was going to require some taming.

To avoid the distracting look of chopped rosemary, we started using a small sprig, intending to discard it once its flavor had permeated the dish. We were already heating a tablespoon of oil to brown the carrots, so we decided to try infusing the oil with the rosemary. Once the oil was strongly perfumed, we discarded the sprig and browned the carrots in the aromatic oil. But by the time we added the broth and let the carrots cook through, the rosemary flavor had pretty much disappeared. Some research explained why the flavor was so fleeting: Most of the aromatic compounds in rosemary are fat-soluble, so when rosemary is heated in oil, these compounds quickly leach out into the oil and then evaporate.

After mulling this over, we tried adding the sprig to the carrots with the broth instead of the oil. The water-rich environment gently extracted flavor from the herb, giving the sweet, toasty carrots a marked but mellow rosemary flavor.

Pan-Roasted Rosemary Carrots

SERVES 2

Stir the carrots gently in step 2 to prevent the rosemary leaves from falling off the stem.

- 1 tablespoon vegetable oil
- 4 carrots, peeled and sliced ½ inch thick on the bias (see photo)
  Salt and pepper
- ½ cup low-sodium chicken broth
- 1 teaspoon brown sugar
- 1 small sprig fresh rosemary

1. Heat the oil in a 10-inch skillet over medium-high heat until shimmering. Add the carrots, ¼ teaspoon salt, and ⅛ teaspoon pepper, and cook, stirring occasionally, until the carrots are golden brown, 8 to 10 minutes.

2. Stir in the broth and sugar, then add the rosemary sprig and bring to a simmer. Reduce the heat to medium-low, cover, and cook, stirring occasionally, until the carrots are tender, 6 to 10 minutes.

3. Uncover, remove and discard the rosemary sprig, and continue to cook until the liquid evaporates, about 1 minute. Season with salt and pepper to taste and serve.

NOTES FROM THE TEST KITCHEN

SLICING CARROTS ON THE BIAS

For a more elegant presentation, cut the carrots on the bias into ovals about ½ inch thick.

BRAISED CAULIFLOWER

CAULIFLOWER AS A SIDE DISH USUALLY CONJURES up images of soggy, overcooked cauliflower doused in a congealed neon-orange cheese sauce—a not-too-distant memory from many childhoods. But cauliflower doesn't have to be prepared this way. When properly cooked and appropriately flavored, cauliflower can be nutty and slightly sweet, and it's the perfect side dish for a simply prepared pork or chicken dish.

Our goal with this dish was to bring out the true flavor of cauliflower—not disguise it with a heavy sauce—so we chose to braise it. We knew that braising cauliflower (cooking it covered with a small amount of liquid) would help develop the flavor of the finished dish because porous vegetables, such as cauliflower, absorb liquid—and therefore flavor—during cooking.

But we quickly learned that simply braising this dense vegetable, with no precooking at all, took too long—even for the half head that we thought was just right for two. Also, it required close monitoring; we had to stand over the stove to make sure the cauliflower did not overcook and become waterlogged. Would sautéing the cauliflower first help to jump-start the cooking process? After a few tests, we knew this was the right path—just a brief sauté of our florets helped to build flavor in the finished dish. And we weren't dirtying an extra pan—we could sauté the cauliflower in the same skillet we would use for the braising.

After nailing down the sauté time (about eight minutes), we worked on our braising technique. We added a small amount (½ cup) of chicken broth to the skillet, then covered the pan. Finally, we had the texture we were after, and the naturally mild flavor of the cauliflower was intensified as well. Not only did the cauliflower absorb the flavors from the braising liquid, but the browned cauliflower also tasted wonderfully nutty and earthy. To boost the flavor even further, we added a clove of garlic and a pinch of red pepper flakes to the skillet before braising the cauliflower. To finish the dish, we stirred in some minced parsley.

With our basic method down, we took things a step further and came up with two variations—one with the tangy flavors of capers and anchovies, and another with curry powder. After just one bite, we knew that cauliflower would never have to be boring—or neon orange—again.

Braised Cauliflower
SERVES 2

For the best texture and flavor, make sure to brown the cauliflower well in step 1.

- 2 tablespoons olive oil
- 1 garlic clove, minced
- Pinch red pepper flakes
- ½ head cauliflower (about 1 pound), trimmed, cored, and cut into 1-inch florets (about 4 cups)
- Salt
- ½ cup low-sodium chicken broth
- 1 tablespoon minced fresh parsley
- Pepper

1. Combine 1 teaspoon of the oil, garlic, and red pepper flakes in a bowl. Heat the remaining 5 teaspoons oil in a 10-inch skillet over medium-high heat until shimmering. Add the cauliflower and ⅛ teaspoon salt and cook, stirring occasionally, until the florets are golden brown, 6 to 8 minutes.

2. Clear the center of the skillet, add the garlic mixture, and cook, mashing the mixture into the pan, until fragrant, about 30 seconds. Stir the garlic mixture into the cauliflower.

3. Add the broth, bring to a simmer, then cover and cook until the cauliflower is crisp-tender, 4 to 5 minutes. Off the heat, stir in the parsley and season with salt and pepper to taste. Serve.

VARIATIONS

Braised Cauliflower with Capers and Anchovies
Follow the recipe for Braised Cauliflower, adding 2 minced anchovy fillets and 2 teaspoons rinsed capers to the garlic mixture in step 1. Stir 1½ teaspoons fresh lemon juice into the cauliflower with the parsley in step 3.

Braised Curried Cauliflower
Follow the recipe for Braised Cauliflower, adding 1 teaspoon curry powder to the garlic mixture in step 1. Substitute ¼ cup plain yogurt for ¼ cup of the chicken broth and 1 tablespoon minced fresh cilantro for the parsley. Stir 1½ teaspoons fresh lime juice into the cauliflower with the cilantro in step 3.

ROASTED BROCCOLI

OVEN-ROASTING IS A GREAT TECHNIQUE FOR coaxing big flavor from vegetables—the dry heat concentrates flavor and caramelizes natural sugars. However, this method doesn't seem to be a natural fit for broccoli, which has an awkward shape, tough stems, and shrubby florets—all attributes that require a moist-heat cooking method so the vegetable can cook evenly. Having come across a few recipes that raved about roasted broccoli, we decided to see what we were missing.

We gathered the recipes we had recently encountered and prepared them. We quickly learned that for the broccoli pieces to brown, they had to be in contact with the baking sheet they were being roasted upon. Aside from the broccoli pieces that were in direct contact with the baking sheet, browning was sparse and the roasted flavor was minimal. Any color that the broccoli did pick up was confined to the florets, which charred and tasted bitter—not very appetizing.

Since we knew that contact with the baking sheet was the key to browning, it made sense that we should try to cut the broccoli in a way that maximized this contact. Working with half a bunch of broccoli, the right amount for two people, we tackled the crown first, lopping it off the stalk, flipping it onto its base, and cutting it crosswise into slabs. Sadly, the cross sections fell apart into a jumble of odd-sized florets that cooked unevenly. Perhaps wedges would work. We started over and cut the crown into uniform wedges. This was much more promising; the florets now held together. Turning our attention to the stalk, we trimmed off the tough exterior, then cut the stalk into ½-inch-thick pieces to help promote even cooking. These came out of the oven evenly cooked and with plenty of flavorful browning.

In the most successful recipes from our initial survey, the broccoli was dressed simply before roasting, with just a sprinkling of salt and pepper and a splash of olive oil, so we followed suit. For oven temperature, we tested everything from 350 degrees to 500 degrees. The upper end delivered the best browning (though it was still spotty), crispest texture, and most vibrant coloring; lower temperatures led to broccoli that was soft and a muddy, drab color. Yet while high heat delivered the best browning, it also increased the risk of charred florets. A couple of recipes suggested blanching or steaming the broccoli before roasting, but we found

that these batches tasted bland, as if the flavor had been washed away; besides, we didn't want to dirty an extra pot or pan for a simple weeknight side for two unless it was absolutely necessary. Eventually, we discovered that a preheated baking sheet cooked the broccoli quickly (in about 10 minutes) and crisped the florets without any charring.

But despite the blazing heat and the fact that we had solved the problem of charred florets, the broccoli still wasn't as browned as we'd hoped. We wondered if a scant amount of sugar added with the salt and pepper would promote browning. The results were the best yet: the blistered, bubbled, and browned stalks were sweet and full-flavored, and the crispy-tipped florets tasted even better, too. To brighten the flavor, we dressed them with a spritz of lemon juice.

Now that we had the basic method down, we looked to create some variations. After our roasted broccoli came out of the oven, we tossed it with a heady combination of olives, garlic, oregano, and a pinch of red pepper flakes. For another variation, we tossed the broccoli with a sautéed shallot, fennel seeds, and thinly shaved Parmesan cheese.

Roasted Broccoli

SERVES 2

Trim away the outer peel from the broccoli stalk; otherwise it will turn tough when cooked.

- ½ large bunch broccoli (about 1 pound)
- 2 tablespoons extra-virgin olive oil
- ¼ teaspoon sugar
- ¼ teaspoon salt
- ¼ teaspoon pepper
- Lemon wedges, for serving

1. Adjust an oven rack to the lowest position, place a foil-lined rimmed baking sheet on the rack, and heat the oven to 500 degrees. Cut the broccoli at the juncture of the florets and stalk, and remove the outer peel from the stalk. Cut the stalk into ½-inch-thick pieces. Cut the crown into 4 wedges if 3 to 4 inches in diameter, or 6 wedges if 4 to 5 inches in diameter. Toss the broccoli pieces with the oil, sugar, salt, and pepper in a bowl.

2. Carefully place the broccoli pieces, flat-side down, on the preheated baking sheet and roast until the stem

ROASTED BROCCOLI

pieces are well browned and tender and the florets are lightly browned, 9 to 11 minutes. Serve with the lemon wedges.

VARIATIONS

Roasted Broccoli with Olives, Garlic, Oregano, and Lemon

Cook 1 tablespoon extra-virgin olive oil, 3 thinly sliced garlic cloves, and ¼ teaspoon red pepper flakes in an 8-inch skillet over medium-low heat until the garlic begins to brown, 5 to 7 minutes. Off the heat, stir in 1 tablespoon chopped pitted kalamata olives, 1 teaspoon fresh lemon juice, and ½ teaspoon minced fresh oregano. Follow the recipe for Roasted Broccoli, tossing the broccoli with the olive mixture before serving.

Roasted Broccoli with Shallot, Fennel Seeds, and Parmesan

Use a vegetable peeler to shave the Parmesan.

Heat 2 teaspoons extra-virgin olive oil in an 8-inch skillet over medium heat until shimmering. Add 1 thinly sliced large shallot and cook until lightly browned, 5 to 7 minutes. Stir in ½ teaspoon coarsely chopped fennel seeds and continue to cook until the shallot is golden brown, 1 to 2 minutes longer. Follow the recipe for Roasted Broccoli, tossing the broccoli with the shallot mixture and ¼ cup thinly shaved Parmesan cheese before serving.

NOTES FROM THE TEST KITCHEN

REVIVING LIMP BROCCOLI

Broccoli seems to turn limp in the fridge in no time at all. We decided to find the best method to revive our sad stalks and tried standing them overnight in three different liquids: plain water, sugar water, and salt water. The sugar, we thought, might act like plant food and revive the vegetable, and the salt might work like a brine, adding moisture and seasoning. The next day, we examined the broccoli raw and then pan-roasted it. The broccoli placed in sugar water was nearly as limp as before, and the broccoli from the salted water was even more dehydrated. In both the cooked and raw states, the broccoli left standing in plain water was the clear winner. So, to keep your broccoli fresh, simply trim the stalk, stand it in an inch of water, and refrigerate it overnight.

BACON-BRAISED GREEN BEANS

GREEN BEANS ARE A STAPLE ON ANY SOUTHERN dinner table. Often, they're prepared the same way collard greens are cooked—simmered for hours in a big pot with water, a ham hock, sugar, and vinegar. Although these beans are more soft than crisp and their color is muted, they boast a deep, sweet, smoky pork flavor. We wanted to adapt this recipe for two, so we began by scaling down the cooking vessel, trading in the big pot for a small skillet.

With a 10-inch pan in hand, we examined the ingredient list. A ham hock needs to simmer for hours to truly offer up its flavor, but we didn't want to spend all day making a simple side for two. We considered some of the boneless pork options, such as salt pork, sausages, ham steak, and boneless pork ribs. But bacon stood out: It has a rich, smoky flavor, and most home cooks already have some in the fridge. For the green beans, we settled on half a pound, a good portion for two, which we trimmed and cut in half.

To impart the most smoky flavor possible to our beans, we cooked two slices of bacon (which we had halved so they'd fit comfortably in our small skillet) until crisp, set the bacon aside, and sautéed some onion in the rendered bacon fat. Next, we added the beans and just enough water to cover the bottom of the pan, brought the liquid to a boil, and simmered the beans, covered, over medium-low heat until they were tender, which took about 12 minutes. A few more minutes of uncovered simmering drove off any excess liquid. Finally, we added the reserved bacon back to the beans.

Although the bites with bacon were good, the bacon flavor just wasn't permeating the beans. For our next test, we left the half slices of bacon in the skillet while the beans cooked and removed the bacon, which had gone flabby and limp, before serving. This infused the green beans with the meaty flavor we wanted, but tasters missed the crisp texture of the bacon. The solution was to split the difference—after cooking the bacon, we kept one slice in the skillet with the beans and removed the other slice, crumbling it for the garnish. Now we had beans with meaty flavor and crisp bacon in every bite. Switching from water to chicken broth provided a further boost of meatiness.

For the vinegar, we preferred cider vinegar over other types for its slight fruitiness. We found it was best to add it twice—once to season the broth and at the end of cooking for brightness. A little brown sugar (preferred over white for its more complex flavor), minced thyme, salt, and pepper rounded out the flavors of our Southern-style braised green beans.

Bacon-Braised Green Beans

SERVES 2

Large, thick green beans hold up best in this preparation.

- 2 slices bacon
- ¼ cup minced onion
- ½ teaspoon minced fresh thyme or ⅛ teaspoon dried
- 8 ounces green beans, trimmed and halved (see note)
- ½ cup low-sodium chicken broth
- 2 teaspoons cider vinegar
- 1 teaspoon brown sugar
  Salt and pepper

1. Cut each slice of bacon in half. Cook the bacon pieces in a 10-inch skillet over medium heat until crisp, about 8 minutes. Transfer 2 pieces of the bacon to a paper towel–lined plate, leaving the remaining 2 pieces and fat in the pan. When the reserved bacon is cool enough to handle, crumble and set aside.

2. Add the onion to the pan with the remaining 2 pieces bacon and cook over medium heat until softened and lightly browned, 5 to 7 minutes. Stir in the thyme and cook until fragrant, about 30 seconds. Add the beans, broth, 1 teaspoon of the vinegar, sugar, and ¼ teaspoon salt, and bring to a simmer. Reduce the heat to medium-low, cover, and cook, stirring occasionally, until the beans are tender, 12 to 15 minutes.

3. Uncover the skillet and remove and discard the bacon pieces. Increase the heat to medium-high and cook until the liquid evaporates, 3 to 5 minutes. Off the heat, stir in the reserved crumbled bacon and the remaining 1 teaspoon vinegar. Season with salt and pepper to taste and serve.

CREOLE-STYLE SAUTÉED CORN

WE LOVE BUTTERED CORN ON THE COB, BUT occasionally this summer classic becomes a little ho-hum. We set out to develop a recipe for a simple sauté that would bring out the natural sweetness of corn and maintain its crisp crunch. For a fresh take on corn, we decided to pair it with bell pepper, onion, and garlic and to spice up the combination with a punch of hot sauce, creating a Creole-inspired side dish.

We started by preparing two ears of corn. To remove the kernels from the cobs, we found it best to place each ear on its end in a large bowl and cut the kernels off with a paring knife. This way, the cob is stabilized at the bottom of the bowl and the kernels end up in a confined space, rather than all over the counter.

With our kernels ready to go, it was time to address flavorings. We started with corn's best friend and melted a pat of butter in our skillet before adding half of a green bell pepper, chopped, along with a clove of garlic, minced thyme, and some scallions; tasters preferred scallions to minced yellow onion, which imparted a brash flavor that seemed out of place in this dish. We then added the corn kernels, browned them lightly for a pleasant nutty quality, and tasted. This dish was less than the sum of its parts.

Looking for ways to enhance this side, we turned to the test kitchen technique for extracting "milk" from corn cobs: We ran the back of a butter knife down the stripped cobs and collected the juice. We then added this corn milk to the skillet with the kernels. This simple step enhanced the corn flavor, imparted a slight creaminess, and helped meld the individual components of the dish. But something was still missing.

Looking to add a smoky, savory note to our dish, we went back to the beginning and started the sauté with two slices of bacon that we had chopped. Instead of sautéing the vegetables in butter, we cooked them in the bacon fat that remained in the pan after we had crisped our bacon. Now every bite of our sautéed corn had a deeper, richer flavor.

When the vegetables were tender, we sprinkled them with the crumbled bacon and seasoned the dish with a sprinkling of hot sauce and a handful of scallion greens. At last, we had a great alternative to corn on the cob—the sweet corn was pleasantly crisp, enhanced by the smoky bacon and a touch of heat, and we didn't have to get our hands dirty eating it.

Creole-Style Sautéed Corn

SERVES 2

Although we prefer the flavor of fresh corn, you can substitute 1½ cups frozen corn; don't thaw it before adding it to the pan. See page 131 for a recipe to use up the leftover green bell pepper.

  2 slices bacon, chopped fine
  ½ green bell pepper, stemmed, seeded, and
     chopped fine
  3 scallions, white parts minced, green parts sliced thin
  1 teaspoon minced fresh thyme or ¼ teaspoon dried
  1 small garlic clove, minced
  2 ears fresh corn, husks and silk removed,
     kernels cut from the cobs and corn milk reserved
     (see photos)
  ½ teaspoon hot sauce
     Salt and pepper

NOTES FROM THE TEST KITCHEN

STRIPPING AND MILKING CORN ON THE COB

1. To remove the corn kernels from the cob, stand the corn upright inside a large bowl and carefully cut the kernels from the cob using a paring knife.

2. Before discarding the cob, scrape any remaining milk from it, using the back of a butter knife, and reserve with the kernels.

---

1. Cook the bacon in a 10-inch nonstick skillet over medium heat until crisp, about 8 minutes. Using a slotted spoon, transfer the bacon to a paper towel–lined plate, leaving the fat in the pan. Return the skillet to medium heat, add the bell pepper and scallion whites, and cook until softened, about 5 minutes. Stir in the thyme and garlic and cook until fragrant, about 30 seconds.

2. Add the corn kernels and corn milk to the skillet and cook until tender and lightly browned, 5 to 7 minutes. Off the heat, stir in the reserved bacon, scallion greens, and hot sauce. Season with salt and pepper to taste and serve.

SAUTÉED SWISS CHARD

LEAFY GREENS FALL INTO TWO DISTINCT categories—tender and mild-flavored, and tough and assertively flavored—that should be handled quite differently. Swiss chard belongs in the tender category, along with spinach and beet greens, all of which taste of the earth and minerals but are still rather delicate. We wanted a preparation for Swiss chard that would bring out its earthy flavor but wouldn't compromise its texture. Because chard has a mild flavor and just a touch of bitterness, it needs little adornment and can pair easily with a wide range of entrées. Plus, a single bunch of chard is the perfect amount for two when served alongside a main course.

Two main varieties of chard are available at the supermarket. There's green chard, which has medium to dark green leaves with thick white stalks, and red or rhubarb chard, which has brilliant red stalks and is most similar to beet greens (not much of a stretch, considering chard is related to beets). Either one will work well here, but the rhubarb chard has a stronger flavor than the green chard.

Both the chard stems and leaves are delicious cooked; there's no need to discard the tougher stems, as some cooks do. But the heartier stems do need to be cooked longer than the leaves, so to prepare the chard, we began by cutting the leaves from the stems. Then we chopped the stems and the leaves and set the leaves aside for the time being.

With our chard trimmed and chopped, we tackled the cooking method. Both boiling and steaming were out, as these methods produced greens that were brightly colored but mushy and bland. Clearly these tender greens, with their high moisture content, did not need any extra liquid to cook. We decided to try sautéing.

We heated a small amount of olive oil, which provided a neutral flavor base, and added the chopped stems to the skillet first since they take a little more time to cook. In just five minutes, the stems had softened. We tossed in the chopped leaves, covered the pan to retain some moisture, and let the greens wilt and become tender. Another five minutes passed, and the greens were just right. We took a shortcut by not fully drying the leaves after washing them, and this omission paid off—slightly dried, damp greens added just enough moisture to ensure that the greens were perfectly tender.

Our sautéed chard was tender and hearty, but the flavor needed a kick. We tried again, this time adding some minced onion to the skillet with the stems; the onion lent a sweet flavor and balanced the slightly more assertive and earthy taste of the chard. We normally favor the addition of garlic and lemon juice to sautéed greens, and this dish proved no exception. A handful of minced thyme and a final drizzle of olive oil were all our chard needed to become a new weeknight favorite.

Sautéed Swiss Chard

SERVES 2

Don't dry the chard greens completely after washing; a little extra water clinging to the leaves will help them wilt when cooking in step 2.

- 2 tablespoons plus 1 teaspoon extra-virgin olive oil
- 1 bunch Swiss chard (about 12 ounces), stems and leaves separated, stems chopped medium and leaves cut into ½-inch pieces (see note; see photos)
- ¼ cup minced onion
   Salt
- 1 garlic clove, minced
- 1 teaspoon minced fresh thyme
- 1 teaspoon fresh lemon juice
   Pepper

1. Heat 2 tablespoons of the oil in a 12-inch skillet over medium heat until shimmering. Add the chard stems, onion, and ¼ teaspoon salt, and cook until softened and lightly browned, 5 to 7 minutes.

2. Stir in the garlic and thyme and cook until fragrant, about 30 seconds. Stir in the chard leaves, cover, and cook until the chard is wilted and tender, about 5 minutes.

3. Off the heat, stir in the lemon juice and season with salt and pepper to taste. Transfer to a serving dish, drizzle with the remaining 1 teaspoon oil, and serve.

NOTES FROM THE TEST KITCHEN

PREPARING SWISS CHARD AND HEARTY GREENS

1. The leaves and stems of Swiss chard and other hearty greens cook at different rates and must be separated prior to cooking. To do this, cut away the leafy green portion from the stem using a chef's knife.

2. Then stack several leaves on top of one another and slice the leaves crosswise in the desired thickness.

3. Finally, gather together the stems and trim and chop them.

TANGY APPLE-CABBAGE SLAW

WHEN MOST PEOPLE THINK OF COLESLAW, THE image that comes to mind is a massive bowl loaded up with pounds of shredded cabbage, several grated carrots, and a pint of mayonnaise. But it doesn't have to be this way—coleslaw's tidy ingredient list makes it easy enough to scale down for two. We also thought a fresher-flavored mayo-free slaw might be in order, one with an oil and vinegar dressing and refreshing bites of apple—a natural pairing with cabbage. We set out to create our own recipe for a tangy slaw that was scaled down to serve two, not 12.

USE IT UP: CABBAGE

Beer-Braised Cabbage
SERVES 2

Strongly flavored beers can make the dish bitter; mild American lagers, such as Budweiser, work best here.

- 2 **tablespoons unsalted butter**
- 1 **small onion, minced**
- ½ **cup beer (see note)**
- 1 **tablespoon whole grain mustard**
- ¼ **teaspoon dried thyme**
- ¾ **small head green cabbage (12 ounces), cored and sliced thin (about 6 cups; see page 241)**
- 2 **teaspoons cider vinegar**
  Salt and pepper

1. Melt the butter in a 12-inch skillet over medium heat. Add the onion and cook until softened, about 5 minutes. Stir in the beer, mustard, and thyme, bring to a simmer, and cook until thickened slightly, 1 to 2 minutes.

2. Stir in the cabbage and vinegar, cover, and cook, stirring occasionally, until the cabbage is wilted and tender, about 8 minutes. Season with salt and pepper to taste and serve.

We began by figuring out just how much cabbage we would need for our scaled-down slaw. For ample servings for two diners, we started with a quarter of a head of green cabbage, which yielded 2 cups of chopped cabbage.

Since cabbage is a relatively watery vegetable, our standard test kitchen protocol calls for salting cut cabbage to draw out excess moisture before dressing it; this prevents the moisture from being released into the dressing later on, thus diluting the dressing and making for a watered-down slaw. Salting the cabbage also wilts it slightly, improving its texture and preventing that unpleasant chewiness. We sprinkled our chopped cabbage with some salt and, after about an hour, it was wilted. After rinsing off the salt and drying the cabbage, we were ready to proceed.

We tested several varieties of apple, but most were mushy and bland when dressed. The one exception was Granny Smith, which tasters loved for its reliably sturdy crunch and tart bite. Grating the apple negated its crunch, but cutting it into matchsticks meant it could be easily mixed with the cabbage while retaining its crispness. Half a large apple provided the right sweet-savory balance with our cabbage.

The classic dressing for this type of slaw calls for sugar, white vinegar, vegetable oil, and various seasonings. We tried swapping out the granulated sugar for more flavorful brown sugar, maple syrup, and honey, but in the end nothing beat the clean sweetness of regular sugar. Cider vinegar contributed a fruity flavor lacking in the traditional white vinegar. A pinch of red pepper flakes, a sliced scallion, and a touch of mustard added some punch. At this point, the dressing tasted pretty good, but it wasn't clinging to the cabbage and apples.

As with our Warm Asian Cabbage Salad with Chicken (page 141), we decided to cook the dressing and pour it—still hot—over the cabbage. We were pleased to discover that the cabbage and apple more readily absorbed a hot dressing—especially if the slaw was allowed to sit for an hour before serving.

This tangy slaw provides a welcome change of pace from the usual mayo slaws and adds a lively note to any dinner.

Tangy Apple-Cabbage Slaw

SERVES 2

Look for a yellowish or light green Granny Smith apple—they are riper (and better-tasting) than dark green Grannies. See page 240 for a recipe to use up the leftover cabbage.

¼   **small head green cabbage (4 ounces), cored and chopped fine (about 2 cups; see photos)**
     Salt
½   **Granny Smith apple, peeled, cored, and cut into thin matchsticks (see note; see photos)**
1   **scallion, sliced thin**
2   **tablespoons cider vinegar**
1   **tablespoon sugar**
1   **tablespoon vegetable oil**
1   **teaspoon Dijon mustard**
     Pinch red pepper flakes
     Pepper

1. Toss the cabbage with ¼ teaspoon salt in a colander set in a bowl. Let sit until wilted, about 1 hour. Rinse the cabbage with cold water, then drain and dry well with paper towels. Transfer to a medium bowl and stir in the apple and scallion.

2. Bring the vinegar, sugar, oil, mustard, and red pepper flakes to a simmer in a small saucepan over medium heat. Pour the mixture over the cabbage and toss to coat. Cover and refrigerate until chilled, at least 1 hour, or up to 1 day. (If refrigerated for longer than 2 hours, let sit at room temperature for 15 minutes before serving.) Season with salt and pepper to taste and serve.

NOTES FROM THE TEST KITCHEN

PREPARING CABBAGE FOR SLAW

1. Cut the cabbage into quarters, then trim and discard the hard core.

2. Separate the cabbage into small stacks of leaves that flatten when pressed.

3. Cut each stack of cabbage leaves into thin strips, about ¼ inch thick. Then, for chopped slaws, cut the strips into ¼-inch pieces.

CUTTING AN APPLE FOR SLAW

1. Cut half of a cored apple into ¼-inch-thick planks.

2. Stack the planks and cut them into thin matchsticks.

GUACAMOLE SALAD

YOU'D BE HARD-PRESSED TO FIND SOMEONE WHO doesn't love guacamole. The mashed avocado dip is always the first thing to go at parties. Recently, we came across a recipe that turned the bright, flavorful ingredients of guacamole into a salad. We were intrigued and set out to make this lively salad that might pair well with simply prepared dishes like grilled steak, chicken, or fish.

We headed into the test kitchen to try out the handful of recipes we'd found in our research. For a dish that seemed simple, the results were disappointing. Most of the salads were encumbered by ingredients that did little for the dish, such as black beans, red bell pepper, and cucumber. Even the best recipe we tested—a straightforward combination of tomato, avocado, cilantro, red onion, garlic, and jalapeño with a lime vinaigrette—needed fine-tuning.

Running through the list of ingredients, we started with the easiest item first: the avocado. One avocado was the perfect quantity for two, so we pitted it and chopped it into bite-sized pieces. For the tomatoes, we turned to grape tomatoes and cherry tomatoes, which have reliable flavor and juiciness year-round. For this salad, we preferred grape tomatoes, which held their shape when mixed with the other ingredients, but both work fine. We settled on 1 cup of grape tomatoes, which we halved so they'd be evenly distributed throughout the salad.

For more potent flavor, we tested onion and garlic. Tasters thought raw onion—even sweet red onion and shallot—was too harsh, but they favored the milder flavor of scallions. We sliced two scallions and toned down their flavor slightly by letting them mellow in some lime juice for a few minutes before combining them with the avocado. Tasters also liked the inclusion of some minced garlic, which gave the salad some depth.

At this point, our salad needed a punch of heat. Jalapeño is standard in guacamole, and we found it important in our salad as well, for both flavor and textural contrast. Instead of mincing the jalapeño, we sliced it into thin strips, ensuring bites with good crunch and a moderate level of heat.

At last, we had arrived at the dressing, which would coat all the ingredients of our salad and help to unify their flavors. We supplemented 1 tablespoon of lime juice with a teaspoon of zest to boost the lime flavor without adding acidity. A tablespoon of olive oil rounded out the dressing, and a small handful of minced cilantro added brightness to the salad.

Tasters liked the combination of flavors and textures, but after five minutes, liquid pooled in the salad bowl and the flavors became diluted. The tomatoes were at fault: They were giving off a lot of moisture. The next time we made the salad, we tossed the tomatoes with a little salt and let them drain in a colander for 15 minutes. Meanwhile, we prepped the rest of the ingredients. When we assembled the dish, we were happy to find that the flavors were assertive and the salad was lightly coated in dressing, not drowning in juice.

Finally, we had elevated guacamole to more than just a dip—and it was every bit as delicious.

Guacamole Salad
SERVES 2

To make this dish spicier, add the chile seeds to the dressing in step 2. You can substitute 6 ounces cherry tomatoes, halved, for the grape tomatoes. Because the avocado will discolor upon standing, the salad should be prepared no more than a few hours ahead.

- 6 ounces grape tomatoes (about 1 cup), halved (see note)
  Salt
- 2 scallions, sliced thin
- 1 tablespoon fresh lime juice plus 1 teaspoon grated lime zest
- 1 small garlic clove, minced
  Pepper
- 1 tablespoon olive oil
- 1 ripe avocado, halved, pitted, and cut into ½-inch pieces (see page 244)
- 1 jalapeño chile, stemmed, seeded (see note), and sliced thin
- 2 tablespoons minced fresh cilantro

1. Toss the tomatoes and ¼ teaspoon salt in a colander set in a bowl. Let drain for 15 minutes.

GUACAMOLE SALAD

2. Meanwhile, combine the scallions, lime juice, lime zest, garlic, ¼ teaspoon salt, and ¼ teaspoon pepper in a medium bowl. Let sit for 5 minutes, then slowly whisk in the oil.

3. Add the drained tomatoes, avocado, jalapeño, and cilantro to the bowl with the dressing and toss to combine. Season with salt and pepper to taste and serve.

NOTES FROM THE TEST KITCHEN

PREPARING AN AVOCADO

1. After slicing the avocado in half around the pit, lodge the edge of the knife blade into the pit and twist to remove. Use a large wooden spoon to pry the pit safely off the knife.

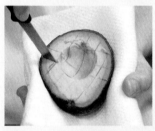

2. Using a dish towel to hold the avocado steady, make ½-inch crosshatch incisions in the flesh of each avocado half with a knife, cutting down to but not through the skin.

3. Separate the diced flesh from the skin with a soup spoon inserted between the skin and the flesh, gently scooping out the avocado cubes.

GREEK RICE SALAD

RICE SALAD IS AN EASY WAY TO TRANSFORM PLAIN white rice into a lively side dish. A well-made rice salad should have light, fluffy grains that are neither mushy nor dry and just the right amount of vinaigrette—not so much that the rice is slippery, and not so little that the dish is dry and flavorless. We set out to make a rice salad for two, and we liked the idea of including the classic ingredients of a Greek salad (cucumbers, tomatoes, feta, olives) to give our dish a Mediterranean tone.

While the concept of a rice salad seems quite simple, the texture of rice—both short- and long-grain—can quickly throw it off target. Both short- and medium-grain rice hold up relatively well as they cool, but they have an inherent stickiness that is out of place in a rice salad. Long-grain rice, though texturally promising when just cooked, tends to turn into a solid, clumpy mess at room temperature. We decided to hedge our bets and proceed with the latter option, hoping to solve the clumping problem. To achieve a tender, fluffy, and light rice salad, we needed a cooking method for long-grain rice that would preserve its fresh-from-the-pan characteristics once cooled.

We started by cooking long-grain rice using the conventional absorption method (simmered in a covered pot with just enough water). As expected, once cooled, the rice solidified into a sticky mass. We tried rinsing the rice before cooking to remove some excess starch. This made for a slight improvement, but it still didn't produce the fluffy texture we wanted once the rice had cooled.

We needed to get rid of even more starch, so we tried cooking the rice as we would pasta: boiling it in a large volume of water until it was just cooked through and then draining it. After a few tests, we found that the rice prepared this way had the light and separate consistency we were looking for and stayed fluffy after it had cooled. But there was one nagging problem: Now the rice was somewhat waterlogged. We came up with a simple solution—we spread the drained rice on a baking sheet to cool off, creating a large surface area that allowed the excess moisture to evaporate. Spreading out the rice also helped it cool more quickly and clump less. After a few tests, we determined that ⅓ cup of rice resulted in the right quantity of cooked rice for two people.

Now that our rice was ready, we could incorporate the other ingredients. First, we prepared our vegetables. We peeled, seeded, and chopped half a cucumber, and we halved some grape tomatoes. Normally we salt tomatoes to extract extra moisture, but we felt that wasn't necessary here because any juice released from the tomatoes would just help to flavor the rice.

As for the dressing, in a few recipes we found the cooled rice was combined with the vegetables before the whole salad was tossed with extra-virgin olive oil and vinegar. But we found that the flavors in these salads never really melded, and the grains were oily. To combat both of these problems, we created a simple vinaigrette (with extra-virgin olive oil, red wine vinegar, and a touch of dried oregano) but added two extra ingredients: some honey and a little crumbled feta cheese. Not only did the feta and honey add flavor and sweetness, but they also helped the vinaigrette emulsify, so that when we dressed the salad, the rice didn't become slick and greasy.

To ensure flavorful vegetables, we tossed them with the dressing and let them sit while we cooked the rice. After we'd combined the rice with the vegetables and dressing, we sprinkled the salad with another handful of crumbled feta for a tangy, briny kick. Now our salad was bright, light, and refreshing.

Greek Rice Salad

SERVES 2

In step 1, do not marinate the vegetables for more than 1 hour or the salad will become soggy. You can substitute 3 ounces cherry tomatoes, halved, for the grape tomatoes.

- 1 ounce feta cheese, crumbled (about ¼ cup)
- 1 tablespoon extra-virgin olive oil
- 1 tablespoon red wine vinegar
- 1 teaspoon honey
- ⅛ teaspoon dried oregano
- 3 ounces grape tomatoes (about ½ cup), halved (see note)
- ½ cucumber, peeled, halved lengthwise, seeded, and cut into ½-inch pieces
- 2 tablespoons chopped pitted kalamata olives
- 1 scallion, sliced thin
- ⅓ cup long-grain rice
    Salt and pepper

1. Whisk 2 tablespoons of the feta, oil, vinegar, honey, and oregano together in a medium bowl until mostly smooth. Stir in the tomatoes, cucumber, olives, and scallion; set aside.

2. Bring 2 quarts water to a boil in a large saucepan. Add the rice and 1 tablespoon salt and cook until just tender, 12 to 14 minutes. Drain the rice, spread on a rimmed baking sheet, and cool to room temperature.

3. Add the cooled rice and remaining 2 tablespoons feta to the bowl with the vegetable mixture and toss to combine. Season with salt and pepper to taste and serve.

TOASTED ORZO WITH PEAS AND MINT

ALTHOUGH MOST COMMONLY BOILED, ORZO, WHICH is a small rice-shaped pasta, can actually be used in a variety of ways, since it can fill the role of either grain or pasta. We decided to try our hand at using orzo in a pilaf, a dish that usually features rice as the starring ingredient. We wanted the texture of a true pilaf, with separate, distinct pieces of orzo. While lots of ingredients pair nicely with orzo's compact, even shape, we especially liked the idea of a dish featuring peas and mint: The dish would be bright, fresh, and redolent of spring.

In a pilaf, the rice is sautéed, or toasted, in fat as a way to give the grain flavor prior to cooking it in liquid. Following this method, we began our testing by softening some onion and garlic in oil, then adding a small amount of orzo (⅔ cup was a good portion for two as a side dish) and sautéing until lightly browned. We then added 2 cups of chicken broth and ½ cup of water (all chicken broth made the dish too salty) and simmered until the orzo was tender before stirring in the peas and mint. As with our Baked Shrimp and Orzo (page 27), we found that stirring the orzo regularly as it cooked caused the release of too much starch into the liquid, making the orzo creamy and risotto-like—not what we had in mind for this dish. For our next test, we tried stirring the orzo with restraint as it cooked—just three times in 15 minutes, which was enough to keep the orzo from clumping. We now had distinct, not clumpy, grains of orzo.

Our texture was spot-on, but with the orzo as the starring ingredient, tasters thought it should have a more distinct flavor. Sautéing the orzo with the aromatics and oil had deepened its flavor, but not enough. We wondered about toasting the orzo in a dry skillet, a method the test kitchen employs to coax more flavor out of nuts and spices. With the skillet empty, we could toast the orzo for a full 8 minutes, until it turned an even golden brown, without burning it. The orzo toasted in a dry skillet had a deeper flavor than the orzo toasted in oil and possessed the full, nutty flavor that the dish needed.

After toasting the orzo, we set it aside and sautéed the aromatics. This time we ditched the oil and used butter instead; we found that the butter was a better complement to the peas and gave the dish a touch of silkiness. We then returned the orzo to the skillet along with the broth, water, and a little white wine for complexity. When the orzo was tender, we folded in ⅓ cup of frozen peas and some mint and cooked the orzo for another minute, just until the peas were warm and tender. The dish was almost perfect, but it needed a small flavor boost. Some lemon juice and lemon zest, stirred in with the peas and mint, further brightened the flavors and reinforced the fresh, springtime theme of our dish.

NOTES FROM THE TEST KITCHEN

ALL ABOUT FROZEN PEAS
For bright green, sweet peas in our Toasted Orzo with Peas and Mint, we depend on the frozen variety. Not only are they more convenient than their fresh, in-the-pod comrades, but they taste better. While this may seem counterintuitive, there is a good reason behind it.

Green peas lose a substantial portion of their nutrients within 24 hours of being picked. This is why most "fresh" peas sold at the supermarket taste starchy and bland—these not-so-fresh peas might be several days old, depending on where they came from and how long they were kept in the cooler. Frozen peas, on the other hand, are picked, cleaned, sorted, and frozen within several hours of harvest, which helps to preserve their delicate sugars and flavors.

Finding good frozen peas is not hard. After tasting peas from the two major national frozen food purveyors, Birds Eye and Green Giant, along with some from a smaller organic company, Cascadian Farm, tasters found little difference among them. All of the peas were sweet and fresh, with a bright green color. So unless you grow your own or can stop by your local farm stand for fresh-picked, you're better off cruising up the frozen food aisle for a bag of frozen peas.

THE BEST CHICKEN BROTH
Store-bought chicken broth is a real time-saver, but which brand is best? Our winning broth, **Swanson Certified Organic Free Range Chicken Broth**, has two important characteristics: less than 700 milligrams of sodium per serving (others contain up to 1,350 milligrams per serving) and a short ingredient list that includes vegetables such as carrots, celery, and onions. Don't be intimidated by the large 32-ounce carton; extra chicken broth can be used in many applications, from cooking rice and grains to making soups and stews.

Toasted Orzo with Peas and Mint
SERVES 2

In step 1, watch the orzo closely toward the end of the toasting time—it can quickly go from browned to burned.

- ⅔ **cup orzo**
- 1 **tablespoon unsalted butter**
- ¼ **cup minced onion**
- 1 **garlic clove, minced**
- 2 **cups low-sodium chicken broth**
- ½ **cup water**
- 2 **tablespoons dry white wine**
- ⅓ **cup frozen peas**
- 1 **tablespoon minced fresh mint**
- 1 **teaspoon fresh lemon juice plus**
  - ½ **teaspoon grated lemon zest**
- **Salt and pepper**

1. Toast the orzo in a 10-inch skillet over medium heat, stirring frequently, until golden brown, 6 to 8 minutes; transfer to a bowl. Melt the butter in the skillet. Add the onion and cook until softened, about 5 minutes. Stir in the garlic and cook until fragrant, about 30 seconds.

2. Add the toasted orzo, broth, water, and wine to the pan, and bring to a simmer. Reduce the heat to medium-low and cook, stirring every 5 minutes, until the liquid has been absorbed and the orzo is tender, about 15 minutes.

3. Stir in the peas, mint, lemon juice, and lemon zest, and cook until heated through, about 1 minute. Season with salt and pepper to taste and serve.

LEMON POTATOES

ON THE MENU AT ANY GREEK RESTAURANT, YOU'RE likely to find lemony, garlicky, golden potatoes—a tasty cross between home fries and roasted potatoes. To get a creamy white interior and crispy browned crust, many recipes call for covering potato chunks with a mixture of olive oil, water, and lemon juice, baking them in a slow oven for up to 1½ hours, then crisping them on a hot griddle. This method makes sense at a restaurant where the potatoes are finished to order, but it's far too time-consuming and laborious when cooking at home for two. We set out to see if we could develop a stream-lined, small-scale version of Greek-style lemon potatoes.

Right off the bat, we knew that low-starch, waxy red potatoes were the best potatoes to use because they hold their shape when cooked. We found that 12 ounces of red potatoes was the right amount for two. For an attractive presentation and easy eating, we sliced the potatoes in half.

For our first test, we decided to use the oven alone and increase the cooking time, baking the potatoes until the liquid evaporated. While the method was easy and the potatoes had good lemon flavor, it still took a good chunk of time to cook the spuds, and even with the extra time in the oven, they lacked a crisp crust. Next, we tried sautéing the potatoes in a skillet, then tossing them with lemon juice and water and letting the excess liquid evaporate. Now the potatoes had great color, but the lemon flavor was washed out. To combine the best facets of each method, we first skillet-simmered the potatoes in water and lemon juice, covered, until tender, then uncovered the pan to let the liquid evaporate. Then we added a little olive oil and browned the potatoes.

At last, our potatoes had good lemon flavor and a crispy crust, but we found that the cut sides of the pota-toes burned slightly and stuck to the pan. Switching to a nonstick skillet and rinsing the raw potatoes to wash off extra starch solved the problem.

For the simmering liquid, an even ratio of water to lemon juice proved too puckery. After several tests, we went with ¾ cup of water to just 1 tablespoon of lemon juice, plus a little grated zest. For added richness and flavor, we replaced the water with chicken broth and added two smashed garlic cloves to the simmering liquid. This worked well, but tasters thought the flavor still needed a punch. We decided to reserve the lemon zest and one of the garlic cloves and toss them, along with a sprinkling of parsley, with the cooked potatoes; this did the trick.

Finally, we had Greek-inspired potatoes that were as bright, creamy, and crispy as the original, but they were now suited to the home kitchen.

Pan-Roasted Lemon Potatoes

SERVES 2

We prefer to use small red potatoes (1 to 2 inches in diameter) in this recipe; however, larger red potatoes, cut into 1-inch pieces, can be substituted. Be sure to rinse the potatoes until the water runs clear to remove excess starch.

- 12 ounces small red potatoes (about 4), halved, rinsed, and drained (see note)
- ¾ cup low-sodium chicken broth
- 1 tablespoon fresh lemon juice plus ¾ teaspoon grated lemon zest
- 1 garlic clove, peeled and smashed, plus 1 garlic clove, minced
     Salt
- 2 tablespoons extra-virgin olive oil
- 1 tablespoon minced fresh parsley
     Pepper

1. Bring the potatoes, broth, lemon juice, smashed garlic clove, and ¼ teaspoon salt to a simmer in a 10-inch nonstick skillet over high heat. Reduce the heat

---

NOTES FROM THE TEST KITCHEN

BUYING AND STORING POTATOES

When buying potatoes, look for firm specimens that are free of green spots, sprouts, cracks, and other blemishes. We generally prefer to buy loose potatoes, so we can see what we are getting. Stay away from potatoes in plastic bags, which can act like greenhouses and cause potatoes to sprout, soften, and rot.

At home, keep potatoes in a cool, dark, dry place and away from onions, which give off gases that will hasten sprouting. Stored in a cool, dark place, most varieties should keep for several months. The exception is new potatoes—because of their thinner skins, they will keep no more than one month. To further extend their shelf life, we tried storing potatoes in a cool, dark place with an apple—a common old wives' tale that we wanted to put to the test. We found that because of the ethylene gas the apple released, it did indeed boost the storage time; these potatoes lasted almost two weeks longer.

to medium-low, cover, and cook until the potatoes are just tender, 12 to 15 minutes.

2. Uncover, increase the heat to medium, and cook, stirring occasionally, until the liquid has evaporated, about 5 minutes. Remove and discard the smashed garlic clove and add the oil to the pan. Arrange all the potatoes cut-side down and continue to cook until deep golden brown, about 5 minutes longer.

3. Transfer the potatoes to a bowl and gently toss with the lemon zest, minced garlic, and parsley. Season with salt and pepper to taste and serve.

SOUR CREAM AND ONION SMASHED POTATOES

MASHED POTATOES ARE THE DEFINITION OF COMFORT food. But who wants to peel potatoes and get out the ricer for a quick weeknight supper for two? More rustic in appearance but quicker and easier to prepare, smashed potatoes are a satisfying stand-in. Add some sour cream and onions, and you've got a slam-dunk on your hands. Unfortunately, most of the smashed potatoes we've tried had an identity crisis, running the gamut from lean and dry to practically mashed. Our goals were clear: We wanted chunks of potato textured with skins, bound by rich, creamy puree, and infused with bold but balanced sour cream and onion flavor. And we wanted to make just enough for two, so we weren't stuck with a week of leftovers.

Putting aside the issue of incorporating the sour cream and onion, we focused on the potatoes. Using the test kitchen's standard mashed potato add-ins—melted butter and half-and-half—we smashed our way through four different varieties: russet, all-purpose, Yukon gold, and Red Bliss. The russets and all-purpose potatoes had strong potato flavor, but their dry texture caused them to crumble quickly when smashed, and their skins were too thick and tough to create a nice counterpoint to their smashed interiors. The texture of the waxy Yukon golds was slightly firmer, but these potatoes broke down too much when smashed. The moist, low-starch red potatoes won out with their tender, thin skins, which worked nicely in a chunky potato side dish. Eight ounces of red potatoes gave us two skimpy portions, so we settled on 12 ounces (about four small potatoes) as a good amount for two.

We tried cooking the potatoes whole and cut into 1-inch chunks. Even though cutting the potatoes into chunks reduced the cooking time, the end result was leaden, soggy smashed potatoes with diluted flavor. Cooked whole, the potatoes retained their creamy texture, as less potato surface was exposed to the water.

Up to this point, we had incorporated our flavorings by draining the potatoes and breaking them up with a rubber spatula before folding in 2 tablespoons each of melted butter and half-and-half (which tasters preferred to cream or milk) until a chunky yet creamy mixture was achieved. Our next step was to add the sour cream, but by the time it was fully incorporated, the potatoes had turned gluey. After several tests, we found that stirring the sour cream directly into the melted butter and the half-and-half before adding the mixture to the cooked potatoes meant less stirring altogether, eliminating the glueyness caused by overworking the spuds. This technique also helped to meld the flavors. For 12 ounces of potatoes, ⅓ cup of sour cream provided sufficient tanginess without being overwhelming.

As for the onion, minced chives proved to be too discreet, no matter how much we added. We had better results with sliced scallions, especially when we sautéed the whites in the melted butter before mixing the butter and scallions with the half-and-half and sour cream. Adding the raw scallion greens at the end added crunch, bite, and color.

Sour Cream and Onion Smashed Potatoes
SERVES 2

If the potatoes are too thick after you fold in the sour cream mixture in step 3, stir in additional half-and-half, 1 tablespoon at a time, until they reach the desired consistency. We prefer to use small red potatoes (1 to 2 inches in diameter) in this recipe; however, if only larger potatoes are available, increase the cooking time by about 10 minutes. See page 249 for a recipe to use up the leftover sour cream.

12   **ounces small red potatoes (about 4) (see note)**
     Salt
2   **tablespoons unsalted butter**
2   **scallions, white parts minced, green parts sliced thin**
⅓   **cup sour cream**
2   **tablespoons half-and-half, plus more as needed**
     Pepper

1. Bring the potatoes, ½ teaspoon salt, and 2 quarts water to a simmer in a medium saucepan over high heat. Reduce the heat to medium and cook until the potatoes are tender, 15 to 25 minutes.

2. Meanwhile, melt the butter in a small saucepan over medium-low heat. Add the scallion whites and cook until softened, 2 to 3 minutes. Whisk in the sour cream, half-and-half, ¼ teaspoon salt, and ⅛ teaspoon pepper until smooth. Remove from the heat and cover to keep warm.

3. Drain the potatoes, return them to the pot, and let the steam escape for 2 minutes. Using a rubber spatula, break the potatoes into large chunks. Fold in the sour cream mixture until incorporated and only small chunks of potato remain. Fold in the scallion greens, season with salt and pepper to taste, and serve.

USE IT UP: SOUR CREAM

Ranch Dressing
MAKES ABOUT 1 CUP

Any combination of soft, leafy herbs, such as cilantro, dill, tarragon, or parsley, can be used in this recipe. This creamy dressing is great for crisp lettuce, such as iceberg and romaine, or served as a dip alongside crudités or potato chips. The dressing can be refrigerated in an airtight container for up to 4 days; whisk to recombine before using.

⅔ cup sour cream

3 tablespoons milk

2 tablespoons minced fresh cilantro, dill, tarragon, or parsley (see note)

1 small shallot, minced

2 teaspoons white wine vinegar

½ teaspoon garlic powder

¼ teaspoon salt

¼ teaspoon pepper

Pinch cayenne pepper

Pinch sugar

Whisk all of the ingredients together in a bowl until smooth.

EASIER FRENCH FRIES

WHILE EVERYONE LOVES CRISP, SALT-FLECKED FRENCH fries, few of us like to cook them. The ingredient list may be simple (potatoes, oil, salt), but the most common method requires rinsing the potatoes to remove excess starch, soaking them in ice water to encourage more even cooking, and deep-frying them in a vat of oil—not once but twice. First the potatoes are fried in moderately hot oil to cook through, then they're fried in hotter oil to render them golden and crisp. In addition to being time-consuming and messy, this technique requires 2 to 3 quarts of oil, which seems wasteful, particularly if you are making just enough fries for two. Over the years, cooks have tried and failed to find an easier method. Nevertheless, we were determined to achieve crisp, slender fries with a tender interior and earthy potato flavor, and without the hassle.

While researching alternative techniques, we came across an impossibly simple-sounding recipe that skipped the rinsing and soaking steps. Bucking tradition even more, it called for submerging the potatoes in a few cups of room-temperature (or "cold") oil, rather than quarts of bubbling hot oil, and frying the spuds over high heat until browned. It seemed worth a try.

We peeled 1½ pounds of russets (our favorite potato for frying because its high starch content translates to crispiness) and cut them into ¼-inch-thick batons. This might sound like a lot of potato, but after squaring off the sides to make for evenly shaped potatoes, we were left with just the right amount for two. For cooking oil, we like both peanut oil and vegetable oil because of their high smoke points and neutral flavor. We combined the potatoes with just enough oil to cover them (3 cups) in a saucepan. Granted, 3 cups of oil is not an amount to sneeze at, but it's still far less than what is used in typical recipes. We cranked up the heat and about 25 minutes later pulled out golden fries that looked identical to classic fries and tasted pretty darn good, albeit a little tough in texture.

Intrigued, we approached our science editor, who surmised that by starting with cold oil, we gave the potato interior an opportunity to soften and cook before the exterior started to crisp. Despite the fact that the temperature of the oil never got as hot as in the traditional method, it was still high enough to trigger the same reactions that led to a golden, nicely crisped crust.

EASIER FRENCH FRIES

Our fries were pretty good, but we still had the nagging issue of toughness to resolve. We wondered if the prolonged cooking time was having an adverse effect on the high-starch russets. We turned to Yukon golds, which have less starch and more water than russets, and found that they worked well in this preparation. The exteriors of the fries were now crisp, with none of the toughness of the russets, and the interiors were creamy. Clearly, the moister, less starchy composition of the Yukon golds could better withstand the long cooking time of this approach. Plus, Yukon golds have such a thin skin that they could be used unpeeled, making the recipe even easier. As an added bonus, our cold-start method produced fries that contained about a third less oil than conventional, twice-fried spuds.

The only remaining problem was fries sticking to the bottom of the pot (and each other). We found that if we didn't touch the spuds for about 20 minutes after putting them in the pot, enough of a crust formed that we could stir them with no ill effect.

NOTES FROM THE TEST KITCHEN

CUTTING POTATOES FOR FRENCH FRIES

1. Square off the potato by cutting a ¼-inch-thick slice from each of its four long sides.

2. Cut the potato lengthwise into ¼-inch-thick planks.

3. Stack three to four planks and cut into ¼-inch-thick batons. Repeat with the remaining planks.

For a final touch, we took a moment to whip up a creamy dipping sauce that provided a more exciting alternative to ketchup. Finally, we had perfect French fries that were remarkably easy to cook and required a minimal amount of oil.

Easier French Fries
SERVES 2

You will need a saucepan with a 4-quart capacity for this recipe; if your pan is larger you may need more oil to cover the potatoes. If desired, serve with Belgian-Style Dipping Sauce (recipe follows) or Garlic Mayonnaise (page 223).

> 1½ **pounds Yukon gold potatoes (about 3 medium), sides squared off, cut lengthwise into ¼-inch-thick batons (see photos)**
> 3 **cups peanut oil or vegetable oil**
> **Kosher salt**

1. Combine the potatoes and oil in a large saucepan. Cook over high heat until the oil has reached a rolling boil, about 5 minutes. Continue to cook, without stirring, until the potatoes are limp but the exteriors are beginning to firm, 12 to 14 minutes.

2. Using tongs, stir the potatoes, gently scraping up any that stick, and continue to cook, stirring occasionally, until the fries are golden and crisp, 5 to 10 minutes longer. Using a skimmer or slotted spoon, transfer the fries to a paper towel–lined plate. Season with salt to taste and serve immediately.

Belgian-Style Dipping Sauce
MAKES ABOUT ¼ CUP

For a spicier sauce, use the larger quantity of hot sauce. The dipping sauce can be refrigerated in an airtight container for up to 4 days; whisk to recombine before using.

> 3 **tablespoons mayonnaise**
> 1 **tablespoon ketchup**
> ¼–½ **teaspoon hot sauce (see note)**
> ¼ **teaspoon minced garlic**
> ⅛ **teaspoon salt**

Whisk all of the ingredients together in a bowl.

PINEAPPLE UPSIDE-DOWN CAKE

CHAPTER 10

DESSERTS

ALL-SEASON PEACH CRISP

A SIMPLE FRUIT DESSERT IS AN ESSENTIAL IN the cooking-for-two kitchen. One of our favorites is peach crisp. Peach crisp should taste like summer, with juicy ripe peaches and a buttery, nutty topping. But summer, for most of us, is a cruelly short season, which means the window for making a crisp with truly great peaches is very brief indeed. We wanted an easy, all-season peach crisp that would highlight the naturally sweet flavor of peaches.

We started our testing with the peaches. Few fruits are as inconsistent in texture and juiciness as the peach. Unripe peaches take forever to cook through and usually produce a dry crisp devoid of flavor; at the other extreme, very ripe peaches overcook easily and produce a soupy mess with a soggy topping. There was no question we needed to find peaches that would produce consistent, reliable results.

At the supermarket, we skipped the produce aisle and instead looked to the freezer case. We wondered if using frozen sliced peaches would help standardize the amount of juice that the peaches released and make our recipe more foolproof. After just one test, we found ourselves fully convinced that frozen peaches far surpassed fresh peaches as the base of our crisp. Not only did they release a consistent amount of juice, but they were always available and perfectly ripe—ideal for an anytime peach crisp. After just five minutes in the microwave and a quick drain (to get rid of excess moisture), the thawed peaches were ready. Best of all, a 1-pound bag of frozen peaches was the perfect amount to fill two ramekins for a pair of individual crisps.

Using frozen peaches had certainly been a good first step in regulating the amount of juice they released, but the peach filling was still causing our topping to turn soggy. We thought about baking the filling and topping separately and then combining them just before serving, but this seemed like too much trouble for such a simple dessert. It occurred to us that maybe the peaches weren't solely to blame. The sugar in the filling was most likely drawing out excess liquid. Perhaps we needed to use even less sugar than we were already using for our scaled-down recipe. When we tried omitting the sugar altogether in our

next test, we were pleased to find that the amount of liquid left in the bottom of our two ramekins was significantly reduced and the topping was much drier. After some testing, we found that just a tablespoon of sugar provided optimal levels of both sweetness and moisture in our filling.

As a final refinement, we experimented with thickening the filling and tried flour, tapioca, and cornstarch. The flour made the filling pasty. Tapioca needed at least 40 minutes in the oven to thicken—far too much cooking time for the peaches, especially since they were already softened. A mere ¼ teaspoon of cornstarch, mixed with the sugar and a bit of lemon juice for some brightness, was enough to quickly thicken the filling without muting the flavor of the peaches.

We moved on to the crunchy, sweet topping that would provide textural contrast to the softer fruit. Early on in our testing, we found that the standard crisp topping (cold butter, sugar, flour, and nuts) sank into our peach filling while it baked. We thought the cold butter might be to blame, so we ditched it. Instead, we melted the butter and combined it with our dry ingredients—to which we had added cinnamon and nutmeg to enhance the flavor of the peaches—until we had small clumps that we could sprinkle over the filling. When we took the ramekins out of the oven 30 minutes later, we were rewarded with a truly crisp topping.

Finally, we had a peach crisp for two that we could enjoy any time of the year.

Individual All-Season Peach Crisps
MAKES 2

You will need two 12-ounce ramekins for this recipe (see page 3). The crisp can also be prepared in a 3-cup baking dish (measuring approximately 7¼ by 5¼ inches; see page 3). Serve with vanilla ice cream or whipped cream (see page 281).

- 1 **pound (3 cups) frozen peaches**
- 2 **tablespoons granulated sugar**
- 1 **teaspoon fresh lemon juice**
- ¼ **teaspoon cornstarch**
-    **Salt**
- ⅓ **cup almonds or pecans, chopped fine**

¼ cup (1¼ ounces) unbleached all-purpose flour

2 tablespoons light brown sugar

⅛ teaspoon ground cinnamon

 Pinch ground nutmeg

3 tablespoons unsalted butter, melted and cooled

1. Adjust an oven rack to the lower-middle position and heat the oven to 400 degrees. Place the peaches in a microwave-safe bowl and microwave on medium until thawed and slightly warm, 5 to 7 minutes, stirring halfway through. Drain the peaches and set aside.

2. Whisk 1 tablespoon of the granulated sugar, lemon juice, cornstarch, and a pinch of salt together in a medium bowl. Add the thawed peaches to the sugar mixture and gently toss to combine. Divide the peaches evenly between two 12-ounce ramekins.

3. Mix the remaining 1 tablespoon granulated sugar, almonds, flour, brown sugar, cinnamon, nutmeg, and a pinch of salt together in a bowl until combined. Drizzle the melted butter over the top and stir until the mixture resembles crumbly wet sand. Pinch the mixture between your fingers into small pea-sized pieces (with some smaller loose bits).

4. Sprinkle the topping evenly over the peaches, breaking up any large chunks. Place the crisps on a rimmed baking sheet and bake until the filling is bubbling around the edges and the topping is deep golden brown, 30 to 35 minutes, rotating the baking sheet halfway through. Let the crisps cool on a wire rack for 15 minutes before serving.

NOTES FROM THE TEST KITCHEN

REVIVING BROWN SUGAR

Every home baker has encountered brown sugar that's so dried out it can't even be scooped. This happens because the moisture in the brown sugar evaporates when the sugar comes into contact with air, eventually causing the sugar to lump together. When this happens, there's an easy way to bring your brown sugar back to life. Place the sugar in a zipper-lock bag, add a slice of bread, and set it aside overnight until the sugar is soft again. Or, for a quicker fix, put the brown sugar in a microwave-safe bowl with the bread, cover the bowl, and microwave on high until the sugar is moist, 15 to 30 seconds.

VARIATIONS

Individual All-Season Peach-Ginger Crisps

Follow the recipe for Individual All-Season Peach Crisps, adding 2 teaspoons finely chopped crystallized ginger to the peaches before microwaving in step 1.

Individual All-Season Peach, Cardamom, and Pistachio Crisps

Follow the recipe for Individual All-Season Peach Crisps, adding ⅛ teaspoon ground cardamom to the sugar mixture in step 2. Substitute ⅓ cup shelled pistachio nuts, chopped coarse, for the almonds in step 3.

SKILLET-ROASTED PEAR HALVES

PEARS TASTE GREAT SIMPLY EATEN OUT OF HAND or with a pungent cheese, but they are also excellent when cooked, because their flavor intensifies, turning sweet and rich. Unfortunately, this often overlooked fruit tends to take a backseat in the dessert world, frequently passed over for more colorful berries or reliable apples. We wanted to give the juicy, sweet pear the attention it deserves by developing an uncomplicated recipe for a roasted pear that would allow the inherent flavor of the fruit to shine through.

We would need only one pear for a dessert for two, so we began by selecting the variety. We immediately narrowed it down to the readily available varieties—Bosc, Anjou, Comice, and Bartlett—and cooked several of each to discern flavor differences among the cooked fruit. The Anjou and Comice pears developed a rather ordinary and mild flavor once cooked. The Bartlett and Bosc varieties fared much better; tasters liked both the sweet, slightly spicy Bosc and the floral Bartlett. We also found that choosing a pear at the cusp of ripeness was key; too ripe and it turned to mush as it cooked, too firm and it never obtained the desired tender texture.

We were ready to roast our pear, but we wondered about incorporating more flavor with a sauce. Caramel complements pears nicely because it brings an appealing nutty contrast to the sweet fruit. We decided to roast our pear until soft and golden, then create a caramel sauce that would cling to the fruit. To be more efficient, we would use a skillet to cook both components, roasting the pear right in the caramel sauce, instead of cooking them in separate pans or baking dishes.

Making caramel can be an intimidating task, especially when making a small amount for two, which can burn much quicker than larger quantities. Many recipes for caramel rely on the use of a candy thermometer to monitor the temperature changes and avoid burning, but it was difficult to obtain an accurate temperature reading for such a small amount of sauce. Instead, we relied on visual clues to tell us when the sauce was done. We brought a mixture of 3 tablespoons each of water and sugar to a boil over medium-high heat until the sugar had completely dissolved; after only a minute the sauce was hot and bubbling.

With our caramel on its way, we added the pear, which we had halved for easy serving, to the skillet and let it cook while the caramel slowly browned. To prevent the caramel from browning too heavily before the pear halves were ready, we reduced the heat to medium and kept the lid on the skillet, which helped slow the evaporation of water and gently softened the pear. After 15 minutes, the pear was almost tender, with a hint of resistance when a fork was inserted. The last thing we wanted was an overcooked, mushy pear, so we moved the halves to a wire rack set inside a baking sheet to drain while we finished the caramel sauce.

For a lusciously rich sauce, we added ⅓ cup heavy cream and shook the pan over medium-low heat until the sauce was smooth and had developed a deep caramel color. Ready to serve our dessert, we reached for the pear halves, but they had turned unappetizingly sticky from being cooked in what was basically sugar candy (our pre-cream caramel sauce). We tried the recipe again, this time stirring the cream into the skillet around the pears as they finished caramelizing, transforming the sticky sugar syrup into a smooth sauce. We then removed the pears from the skillet to let them drain for a few minutes before drizzling them with the caramel sauce.

For a restaurant-worthy presentation, we trimmed the bottoms of the pear halves before cooking them, so that they would stand upright on the plate. One bite told us we had done right by this fruit—it was sweet and juicy and perfectly balanced by the luxurious caramel.

Skillet-Roasted Pear Halves with Caramel Sauce

SERVES 2

For this dessert, the pear should be ripe but firm, which means the flesh at the base of the stem should give slightly when gently pressed with a finger. Trimming ¼ inch off the bottom of each pear half allows the halves to stand up straight when served, making for an attractive presentation. Use caution around the caramel—it is extremely hot. See page 229 for a recipe to use up the leftover heavy cream.

- 3 **tablespoons water**
- 3 **tablespoons sugar**
- 1 **large ripe but firm Bartlett or Bosc pear (see note), halved and cored, ¼ inch trimmed from the bottom (see page 257)**
- ⅓ **cup heavy cream**
  Salt

1. Set a wire rack inside a foil-lined rimmed baking sheet and set aside. Pour the water into a 10-inch non-stick skillet, then pour the sugar into the center of the pan (don't let it hit the pan sides). Gently stir the sugar with a clean spatula to wet it thoroughly. Bring to a boil over medium-high heat and cook, without stirring, until the sugar has dissolved completely and the liquid is bubbling, about 1 minute.

2. Gently add the pear halves to the skillet, cut-side down, cover, and reduce the heat to medium. Cook until the pear halves are almost tender and a fork inserted into the center meets slight resistance, 13 to 15 minutes, reducing the heat as needed to prevent the caramel from getting too dark.

3. Uncover, reduce the heat to medium-low, and cook until the sauce is golden brown and the cut sides of the pear halves are beginning to brown, 2 to 3 minutes. Pour the heavy cream around the pear halves and cook, shaking the pan, until the sauce is a smooth, deep caramel color and the cut sides of the pear halves are golden brown, 2 to 3 minutes.

4. Off the heat, transfer the pear halves, cut-side up, to the prepared wire rack and cool slightly. Season the sauce with salt to taste, then transfer to a bowl. Using tongs, carefully (the pear halves will still be hot) stand the pear halves upright on individual plates, drizzle with the caramel sauce, and serve.

PREPARING A PEAR FOR SKILLET-ROASTING

1. Halve the pear from the stem to the blossom end. For a clean look, remove the core using a melon baller.

2. After removing the core, use the edge of the melon baller to scrape away the interior stem of the pear, from the core to the stem.

3. So that the pear can be served standing upright, trim ¼ inch off the bottom of each pear half.

BERRY GRATINS

PICKED AT THE PEAK OF RIPENESS, FRESH BERRIES are good enough to eat plain or with a dollop of whipped cream and a dusting of sugar. But when the occasion demands a more dressed-up dessert, our thoughts turn to berry gratin. This dessert is made by spreading fruit in a shallow baking dish, covering the fruit with a topping, and then baking the dish until the fruit releases its juice and the topping forms a lightly browned crust. Possible toppings run the gamut from bread or croissant crumbs and ground almonds to pastry cream. But we wanted the ultimate choice: the ethereally light and creamy Italian custard, zabaglione.

Rich, luscious zabaglione is made from just three ingredients: egg yolks, sugar, and Marsala wine. But in spite of the compact ingredient list, there's a catch:

These items are whisked together over heat, so you have to be careful not to overcook the mixture and to whisk for just long enough to transform the egg yolks to the ideal creamy texture.

To start, we focused on the base of the gratin—the berries—and would fuss with the zabaglione preparation and flavorings later. We decided that two 6-ounce broiler-safe gratin dishes would work best for individual gratins. For the berries, we thought a combination of raspberries, strawberries, blueberries, and blackberries provided a good mix of sweet and tart; however, if you have only one kind, that works fine, too. We divided 1½ cups of berries between the dishes, spooned a basic zabaglione (made from an egg yolk, 1 teaspoon of sugar, and a single tablespoon of sweet Marsala wine) over the berries, and baked the gratins in a 400-degree oven until the custard developed a golden brown crust. Unfortunately, just beneath the browned custard lurked soupy, overcooked berries. We didn't want to completely cook the berries; we sought to just warm them through while preserving their fresh flavor.

Thinking that increasing the heat might help brown the zabaglione before the berries were overcooked, we tried varying oven temperatures. But even at 500 degrees, the berries were still turning mushy in the time it took to brown the topping. Only when we switched to the broiler were we able to produce a lightly browned crust and gently warmed berries. Two minutes under the broiler was just enough time to develop good caramelization. Tossing the berries with a teaspoon of sugar before placing them in the gratin dishes drew out just enough juice during the brief time in the oven.

With the broiling technique nailed down, we could now concentrate on the zabaglione. Up to this point, we had been following the traditional method of combining the yolk, sugar, and Marsala in a bowl, setting the bowl over a pot of simmering water, and whisking constantly until the zabaglione developed a soft, creamy consistency. But our working method proved finicky, producing varying results—from hard custards with a scrambled yolk to weak foams that quickly deflated—when performed by different test cooks.

After numerous tests, we were able to make three small but significant modifications that made our technique foolproof. First, we warded off a scrambled yolk by turning the heat down slightly, keeping the water beneath the bowl at a bare simmer. Second, to get the proper texture in our zabaglione—a soft, creamy foam—we didn't stop whisking when soft peaks formed; instead, we waited until the custard became slightly thicker, so it retained some body when it went into the oven. Finally, the addition of a little whipped cream, folded into the cooked and cooled zabaglione base, ensured that the zabaglione remained light and creamy once broiled.

The next factor to address was flavor. Tasters found the zabaglione made with Marsala wine to be a bit overpowering on top of the berries. No worries—we had an entire liquor cabinet at our disposal. After several tests, we found that a dry white wine tasted best and its clean flavor allowed the berries' flavor to shine. However, without the Marsala, our zabaglione was lacking sweetness; adding an extra teaspoon of sugar to the mix remedied this problem.

We spooned the zabaglione over the berries and were pleased—finally, we had a light, smooth, and creamy concoction cut with a touch of dry white wine. The only thing missing was the browned topping. When we sprinkled the zabaglione with a mixture of brown and white sugar and let the gratins rest for 10 minutes before broiling so the sugar could really sink in, our finished gratins were covered in a lightly caramelized, but not overly crisp, crust.

Our arms were a bit achy from whisking, but we had achieved our goal: an elegantly simple dessert of tender, juicy berries covered with a crown of rich zabaglione.

NOTES FROM THE TEST KITCHEN

THE BEST MINI GRATIN DISHES
For our Berry Gratins, we wanted broiler-safe 6-ounce gratin dishes that were shallow enough to ensure maximum surface area for the lightly browned, nicely crisp crust. We tested four dishes; one was flimsy, and a few were ridiculously pricey. Our favorite, **Le Creuset Petite Au Gratin Dish**, $9.95, heated evenly and offered a generous surface for good browning. Its protruding handles were easy to grasp, and the enamel-coated stoneware was sturdy and easy to clean, stack, and store.

Berry Gratins
SERVES 2

Although we prefer to make this recipe with a mixture of raspberries, blackberries, blueberries, and hulled and quartered strawberries, you can use 1½ cups of just one type of berry. Do not use frozen berries. You will need two shallow 6-ounce broiler-safe gratin dishes for this recipe (see page 3). The gratins can also be prepared in a 3-cup broiler-safe baking dish (measuring approximately 7¼ by 5¼ inches; see page 3). Make sure to cook the egg mixture in a glass bowl over water that is barely simmering. To prevent scorching, pay close attention to the gratins when broiling. See page 229 for a recipe to use up the leftover heavy cream.

BERRY MIXTURE
- 1½ cups (7½ ounces) mixed berries, room temperature (see note)
- 1 teaspoon granulated sugar
- Pinch salt

ZABAGLIONE
- 1 large egg yolk
- 1 tablespoon granulated sugar
- 1 tablespoon dry white wine
- 2 teaspoons light brown sugar
- 2 tablespoons heavy cream, chilled

1. FOR THE BERRY MIXTURE: Gently toss the berries, granulated sugar, and salt together in a bowl. Divide the berry mixture evenly between two shallow 6-ounce broiler-safe gratin dishes and set aside.

2. FOR THE ZABAGLIONE: Whisk the egg yolk, 2 teaspoons of the granulated sugar, and wine together in a medium glass bowl until the sugar is dissolved, about 1 minute. Set the bowl over a small saucepan of barely simmering water (the water should not touch the bottom of the bowl) and cook, whisking constantly, until the mixture is frothy.

3. Continue to cook, whisking constantly, until the mixture is thickened slightly and creamy and forms loose mounds when dripped from the whisk, 5 to 10 minutes longer. Remove the bowl from the saucepan and whisk constantly for 30 seconds to cool slightly. Transfer the bowl to the refrigerator and chill until completely cool, about 10 minutes.

BERRY GRATIN

4. Meanwhile, position an oven rack 6 inches from the broiler element and heat the broiler. Combine the remaining 1 teaspoon granulated sugar and brown sugar in a bowl.

5. In a separate bowl, whisk the heavy cream to soft peaks, 30 to 90 seconds. Gently fold the whipped cream into the cooled egg mixture with a rubber spatula until just incorporated and no streaks remain. Spoon the zabaglione over the berries and sprinkle the sugar mixture evenly over the top; let sit at room temperature until the sugar dissolves into the zabaglione, about 10 minutes.

6. Place the dishes on a rimmed baking sheet and broil until the sugar is bubbly and caramelized, 1 to 4 minutes. Serve immediately.

NOTES FROM THE TEST KITCHEN

STAGES OF ZABAGLIONE
As zabaglione cooks, it gradually transforms from liquid and thin to creamy and thick. It's important to pay attention to the visual clues to know when it's ready.

1. At the beginning, the mixture is fluid and loose. Whisking develops foamy air bubbles, which lighten the mixture as it heats.

2. With further whisking and cooking, the mixture expands, thickens, and begins to turn creamy.

3. Finally, the zabaglione becomes glossy and creamy, with a thicker consistency.

SKILLET CHERRY COBBLER

CHERRY COBBLER MAY BE A SIMPLE DISH IN THEORY— saucy cherries are baked under a fleet of sweet biscuits—but that doesn't mean it's foolproof. Too often this dessert can suffer from all manner of problems, with bland cherry flavor and dense biscuits leading the list. We hoped to develop a foolproof recipe for cherry cobbler that would serve two—one that we could make any time of year, not just during cherry season. And to streamline our cobbler, we would make it entirely in a small skillet.

First we had to decide on the perfect cherry for this cobbler. Sour cherries were the obvious choice, as they have sufficient acidity to cook up well and become truly flavorful with a touch of sugar and some heat. Sweet cherries, like Bing cherries, are better for snacking because they lose their cherry flavor when cooked. Since fresh sour cherries have such a short season, we knew that using jarred or canned sour cherries would be easier—they're always in season and already pitted, plus they're usually packed in a juice that can be used to flavor the sauce.

We tested several canned and jarred varieties and found jarred Morello cherries to be the best of the bunch; they were plump, meaty, and tart, right out of the jar. Eight ounces of jarred cherries was an ample amount for two people, and we reserved ¼ cup of the juice for the sauce. Setting the cherries aside for the time being, we now needed to thicken the juice to form the base of our rich, saucy cobbler. We got out an 8-inch skillet, added the juice, and stirred in a single tablespoon of cornstarch. For sweetness, we found that ¼ to ⅓ cup of sugar was the right amount, depending on the brand and sweetness level of the cherries. To add depth to the cherry flavor, we also added some red wine, a dash of vanilla, and a small cinnamon stick, then cooked the mixture until it had thickened. Off the heat, we removed the cinnamon stick and stirred in the cherries. Since jarred (and canned) cherries have been processed, they are already cooked, so the less heat they're exposed to thereafter the better. By fully cooking the sauce on the stove, we could also lessen the baking time—the sauce wouldn't have to cook in the oven—ensuring that the topping wouldn't burn.

Moving on to the cobbles, we knew we wanted them to be light but browned and crisp. We avoided using eggs, which in the past we had learned can give biscuits a dense texture, and added buttermilk, which has the opposite effect, creating biscuits that are light and tender. We tested several biscuit variations and settled on a fairly standard mix of all-purpose flour, butter, baking powder and soda, sugar, salt, and buttermilk.

Our biscuit dough was ready to go, so we simply dropped large spoonfuls of it over the filling. But after our first test, we found that these large drops took too long to bake through, and the undersides remained raw and gummy. For the next test, we dropped small scoops of biscuit dough evenly over the fruit for a truly cobbled effect. These mini cobbles worked perfectly and cooked through in just 20 minutes without issue. To give the topping a bit more oomph, we sprinkled turbinado sugar over the tops before baking, resulting in a crispy texture.

With our topping perfected and our juicy cherry filling hot and bubbling, we let the finished cobbler sit for a short time before we dug in. The biscuits were brown and crisp, and the cherries were just right, somewhere between sweet and tart. Our cobbler was ready in minutes, and since we used jarred cherries, it could satisfy our dessert cravings even in the middle of winter.

Skillet Cherry Cobbler

SERVES 2

You will need an 8-inch ovensafe skillet for this recipe. We prefer the tart flavor and meaty texture of Morello cherries in this recipe, but if you can't find them, look for other brands of jarred or canned sour cherries in light juice; do not substitute maraschino cherries. The amount of sugar you use in the filling will depend on the sweetness of your cherries. We prefer the crunchy texture of turbinado sugar sprinkled over the biscuits before baking, but granulated sugar can be substituted. See page 215 for a recipe to use up some of the leftover buttermilk.

TOPPING

- ½ cup (2½ ounces) unbleached all-purpose flour
- 3 tablespoons granulated sugar
- ½ teaspoon baking powder
- ⅛ teaspoon baking soda
- ⅛ teaspoon salt
- ¼ cup buttermilk
- 2 tablespoons unsalted butter, melted and cooled

FILLING

- ¼–⅓ cup (1¾ to 2⅓ ounces) granulated sugar
- 1 tablespoon cornstarch
  Pinch salt
- 1⅓ cups (about 8 ounces) drained jarred or canned sour cherries, ¼ cup juice reserved (see note)
- ¼ cup dry red wine
- ¼ teaspoon vanilla extract
- 1 small cinnamon stick
- 1 teaspoon turbinado sugar (see note)

1. FOR THE TOPPING: Adjust an oven rack to the middle position and heat the oven to 400 degrees. Whisk the flour, granulated sugar, baking powder, baking soda, and salt together in a medium bowl. Stir in the buttermilk and melted butter until a dough forms. Cover and set aside.

2. FOR THE FILLING: Whisk the granulated sugar, cornstarch, and salt together in an 8-inch ovensafe skillet. Whisk in the reserved ¼ cup cherry juice, wine, and vanilla, then add the cinnamon stick. Bring the mixture to a simmer over medium-high heat and cook, whisking frequently, until thickened slightly, 1 to 3 minutes. Off the heat, remove the cinnamon stick and stir in the cherries.

3. Using a spoon, scoop and drop 1-inch pieces of the dough, spaced about ½ inch apart, over the cherry filling in the skillet, then sprinkle with the turbinado sugar. Transfer the skillet to the oven and bake until the biscuits are golden brown and the filling is thick and glossy, 20 to 25 minutes. Let the cobbler cool in the skillet for at least 15 minutes before serving.

ICEBOX STRAWBERRY PIE

THERE ARE COUNTLESS STYLES OF BERRY PIES, BUT one of our favorites is a diner-style strawberry pie. Unlike typical berry pies, this one isn't baked. Instead, a cooked strawberry filling is poured into a prebaked pie crust and chilled. Ideally, the end result is a homogenous pie bursting with bright, fresh strawberry flavor, but this outcome is sadly a rarity. Instead, strawberry pies are often loaded with artificial flavor and have textures ranging from soupy to gelatinous. We wanted a pie with a filling that was firm but not rubbery and had a distinct fresh strawberry flavor. And while we couldn't wait to dig in, we wanted a petite pie for two, so we wouldn't be eating leftovers all week.

We settled on using a 6-inch pie plate for our small pie. For the pie dough, we followed the standard formula of flour, fat, and water, ultimately settling on 4 tablespoons of butter and 2 tablespoons of shortening to 1 cup of flour, which provided the most buttery flavor and tender texture without compromising the structure of the dough. After rolling out the dough and fitting it into the pie plate, we allowed the crust to chill for 20 minutes (to prevent the crust from shrinking while it baked), then prebaked it in a 375-degree oven until deep golden brown in color.

With the pie crust baked and cooled, we were ready to start on the filling. Most of the recipes we found were virtually identical. Water and sugar are heated with a small amount of cornstarch until thickened. Fresh berries are stirred into the cooled mixture—with a few drops of food coloring for that trademark ruby shade—and the mixture is poured into the pie shell. Some versions had one significant variation—adding boxed strawberry Jell-O to the mix. For our first test, we tried a cornstarch-only version, which thickened nicely; once refrigerated, however, the filling began to weep and create a watery mess at the bottom of the pie plate. At the other end of the spectrum, the pie made with Jell-O was disagreeably bouncy and, worse, had a fake strawberry taste. But getting the texture just right was the least of our problems—all of the recipes provided modest berry flavor at best. We decided to start by fixing the flavor of our pie—we'd have to sort out the textural problems later.

Right off the bat, we decided the red dye and its artificial hue had to go. That settled, we began to question the water added to the filling. Like most soft fruits, strawberries are naturally moist, so shouldn't we concentrate their juice instead of diluting it with water? We headed in a new direction, beginning our testing by simmering 1 pound of sliced fresh berries in a dry saucepan. The berries released their juice, and after 20 minutes our mixture was thick and flavorful. All good, except for one thing: Tasters missed the freshness of uncooked berries.

The next time we made the pie, we cut back on the amount of fruit slightly (1 pound was a tight squeeze in our pie plate) and divided the fruit, cooking down 8 ounces of frozen berries—they worked as well as fresh for cooking—and stirring in 5 ounces (1 cup) of fresh berries off the heat. We poured this mixture into the shell and chilled the pie. This pie had all the berry flavor we could want, plus some added brightness from a squirt of lemon juice. As the pie chilled, however, the uncooked berries softened gently, making the filling watery.

Thinking about the composition of strawberries, we recalled that they are low in pectin, a natural thickener found in citrus fruits and many other plants. To make up for this lack of pectin, we traded in the strawberry Jell-O for unflavored gelatin. We tested various quantities and found that ¾ teaspoon produced a clean-slicing yet not bouncy pie.

NOTES FROM THE TEST KITCHEN

THE BEST FROZEN STRAWBERRIES

Our Icebox Strawberry Pie recipe calls for 8 ounces of frozen strawberries. Would the brand of berry matter? We thawed and sampled three national brands, both plain and cooked in the pie. Tasted plain, each brand had a surprisingly different flavor (one even tasted "pickled"), and textures ranged from mushy to firm and sizes from small to exceptionally large. Once cooked in the pie, the flavor variations were less pronounced but didn't disappear.

In the end, tasters preferred the only brand with no off-flavors: **Cascadian Farms Frozen Premium Organic Strawberries**. They were also the plumpest, juiciest berries, with good strawberry flavor and a "balanced sweetness."

Diner-style strawberry pies typically get a squirt of canned whipped topping, but we hadn't come this far only to reach for the canister now. We could have simply garnished the pie with dollops of fresh whipped cream, but we wanted something more substantial. Instead, we whipped heavy cream and cream cheese with small amounts of vanilla and sugar. Now our pie had a slightly tangy, rich topping that balanced the sweetness and lightness of the berries.

Icebox Strawberry Pie

SERVES 2

You will need a 6-inch pie plate for this recipe (see page 3). If desired, you can substitute 1 round of store-bought pie dough, such as Pillsbury Just Unroll!, for the homemade pie dough. If the pie dough becomes too soft to work with, simply refrigerate it until firm. In step 4, be sure to cook the strawberry mixture until it measures ½ cup in a liquid measuring cup. See page 229 for a recipe to use up the leftover heavy cream.

    1 recipe Homemade Pie Dough (recipe follows; see note)

FILLING

    8 ounces (1⅓ cups) frozen strawberries
  1½ teaspoons fresh lemon juice
    1 teaspoon water
    ¾ teaspoon unflavored gelatin
    ⅓ cup (2⅓ ounces) sugar
       Pinch salt
    1 cup (5 ounces) fresh strawberries,
       hulled and sliced thin

TOPPING

    ½ cup heavy cream, chilled
    1 ounce cream cheese, softened
    1 tablespoon sugar
    ¼ teaspoon vanilla extract

1. Roll out the dough into a 10-inch round, about ⅜ inch thick, on a lightly floured counter. Following the photos on page 264, fit the dough into a 6-inch pie plate and trim, fold, and crimp the edge. Cover loosely with plastic wrap and freeze for 20 minutes.

2. Adjust an oven rack to the lower-middle position and heat the oven to 375 degrees. Line the chilled pie shell with a sheet of lightly greased foil and fill with pie weights. Bake until the pie dough looks dry and is light in color, 25 to 30 minutes.

3. Remove the pie weights and foil and continue to bake the pie shell until deep golden brown, 10 to 12 minutes longer. Transfer the pie plate to a wire rack and let cool to room temperature.

4. FOR THE FILLING: While the pie shell bakes, cook the frozen strawberries in a small saucepan over low heat until the berries begin to release their juice, about 3 minutes. Increase the heat to medium-low and continue to cook, stirring frequently, until the mixture measures ½ cup and is thick and jam-like, 10 to 15 minutes longer.

5. Meanwhile, combine the lemon juice, water, and gelatin in a bowl. Let sit until the gelatin is softened and the mixture is thickened, about 5 minutes. Stir the gelatin mixture, sugar, and salt into the cooked berry mixture, return to a simmer, and cook for about 1 minute. Transfer to a medium bowl and cool to room temperature, about 30 minutes.

6. Fold the fresh strawberries into the cooled filling. Spread the filling evenly in the cooled pie shell and refrigerate until set, at least 4 hours, or up to 24 hours.

7. FOR THE TOPPING: Whip the cream, cream cheese, sugar, and vanilla together in a large bowl with an electric mixer on medium-low speed until combined, about 1 minute. Increase the speed to high and continue to whip the cream mixture to stiff peaks, 2 to 3 minutes longer. Spread the topping over the pie and serve.

Homemade Pie Dough

MAKES ENOUGH FOR ONE SINGLE-CRUST 6-INCH PIE

If you don't have a food processor, see the hand mixing instructions on page 264.

    1 cup (5 ounces) unbleached all-purpose flour
    ½ teaspoon salt
    2 tablespoons vegetable shortening,
       cut into ½-inch pieces and chilled
    4 tablespoons (½ stick) unsalted butter,
       cut into ¼-inch pieces and chilled
  3-5 tablespoons ice water

1. Process the flour and salt together in a food processor until combined. Scatter the shortening over the top and process until the mixture resembles coarse cornmeal, about 10 seconds. Scatter the butter pieces over the top and pulse until the mixture resembles coarse crumbs, about 10 pulses. Transfer the mixture to a medium bowl.

2. Sprinkle 3 tablespoons of the ice water over the mixture. Using a stiff rubber spatula, stir and press the dough until it sticks together. If the dough does not come together, stir in the remaining water, 1 tablespoon at a time, until it does.

3. Turn out the dough onto a clean counter. Shape into a ball and flatten into a 5-inch disk. Wrap with plastic wrap and refrigerate for 1 hour. Before rolling out the dough, let it sit on the counter to soften slightly, about 10 minutes. (The wrapped dough can be refrigerated for up to 2 days, or frozen for up to 1 month. If frozen, let the dough thaw completely on the counter before rolling it out.)

NOTES FROM THE TEST KITCHEN

FITTING PIE DOUGH INTO A PIE PLATE

1. Loosely roll the dough around a rolling pin, then gently unroll it over the pie plate.

2. Lift the dough and gently press it into the pie plate, letting the excess hang over the plate.

3. Trim the pie dough so that it hangs over the pie plate by ½ inch, then tuck the dough underneath itself to form a tidy, even edge that sits on the lip of the pie plate.

4. Use the index finger of one hand and the thumb and index finger of the other to create fluted ridges perpendicular to the edge of the pie plate.

HAND MIXING DOUGH

Both our Homemade Pie Dough (page 263) and Empanada Dough (page 172) are mixed in a food processor. But if you don't have a food processor, you can mix the dough by hand.

For the Homemade Pie Dough: Freeze the butter in its stick form until very firm. Whisk together the flour and salt in a medium bowl. Add the chilled shortening and press it into the flour using a fork. Grate the frozen butter on the large holes of a box grater into the flour mixture, then cut the mixture together, using two butter or dinner knives, until the mixture resembles coarse crumbs. Add the water as directed.

For the Empanada Dough: Freeze the butter in its stick form until very firm. Whisk together the flour, sugar, and salt in a medium bowl. Grate the frozen butter on the large holes of a box grater into the flour mixture, then cut the mixture together, using two butter or dinner knives, until the mixture resembles coarse crumbs. Add the water as directed.

THE BEST ROLLING PIN

For the most part, rolling pins can be divided into two distinct styles: American-style pins that have handles affixed to a largish cylinder and French-style pins that are simple tapered cylinders. We tested several of each on three kinds of dough: a pie dough, a delicate sugar cookie dough, and a resilient yeasted coffee cake dough. For all three doughs, we were looking for a fast, easy roll—one that allowed us to feel the dough and did not require the application of too much pressure. We favored the French-style pins because the tapered ends make it easy to roll out dough to a consistently even thickness. Our favorite pin is **Fante's Large French Rolling Pin with Tapered Ends**, $6.99. Its subtle taper provides a large, flat rolling surface at the center of the pin, making for increased efficiency and easier rolling.

LEMON–POPPY SEED POUND CAKE

LEMON–POPPY SEED POUND CAKE SHOULD BE EASY to make. After all, there are no tricky ingredients to deal with—the batter is just eggs, butter, flour, sugar, lemon, and poppy seeds. But often the end result is a heavy cake that is dry and disappointing. What we wanted was a fine-crumbed, rich, moist cake full of bright lemon flavor. And while most recipes yield a 9 by 5-inch loaf, we set our sights on a mini version for two.

We started with the traditional method of creaming butter, sugar, and lemon zest until fluffy and light in color, adding the eggs, then folding in cake flour (all-purpose flour was too protein-rich and delivered dry, tough cakes) and adding the poppy seeds. Working with a 5½ by 3-inch loaf pan, we found that ½ cup of cake flour, ⅓ cup of sugar, 4 tablespoons of butter, and an egg filled the pan nicely. Several recipes we found called for only lemon zest, but we felt the addition of lemon juice helped bring out the tart flavor we were looking for; ½ teaspoon of fresh juice and 1½ teaspoons of zest did the trick. We also added a splash of vanilla and a sprinkling of salt to enhance the overall flavor of the cake. As for the hallmark poppy seeds, 4 teaspoons was plenty to make their presence known without becoming overwhelming.

Baked in a 325-degree oven, the cake was off to a good start, with a tender crumb, golden buttery interior, and a pleasant hint of lemon. But the method seemed tricky, often producing a curdled batter if the egg wasn't incorporated enough into the whipped butter. This resulted in cakes with mottled crusts and dense interiors. In addition, the poppy seeds tended to sink to the bottom. There had to be a simpler and more foolproof way to make a great lemon–poppy seed pound cake.

We thought adding the butter melted might work better, so in our next test, we mixed the eggs, sugar, lemon juice, and zest by hand, then whisked in the melted butter and finally the flour. Now we were getting somewhere. Melting the butter made it easier to incorporate it; also, this method enabled us to assemble the batter and get it into the oven much quicker. We still had some issues with texture—tasters felt the cake was now a little dense—but we decided to press forward in this direction.

Looking to create a slightly finer crumb, we tried changing the amount of butter in the cake, but this experimentation only caused the cake to become either too greasy or too dry. And when we played around with the number of eggs, the cake became too spongy. We found the answer in a can of baking powder. With just ¼ teaspoon, we instilled the cake with enough levity to produce the fine crumb we were after.

Our cake now had the tender texture and bright flavor we wanted, but there was still the issue of the poppy seeds clumping and sinking to the bottom of the pan. In the past, when making cakes that contain berries, we have tossed the berries with a little flour to help keep them suspended in the batter. Trying this method with our poppy seeds, we were met with equal success; the seeds now remained evenly dispersed throughout the cake.

Brushed with a simple lemon glaze before serving (after being poked with a toothpick so the glaze would really soak in), our mini pound cake delivered the buttery, rich, and poppy seed–speckled crumb we were after.

Lemon–Poppy Seed Pound Cake

MAKES ONE 5½ BY 3-INCH LOAF

You will need a 5½ by 3-inch loaf pan or a pan of similar size for this recipe (see page 3). Substituting all-purpose flour for cake flour will result in a denser cake.

CAKE

- ½ cup (2 ounces) cake flour
- ¼ teaspoon baking powder
- ⅛ teaspoon salt
- ⅓ cup (2⅓ ounces) sugar
- 4 tablespoons (½ stick) unsalted butter, melted and cooled
- 1 large egg
- 1½ teaspoons grated lemon zest plus ½ teaspoon fresh lemon juice
- ¼ teaspoon vanilla extract
- 4 teaspoons poppy seeds

GLAZE

- 2 tablespoons sugar
- 1 tablespoon fresh lemon juice

1. FOR THE CAKE: Adjust an oven rack to the middle position and heat the oven to 325 degrees. Grease and flour a 5½ by 3-inch loaf pan.

2. Whisk the flour, baking powder, and salt together in a bowl. In a medium bowl, whisk the sugar, melted butter, egg, lemon zest, lemon juice, and vanilla together. In another bowl, combine 1 tablespoon of the flour mixture and the poppy seeds.

3. Add half of the remaining flour mixture to the sugar mixture and whisk to combine until just a few streaks of flour remain. Repeat with the remaining flour mixture, then add the poppy seeds and continue to whisk gently until most of the lumps are gone (do not overmix).

4. Give the batter a final stir with a rubber spatula to make sure it is thoroughly combined. Scrape the batter into the prepared pan and smooth the top. Wipe any drops of batter off the sides of the pan and gently tap the pan on the counter to settle the batter. Bake the cake until a toothpick inserted into the center comes out with a few crumbs attached, 30 to 40 minutes, rotating the pan halfway through. Transfer the cake to a wire rack and let cool for 10 minutes.

5. FOR THE GLAZE: Meanwhile, combine the sugar and lemon juice in a microwave-safe bowl and microwave on high until the sugar dissolves and the mixture thickens slightly, about 1 minute, stirring halfway through.

6. Run a small knife around the edge of the cake to loosen, then flip it out onto a wire rack. Turn the cake right-side up and poke the top and sides with a toothpick. Brush the warm glaze all over the cake. Cool the cake to room temperature, about 1 hour, before serving.

NOTES FROM THE TEST KITCHEN

KEEPING EGGS FRESH

Although perishable, properly stored eggs will last up to three months, but both the yolks and the whites will become looser and their flavor will begin to fade. To be sure that you have fresh eggs, check the sell-by date on the side of the carton. Legally, eggs may already be up to two months old by the end of the "sell by" date, so it's best to check for freshness yourself. If an egg has an unpleasant odor, discard it.

To ensure freshness, store eggs in the back of the refrigerator (the coldest area), not in the door (which is actually the warmest part of the refrigerator), and keep them in the carton. It holds in moisture and keeps the eggs from drying out; the carton also protects the eggs from odor.

LEMON PUDDING CAKE

LIKE MAGIC, PUDDING CAKES SEPARATE INTO two layers during baking: airy and cakey on top, dense and custardy below. Somewhere between a cake and custard, pudding cakes have very little flour, quite a bit of egg, and a lot more liquid than you might expect. In fact, it's the water in that liquid that sinks to the bottom, taking the batter with it; the egg whites float to the top. The science of this cake is certainly amazing, but the lively sweet-tart flavor and exquisite texture of one of our favorite pudding cakes—lemon—are what had us eager to create a version for two.

Gathering a handful of recipes, we discovered that most contained the same basic ingredients (butter, sugar, milk, eggs, flour, and lemon juice) and used a water bath technique for baking, but the pudding cakes that emerged varied remarkably. Older recipes produced short, squat cakes with barely perceptible layers. Newer recipes had more height, though the bottom layer in some was more sauce than pudding. Likewise, the flavors varied. Many were merely sweet, a few hinted at lemon, and one tasted of sour egg. We wanted a pudding cake with rich, creamy pudding, a delicate, tender cake, and bright, balanced lemon flavor.

The best recipe we found began with creaming butter with sugar; egg yolks and flour were added, milk and lemon juice were poured in, then stiffly beaten egg whites were folded in. This version had good height and clear separation between the pudding and cake layers, but it didn't taste especially lemony. We decided this would be the best recipe to start with; we hoped the lemon flavor would be an easy fix.

We developed a version using roughly one-quarter of the original recipe—but scaled down the lemon juice a little less, settling on ¼ cup. The flavor was now bracing, but not off-putting when balanced by ½ cup of sugar. Still, tasters demanded more citrus. To coax more flavor from the lemons, we creamed varying amounts of grated zest (which has a high concentration of flavorful lemon oil) with the butter—just 2 tablespoons—and sugar; ultimately, we used 2 teaspoons of zest. As in our Lemon–Poppy Seed Pound Cake (page 265), the lemon zest gave the finished dessert the kick it needed.

While tasters enjoyed the flavor of this cake, they found that the bottom layer was soupy. Thinking that the ratio of liquid ingredients to dry was off because we

LEMON PUDDING CAKE

had scaled down the recipe, we increased the amount of flour. The bottom layer thickened from the added starch, but the lemon flavor dulled appreciably and the top layer became gummy. Next we tried substituting cornstarch (which is virtually tasteless) for some of the extra flour. A mere ½ teaspoon gently firmed the pudding layer without muddying the lemon flavor.

We were close, but during a trial run, we noticed that when the cake was in the oven, the top layer first puffed and swelled, and then—about halfway through baking—deflated. From our experience baking soufflés, we immediately suspected that we would need to stabilize the egg whites. Our first instinct was to add lemon juice to the whites as we were whipping them, because the acid would help to stabilize them. For some reason, this had no effect on our pudding cake. Reading up on the science behind this, we learned that merely by folding the whites into the acidic batter, they stabilized, which meant that adding acid to the whites alone wasn't doing much. But our research paid off, because we were reminded that beating sugar into egg whites as they are whipped also helps stabilize them.

For our next test, we added most of the sugar (6 tablespoons) to the egg whites and added the remaining sugar (2 tablespoons) to the batter before folding in the whipped whites. Sure enough, now when we baked our lemon pudding cake it was almost magical, emerging with a high, golden, and fluffy top floating over a creamy lemon custard.

Lemon Pudding Cake

SERVES 2

You will need a 3-cup baking dish (measuring approximately 7¼ by 5¼ inches) or a pan of a similar size for this recipe (see page 3). It's important to use a metal pan for the water bath—a glass baking pan may crack when you add the boiling water. This dessert is best served warm or at room temperature.

2 **large eggs, separated, room temperature**
½ **cup (3½ ounces) sugar**
4 **teaspoons unbleached all-purpose flour**
½ **teaspoon cornstarch**
2 **tablespoons unsalted butter, softened**
2 **teaspoons grated lemon zest plus**
   ¼ cup fresh lemon juice from 2 lemons
½ **cup whole milk, room temperature**

1. Adjust an oven rack to the lowest position and heat the oven to 325 degrees. Grease a 3-cup baking dish. Bring a kettle of water to a boil. Following the photos on page 269, place a kitchen towel in the bottom of a 13 by 9-inch metal baking pan and set the baking dish on the towel.

2. In a large bowl, whip the egg whites with an electric mixer on medium-low speed until foamy, about 1 minute. Increase the speed to medium-high and whip the whites to soft, billowy mounds, about 1 minute. Gradually whip in 6 tablespoons of the sugar and continue to whip the whites until they are glossy and form stiff peaks (see page 272), 2 to 6 minutes longer. Transfer the whipped egg whites to a bowl and set aside (do not wipe out the mixing bowl).

3. Whisk the flour and cornstarch together in a bowl. In the large mixing bowl, beat the remaining 2 tablespoons sugar, butter, and lemon zest together with an electric mixer on medium speed until light and fluffy, 3 to 6 minutes, scraping down the bowl as needed. Beat in the yolks, one at a time, until combined, about 30 seconds, scraping down the bowl as needed. Reduce the mixer speed to low and slowly add the flour mixture until combined, about 30 seconds. Gradually mix in the lemon juice and milk until just incorporated.

4. Using a rubber spatula, fold one-third of the whipped egg whites into the batter to lighten, then gently fold in the remaining egg whites until no white streaks remain. Pour the batter into the prepared baking dish and gently smooth the top.

5. Transfer the 13 by 9-inch baking pan to the oven and carefully pour enough boiling water into the pan to reach halfway up the sides of the baking dish. Bake until the surface is golden brown and the edges are set (the center should jiggle slightly when gently shaken), about 1 hour.

6. Carefully remove the baking dish from the water bath and let the cake cool, about 30 minutes, before serving.

TWO WAYS TO SEPARATE EGGS

A. To separate eggs, you can use the broken shells or your hand. To use the broken shell halves, gently transfer the egg white from one shell half to the other, so it will drip into a bowl and leave the intact yolk behind.

B. To use your hand (make sure it's very clean), cup your hand over a small bowl, then transfer the egg into your palm and slowly unclench your fingers to allow the white to slide through, leaving the yolk intact in your palm.

MAKING A WATER BATH

1. To prevent the baking dish from sliding, line the bottom of a 13 by 9-inch metal baking pan with a kitchen towel. Then place the baking dish on top.

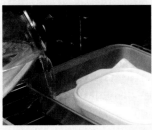

2. After adding the batter to the baking dish set inside the large baking pan, transfer the pan to the oven. Then carefully pour boiling water into the baking pan, halfway up the sides of the baking dish.

3. After baking, promptly remove the baking dish from the water. Let the water cool before moving the water bath.

PINEAPPLE UPSIDE-DOWN CAKE

ONE OF THE MOST BELOVED AMERICAN CAKES IS pineapple upside-down cake. The recipe is pretty simple: The fruit is cooked with sugar and butter, spread out on the bottom of a cake pan, then topped with a basic batter before being baked and served upside down so the fruit crowns the cake. But as every cook knows, simple doesn't always translate to success. The pineapple is typically pale, and there's hardly enough of it in the cake to support the title. As for the cake itself, though a sturdy texture is a must to support the fruit, most recipes overcompensate and bake up dry and dense. We sought to correct these problems, while also downsizing our cake for two.

Before we addressed size issues, we needed a solid foundation. We started by preparing a lineup of cakes that ranged from tender and fluffy to leaden in texture. Tasters preferred a moist butter cake (which used butter as the fat, a few eggs, a good amount of flour, sugar, baking powder, and some milk), as the richness of this style of cake balanced the acidity of the pineapple. Creaming the butter and sugar before adding the wet and dry ingredients ensured that the cake was light and tender, but still sturdy enough to support the heavy fruit topping.

After numerous tests, we adjusted the ingredient amounts for this standard-sized cake and cut the yield of the batter by about half, which fit nicely in a 6-inch round cake pan. For the main players in our cake, we ultimately settled on ¾ cup of flour, an egg, ⅓ cup of sugar, and 3 tablespoons of milk. Tasters liked the moist crumb and light sweetness of this cake, which needed about 45 minutes in a 350-degree oven to come out perfect (down from 375 degrees for the 9-inch cake). Now it was time to address the pineapple topping.

Many pineapple upside-down cake recipes call for cooking the pineapple in sugar and butter on the stovetop. We started by following this method, but since we were cooking just a few pineapple rings for our scaled-down cake, it seemed a shame to dirty an extra pan. We decided instead to use the preheated oven to melt the butter directly in the cake pan; then we could stir in a small amount of brown sugar until it dissolved and set the pineapple rings right on top. With our pineapple topping ready to go, we spooned our cake batter on top and set the timer. Now when the cake was finished, the pineapple was lightly caramelized and had a smooth syrup to go with it—all without the assistance of a skillet. The only complaint from tasters was that the cake could use more of its namesake

ingredient. Up until this point, we had been using a quarter of a small pineapple, but tasters were not satisfied until we packed twice as much into the cake pan. There was just one problem: Using this much pineapple made it nearly impossible to create a flat layer of fruit, thereby compromising the distribution of batter in the cake pan. How could we cram more pineapple into our 6-inch cake pan and still end up with an evenly cooked and attractive cake that didn't have a messy pile of fruit on top? We ultimately decided to trade the traditional pineapple rounds for small chunks of pineapple, which created a level layer of pineapple for the batter to rest on and also satisfied our tasters' craving for more fruit.

Once baked, the cake needed a 10-minute rest in the pan before being flipped onto a serving platter. This was just enough time for the cake to set up and for the syrup in the topping to thicken slightly. Slices of our pineapple upside-down cake were greeted by oohs and aahs from tasters, who were thrilled with both the flavor and the appearance of this scaled-down classic dessert.

NOTES FROM THE TEST KITCHEN

CUTTING PINEAPPLE INTO CHUNKS

1. After trimming off the bottom and top of the pineapple, set the fruit on its bottom and cut off the skin in thin strips, top to bottom, with a sharp knife.

2. Halve the pineapple lengthwise; reserve one half for future use. Cut the remaining pineapple half into two pieces, lengthwise, then cut the tough core from each piece. The pineapple can now be cut into ½-inch chunks.

THE BEST RUBBER SPATULAS

We evaluated 10 heatproof rubber (also called silicone) spatulas, all dishwasher-safe, running each through nine tests, including lifting omelets, scraping the bowl of a food processor, making a pan sauce, and stirring risotto. We also simmered the spatulas in a pot of tomato-curry sauce and then ran them through the dishwasher to see if they would come through clean and odor-free. Our favorites are the **Rubbermaid Professional 13½-Inch Heat Resistant Scraper**, $23.50 (left), and the **Tovolo Silicone Spatula** (right), which at $8.99 is our best buy. The Rubbermaid is a practical, no-nonsense spatula that aced every cooking test, with a great balance of flexibility and firmness in both the head and the handle. The Tovolo passed every performance test, scraping, stirring, folding, and sautéing like a champ. It also withstood our attempts to stain and melt it. The Tovolo's good looks and nice price make it hard to resist, but, in the end, the larger overall size and sturdiness of the Rubbermaid won our highest accolades.

Pineapple Upside-Down Cake

SERVES 2

You will need a 6-inch round cake pan for this recipe (see page 3). To ensure a clean release, cool the cake in the pan for no more than 10 minutes before inverting it. Do not substitute canned pineapple.

  6 **tablespoons (¾ stick) unsalted butter,**
     cut into 6 pieces and softened
  ⅓ **cup packed (2⅓ ounces) light brown sugar**
  ½ **small pineapple, peeled, cored, and cut into**
     ½-inch chunks (about 1½ cups) (see note)
  ¾ **cup (3¾ ounces) unbleached all-purpose flour**
  ¾ **teaspoon baking powder**
  ¼ **teaspoon salt**
  ⅓ **cup (2⅓ ounces) granulated sugar**
  1 **large egg, room temperature**
  ½ **teaspoon vanilla extract**
  3 **tablespoons whole milk, room temperature**

1. Adjust an oven rack to the lower-middle position and heat the oven to 350 degrees.

2. Place 2 tablespoons of the butter in a 6-inch round cake pan and place in the oven until the butter melts, 2 to 4 minutes. Stir the brown sugar into the melted butter in the cake pan, then, using a spatula, pat the mixture into an even layer. Set the pineapple chunks on top of the sugar and press into a single layer.

3. Whisk the flour, baking powder, and salt together in a bowl. In a large bowl, beat the remaining 4 tablespoons butter and granulated sugar together with an electric mixer on medium speed until light and fluffy, 3 to 6 minutes. Beat in the egg until combined, about 30 seconds. Beat in the vanilla.

4. Reduce the mixer speed to low and beat in one-half of the flour mixture, followed by the milk, scraping down the bowl as needed. Beat in the remaining flour mixture until just combined (the batter will be thick).

5. Give the batter a final stir with a rubber spatula to make sure it is thoroughly combined. Scrape the batter into the pan over the pineapple and smooth the top. Gently tap the pan on the counter to settle the batter. Bake the cake until a toothpick inserted into the center comes out with a few crumbs attached, 45 to 50 minutes, rotating the pan halfway through. Transfer the cake to a wire rack and let cool for 10 minutes.

6. Place a serving plate over the top of the cake pan, invert the cake, and let sit until the cake releases itself from the pan (do not shake or tap the pan), about 1 minute. Gently remove the cake pan, replacing any pineapple chunks that fall off. Cool the cake completely, about 1 hour, before serving.

ANGEL FOOD CAKES

AT ITS BEST, AN ANGEL FOOD CAKE SHOULD BE TALL and perfectly shaped, have a snowy-white, tender crumb, and be encased in a thin, delicate, golden crust. Achieving these results seems pretty straightforward; you whip egg whites with sugar and cream of tartar until soft peaks form, fold in flour and flavorings, and bake. But try finding a reliable recipe for angel food cake and you will quickly immerse yourself in hundreds of variations on the same theme, producing widely varying outcomes. We sought a foolproof recipe for angel food cake that would ensure a tender and statuesque cake with a delicate crumb every time.

Angel food cake requires a specific pan, a tube pan, and up to this point we had seen only 9- and 10-inch pans that hold 12 or more cups of batter for a standard-sized cake. But after checking a few local kitchen supply and retail shops, we found miniature tube pans that hold approximately 2 cups of batter; we bought two pans, perfect for a pair of cakes. With the right baking equipment in hand, we headed into the test kitchen to develop a recipe for a reliable cake batter.

Even as experienced bakers, we grew intimidated by the many dire warnings we came across while researching recipes—many of them just didn't ring true. To begin with, we found that cold egg whites would whip to the same volume as room-temperature eggs; they just take a few minutes longer (which is why we suggest using room-temperature eggs). And we didn't need to panic if we slightly underbeat or overbeat the whites—we tried both during our tests, and our cakes turned out respectably regardless. Finally, while baking the cake, we didn't need to tiptoe around the kitchen as many recipes led us to believe. In fact, we could jump up and down and the cake wouldn't fall.

However, we did identify certain claims that weren't just old wives' tales. We tested both cake flour and all-purpose flour and found that the cake flour, which is finer, did in fact produce a more delicate crumb. Also, being extra-careful and taking our time when separating the eggs were essential—the merest speck of yolk in the egg whites prevented them from whipping to peaks. And cream of tartar, which is acidic, proved its mettle, offering some insurance against deflated whites. For our two cakes, we found that three large egg whites provided the right volume, and ½ teaspoon of cream of tartar was sufficient to stabilize them. We also learned that inverting the cakes while they rested was imperative in preventing them from collapsing under their own weight. While traditional tube pans typically have feet, which enable them to sit upside down without squishing the risen cake, our mini pans did not, so we had to improvise. We found two methods that work equally well. First, a chopstick inserted into an empty beer bottle (any similarly shaped glass bottle will work) provided a good way to support an upside-down pan; the weight of the bottle kept it from tipping over while supporting the cake pan, and the chopstick ensured that the pan didn't fall off. (If you use this method, just make sure you have two bottles and two chopsticks on hand.) Alternatively, you could rest the cake pans on two kitchen funnels, set upside down on the counter.

We had seen that angel food cake wasn't that difficult to make, but it was exacting. Having proportionally scaled down the amount of cake flour we had found in other recipes, we were working with ¼ cup of cake flour, but this produced cakes that were slightly wet and spongy. One-third cup was an improvement, but the cakes were still somewhat spongy; ½ cup, however, made for dry cakes that were too firm. In the end, we determined that 6 tablespoons of cake flour (¼ cup

plus 2 tablespoons), while fussy, was the right amount, producing two flawlessly tender cakes time and again.

After several days of baking, we finally had the reliable recipe we were after. For our main recipe, tasters had enjoyed just a dash of vanilla added to the mix, but we also created two variations, one with chocolate and the other with espresso powder, that piqued their interest. Served with fresh berries, our cakes were certainly worthy of angelic praise.

NOTES FROM THE TEST KITCHEN

WHIPPING EGG WHITES

Perfectly whipped egg whites begin with a scrupulously clean bowl, as fat inhibits egg whites from whipping properly. The best choice for the bowl is stainless steel. Wash the bowl in hot, soapy water, rinse with more hot water, and dry with paper towels. (A dish towel may have traces of oil within its fibers that could be transferred to the bowl.) With the whites in the bowl, start with your mixer on medium-low speed and whip the whites until foamy, about 1 minute. Then increase the mixer speed, add sugar if required, and continue to whip the whites to their desired consistency. For soft peaks (left), whip until the whites droop slightly from the tip of the whisk or beater. For stiff peaks (right), whip until the whites stand up tall on their own on the tip of the whisk or beater.

SOFT PEAKS   STIFF PEAKS

TWO WAYS TO COOL ANGEL FOOD CAKES

A. Place a clean chopstick in an empty beer bottle, then repeat this setup. Invert each cake over a chopstick, balancing it on the mouth of the bottle, so it is hanging upside down. Let the cakes cool completely.

B. Alternatively, you can use two 5- or 6-inch kitchen funnels. Set them on the counter, upside down, then rest one cake pan on each funnel. Let the cakes cool completely.

Angel Food Cakes

SERVES 2

You will need two 2-cup tube pans for this recipe (see page 3); you will also need either two chopsticks and two empty beer bottles (or two similarly shaped glass bottles) or two 5- or 6-inch kitchen funnels for cooling the cakes. If your tube pans do not have removable bottoms, line the bottoms of the pans with parchment paper. In either case, do not grease the pans (or the paper). See page 274 for a recipe to use up the leftover egg yolks. Serve with fresh berries and whipped cream (page 281), if desired.

  6 tablespoons (1½ ounces) cake flour
  ½ cup (3½ ounces) sugar
     Pinch salt
  3 large egg whites, room temperature
  ½ teaspoon cream of tartar
  ¼ teaspoon vanilla extract

1. Adjust an oven rack to the lower-middle position and heat the oven to 325 degrees. Whisk the flour, ¼ cup of the sugar, and salt together in a bowl.

2. In a large bowl, whip the egg whites and cream of tartar with an electric mixer on medium-low speed until foamy, about 1 minute. Increase the speed to medium-high and whip the whites to soft, billowy mounds, about 1 minute. Gradually whip in the remaining ¼ cup sugar and continue to whip the whites until they are glossy and form soft peaks (see photos), 1 to 3 minutes longer.

3. Whisk the vanilla into the whipped egg whites by hand. Sift one-half of the flour mixture over the egg whites, then gently fold to combine with a large rubber spatula until just a few streaks of flour remain. Repeat with the remaining flour mixture.

ANGEL FOOD CAKES

4. Divide the batter evenly between two 2-cup tube pans and smooth the tops. Wipe any drops of batter off the sides of the pans. Bake the cakes until a toothpick inserted into the centers comes out clean and any cracks in the cakes appear dry, 30 to 35 minutes.

5. Following the photos on page 272, invert each cake pan over an empty beer bottle with a chopstick set inside or over an upside-down kitchen funnel. Let the cakes cool completely, upside down, about 1 hour.

6. Run a small knife around the edges of the cakes to loosen. Gently tap the pans upside down on the counter to release the cakes. Turn the cakes right-side up onto serving plates and serve.

USE IT UP: EGG YOLKS

Lemon Curd
MAKES 1 CUP

This tangy curd is great served with fresh berries, scones, shortbread, or buttered toast.

- ⅔ cup (4⅔ ounces) sugar
- ¼ cup fresh lemon juice from 2 lemons
  Pinch salt
- 3 large egg yolks
- 4 tablespoons (½ stick) unsalted butter, cut into ½-inch pieces and frozen
- 2 tablespoons whole milk or half-and-half

1. Cook the sugar, lemon juice, and salt together in a small saucepan over medium-high heat, stirring occasionally, until the sugar dissolves and the mixture is hot (do not boil), about 1 minute.

2. In a bowl, whisk the egg yolks until combined, then slowly whisk in the hot lemon mixture. Return the mixture to the saucepan and cook over medium-low heat, stirring constantly, until the mixture is thickened and a rubber spatula scraped along the bottom of the pan leaves a trail, 3 to 5 minutes.

3. Off the heat, stir in the frozen butter and milk until incorporated. Strain the curd through a fine-mesh strainer into a bowl and press plastic wrap directly onto the surface. Refrigerate the curd until it is firm and spreadable, about 1½ hours.

VARIATIONS
Chocolate-Almond Angel Food Cakes
Follow the recipe for Angel Food Cakes, substituting ¼ teaspoon almond extract for the vanilla extract and adding ½ ounce finely grated bittersweet chocolate with the flour mixture in step 3.

Café au Lait Angel Food Cakes
Follow the recipe for Angel Food Cakes, adding ½ teaspoon instant espresso powder to the flour mixture in step 1. Substitute ½ teaspoon coffee liqueur, such as Kahlúa, for the vanilla extract in step 3.

GINGERBREAD CAKES

TRADITIONAL GINGERBREAD CAKE IS EASY TO MAKE. Most recipes instruct you to combine butter, sugar, eggs, flour, leavener, warm spices, molasses, and water, then pour the batter into a cake pan and bake. But what's not easy is keeping the cake moist and tender while also getting the balance of spices just right—most recipes we've sampled produced cakes that were dry and far too sweet, with unbalanced spicing dominated by the dusty burn of powdered ginger. Without unduly complicating the recipe, we wanted to turn this neglected cake into a moist, boldly flavored, yet balanced cake for two.

Most gingerbread cakes are made in square or round cake pans, but since we were already scaling down the recipe, we thought we could take some creative license when it came time to select the baking vessel. We opted for another pan that would make for a lovely little cake, perfect for the finale of a fancy holiday dinner. After a bit of shopping, we found individual Bundt pans at a local retail store; we purchased two of them and headed back to the test kitchen.

Working with a basic gingerbread cake formula, we scaled down the ingredients and found that ⅓ cup of all-purpose flour, 3 tablespoons of sugar, 2 tablespoons of butter, and an egg filled the pans nicely. Creaming the butter and sugar with an electric mixer made the cakes a little too light and fluffy. Searching for a denser, moister texture, we tried a dump-and-stir mixing method where the butter was replaced with an equal volume of vegetable oil, but that made for greasy cakes that lacked richness. We tried the same method using melted butter, which proved the best path to moist, dense, rich cakes.

Recipes we found typically called for a liquid combination of mild molasses and water, though we did find a few that used milk. To start, tasters found the molasses flavor to be weak, so we quickly switched from mild to robust molasses. For the other liquid ingredient, we gave both milk and water a shot but found that the milk muted the spice flavor; water worked better, and since we needed only a tablespoon, it was also the most sensible choice.

As for the spices, ¼ teaspoon of ground ginger gave the cakes some bite, and the same amount of cinnamon and ⅛ teaspoon of allspice supported the ginger flavor nicely. A surprising ingredient, pepper, helped draw out even more of the ginger's pleasing burn. Even though the flavor was good, we wanted to take the spice flavor even further. We tried cooking the spices in melted butter, a technique we use in the test kitchen for savory spiced dishes like curry and chili. The flavors bloomed, but tasters still wanted more ginger. Here, we turned to grated fresh ginger, which added an unmistakable zing that the dried spice alone couldn't muster.

After 25 minutes in a 375-degree oven, our cakes were moist, tender, and boldly spiced. With a glaze of confectioners' sugar, water, and a little bourbon for a festive kick, these gingerbread cakes were worthy of any holiday table.

NOTES FROM THE TEST KITCHEN

ALL ABOUT MOLASSES

Thick, sticky-sweet molasses is a by-product of the sugar-refining process—it is the liquid that is drawn off after the cane juice has been boiled and has undergone crystallization. Once the sugar crystals are removed, the remaining liquid is packaged and sold as mild (or light) molasses, or it is boiled again and marketed as robust or full-flavored molasses. If the molasses is reduced a third time, it is labeled blackstrap. With each boil, the molasses becomes darker, more concentrated in flavor, and more bitter. We prefer robust molasses in our Bold and Spicy Gingerbread Cakes, as its bold flavor pairs best with the spices; mild molasses would be too tame for this cake, and blackstrap molasses would impart an assertive, overpowering bitterness.

Bold and Spicy Gingerbread Cakes

SERVES 2

Be sure to use finely ground pepper. You will need two 1-cup Bundt pans for this recipe (see page 3). Don't be tempted to make the cake in another pan; the batter was designed to work in a Bundt pan that has a center tube to facilitate baking. If desired, you can substitute water for the bourbon.

CAKE

⅓ cup (1⅔ ounces) unbleached all-purpose flour
¼ teaspoon baking powder
⅛ teaspoon baking soda
⅛ teaspoon salt
2 tablespoons unsalted butter
¼ teaspoon ground ginger
¼ teaspoon ground cinnamon
⅛ teaspoon ground allspice
  Pinch pepper (see note)
1 large egg, room temperature
3 tablespoons granulated sugar
½ teaspoon grated or minced fresh ginger
2 tablespoons robust or dark molasses
1 tablespoon water

GLAZE

½ cup (2 ounces) confectioners' sugar
1½ teaspoons water
1 teaspoon bourbon (see note)

1. FOR THE CAKE: Adjust an oven rack to the middle position and heat the oven to 375 degrees. Grease and flour two 1-cup Bundt pans.

2. Whisk the flour, baking powder, baking soda, and salt together in a bowl. Melt the butter in a small saucepan over medium heat until bubbling. Stir in the ground ginger, cinnamon, allspice, and pepper, and cook until fragrant, about 30 seconds. Remove from the heat and let cool slightly.

3. Whisk the egg, granulated sugar, and fresh ginger together in a medium bowl until light and frothy. Whisk in the melted butter mixture, molasses, and water until smooth and thoroughly combined. Gently whisk in the flour mixture until just incorporated.

4. Give the batter a final stir with a rubber spatula to make sure it is thoroughly combined. Divide the batter evenly between the prepared pans and smooth the tops. Wipe any drops of batter off the sides of the pans and gently tap each pan on the counter to settle the batter. Place the pans on a rimmed baking sheet and bake the cakes until a toothpick inserted into the centers comes out with a few crumbs attached, 20 to 25 minutes, rotating the baking sheet halfway through.

5. Let the cakes cool in the pans for 10 minutes, then flip them out onto a wire rack set inside a foil-lined baking sheet. Let the cakes cool completely, about 30 minutes.

6. FOR THE GLAZE: Whisk the confectioners' sugar, water, and bourbon together in a bowl until smooth. Pour the glaze over the cooled cakes. Let the glaze set for 15 minutes before serving.

CARROT CAKE

A CLASSIC CONFECTION FROM THE AMERICAN landscape, carrot cake was once a proud addition to the dessert table. But peek under the luscious, rich cream cheese frosting, and today's versions are nothing more than a good spice cake gone bad—far too oily, with a saturated crumb caused by an overabundance of shredded carrot. We set our sights on creating a truly great carrot cake that was moist (not soggy) and rich (not greasy) with a balance of spices—and it had to be scaled down to serve two.

We started with a carrot cake from our own archives. The ingredients were straightforward—all-purpose flour, white and brown sugar, eggs, vegetable oil, shredded carrot, baking powder, baking soda, and warm spices such as cinnamon and nutmeg—and the method couldn't have been easier: Just dump and stir. Best of all, this cake boasted a moist, rich crumb that harked back to the cake's better years. But things quickly went downhill once we scaled back the ingredient amounts to accommodate a 3-cup baking dish (which is about a third of the capacity of the original 13 by 9-inch

baking dish). Now when tasters sampled the cake, they found the crumb to be greasy and damp. We felt confident that with a few tweaks to our working recipe, our cake would once again be a success. We would focus first on the cake, then create a silky cream cheese frosting to go with it.

While the oil in carrot cake recipes is responsible for much of the moisture, we knew that just a bit too much took the cake from light and moist to heavy and slick. We were working with ½ cup of vegetable oil (to ⅔ cup of flour, ⅓ cup of granulated sugar, a couple of tablespoons of brown sugar, and an egg) and decided to experiment with various amounts until we achieved the optimal texture. Reducing the amount of oil by 1 tablespoon at a time, we eventually settled on ¼ cup of oil. Any more than this and the cake was still too dense and greasy; any less and tasters found the cake too lean. But even with the oil issue settled, our cake still seemed a little soggy.

While the carrots contribute sweetness and flavor to their namesake cake, they also add a lot of moisture, so we turned our attention there. Previous testing had shown us that cooking the shredded carrots ahead of time to reduce some of their inherent moisture was a step in the wrong direction. Doing this released some of the moisture, but it also turned the carrots to mush once baked in the cake. The flavor of the cake suffered, too. Adding fresh grated carrot was clearly the way to go, but this meant we needed to use a judicious amount in order to avoid a soggy cake. After several attempts, we found that one small carrot was just the right amount to produce a moist, flavorful crumb and still maintain enough carrot presence.

Our cake was now good enough to eat on its own, but there was no way we were going to pass up the frosting. We made several frostings with varying amounts of cream cheese, butter, and confectioners' sugar until we reached the proper amounts. Our winning combination contained 4 ounces of cream cheese, 2 tablespoons of butter, and ½ cup of confectioners' sugar. We added vanilla for depth of flavor, but it wasn't until we added a pinch of salt that the frosting really shone on top of the cake.

Carrot Cake with Cream Cheese Frosting

SERVES 2

We recommend using a small offset spatula to easily and neatly frost the cake. You will need a 3-cup baking dish (measuring approximately 7¼ by 5¼ inches) or a pan of a similar size for this recipe (see page 3).

CAKE

- ⅔ cup (3⅓ ounces) unbleached all-purpose flour
- ½ teaspoon ground cinnamon
- ¼ teaspoon baking powder
- ⅛ teaspoon baking soda
- ⅛ teaspoon salt
- ⅛ teaspoon ground nutmeg
  Pinch ground cloves
- ⅓ cup (2⅓ ounces) granulated sugar
- ¼ cup vegetable oil
- 1 large egg, room temperature
- 2 tablespoons light brown sugar
- 1 small carrot, peeled and shredded

FROSTING

- 4 ounces cream cheese, softened
- 2 tablespoons unsalted butter, cut into 3 pieces and softened
- ½ teaspoon vanilla extract
  Pinch salt
- ½ cup (2 ounces) confectioners' sugar

1. FOR THE CAKE: Adjust an oven rack to the middle position and heat the oven to 350 degrees. Grease a 3-cup baking dish.

2. Whisk the flour, cinnamon, baking powder, baking soda, salt, nutmeg, and cloves together in a bowl. In a medium bowl, whisk the granulated sugar, oil, egg, and brown sugar together until smooth and thoroughly combined. Gently whisk in the flour mixture until just incorporated. Stir in the carrot.

3. Give the batter a final stir with a rubber spatula to make sure it is thoroughly combined. Scrape the batter into the prepared pan and smooth the top. Wipe any drops of batter off the sides of the pan and gently tap the pan on the counter to settle the batter. Bake the cake until a toothpick inserted into the center comes out with a few crumbs attached, 30 to 40 minutes,

rotating the pan halfway through. Cool the cake in the pan for 10 minutes, then flip it out onto a wire rack, turn the cake right-side up, and let cool for at least 1 hour.

4. FOR THE FROSTING: Meanwhile, beat the cream cheese, butter, vanilla, and salt together in a large bowl with an electric mixer on medium-high speed until smooth, 1 to 2 minutes. Reduce the speed to medium-low, slowly add the confectioners' sugar, and beat until smooth, 2 to 3 minutes. Increase the speed to medium-high and beat until the frosting is light and fluffy, 2 to 3 minutes. Spread the frosting evenly over the top of the cake and serve.

NOTES FROM THE TEST KITCHEN

DOES VANILLA EXTRACT EVER GO BAD?

Some people bake enough cookies and cakes to blow through a whole bottle of vanilla extract in just a month, but when cooking for two, you are more likely to keep the same bottle for much longer. Does vanilla extract ever go bad or lose potency? We located three-year-old and 10-year-old bottles of vanilla extract and compared them with a fresh bottle of the same brand in cupcakes, vanilla frosting, and chocolate chip cookies. Although the older bottles took a bit of effort to open, once the extract was incorporated into recipes, tasters could detect no difference between the old and the new. Vanilla extract has a minimum alcohol content of 35 percent, which, according to Matt Nielsen of vanilla manufacturer Nielsen-Massey, makes it the most shelf-stable form of vanilla. It will last indefinitely if stored in a sealed container away from heat and light.

THE BEST CREAM CHEESE

There aren't too many options at the supermarket when shopping for cream cheese. Whenever we need cream cheese in the test kitchen, we instinctively reach for Philadelphia brand. But is Philadelphia the best, or just the most familiar and widely available?

To find out, we compared Philadelphia cream cheese with two other brands, Horizon and Organic Valley. We tasted them plain and in cheesecake. Tasters judged the cream cheeses on richness, tanginess, creaminess, and overall quality, and one product swept both the plain and cheesecake tastings. **Philadelphia** brand once again trumped the competition, appointed as the cream cheese of choice in the test kitchen for its milkiness and deep flavor.

INDIVIDUAL FALLEN CHOCOLATE CAKES

FALLEN CHOCOLATE CAKE IS AN INTENSE, RICH chocolate cake that ranges in texture from a dense, brownie-like consistency to something altogether more ethereal. We thought this cake would make the perfect dessert for two—only a handful of ingredients are required, and the finished cakes look so posh, they have the ability to transform any Tuesday night supper into a special-occasion dinner.

To begin, we had to decide on the basic method. Melting chocolate and butter together is the standard protocol found in most recipes, but from there we had two choices: We could whip the egg yolks and whites separately and then fold them together, or we could whip whole eggs and sugar to create a thick foam. The latter method proved superior, as it delivered the rich, moist texture we were looking for, and it kept the recipe simple and streamlined. That left us with a recipe that consisted of melting chocolate and butter; whipping whole eggs, sugar, and flavorings into a foam; and then folding the two together.

Our next step was to determine how much of each ingredient we would need for two cakes. After considerable testing, we decided that 2 tablespoons of melted butter and 2 ounces of bittersweet chocolate made the dessert just moist enough and delivered a good jolt of chocolate without being overbearing. The egg quantity, however, was perhaps the most crucial element, affecting texture, richness, and moisture. We tested cakes made with two whole eggs (these had a light and spongy texture), one whole egg plus one yolk (these were moist and dark), and one whole egg (rich but light, moist, intense, and dark). The single whole egg gave us the best cakes overall, with both the flavor and texture we were after. And although some recipes use very little or no flour, we found that a modest amount (a mere tablespoon) gave the cake some structure and lift—making it less fudge-like and more cake-like.

To bake the cakes, we greased two 6-ounce ramekins and dusted them with cocoa powder for an extra boost of chocolate on the cakes' exterior. With the dishes ready and the batter portioned, we turned our attention to oven temperatures, baking the cakes at 350, 400, and 450 degrees. At the highest temperature, we found that the tops were slightly burned and the centers were a bit too runny. At 350 degrees, the dessert took on a more cake-like quality, but not in a good way—the cakes were now too dry. Choosing the middle ground, we found that 400 degrees (for 10 minutes) worked best, yielding a light, cake-like perimeter around a moist well of intense, gooey chocolate.

When it came to unmolding our cakes, we found it best to start by running a small knife around the edges; then we could gently invert each ramekin onto its own plate. Lifting the ramekins too soon often resulted in cracked cakes, so we let the ramekins rest on the plates for a minute until the cakes completely separated from the baking dishes.

With a dusting of confectioners' sugar and a few berries sprinkled on top, these ultra-chocolaty, molten-in-the-middle cakes will turn any dining room into a four-star restaurant.

Individual Fallen Chocolate Cakes

SERVES 2

These elegant cakes are slightly underbaked so that their centers remain a little saucy. Greasing the ramekins with butter and dusting with cocoa powder help to ensure that the cakes release from the ramekins cleanly. The cakes are best served warm with a dollop of whipped cream (see page 281) and fresh berries. You will need two 6-ounce ramekins for this recipe (see page 3).

2 tablespoons unsalted butter, softened,
   plus extra for the ramekins
   Cocoa powder, for the ramekins
2 ounces bittersweet or semisweet chocolate,
   chopped
¼ teaspoon vanilla extract
1 large egg
2 tablespoons granulated sugar
   Pinch salt
1 tablespoon unbleached all-purpose flour
   Confectioners' sugar, for dusting (optional)

INDIVIDUAL FALLEN CHOCOLATE CAKE

1. Adjust an oven rack to the middle position and heat the oven to 400 degrees. Grease two 6-ounce ramekins with butter and dust with cocoa powder.

2. Combine the butter and chocolate in a medium microwave-safe bowl and microwave on high until melted, 1 to 3 minutes, stirring often. Stir in the vanilla.

3. In a large bowl, whip the egg with an electric mixer on medium-low speed until foamy, about 1 minute. Increase the speed to medium-high and whip the egg to soft, billowy mounds, about 1 minute. Gradually whip in the granulated sugar and salt; continue to whip the egg until very thick and pale yellow, 5 to 10 minutes longer.

4. Scrape the whipped egg mixture on top of the chocolate mixture, then sift the flour over the top. Gently fold the mixtures together with a large rubber spatula until just incorporated and no streaks remain.

5. Divide the batter between the prepared ramekins, smooth the tops, and wipe any drops of batter off the sides. Place the ramekins on a rimmed baking sheet and bake the cakes until they have puffed about ½ inch above the rims of the ramekins and jiggle slightly in the center when shaken very gently, 10 to 13 minutes.

6. Run a small knife around the edges of the cakes. Gently invert each ramekin onto an individual serving plate and let sit until the cakes release themselves from the ramekins, about 1 minute. Remove the ramekins, dust the cakes with confectioners' sugar (if using), and serve immediately.

NOTES FROM THE TEST KITCHEN

GETTING THE TEXTURE RIGHT

When a perfectly cooked Fallen Chocolate Cake is cut, just a bit of uncooked batter will run out from the center (bottom). If the cake is underbaked (top), a puddle of uncooked batter will flow from the center of the cake. Alternatively, if the cake is over-baked (middle), it will be too dry.

PROBLEM:
Underbaked and Puddling

PROBLEM:
Overbaked and Dry

JUST RIGHT:
Set Up yet Saucy

OUR FAVORITE DARK CHOCOLATE

We've tasted, and baked with, lots of chocolate that falls into the "gourmet" category, and although many brands have distinctive flavors that tasters liked in particular desserts, two chocolates consistently produce great results in a variety of baked goods—**Callebaut Intense Dark Chocolate L-60-40NV** (left) and **Ghirardelli Bittersweet Chocolate Baking Bar** (right). Tasters found Callebaut to have a "complex flavor, creamy and thick," with a pleasant balanced sweetness and bitterness. Ghirardelli scored well for its blend of tastes; tasters discerned "coffee, smoke, and dried fruit" in this rich, creamy chocolate. Both chocolates are widely available.

STORING CHOCOLATE

Although you might not often find yourself with extra chocolate, it's important to know how to store it should the occasion arise. To start, never store chocolate in the refrigerator or freezer, as cocoa butter can easily pick up off-flavors from other foods. If chocolate is exposed to rapid changes in humidity or temperature, sugar or fat may dissolve and migrate, discoloring the surface. This condition, known as bloom, is cosmetic and not harmful—bloomed chocolate is safe to eat and cook with. To extend the shelf life of chocolate, we recommend wrapping it tightly in plastic wrap and storing it in a cool, dry place. Dark chocolates will last for several years, but milk and white chocolates last for only six months to a year.

VARIATION

Individual Fallen Chocolate-Orange Cakes

Follow the recipe for Individual Fallen Chocolate Cakes, stirring ½ teaspoon grated orange zest and 1 teaspoon orange-flavored liqueur into the melted chocolate with the vanilla in step 2.

Whipped Cream

MAKES ABOUT ¾ CUP

The whipped cream can be refrigerated in a fine-mesh strainer set over a small bowl, wrapped tightly with plastic wrap, for up to 8 hours. See page 229 for a recipe to use up the leftover heavy cream.

- ⅓ cup heavy cream, chilled
- 1 teaspoon sugar
- ¼ teaspoon vanilla extract

Whip the cream, sugar, and vanilla together in a large bowl with an electric mixer on medium-low speed until frothy, about 1 minute. Increase the speed to high and continue to whip the cream to soft peaks, 1 to 3 minutes longer.

PECAN TARTS

FEW DESSERTS CREATE A HOMEY FEELING THE WAY pecan pie does—the chewy brown sugar filling and deep pecan flavor are an ideal combination that makes for a soul-satisfying dessert. We were interested in transforming the traditional pecan pie into two individual tarts that still delivered its warm, rich flavors.

Working from the ground up, we considered the tart dough first and decided that an all-butter crust would provide the crispy texture and buttery flavor we wanted. Unlike traditional tart dough recipes that call for rolling and fitting a single tart shell into a pan, our recipe was much less demanding. We simply mixed the dough, tore it into small pieces, then patted it into two 4-inch tart pans. Once fully baked and cooled, the tart shells were ready for their pecan filling.

Usually the dough is the more challenging component of any tart recipe, but we knew we had our work cut out for us with the filling. Pecan pie filling is notorious for being too sweet. The other major complaint is the texture—too often the filling is gritty and separated. We planned to focus our attention on creating a smooth, cohesive, lightly sweetened filling first; then we could finesse the flavors.

We started by following our method for making pecan pie filling—cooking butter and brown sugar together until the sugar dissolves. For the sugar, we used brown sugar instead of granulated sugar because it has a less overt sweetness and undertones of caramel that complement the pecans. We also added corn syrup as we'd learned from past experience that corn syrup made the filling less likely to seize or become gritty; it also offered a moderate level of sweetness, which we aimed to accentuate only slightly. Then off the heat, it was time for the egg yolks—or in this case, egg yolk, as we needed just one in our tart filling to ensure that the filling sets up and help to avoid separation. In the end we had a custard filling that was smooth and sweet, but not cloying.

For the pecans, we tested tarts made with whole pecan halves, chopped pecans, and a combination of chopped and whole nuts. We had no problem deciding on our preference. We found whole pecans too much of a mouthful, and we had difficulty cutting through them with a fork as we dug in. Chopped nuts were easier to slice through and eat. Tasters insisted on packing in as many as possible—we found that ½ cup was the most we could add and still allow room for the filling.

Now all we had to do was tweak the flavors. Tasters asked for a darker and richer filling, so our thoughts turned to using dark brown sugar instead of light brown sugar. The candy-like flavor of dark brown sugar was perfect but a bit too sweet. A pinch of salt kept the filling from being cloying. For more richness, we doubled the amount of butter to 2 tablespoons.

With the tart shells already baked and the filling partially cooked, our pecan tarts needed only 10 minutes in a 325-degree oven to set up completely. After waiting an hour for the tarts to cool, tasters dug in; after just one bite, they raved about the bold pecan filling and tender tart crust. Taking a bite ourselves, we knew we had created a pecan tart recipe we would be making again and again.

Pecan Tarts

SERVES 2

Serve with vanilla ice cream or whipped cream (page 281). The tart shells can be made up to a day ahead of time.

- ¼ **cup packed (1¼ ounces) dark brown sugar**
- 3 **tablespoons light corn syrup**
- 2 **tablespoons unsalted butter**
- **Pinch salt**
- 1 **large egg yolk**
- ½ **teaspoon vanilla extract**
- ½ **cup pecans, toasted (see page 210) and chopped coarse**
- 1 **recipe All-Butter Tart Shells (see page 124), fully baked and cooled**

1. Adjust an oven rack to the middle position and heat the oven to 325 degrees.

2. Heat the brown sugar and corn syrup together in a small saucepan over medium heat, stirring occasionally, until the sugar dissolves, about 2 minutes. Off the heat, whisk in the butter and salt until the butter is melted. Whisk in the egg yolk and vanilla until combined. Stir in the pecans.

3. Divide the pecan mixture evenly between the cooled tart shells. Place the tart shells on a rimmed baking sheet and bake until the filling is set and the centers jiggle slightly when the tarts are gently shaken, 10 to 15 minutes.

4. Let the tarts cool completely on a wire rack, about 1 hour. To serve, remove the outer metal ring of the tart pan, slide a thin metal spatula between the tart and the tart pan bottom, and carefully slide the tart onto a plate.

CRÈME BRÛLÉE

THE CLASSIC FRENCH DESSERT, CRÈME BRÛLÉE, should have a crackling-crisp bittersweet sugar crust over a chilly custard of balanced egginess, creaminess, and sweetness. Unfortunately, the opposite is more common: The custard's texture is typically leaden, not light and creamy, and the flavors are muted and dull. And the topping has its own issues, too; if it isn't a paltry sugar crust, it's one so thick it requires a pickax. We set out to fix these problems and create the perfect crème brûlée for two.

First we sought to settle the issue of eggs. Firmer custards, such as crème caramel, are made with whole eggs, which help the custard to achieve a clean-cutting quality. Crème brûlée should be richer and softer—with a pudding-like texture—in part because of the use of yolks. For two servings, set in 6-ounce ramekins, we started with a single cup of heavy cream as the dairy ingredient and began varying the number of yolks. The custard refused to set at all with as little as one yolk; with two (a common amount for a single cup of cream), it was better, but still rather slurpy. With three, however, we struck gold. The custard maintained a thick texture without turning rubbery.

Next we tested various sugar quantities, from 1 tablespoon to ¼ cup. Three tablespoons was the winner. With more than that, the crème brûlée was too sweet; with less, the simple egg and cream flavors tasted muted and dull. We also found that a pinch of salt heightened the flavors and that a vanilla bean, which we steeped in some of the cream, proved superior to extract.

With the proportions in place, we refined our cooking technique. After heating half the cream with the sugar and the vanilla bean so the sugar could dissolve and the flavor of the vanilla bean would be released, we added the remaining cold cream to bring the temperature down before whisking in the yolks. This technique created a silky, fine custard—and required little time to complete. The next step was baking our custards.

Having baked several custards by this point, we were well aware that the baking time and temperature could make the difference between a great dessert and a

CRÈME BRÛLÉE

NOTES FROM THE TEST KITCHEN

REMOVING SEEDS FROM A VANILLA BEAN

1. Use a small knife to cut the piece of vanilla bean in half lengthwise.

2. Then scrape the vanilla seeds out of the bean using the blade of the knife.

HOW TO BRÛLÉE

To caramelize the topping, ignite the torch and sweep the flame from the perimeter of the custard toward the middle, keeping the flame about 2 inches above the ramekin, until the sugar is bubbling and golden.

THE BEST TORCH

A torch is about the only way to effectively caramelize the sugar topping on crème brûlée. We tested four brands of small butane kitchen torches and a hardware-store propane torch—the favorite choice of professional cooks—and found only one butane torch we liked as well as the propane torch. A propane torch is not a tool for the fainthearted: It puts out a powerful flame and therefore caramelizes the sugar much faster than the lower-power kitchen models. Of the mini kitchen torches, the **Bernzomatic 3 in 1 Micro Torch**, $28.99, came out ahead of other brands. This butane-powered torch performed admirably and is easy to use.

mediocre, or even disappointing, one. After considerable experimentation, we determined that baking the custards at 300 degrees for about 30 minutes produced the best results. Using a water bath, to maintain an even, gentle heating environment, also ensured that the custards cooked evenly and remained creamy and smooth. To do this, we simply placed the ramekins in a metal baking pan, then filled the pan with boiling water until it reached halfway up the sides of the ramekins. We found that lining the baking pan first with a towel further ensured that the bottoms of the custards didn't overcook.

Out of the oven and chilled in the refrigerator until completely set, our custards were now ready for their crowning touch—the caramelized top. For an incredibly crackly crust, we found that turbinado sugar worked best, though granulated sugar could be substituted in a pinch. For caramelizing the sugar, we attempted to use the broiler, but the inadequate heat produced uneven browning. A torch accomplished the task much more efficiently and took just seconds to give our custards their sunset-colored toppings.

After extensive testing, our efforts were rewarded. Tasting our finished dessert, we found that beneath a shatteringly crisp crust was a combination of creamy, sweet, and smooth—in essence, the perfect crème brûlée.

But never satisfied—even with perfection—we set out to create a simple variation. For another sophisticated dessert, we added a bit of instant espresso for a crème brûlée that will make coffee lovers swoon.

Crème Brûlée

SERVES 2

We developed this recipe using two 6-ounce ramekins (see page 3). If using shallow ramekins, which normally hold 4 to 5 ounces, you will have custard left over; note also that the custards will bake more quickly and give you more surface area for the caramelized sugar topping. If you don't have a vanilla bean, stir ½ teaspoon of vanilla extract into the yolk mixture in step 3 and skip the 15-minute steeping in step 2. For the caramelized sugar topping, we like to use turbinado sugar, but granulated sugar can be substituted. Be sure not to overcook the custards; they will look barely set once they are ready to come out of the oven. It's important to use a metal pan for the water bath—a glass baking pan may crack when you add the boiling water.

1 cup heavy cream, chilled

3 tablespoons granulated sugar

1 (3-inch) piece vanilla bean, halved lengthwise, seeds removed and reserved (see note; see page 284)

   Pinch salt

3 large egg yolks, room temperature

1 tablespoon turbinado sugar (see note)

1. Adjust an oven rack to the middle position and heat the oven to 300 degrees. Bring a kettle of water to a boil. Place a kitchen towel in the bottom of an 8-inch metal baking pan and set two 6-ounce ramekins on the towel (see page 269).

2. Combine ½ cup of the cream, granulated sugar, vanilla bean and seeds, and salt in a small saucepan. Bring the mixture to a simmer over medium heat, stirring occasionally to dissolve the sugar. Remove the pan from the heat, cover, and let steep for 15 minutes.

3. Stir in the remaining ½ cup cream. Place the egg yolks in a medium bowl and slowly whisk in ½ cup of the cream mixture until smooth. Whisk in the remaining cream mixture until thoroughly combined. Strain the custard through a fine-mesh strainer into a liquid measuring cup. Pour the custard into the ramekins.

4. Transfer the baking pan to the oven and carefully pour enough boiling water into the pan to reach halfway up the sides of the ramekins. Bake the custards until the centers are just barely set, 30 to 35 minutes (25 to 30 minutes for shallow dishes).

5. Carefully remove the ramekins from the water bath and let the custards cool to room temperature,

USE IT UP: VANILLA BEAN

Vanilla Sugar
MAKES 1 CUP

This flavored sugar is great for sweetening coffee and tea or for sprinkling onto fresh fruit. The sugar can be stored at room temperature in an airtight container for up to 6 months.

1 (3-inch) piece vanilla bean, halved lengthwise, seeds removed and reserved (see page 284)

1 cup (7 ounces) granulated sugar

Process the vanilla bean, seeds, and sugar in a food processor until combined, 30 seconds to 1 minute.

about 1 hour. Cover the ramekins tightly with plastic wrap and refrigerate until cold, at least 2 hours, or up to 1 day.

6. Just before serving, uncover the ramekins and gently blot the tops dry with a paper towel. Sprinkle each ramekin evenly with the turbinado sugar, then shake the ramekin to spread the sugar in an even layer. Pour out any excess sugar and wipe away the excess from the inside rim of the ramekin. Following the photo on page 284, ignite a torch and caramelize the sugar. Refrigerate the ramekins, uncovered, to rechill the custards for up to 45 minutes (but no longer), or serve immediately.

VARIATION

Espresso Crème Brûlée
Follow the recipe for Crème Brûlée, adding ½ teaspoon instant espresso or instant coffee to the egg yolks in step 3.

Conversions & Equivalencies

SOME SAY COOKING IS A SCIENCE AND AN ART. We would say that geography has a hand in it, too. Flour milled in the United Kingdom and elsewhere will feel and taste different from flour milled in the United States. So, while we cannot promise that the loaf of bread you bake in Canada or England will taste the same as a loaf baked in the States, we can offer guidelines for converting weights and measures. We also recommend that you rely on your instincts when making our recipes. Refer to the visual cues provided. If the bread dough hasn't "come together in a ball," as described, you may need to add more flour—even if the recipe doesn't tell you so. You be the judge.

The recipes in this book were developed using standard U.S. measures following U.S. government guidelines. The charts below offer equivalents for U.S., metric, and Imperial (U.K.) measures. All conversions are approximate and have been rounded up or down to the nearest whole number. For example:

1 teaspoon = 4.929 milliliters, rounded up to 5 milliliters
1 ounce = 28.349 grams, rounded down to 28 grams

VOLUME CONVERSIONS

U.S.	METRIC
1 teaspoon	5 milliliters
2 teaspoons	10 milliliters
1 tablespoon	15 milliliters
2 tablespoons	30 milliliters
¼ cup	59 milliliters
⅓ cup	79 milliliters
½ cup	118 milliliters
¾ cup	177 milliliters
1 cup	237 milliliters
1¼ cups	296 milliliters
1½ cups	355 milliliters
2 cups	473 milliliters
2½ cups	592 milliliters
3 cups	710 milliliters
4 cups (1 quart)	0.946 liter
1.06 quarts	1 liter
4 quarts (1 gallon)	3.8 liters

WEIGHT CONVERSIONS

OUNCES	GRAMS
½	14
¾	21
1	28
1½	43
2	57
2½	71
3	85
3½	99
4	113
4½	128
5	142
6	170
7	198
8	227
9	255
10	283
12	340
16 (1 pound)	454

CONVERSIONS FOR INGREDIENTS COMMONLY USED IN BAKING

Baking is an exacting science. Because measuring by weight is far more accurate than measuring by volume, and thus more likely to achieve reliable results, in our recipes we provide ounce measures in addition to cup measures for many ingredients. Refer to the chart below to convert these measures into grams.

INGREDIENT	OUNCES	GRAMS
Flour		
1 cup all-purpose flour*	5	142
1 cup cake flour	4	113
1 cup whole wheat flour	5½	156
Sugar		
1 cup granulated (white) sugar	7	198
1 cup packed brown sugar (light or dark)	7	198
1 cup confectioners' sugar	4	113
Cocoa Powder		
1 cup cocoa powder	3	85
Butter†		
4 tablespoons (½ stick, or ¼ cup)	2	57
8 tablespoons (1 stick, or ½ cup)	4	113
16 tablespoons (2 sticks, or 1 cup)	8	227

* U.S. all-purpose flour, the most frequently used flour in this book, does not contain leaveners, as some European flours do. These leavened flours are called self-rising or self-raising. If you are using self-rising flour, take this into consideration before adding leavening to a recipe.
† In the United States, butter is sold both salted and unsalted. We generally recommend unsalted butter. If you are using salted butter, take this into consideration before adding salt to a recipe.

OVEN TEMPERATURES

FAHRENHEIT	CELSIUS	GAS MARK (imperial)
225	105	¼
250	120	½
275	130	1
300	150	2
325	165	3
350	180	4
375	190	5
400	200	6
425	220	7
450	230	8
475	245	9

CONVERTING TEMPERATURES FROM AN INSTANT-READ THERMOMETER

We include doneness temperatures in many of our recipes, such as those for poultry, meat, and bread. We recommend an instant-read thermometer for the job. Refer to the table above to convert Fahrenheit degrees to Celsius. Or, for temperatures not represented in the chart, use this simple formula:

Subtract 32 degrees from the Fahrenheit reading, then divide the result by 1.8 to find the Celsius reading.

EXAMPLE:

"Roast until the thickest part of a chicken thigh registers 175 degrees on an instant-read thermometer." To convert:

175° F – 32 = 143°
143° ÷ 1.8 = 79° C (rounded down from 79.44)

Index

NOTE: *ITALICIZED* PAGE REFERENCES INDICATE COLOR PHOTOGRAPHS.